In the Country

Nicholas Dawidoff graduated from Harvard and spent a year in Asia as a Henry Luce Scholar. He has written for the *New Republic*, *The New York Times Magazine* and the *New Yorker*. His previous book, *The Catcher Was a Spy*, was published in 1994. He lives in New York City.

In the Country of Country

NICHOLAS DAWIDOFF

faber and faber

First published in Great Britain in 1997
by Faber and Faber Limited
3 Queen Square London WC1N 3AU
This edition published in 2005

Printed in England by Mackays of Chatham plc, Chatham, Kent

© Nicholas Dawidoff, 1997

Nicholas Dawidoff is hereby identified as author of this
work in accordance with Section 77 of the Copyright,
Designs and Patents Act 1988

A CIP record for this book
is available from the British Library

ISBN 0–571–22719–8

2 4 6 8 10 9 7 5 3 1

For Sally Dawidoff and for Robert Dawidoff

Fruit packers take a break,
Copiah County, Mississippi, 1936.

And perhaps a man brought out his guitar to the front of his tent. And he sat on a box to play, and everyone in the camp moved slowly in toward him, drawn in toward him. Many men can chord a guitar, but perhaps this man was a picker. There you have something—the deep chords beating, beating while the melody runs on the strings like little footsteps. Heavy hard fingers marching on the frets. The man played and the people moved slowly in on him until the circle was closed and tight, and then he sang, "Ten-Cent Cotton and Forty-Cent Meat." And the circle sang softly with him. And he sang, "Why Do You Cut Your Hair, Girls?" And the circle sang. He wailed the song, "I'm Leaving Old Texas," that eerie song that was sung before the Spaniards came, only the words were Indian then.

And now the group was welded to one thing, one unit, so that in the dark the eyes of the people were inward, and their minds played in other times, and their sadness was like rest, like sleep. He sang the "McAlester Blues" and then, to make up for it to the older people, he sang "Jesus Calls Me to His Side." The children drowsed with the music and went into the tents to sleep, and the singing came into their dreams.

And after a while the man with the guitar stood up and yawned. Good night, folks, he said.

And they murmured, Good night to you.

And each wished he could pick a guitar, because it is a gracious thing.

—JOHN STEINBECK, *The Grapes of Wrath*

CONTENTS

CONTENTS

In the Country of Country

Crossville,
the crossroads of East Tennessee.

THE SPIRIT OF JIMMIE RODGERS

PROLOGUE

My object was not to see the inns and the turnpikes,
but to see the country.

—WILLIAM COBBETT, *Rural Rides*

ON A LATE MAY DAY in Meridian, Mississippi—warm enough that people were dusting off the line about its being so hot that they'd seen a dog chasing a cat and both were walking—I was on my way to the home of Johnnie and Carolyn Shurley. Johnnie is a retired box-factory worker and a pretty good amateur guitar player. Carolyn used to work as a die coordinator and forklift driver at the box factory. They live outside the city, in the hamlet of Arundel, Mississippi, and had invited me to a party. People would be there, they said, who knew about Jimmie Rodgers.

Rodgers was "The Father of Country Music," a sickly man who recorded songs of such power that today, more than sixty years after he was buried in Meridian, some of the finest living American singers and songwriters like Hank Snow, Merle Haggard, Doc Watson, Jimmie Dale Gilmore—who is named for Rodgers—and Iris DeMent mention him right away when they begin talking about the music that means a lot to them.

It was quiet out in the country, and as I parked I could hear the sounds of string music coming from behind the Shurleys' house. Close to forty casually dressed men and women were out back, eating hamburgers, singing, and dancing. The musicians sat in a circle together and played their fiddles, mandolins, dobros, guitars, and an upright bass, taking frequent breaks to sample some homemade ice cream or fish out a can of soda pop from a tub packed with melting ice. There wasn't any alcohol because, as people were quick to explain, unlike Jimmie Rodgers, who loved "a squirt," the Shurleys don't drink.

Stories were unfolding even as the music played. Some of them were about snakes—a man named Cookie said that it was already a good year for them because of the warm winter—and others concerned feuds. One well-known local hostility began at a square dance when a young man drew up some water from a well and drank straight out of the bucket instead of using a dipper. There was a woman standing in line behind him, and first by not stepping aside and letting her have a drink before he took his, and then by going ahead and slaking his thirst in such a crude fashion, the young man had insulted her twice. These were mortal breaches of decorum. The young man was stabbed and ended up "down by the creek trying to hold his insides in," according to Larry Finch, a friendly shop owner with a lazy eye and a gum-thick drawl. Many classic country songs have been inspired by real-life tragedies just like this one, and when I mentioned this connection to Finch he said, "It sounds very much like a Jimmie Rodgers song, and if Jimmie had known about it he might have made a song out of it."

As the Shurleys had promised, Rodgers was another popular subject for the raconteurs. He grew up around Meridian, and many of those at the gathering had relatives or friends who had known him. Meridian thinks of itself as an upstanding place; there used to be a welcome sign on the outskirts of town proclaiming "The Largest Percentage of Churchgoers in the World." Rodgers, meanwhile, left behind a number of bawdy songs bragging about his life as a hard-drinking, hard-loving-rascal—in "Blue Yodel 10" he wrote, "It's my regular grinding gets me by in this world"—and people at the party still weren't quite ready to forgive him for his cheek. Johnnie Shurley said that his father had worked on the Southern Railroad in Meridian for fifty years and got to know Rodgers, a sometime brakeman, around the railroad yards. Shurley pointed to one of the high hills visible from Arundel and said that Rodgers and his friends would go out there to a settlement at Arundel Springs and "drink, they'd shoot dice—a little bit of everything, I guess. You couldn't come into the city doing things like that."

The stories only got worse. Rodgers was depicted as a lout by a retired pipe fitter and reviled as "a drunk on the street, a tramp" by a white-

The Father of Country Music in his brakeman's cap.
"Our musical heritage is Jimmie Rodgers."

haired woman who was explaining that "my daddy used to drink with him," when a woman got to her feet and sang "Give Me the Roses While I Live." Then nearly everyone joined in as the band struck up "Will the Circle Be Unbroken?" a Carter Family song as familiar to Southern country people of a certain generation as "When Irish Eyes Are Smiling" used to be in Hell's Kitchen.

The last person I spoke with about Rodgers was Larry Finch. Like many people I met over the past few years, he wanted to know what a "Yankee" was doing traveling through the South, asking people about old-time country music. I explained I that grew up in a small New England city, but I got to know country music in the traditional way—it was handed down to me by a relative. As a student at Cornell, my uncle Robert made himself a little pocket money by singing country songs in small clubs and at parties in and around Ithaca. He loved country music, especially Rodgers's, Bill Monroe's, Bob Wills's, Haggard's, and George Jones's, and because we were close, he wanted me to like it too. When he decided I was old enough—about eleven—he began sending me records. As conversions go, this one went pretty smoothly. I listened to The Carter Family sing "Keep on the Sunny Side," which begins "There's a dark and a troubled side of life/ There's a bright and a sunny side too," in their lilting, stoical way, and I couldn't get enough of it after that.

The best country music affected me the same way great books did, informing my own experiences even as they gave me a sense of being transported to new places, set down among people who might be said to have nothing to do with my own existence. There was so much soul to the songs that even as a child, I had a strong feeling for the world they described and a corresponding curiosity about it. The young singer and fiddle player Alison Krauss once told me that something similar had happened to her. Krauss grew up in an Illinois college town listening to traditional country music. The songs made the places they described seem almost mythic to her and she wanted to see them. Describing her first trips through the South she said, "As we were driving, Barry, our bass player, would say 'That's Cumberland Gap,' and I'd say '*Cumberland Gap!*' Or the Smoky Mountains. Pretty neat. Still gives me the heebie-jeebies!"

I explained all this to Finch. Then I told him that my aim was to visit with some of the finest living American country musicians to learn about their lives in music. I also intended to go to some of the places where great country music comes from, and to spend time with people who have grown up with it. It is my belief that country music is a piece of our social history, that it describes in its songs the experiences of people who weren't often written up in the newspapers. In an informal way, country music tells us much about how these Americans—the men and women Hank Williams referred to as "the common people"—felt about life as the century unfolded. Although it was impossible to have a conversation with Jimmie Rodgers the way I could with all the living musicians I was writing about, he was such an influential figure that it seemed important to begin by walking over his home ground and spending some time in Meridian.

Finch nodded. He said that in his family, the songs everyone knew were Rodgers's. "My aunt Snook, she yodeled like Jimmie Rodgers," he said. "She loved Jimmie Rodgers. All the family did back then." His grandmother, he said, played the guitar and the pump organ. His great-uncle was a respected Mississippi fiddle player. A grandfather played the harmonica, and Finch's father knew his way around both a harmonica and a mandolin. Finch himself learned to play the banjo, "Uncle Dave Macon style," he said, on an instrument that had once belonged to Rodgers. "My mother never did play," he said, "but she loved the music. My father, he loved music so much. I still have the first banjo he gave me. My mother was from here. Her family had all of Jimmie Rodgers's records and a Victrola. When they got a radio, they sold all the records and the Victrola for five dollars." He put his lips together and shook his head.

"Our musical heritage is Jimmie Rodgers," Finch went on. "He is the reason that around here we appreciate music so much. We're agricultural people. We couldn't get into town much and we couldn't afford a movie if we did. Our entertainment was music. Saturday nights we'd go to somebody's house, take all of the furniture out of the room, roll up the carpet, and have an old-fashioned square dance. Pass the jug, you know."

I found his description uncannily like the first verse from the song "Mama's Opry," which the young singer Iris DeMent wrote not long ago about her mother:

> She grew up plain and simple in a farming town
> Her daddy played the fiddle and used to do the callin' when they had
> hoedowns
> She said the neighbors would come and they'd move all my grandma's
> furniture 'round
> And there'd be twenty or more there on an old wooden floor
> Dancin' to a country sound

The Carters and Jimmie Rodgers played her favorite songs
And on Saturday nights there was a radio show and she would sing along
And I'll never forget her face when she revealed to me
That she'd dreamed about singin' at "The Grand Ol' Opry."

I was thinking that Iris DeMent had brought the history of country music into perfect continuum when I realized that Finch was gazing at me and grinning. "Do you know what the Southern definition of a true music lover is?" he asked. "It's a man who, if he hears a woman singing in the shower, puts his ear to the keyhole."

By ten, everybody had gone home. They were working people, someone said, and they got to bed early.

The Father of Country Music was a city boy. Although it is true that Jimmie Rodgers was born in the deep-country village of Pine Springs, Mississippi, in 1897, and after his mother died spent the better part of several years living there with his spinster aunt Dora, he claimed Meridian as his hometown. During his career Rodgers recorded a range of material, including plantation melodies, old river ballads, sentimental weepers, novelty numbers, swinging Dixieland-style "jazz junk," and, in what would become his seminal contribution to American music, a brilliant collection of country blues. In his pre-radio, pre-Victrola childhood, a lot of what Rodgers learned about the rich variety of popular music that his own music drew from was taught to him by the town.

Today Meridian, which hugs the southwestern Alabama border, is a subdued place. In the first part of the century, however, it pulsed. This could be credited to the surveyors; Meridian was the spot on the map where the north–south and east–west railroad lines happened to cross. During the Civil War it was an obvious target for Federal troops and, sure enough, in 1864, the cigar-puffing Union general William Tecumseh Sherman razed it so thoroughly that his wire to the War Department said: "Meridian . . . no longer exists." But the city rebuilt its depots, roundhouses, and hotels and then grew so rapidly that by the time Jimmie Rodgers was a young man, it had nearly 50,000 residents. There was also a large floating population. The dozens of passenger trains and thousands of boxcars rolling in every day meant that Meridian was filled with ticketed travelers, train crews, and hobos riding the rods.

Rodgers grew up a streetwise Meridian kid with a passion for trains and a precocious enthusiasm both for wayfaring people and, by extension, for the transient existence that would become a central theme in his life and music. His father, Aaron Rodgers, was a section foreman on the Mobile and Ohio line. Sometimes Aaron Rodgers took his son with him out to the tracks and put him to work bringing water to the black work crews who repaired worn ties and damaged rails, cleared brush, and shoveled gravel ballast. These men, known as "gandy dancers," toiled most effectively when they moved their tamping picks and spike mauls in unison. One way they kept themselves aligned was by singing in rhythm. The foreman sent along a command to a "caller," who configured this order into cadences similar to what you might hear from a drillmaster. "If you really wanted to move that track, you made a sexy call," a former gandy dancer named Cornelius Wright told the cultural researcher Maggie Holtzberg-Call. "And they had the language for it. Some callers would talk about the lingerie that a woman wore. Now that caused the crew to really shift that track."

When Rodgers went back out to Pine Springs, other kids sometimes felt that he was "stuck-up" because, as the child of one of his schoolmates told me at the Shurleys' party, Rodgers didn't like to play baseball and wore shoes in warm weather while everybody else went barefoot. They misunderstood. There was nothing highfalutin about Jimmie Rodgers. As the title of one of his great songs suggests, he was a cheerful sort, happy to bend an elbow in the company of all sorts of rounders and roustabouts

"Hey little water boy, bring that water 'round."
A southeastern railroad crew laying track in the summer heat.

with "rough and rowdy ways." This sort of frowsy living began early in his life, well before Rodgers became a railroad man himself. (He would hold jobs as a brakeman—his sobriquet was "The Singing Brakeman"—a flagman, and a baggage handler.) His foremost biographer, Nolan Porterfield, says the youthful Rodgers found a number of ways—running errands, vamping whenever anyone would let him—to spend time in Meridian's barbershops and its billiard halls. He also frequented the city's opera house, its vaudeville theaters, and its hotel lobbies, where he would have encountered plenty of jazz and parlor music. All around the water tank, out beside the tracks, and in the more lowdown joints on Fifth Street, he heard the blues.

By spending so much time around work gangs, porters, and switchmen on the job and inside their places of pleasure—mostly in Meridian's black neighborhoods—Rodgers heard a lot of bright talk about what he said were the railroad man's three favorite conversational topics: whiskey, women, and back pay. These experiences infused his songs with bluesy lyrics that ranged from the gently ribald—"I'm a do-right papa and got a home everywhere I go"—to the directly autobiographical: "Hey little waterboy, bring that water 'round/If you don't like your job, set yo' water bucket down." More generally, he absorbed both the lively and the plaintive rhythms of black popular music. Later, people who heard the Father of Country Music sing called him everything from "a white man gone black" to "a busboy in a roadside café singing nigger blues."

A persistent fiction holds that country music is of pure white, Southern, rural origins. In fact, right from its commercial beginnings, country was a hybrid form conflating many extant styles of popular and religious music with whatever individual innovations people like Rodgers brought to it. By writing songs that drew from the full spectrum of music that he knew, Rodgers was creating a truly American music and setting a precedent that would be followed by a number of the most progressive and influential figures in country music history. A.P. Carter, Bill Monroe, Bob Wills, Hank Williams, Johnny Cash, Brenda Lee, and Buck Owens—to name just a few—all had black musical mentors. In the 1950s, a young country singer named Elvis Presley took the situation a step further, raunching up his chops into rock 'n' roll because he couldn't get enough of the blues he'd heard pouring out of the juke joints as a boy in Tupelo, Mississippi. Country music has satisfied many needs. One of them was that for a time it enabled poor Southern white people to hear strains of the black working-man's music while keeping their distance from poor working-class blacks.

*Arnold Schultz (left), who taught Bill Monroe the blues, and
the fiddle player Clarence Wilson. "If Chuck Berry had been white,"
says Buck Owens, "he'd have been a country singer."*

It has worked the other way too. For much of this century, the Saturday night radio broadcasts of the *Grand Ole Opry* music variety show from the Ryman Auditorium in Nashville—the mother church of country music—claimed the largest listening audience in the world. In the late 1930s, among the many blacks who never missed a week of it was a young boy in Greenville, Florida, who would grow up to record *Modern Sounds in Country and Western Music,* a series of brilliant R&B–informed interpretations of classic country songs: Ray Charles. Outside the only house left in Meridian where Jimmie Rodgers once lived, I met a black woman named Earlean Garry, who told me, "I love his music. I still listen to it. Listened to it growing up."

The first country record was produced in 1923. Four years later, a New York businessman named Ralph Peer, out scouting talent for the Victor Talking Machine Company, arrived in the Tennessee-Virginia border town of Bristol to audition local people who sang what he called "hillbilly music." He set up his equipment in an old furniture store, sent out word through the newspapers of the $50-a-side fees he was paying, and hoped for the best. It turned out well for him. Among the singers and musicians who showed up were a dusty couple from the backwoods Appalachian settlement of Maces Springs, Virginia, and their very pregnant sister-in-law: A.P., Sara, and Maybelle Carter. Lured over from North Carolina, where he was working at the time, was Jimmie Rodgers. They became America's first great country music recording stars.

Rodgers and the Carters both sang, with sincerity and feeling, simply worded songs about common people—a reasonable barebones description of country music. But The Carter Family's wistfully melodic portraits of family, faith, home, and heart held to a somewhat narrower and more bucolic course than Rodgers's music did. He too could deliver poignant sentiment in something like "Treasures Untold" or "Miss the Mississippi and You," but Rodgers was also not above singing about drinking, jailhouses, dice throwers, and a pretty woman's drop-stitch stockings.

There was gritty experience and plenty of pluck in Rodgers's music, as he made clear in his first "Blue Yodel": "If you don't want me Mama/You sure don't have to stall/'Cause I can get me more women/Than a passenger train can haul." Lines like this were followed up with a few of his distinctive yodels. Rodgers wasn't much of a guitar player and so, in a sense, the yodel was his best instrument. Because its falsetto delivery was so different from his singing voice, it was a fine way to apply a certain accent to whatever he was singing about. Beyond this, his skill was *sui generis;* with the possible exception of the mysterious blackface singer Emmett Miller, nobody could yodel like "America's Blue Yodeler." Which prompted some lurid speculation. There were people who believed Rodgers's magnificent yodeling was a by-product of the tuberculosis that was beginning to kill him.

Many of the millions of records Rodgers sold beginning in 1927 were purchased during the Depression when, an old saw has it, the typical Southern shopping list was a pound of butter, a slab of bacon, a sack of flour, and the new Jimmie Rodgers record. His skill at the acrobatic yodel tends to distract from what a fine singer and writer Rodgers was. He had a wonderful drawling tenor, one that could croon like a young mother or strut like a street-corner swell. He understood as well that there were many ways for a vocalist to wring feeling from a lyric. Rodgers had a manner of *lingering* on a chosen word or syllable, a casually stylized approach to singing that presaged the techniques of Hank Snow, Ernest Tubb, Lefty Frizzell, and Merle Haggard.

As for his writing, the "T.B. Blues" ("When it rained down sorrow, it rained all over me") and the first "Blue Yodel" ("T for Texas, T for Tennessee/T for Thelma, the girl that made a wreck out of me") attest to how nimbly his mind could range from pathos to humor. That Rodgers sang so beautifully about a sickness that choked his lungs with blood— audiences took to yelling at him, "Spit 'er up, Jimmie, and sing some more"—makes "T.B. Blues" among the more stirring recordings in country music history. It is one of those horribly sad and yet oddly bracing songs anyone can understand: "I'm fighting like a lion, looks like I'm going to lose/'Cause there ain't nobody ever whipped the T.B. blues." "T.B. Blues" makes it clear that while the Father of Country Music sang songs from life as he knew it, those songs were about common people everywhere, for common people everywhere.

Rodgers died in 1933 at the Taft Hotel in New York, two days after making his final recording. His casket was put on a train that his sister-in-law, Mildred Pollard, met in Washington, where she was a student. She says that, like the rest of the country, the nation's capital was in mourning for him. "After he died, all over Washington, D.C., everywhere you went you could hear Jimmie singing," Pollard told me. "You couldn't walk anywhere in Washington without hearing Jimmie all day long."

Halfway through the 1990s, country music was as popular as it had ever been. In just a few years, record sales had quadrupled to over $2 billion annually, and more people—seventy million of them—listened to country on the radio than any other form of music. Country was now fashionable in places—New York City, Los Angeles, Cleveland, Seattle—and among people—well-educated professionals, teenagers—that contradicted old assumptions about the music.

The country charts were dominated by a series of handsome, video-friendly young swains dressed in boots, snug jeans, and the inevitable Stetsons that won them their nickname, "the hat acts." The music was similarly homogenized. Blending down-home lyrics with fusillades of rock 'n' roll guitar, "Real" or "Hot" Country, as it became known, attracted great clumps of suddenly intrigued crossover customers who hadn't been exposed to country before and were charmed by all the quaint lines about boots, hound dogs, and achy-breaky hearts. From Tracy Byrd to Tracy Lawrence, the voices that sold were clear, smoothly drawling tenors and baritones. Nice enough nearly all of them, but mostly quite similar and decidedly lacking in character. Ear candy, they call it in Nashville. A Madison Avenue advertising man put it to me: "It's slick stuff and it sells. That's the American way." In the best pop tradition, Real Country has also proven to be quite ephemeral stuff. Almost everything coming out of Nashville that spins off the radio and onto the charts soon fades away. The songs don't last because they are devoid of passion and authentic feeling.

In the vanguard of Real Country has been a young man who grew up in the suburbs of Oklahoma City listening to glam-rock bands like Kiss and Queen. Garth Brooks went to Oklahoma State, where he studied marketing and advertising. This education has helped him to conceive baroque, carefully choreographed stage shows that feature as many as five guitar players, colored lights, smoke machines, rope ladders, and swings. As for his music, it has anthemic titles such as "American Honky Tonk Bar Association" and "Friends in Low Places," with choruses like "I'm not big on social graces/Think I'll slip on down to the oasis/Oh I've got friends in low places." There are women who would "give half of Texas just to change the way he feels" and men like "Papa" who "was a good 'n/But the jealous kind." Vigorously though he drops his y'alls, Brooks's songs seem carefully assembled from a series of generic boxes stamped "Country Lyrics." Alas, *Poeta nascitur, non fit*—a poet is born, not made.

Brooks delivers his lines in a voice that is certainly pleasant, but limited in range and not especially distinctive. The real problem is, I suppose, that his songs lack both the rough edges and the feel for pressing experience that you find in the singing of people like George Jones, Merle Haggard, and Johnny Cash. Their lives really have been hard, something that's obvious from their singing. With Brooks there is often the sense that he is aping something he saw somebody else try. On stage, at the climax of a song, he will sometimes smash his guitar to pieces—traditionally a rock 'n' roll gesture made famous by the likes of Pete Townshend. When Ira Louvin destroyed his mandolin or Johnny Cash kicked out the footlights at *The Grand Ole Opry,* it was no contrived bad-boy rock act, but spasms of misery from men whose music also suggested their tortured souls. Brooks is a pop star masquerading as a country singer, a yuppie with a lariat.

But he sells. His albums *No Fences* and *Ropin' the Wind,* with combined receipts of around twenty million copies, are the two best-selling country records in history. Just thirty-three, Brooks has already outsold Michael Jackson and every other American popular singer. (Only the Beatles have sold more in the United States.) His fans are deliriously loyal. One of them, an Iowa dairy farmer's wife, stood in a large cooler at the Iowa State Fair and sculpted a life-size replica of the singer from four hundred pounds of her husband's sweet butter.

I was eager to see what the fuss was about, and so I went to Fan Fair, the country music industry's self-described "lovefest" between fans and their favorite singers, held annually at the Tennessee State Fairgrounds in Nashville. At Fan Fair you can take in concerts given from a stage set up at the center of a stock-car track, savor home-style barbecue and bean lunches, and peruse gift shops flogging Tanya Tucker sneakers. But at $90 a ticket, what really tempts people is the opportunity to mingle with the big stars of the moment, who are all there, perched in lavishly appointed booths in the sheep and swine barns, ready to shake and hug, exchange endearments, and sign photographs of themselves.

At Brooks's booth, a buzzing crowd was on hand. The singer's signature black Stetson was visible. So too was one of his blue western-style shirts and a pair of battered boots. Everything, in short, was there except Brooks himself, who was "taking it easy" at his parents' house in Oklahoma, according to Tami Rose, the editor of *The Believer,* the official Garth Brooks quarterly magazine. In his stead, Brooks had sent along a life-size cardboard cutout of himself. This virtual Garth couldn't sign autographs, but fans were invited to slip into the authentic, guaranteed-to-have-been-worn-by-Garth boots, shirt, and hat and pose for a photograph beside it. Then they could walk over to a video camera and record a personal message that the singer had promised he would watch. I didn't doubt it. This is, after all, someone who claims he reads all his fan mail and who writes music that, well, sounds like it.

The biggest reason for Real Country's success is that it's what gets played on country radio—to the exclusion of everything else. Most large country radio stations rely on a standardized playlist that is distributed all over the United States. Even if disc jockeys at country stations wished to stray from the sheet and play records by other singers, they couldn't, something Iris DeMent's husband Elmer discovered after a man at a country radio station rejected DeMent's latest single. "I'll tell you why we won't play this," the radio man said. "It's too country. We only play Real Country."

DeMent is writing country songs that Merle Haggard thinks are as good as anything he knows, yet most people who say they love country music have never heard of her. As for Haggard, his most recent release, *1996*, is among the better records this gifted man has yet recorded. But he is approaching sixty now, with cracks in his face and gray in his thinning hair, so you won't hear "Truck Driver's Blues" or any of the other new Haggard songs on country radio. In this day when brilliant marketing has helped so many new people to discover country music, they aren't exposed to the best of it.

Older country fans know very well what they're missing. In a recent letter to *Newsweek* following the publication of an article in which Haggard fretted that perhaps he was a "has-been," a man named Jim Dennis wrote to complain: "Much of country music today is dominated by young soap-opera look-alikes singing pop-oriented radio fluff. Merle gives off something that is missing in today's society—genuineness. He has lived through a lot and sings about it all with convincing authenticity."

Another correspondent, William D. Gibson, responded to the same article with what approached an epistolary dirge: "Country ain't country no more," he said. "[The true] country tells a story, relaxes the listener, rips at your heart, brings tears to your eyes, and buoys your spirit. The new stuff has crummy lyrics and even worse sound. And the new singers are a bunch of wimp wanna-bes. Though they do make a helluva lot of money, they're not country and never will be."

The story of country music parallels the extended migration that began when large numbers of people left northern England, Ireland, and Scotland late in the eighteenth century and met with a cool welcome in Amer-

*Hank Williams always slouched when he sang, physical evidence that
the world rested heavy on him. "Ol' Hank, he was all right,"
says Kitty Wells. "The people loved him."*

ican port cities like Philadelphia. They pushed out into the hills of Virginia and North Carolina and, as work and farmland grew scarce, made their way by mule, wagon, railroad, and then, during the Dust Bowl, by wounded automobile, into the middle and deep South, across into Arkansas, Missouri, and Texas, and finally all the way to New Mexico and California. It's no accident that you can still hear a lot of North Carolina and Alabama in the voices of some Texas and California country singers.

For many poor farmers beaten down by debt, drought, declining cotton prices, skinflint landowners, costly newfangled machinery, and swarming insects, the migration concluded with a trudge into town. To be sure, many country singers and fans were farm people, but a lot of the music was also prompted by the dislocation and rural nostalgia working-class Southern Americans felt as industrial jobs called them to booming cities like Memphis, Nashville, Birmingham, Atlanta, Charleston, Norfolk, Chicago, Detroit, and Los Angeles. As Lov Bensey in Erskine Caldwell's *Tobacco Road* says of his father-in-law, Jeeter Lester, who refuses to leave his failing farm for a city job in the mill, "He was a man who liked to grow things in the ground. The mills ain't no place for a human who's got that in his bones."

It wasn't so much that the music was Southern that made it so important to people. The point was more that country took into account an audience who thought of life as a struggle. (As the guitar player and record producer Chet Atkins said, "There was no reason why it should be limited to the South. They didn't have a monopoly on the hard times.") Or, as Hank Williams put it in his famous comments to *Nation's Business* magazine, "He sings more sincere than most entertainers because the hillbilly was raised rougher than most entertainers."

Williams and Jimmie Rodgers are gone, but many of country's greatest musicians are still out there, and that's who I set out to find. I spent the past few years traveling around the United States—in the country of country—talking with country singers, musicians, and songwriters whose music I admire about their lives, the places they come from, and their work. The oldest living person I spoke with, Bill Monroe, was born in 1911, and the youngest, Iris DeMent, fifty years later. And so in a loose sort of way this is a history of the recorded genre. Yet country is deceptively simple music and I don't pretend to offer either a formal or a comprehensive study. I couldn't fit everyone in, and many fine living performers, like Hank Snow, Jimmy Martin, Dolly Parton, Eddy Arnold, and Ray Price, are not included.

Country musicians are generally very aware of their place in the history of the music. The ones I met talked a lot about the music that influenced their own. I hope some of the people they bring up in these conversations—great country performers of the past like "Uncle" Dave Macon, Maybelle Carter, Bob Wills, Patsy Montana, Roy Acuff, Alton Delmore, Ernest Tubb, Hank Williams, Lester Flatt, Lefty Frizzell, Faron Young, and, of course, Jimmie Rodgers—will become slightly more familiar.

Many of the musicians I met began performing in a day when playing country music got you derided as a hillbilly or worse. That they kept to it was, for them, a point of pride. Country music was a way to express frustration at the social exclusion experienced by people they knew, and also a means of solidarity for people who felt marginalized by American society. To now find themselves displaced by tricked-up imitations of their own music is a bitter turn of events.

The situation led to discussions of what country music is. People came to various conclusions, but along the way most of them ended up explaining why, to them, Real Country isn't really country. They don't dismiss it because it's commercial; from Jimmie Rodgers's day on, country has always been commercial music. Their concern is more that Real Country doesn't meet Hank Williams's prescription: it doesn't sound sincere. The spirit of Jimmie Rodgers is suddenly missing from mainstream country. Or as George Jones put it, "They've taken the heart and soul out of country music." Almost without exception, the country musicians I spoke with told me that country music "has to be played with feeling." Yet if you ask any of them what this means, the answer is always a variation on the response Fats Waller gave to a woman who wondered about the meaning of jazz: "If you don't know by now, I can't tell you," he said. I hope some feeling for the feeling comes through in what follows.

Crowds in the 1940s, waiting to enter the Ryman Auditorium for a performance of The Grand Ole Opry. *People across the country looked forward all week to the Saturday night radio broadcasts. One of them was Harlan Howard: "I was just a bored kid on a farm. It was a little lonesome."*

PART ONE

NASHVILLE CATS

Harlan Howard teaching Waylon Jennings (right) a song in the 1960s.
"I'm looking for lines you don't expect."

HARLAN HOWARD

NOTES ON
PAPER NAPKINS

"If you want to make a living writing country music songs, stay away from Nashville. They'll just break your heart," Willie Nelson told Waylon Jennings over a bottle of tequila in 1965. "Upon hearing my advice," continued Nelson, "Waylon did what any good songwriter would do. He went to Nashville." From Roger Miller and Kris Kristofferson to Lucinda Williams and Guy Clark, they all do; that's where the cupboard is. For decades Nashville has been Grub Street to a surfeit of young song hustlers who grew up somewhere else and arrived in town by bus or by '41 Buick to try out a trunkful of lines as supple as "I'm so lonesome I could cry" or as crass as "She broke my heart (I broke her jaw)" on anyone who will lend an ear. Since songwriters—like gold miners—are notoriously blowsy and busted, usually it's only other songwriters who do the listening. "Sitting around talking to writers in Nashville is the most depressing thing in the world," Nelson said to Jan Reid. "There are just so many of them—and it gets to the point where it's niggers and dogs and writers stay off the grass."

In recent years the genteel old Southern city of Nashville has finally recovered from the embarrassment of being "Hillbilly Heaven." But if the prosperous executives on Music Row are now gingerly embraced by the Belle Meade gentry, country music songwriters are still regarded as a raffish, somewhat tawdry lot. Nashville is a suburb at heart, a green expanse of gentle hills where, just a few blocks from downtown, you can see possum and deer slipping across front lawns. Most people drive everywhere they go and eat dinner at home, and so the city's public transportation and restaurants are limited. Several fine universities, including Vanderbilt and Fisk, are in Nashville, and the city still likes to think of itself as "The Athens of the South"—in a park off West End Avenue is a full-scale replica of the Parthenon replete with a 42-foot-high statue of Athena—but this is a homogenized place. Nashville has never really desegregated: its black residents rarely venture into white neighborhoods. There are plenty of tony shopping centers and golf courses in Music City, but very little soul.

The veteran producer Jim Rooney thinks the presence of all the songwriters adds verve to the setting. "They've always given leavening to a town that might otherwise be a little on the flat side," he says. Part of this is that the precarious nature of the work stimulates quirky behavior. Coming up with three-minute hit after three-minute hit is a struggle for even the most prolific songwriters, and so they develop odd tics to urge the business along. Sometimes when he was dry on inspiration, John D. Loudermilk, who wrote "Tobacco Road" and "Talk Back Trembling Lips," consulted a weather map and left town to chase hurricanes. Dallas Frazier—"There Goes My Everything" and "Beneath Still Waters"—used to jump in a sedan with a friend and a sixpack of beer and drive haphazardly through Tennessee farmland until he was lost on the back roads. Kris Kristofferson—"Sunday Morning Coming Down," "Me and Bobby McGee," "Help Me Make It Through the Night"—went for helicopter rides. When Harlan Howard, the sixty-eight-year-old writer of more than four thousand country songs, fifty or more of which became *Billboard* top-ten hits, has been keeping too much company with a blank sheet of paper, he heads off to a cocktail lounge for a little eavesdropping.

The dean of Nashville songwriters first came to the city thirty-five years ago with a U-Haul trailer hitched to the back of a shiny new white Cadillac Coupé de Ville. Howard bought the car after "Heartaches by the Number," a song he'd written while working as a forklift operator in a California factory, went number-one on both the country and pop charts. Howard hasn't let the Nashville skyline out of his sight since. Nor has he driven anything but a Cadillac.

"I love Cadillacs and this one's paid for," Howard was saying from behind the wheel of a red '88 Eldorado at the stroke of noon on a summertime Nashville Friday. Over the years, he has developed a philosophy of sorts about life as a Nashville songwriter. He believes, for example, in a revision of Samuel Johnson's bon mot "No man but a blockhead ever wrote, except for money," which holds that "A good writer is a broke writer." He is also convinced that if a songwriter has not successfully sold a tune to a producer by noon on a Friday when there are golf courses open in Nashville or in Florida, he will have no luck with it at least until Monday and is best advised to take cover in a nearby saloon.

That morning, Howard had been fooling around with something he was calling "I'm the Only Thing Bluer Than Her Eyes." But now, the pitching hour having passed, we were driving the six blocks from his office to Sammy B's on the Row, a bar where Howard "does a lot of business," to meet some "juveniles." To Howard, a "juvenile" is a younger songwriter. At this point, his is a profession with very few adult offenders.

Sammy B's is a dimly lit room centered by a mahogany bar guarding a generous stock of tequila. Howard's seat of choice—which he and other writers call "the pole position"—is at the end of the bar closest to the front door. Howard likes it because "it's where you can talk to people." More important, it's the best spot for listening in on conversations. For Howard has filched his share of lyrics from taprooms. In 1957, he was sitting in a Los Angeles joint called George's Roundup waiting for a friend when he overheard a man who was quarreling with his date tell her, "Well, you can just pick me up on your way down." Howard picked up a paper bar napkin, set the line down on it, and he had the title of one of his best-known songs.

As it happened, the pole position at Sammy B's was unoccupied—not that Howard should have anticipated otherwise: the proprietor has bolted a small engraved metal plaque to the mahogany that says "Reserved for Harlan Howard." Settling onto his stool, Howard cast an affectionate eye toward the tequila. "I'm not hungry but I'm thirsty," he growled happily, ordering up a shot along with a beer to chase it. He didn't exactly nurse them. "Drinkin's kinda like goin' fishin'—makes me forget I'm a writer," he likes to say. "When I'm drinkin', I'm not writin'. I'm celebratin' or grievin' or stuck."

Howard is a rolled-up-shirtsleeve of a man with a pair of narrow slits for eyes in a face that vodka and tequila have stained red. He prefers to forgo socks but flashes his broad, boyish grin often, as if in compensation. His thick hair is white and his ample prizefighter's nose makes waitresses feel softly toward him even before he tips them too much. "I got a hell of a nose," he will sometimes say, without provocation.

He said he was reconsidering his song title. "I may call it 'Bluer Than Her Eyes,' " he said. "Shorter is usually better. Fits on the label, for one thing. Of course I called one song 'Blame It on Your Lyin', Cheatin', Cold Dead Beatin', Two Timin', Double Dealin', Mean Mistreatin', Lovin' Heart.' Actually, we called it 'Blame It on Your Heart,' and had a number-one record. I wanted to call it 'Blame It on Your Etc. Heart.' Patty Loveless did it."

By this time, the juveniles were arriving. Howard effortlessly dispensed with his latest tequila and moved himself from the bar to a table. He sat down near Ralph Murphy and Pat Alger. Murphy is a slender man of fifty-two with gunmetal streaks in his longish hair who has written hits for Crystal Gayle and Ronnie Milsap. Alger is rosy and plump, which seems about right in someone who sometimes writes for Garth Brooks. Murphy, with some glee, described how he came to know Howard. "We hung out at bars together and somebody would be talking," he said. "A killer line would come out and you'd see hands creeping out for bar napkins to scribble on. From the end of the bar would come a low voice: Harlan saying, 'I wrote it already.' Years later he said to me, 'Ralph, remember all those songs I told you I already wrote? I went home and wrote them.' " Murphy shook his head. "Cagey bastard," he said.

As Howard had promised, money turns out to be much on a songwriter's mind, a fact that seems to point to both the abiding incredulity writers have at the notion that they can earn large sums with the idle thoughts they scribble on napkins, and the inverse recognition of how difficult it is to make a living flogging songs. Even before their hamburgers and sandwiches arrived, the songwriters were discussing who would pick up the tab. It was an animated conversation. "We got this deal," Howard explained. "Whoever's got the hottest song on the *Billboard* buys, even though you don't get paid for a year. One day we were desperate. Then a kid named Ronnie Rogers comes in and says, 'I got a hold by [the band] Alabama.' We said, 'He's buying!' We stuck him with three hundred bucks worth of booze. We felt so good, we almost felt we had a hit ourselves."

Murphy was smiling. "We have a lifeboat mentality," he said. "One thing you notice about everybody in Nashville who's a writer is that nobody's from here. Most of us spent a lot of years trying to get here. This is the last Tin Pan Alley." He looked over at Howard and went on: "You can be seventy and still be having hits. Nashville's a real family of writers. Most writers have a piece missing. Either they're from broken homes or they're orphans. They write to be loved."

◆ ◆ ◆

Howard was a Michigan farmboy orphan. He might have come from West Virginia—generations of Howards and Steeds had lived either in Huntington or across the river into Kentucky. But the Depression hit Appalachia with punishing force and, as Howard later described the situation in the original version of his song "Busted," his father, Ralph Howard, and many Kentucky, Ohio, and West Virginia blue-collar families found themselves moving on: "Our friends are all leaving this old mining town, they're busted/They're heading up north where there's work to be found, and trusted/Lord I hate to give up this acre of land/It's been in the family since mining began/But babies get hungry, they don't understand that Dad's busted."

By the early 1930s, the famous "Illinois Central" black migration from the Mississippi Delta to the "Promised Land" of the industrial Midwest—which Howard describes in "Mississippi Delta Land," his account of an illiterate, landless farmer who heads north to Chicago—was comple-

Auto workers outside the Ford plant in Detroit. Many of them were Southerners pushed north by the Depression.

mented by a parallel diaspora of working-class Southern whites, also looking for jobs in the factories of Cleveland, Chicago, and Detroit. Ralph Howard found $5-a-day work in Henry Ford's Michigan auto plants, but his marriage didn't last. When he and Evelyn split up, the family began dispersing as well. From 1933 until 1944, when he turned seventeen and enlisted, the way to find Harlan was either through the Michigan Children's Institute or the Children's Aid Society.

The state paid families $7 a month to keep a child in those days, and Howard was the ward of a succession of them. Mostly these were elderly couples who lived on farms outside Lansing and wanted a young pair of hands to help out with the chores. Howard was a willing laborer, but he found life on the farm dreary. The winters were long, the company sparse, and the diversions few.

There were exceptions, however. When they moved north, Southerners brought their culture with them. Sprinkling the Michigan countryside were Baptist churches and "meat-and-three" restaurants serving everything you'd find in Georgia but the grits. On weekends, traveling evangelical preachers sponsored outdoor revival meetings. And through the radio came country music. It was over a Philco radio on the potato and wheat farm owned by the Whitney family of Leslie, Michigan, that Harlan Howard first heard the low, cracked voice of "The Texas Troubadour," Ernest Tubb, singing "When the World Has Turned You Down" during a broadcast of *The Grand Ole Opry*. He was hooked.

The Whitneys had already gone to bed by early evening on Saturday nights when the show aired, and so Howard would creep downstairs to the den next to their bedroom where the radio was kept, turn the volume down low, and listen with his ear pressed against the speaker. Soon—he didn't quite know why—Howard was copying Tubb's song lyrics onto scraps of paper. "I couldn't get 'em down fast enough, so I started writing my own verses," he says. "I'd turn off the radio after I got the melody. It was like a little adventure. In those days you couldn't tell where his stuff stopped and mine began. I was still a kid, a virgin, and would be for a long time, but he'd sing those love songs and they'd move me." Plenty of other performers worked the *Opry* in addition to Tubb, and Howard got to like Roy Acuff's wistful ballads and Bill Monroe's backwoods tragedies too. "When all these other people started singing wonderful songs, I decided what I really loved was a good sad country love song. My hobby became country music. Kind of a funny way to get into a profession. I was just a bored kid on a farm. The nearest kid was four years older than me and he lived half a mile away. Not being with your family and not having other children to play with, it was a little lonesome."

At seventeen, Howard left Michigan for the Army paratrooper training school at Fort Benning, Georgia, where, among other things, he learned to play the guitar. On weekends he hung out with two Southern boys who taught him a few chords on a six-string borrowed from the PX. "I got two hit titles out of the Army," Howard says. " 'Heartaches by the Number,' because everything in the Army is by the number, and I turned above and beyond the call of duty into 'Above and Beyond the Call of Love.' You take things that are part of your life and turn 'em into love songs."

In 1949, his stretch completed, he went back to Michigan and took a job "doing flunky-type work" in a foundry in Port Huron, which paid for his first guitar. His mother had been remarried, to a man who lived in Port Huron, and so Howard had a new family there. On weekends he took to helping his stepbrother, Joe, cleaning and updating the jukeboxes in the restaurants and taverns in and around the city. "I'd always get acquainted with the waitresses and bartenders," he says. "They have so many stories. To this day I know every bartender and waitress in Nashville. They're my friends. I'm an old factory worker. I draw a lot from those friendships. It gives me a focus when I say 'Who the hell am I writing these songs for?' "

Howard was working in a factory that supplied General Motors plants with parts in 1953, when he met a waitress named Trudy and married her. Besides conducting a courtship, he'd been practicing his guitar and reading about the country music people like Tex Ritter were making in Southern California. Howard had always hated Michigan winters. "I said to my wife, let's move to California," he says. "They've got factories. They've got country music." Two years after their wedding, he and Trudy drove west.

California did have factories and Howard worked in a lot of them. He never earned much more than minimum wage, but the situation had its advantages. "Not having any skills to make big bucks like the tool-and-die guys, all the jobs I took were low-paying jobs, like being an oiler," he says. "I'd walk around with a squirt can and a can of oil to the huge punch presses and keep them oiled. Once that was done I'd sit in a tool crib until the machines started getting hot again. I had six hours out of eight to goof off, so I'd write songs on the back of production sheets. I had free paper. I was paid. I had free time. I'd come home with a whole pocket stuffed full of lyrics. I never took a punch-press job or anything where I'd have to stand in one place. I did things like bring parts to a handful of guys on an auto production line. Somebody has to bring the guys on the line their parts, except that once I'd gone out there, I'd have four hours to write. I'd go hide behind some boxes and write songs."

This wasn't going over very well at home. "My wife didn't like the fact that all I wanted to be was a country music songwriter," he says. "She wanted me to go back to school and get a profession. She told me she'd work two jobs if I'd be an architect. God!" he was nearly shouting. "She called it *hillybilly* music. That pissed me off. She was talkin' about something I loved. It was like a satanic force in my house." Another of Howard's rules of songwriting is that the work makes for divorces by the number, and soon enough he had his first.

He moved into a boarding house, took a new job driving a forklift truck in a book bindery, and began getting to know the West Coast country crowd. He did it methodically, knocking on every door along Selma Avenue in Hollywood, where most country music singers picked up their business mail. When he walked into the offices of Red River Songs to find Tex Ritter and Johnny Bond with their boots on the desk and hats on their heads, it was Howard's good fortune that the cowboys were in jovial humor. They told Howard to play them a few songs and then asked him to send them a tape, which, after some cajoling, they listened to. Soon Howard was writing, in effect, a country song version of a Robert Service poem, the only western tune Howard ever wrote. He called it "The Blizzard," and in 1961, "Cowboy" Jim Reeves would ride it to number one.

Howard had never lived in West Texas, much less taken a dog and a lame pony seven miles through a driving prairie snowstorm, but he says this lack wasn't important in writing "The Blizzard," just as it didn't matter that he had yet to set foot in Maryland when he wrote the mournful "Streets of Baltimore." "I can't write about anything I don't know a little about," he says. "Michigan has some of the worst blizzards you've ever seen. But most of my songs aren't story songs. Most are emotion songs and the emotions are things I've felt. You know, I'm not even born in the right place," he says. "I'm supposed to be from Texas or Alabama. A hillbilly from Michigan? Give me a break. But I'm one of the countriest of all of them and I got the songs to prove it."

Harlan Howard's best songs work around the idea of revealing how people behave when they think nobody is watching and what those actions say about them. As he says in "Sunday Morning Christian," "it's a long time till Sunday." In "The Blizzard," the tragic cowboy perishes in the cold a hundred yards from his beloved Mary Anne's door, because he loyally waits for his dog to catch up. In "Heartaches by the Number," a woman tells the man who is infatuated with her what he wants to hear, but she doesn't mean it:

> *Heartache number three was when you called me*
> *And said that you were coming back to stay*
> *With hopeful heart I waited for your knock on the door*
> *I waited but you must have lost your way.*

The language in Howard's songs is always plain, and never once is a love-blinded sap taken to task for being slow to recognize that he is being fooled by a crafty vixen. The just are celebrated, even when—especially when—they are good-hearted hellraisers, like Harlan Howard himself.

Another friendship Howard struck up in Los Angeles was with the singer and bandleader Wynn Stewart. When the factory shut down for the evening, Howard would go to the nightclubs where Stewart had gigs and listen in on nearby conversations while waiting for Stewart to finish up. Then they'd get pancakes and coffee together. Sometimes Stewart's girlfriend would meet them, and once she brought along a friend of *hers* who became Jan Howard after the Howards' wedding in Las Vegas. They'd been married for a little while when one morning, Howard overheard his shy new wife quietly singing to herself in the kitchen and, impressed, began using her to do the demos on the "girl" songs he wrote. Soon she had a recording contract. Jan Howard performs on *The Grand Ole Opry* to this day.

Howard says that so much was going on in his life between 1955 and 1956 that "it all gets jumbled." Stewart took him up to Bakersfield to meet "a good ol' country boy" named Buck Owens. After that, on weekends Howard was driving to Bakersfield on his own, staying with Owens and writing songs. One of them, about divorce, was called "Daddy for a Day." It didn't take until a year later, when Howard revised it into "Mommy for a Day," and Kitty Wells scooped it up. Owens eventually put the song into Capitol wax himself. Meanwhile, Freddie Hart recorded Howard's "The Wall" and "Chain Gang," Stewart did "You Took Her off My Hands," and both Stewart and Owens sang a version of "Above and Beyond the Call of Love."

A songwriter makes his money through a publisher, who licenses the songs for recording and broadcast and collects royalties on them, giving the songwriter his percentage. Until now Howard had no deal. Then one day, a songwriter and bricklayer named Lance Guynes visited Howard at his frame house not far from the poker clubs in Gardena, California. They sang some songs for each other. Howard sang "Pick Me Up on Your Way Down." Guynes was very impressed. He told Howard about a small publishing firm in Nashville called Pamper Music, run by Hal Smith, Ernest Tubb's old fiddle player. "I'll send it to them for you," Guynes offered, and Howard told him to go right ahead.

Howard was still working in the book bindery a few weeks later when he received the first telephone call he'd ever taken on the factory floor. "The punch presses were so loud I could barely hear," he says. "This guy was saying 'My name is Ray Price. I love your songs. 'Pick Me Up on Your Way Down' is my favorite. Charlie Walker, Ernest Tubb, and I fought over it. Finally we decided that the decent thing to do was to give it to Charlie, because he needed a hit. I'm going in to record in a week or two. Have you got any new songs?" Howard sent him three the next day. He can't remember anymore what the first two were called, but the third was "Heartaches by the Number," and when Price's and Guy Mitchell's renditions topped the country and pop charts simultaneously, Howard was the only forklift driver in America who could switch on his car radio during the drive home from work, press all five preset station buttons, and hear a song he'd written playing on every one. Howard had kids in school. Once they got out in June, it was on to Tennessee.

Over the next fifteen years Howard was, he puts it, "hot as hell." He worked in a perpetual frenzy, writing two or three songs a day, five days a week. Most he called "practice songs." With the rest he made himself a fine living, pitching them to Owen Bradley at Decca, Chet Atkins at RCA, Don Law at Columbia, and Ken Nelson, who would come into town from the Capitol Records headquarters in L.A. "Chet and Owen were my main men," Howard says. "Chet was always very much a melody man, maybe because he was a guitar player. Owen was a word stickler. You learn to know your opponents, and they are opponents. All producers aren't the same. You'd analyze the song at home, decide who would like it, and then you'd go in. I'd sometimes get rejected one place, take it to the other, and get me a hit record. Nashville was kind of like a little family then. You didn't even need appointments. I'd go by Owen's office and his secretary would just buzz me up. He had thirty singers. I'd bring a song and he'd decide who it was for."

Howard regards the 1960s as a halcyon time to be a napkin scribbler. In his view, 1960 was the birth of what he calls "Left Bank Paris," alongside the Cumberland River. Nashville was a writer's town and Howard had a high time barstooling it with Willie Nelson, Hank Cochran, Mel Tillis, Roger Miller, and young Waylon Jennings in from Lubbock, Texas, by way of Arizona. Singers, as always, loved him too, and he counted Faron Young, Jim Reeves, Webb Pierce, Lefty Frizzell, and his favorite, Patsy Cline, among his cronies.

The rendezvous was always Tootsie's Orchid Lounge, a seedy café just across Broadway from the Ernest Tubb Record Shop and down the alley from the Ryman Auditorium—the *Opry* site. Tootsie was Hattie Louise Bess, a heavyset, maternal woman—the place had once been known as Mom's—willing to extend credit to a songwriter who hadn't had a hit in a while. She was also generous with a sharp hatpin or even her nightstick when someone was slow to withdraw at closing time. (On the night a famous sideman was inspired to slap his virility down on the bar she chose the nightstick, forever putting an end to *that* method of payment.) While the regular crowd drank downstairs, the songwriters sipped beer, ate red beans and corn bread, and swapped songs on the second floor. "It was so neat then," Howard says. "Hank Snow and Ernest Tubb had record deals and they'd ask you for a ballad or a sad song. One night George Hamilton IV told me he needed a song and I took him 'Three Steps to the Phone.' He got a top-five hit with it. Patsy's in there on *Opry* night in her stage dress—at first in her cowgirl-type thing, and then gowns. Patsy and Hank Williams, biggest heroes I know of in country music. She was a good old girl. She liked songwriters. Patsy loved Hank Cochran, Roger Miller, Willie Nelson, Mel Tillis, and me because we were lighthearted, not too serious. All of us were always getting divorced because you can't be at Tootsie's every night missing dinner and stay married. We weren't bad. We didn't have other women. We didn't talk so much, either. Hell, we'd sing. Somebody'd always bring along a guitar and it would kind of go around the room. I didn't sing much—I've never really liked to sing—but when Willie Nelson got the guitar, he'd keep it a long time. It never occurred to me then that he wanted to be a singer. Now I realize that was a thrill for him."

Most people stayed in town for a while and then moved on. Roger "King of the Road" Miller got hot and left for California. Kris Kristofferson didn't stop there, going all the way to Hawaii. Willie Nelson went home to Texas. Hank Cochran bought himself a Tennessee farm. Mel

Reunion at Tootsie's: Bobby Bare, Kris Kristofferson, Harlan Howard,
Willie Nelson, and Billy Walker in 1994. "All of us were always getting
divorced because you can't be at Tootsie's every night and stay married."

Tillis has ended up playing two shows a day in the theater he built atop an
Ozarks hogback in Branson, Missouri. Howard remains on Sixteenth
Avenue South. The man who wrote "I Fall to Pieces" with Cochran for
Patsy Cline was around to write for Patty Loveless, Wynonna Judd, and
Mel's daughter, Pam Tillis. "I wanted to be as professional as the great Tin
Pan Alley writers were, but I wanted to do it here, in country music,
because that's what moved me," he says. "I wanted to take the profession-
alism of the old Brill Building, Jerome Kern, Irving Berlin, Hoagy Car-
michael, and couple that with the soul of Ernest Tubb. Tubb wrote from
the heart and he touched people. That's all I'm still wanting to do. We've
all been through the stuff bein' hillbillies, siderunners—that's a guy with
one leg shorter than the other from running alongside a hill. I've always
laughed at Nashville laughing at us. They really don't understand how
neat it is, how soulful. Ray Price or Eddy Arnold putting a tear in your
eye—that's emotion same as in a great book or movie."

Howard has no truck with songwriters who treat country music lightly by relying on puns and quips. "A hook is like a punchline joke," he snaps. "Who'd want to hear a joke over and over again? When Hank Williams said, 'Your cheatin' heart will make you weep' or Irving Berlin says, 'I'm dreaming of a white Christmas,' or in 'I Fall to Pieces,' you make a statement right up front, and explain why you said that. It's not always trying to be clever. I don't write a lot of funny songs. It's always hard to have depth and soul in a song and be clever at the same time."

Brevity is a Harlan Howard specialty. He uses the minimal possible number of chords and lets his melodies follow the lyrics. That's to say that a joyful line never comes with a dirgelike melody. When the song says "Pick me up on your way down," the melody rises and then falls sharply. When someone is "feeling mighty low," the last chord tumbles. Howard even tries to avoid instrumental bridges—he calls them "releases"—but generally includes one because he wants to give his listener a moment to reflect on previous verses, much in the way a prose writer might follow a complex thought with a terse sentence.

"I'm looking for lines you don't expect coming at you," he says. "I'm driving along in my car sometimes, listening to the radio, and I can predict what the next line and the next line of a new song will be—I can tell you what the writer's going to say before he gets there. And I'm right. And if I can predict it, anybody can predict it, and that's mediocre writing. I love to play with words, to condense things, to put a whole half story in one line. People tell me that when they hear a Harlan Howard song on the radio, they know I wrote it. I got a little something going—it might be simplicity. I don't waste a lot of words. Kris Kristofferson was much more of a poet than I am. I admire his imagery. You can make anything you want of his songs. I'm more straight-ahead, like Hank Williams or Fred Rose."

His message is pretty direct, too. Howard says there is an implicit morality in country music, a basic Protestant system that defies the hypocrisy he tweaks in "Sunday Morning Christian." "Good is good, bad will suffer and your cheatin' heart will make you weep," he recites. "Most people don't understand that Hank Williams was preaching to them just as fervently as a Baptist preacher on Sunday. I like that thread—good is good, bad gets your ass kicked. I believe it." The villains in Howard's songs are never difficult to spot, and they are always punished, if not within the song, then because of the song.

As Howard sees it, the country writer's special province is the love song. Country is booming now, he says, because Americans crave love songs as naturally as they do seconds on Thanksgiving, and other forms of popular music haven't been supplying them. "But guess who's here and can write the shit out of 'em?" he exults. "Me and my friends! Us, a bunch of guys sitting around getting divorced because they're writing about love. The world needs love songs. We're accidentally locked into the need for a mate."

After thirty-five years in Nashville, Howard's life there has changed very little save that the trappings are now a little sleeker. He keeps getting married and divorced; he is currently six years into his fifth marriage to "a wonderful, wonderful" woman named Melanie who is half his age and who is so nice to him that when Howard talks about her he sounds as though he can't quite believe his good fortune. Every year he has a birth-day bash, and though it used to be an intimate reunion of the old Tootsie's crowd, these days it's held outside, on a huge parking lot across the street from Mickey Gilley's nightclub and behind the Conway Twitty Gift Shop.

Howard even has an office in a house just off Music Row, with a var-nished wood and brass desk, faux Persian carpet, lamps with fox-hunting scenes on the shades, and a gleaming ceiling fan. Fox-hunting scenes? Putting Harlan Howard in a fancy office is a little like asking Damon Runyon to conduct business from a tearoom. Howard looks sheepish the whole time he's inside the place, swears a bit more here even than usual, and really seems like himself only when he's safely behind a table at Sammy B's.

At Sammy B's the plates have been cleared and all the writers now have a glass of beer and a package of cigarettes in front of them. It is midafter-noon and the discussion is careening back and forth between two of their favorite topics: Nashville and divorces. Songwriters snicker a bit at singers who may make the big money, but have to spend their lives singing the same songs over and over again while living what Howard thinks is "an awful life," spent in "cramped buses and staying in those terrible motels." Songwriters, he believes, can keep their minds open to new ideas and see their friends all over Nashville anytime they get lonely.

"This may be the most unique creative community in the world," says Ralph Murphy. Murphy is getting a little maudlin, which nobody holds against him, particularly because he has just picked up the check. "I've lived in New York. I've lived in L.A.," he says. "Everybody marvels at the sense of cooperation here. It's competitive, but it's healthy. The interesting thing about Harlan is that he's been able to sustain that competitive desire for decades. And even for Harlan, the rejection he's had compared to the amount of success is incredible. There are famous songs, but not many famous songwriters."

And then Murphy is talking about divorces. "Harlan figures it this way," he says. "He writes three number-one records when he falls in love and three number-one records when he gets divorced. You always fall in love. And then you're so down. You keep writing because you hope you'll figure it out some day."

Howard shakes some salt into his beer and nods. "Ex-wives give me the titles," he says. "Where the hell do you think those songs come from? They didn't come from the factory. All there is in a fork truck is three forks."

Murphy looks over at me. "You married?" he asks.

I say that I'm not. The songwriters all just stare at me, expectantly, but I'm not even divorced yet.

"C'mon, you cute bastard," says Howard.

"Well," I say. "I just got a telephone call last night from an old girl-friend telling me she was getting married."

"How'd you feel about it?" Murphy asks.

"Better him than me," I say.

"Umm," says Murphy, pulling out a scrap of paper.

"I already wrote it," says Howard.

Chet Atkins. "I was original—my style sounded like two bad guitar players."

CHET ATKINS

TAKING OUT THE TWANG

"I've always had a country aroma," the brilliant guitar player Chet Atkins was saying. "You know, that's where I first got slightly famous. But I didn't want to be pigeonholed. I wanted to play all kinds of music. When I became a professional I could play only three tunes: 'Seein' Nellie Home,' 'Bye Bye Blues,' and 'When You and I Were Young, Maggie.' It's popular in Ireland, that song. A fellow I worked for in Knoxville in 1944 told me, 'You're our new soloist, you have to play two or three new songs a week.' So I gradually learned to play while I was making a living at it. I think if people knew how far I've come they'd be amazed. I don't know how the hell I did it. I was shy and backward. I got fired a lot. I was original—my style sounded like two bad guitar players. Everybody was playing with a straight pick. I was playing guitar with my thumb and three fingers, which turns out to be a pseudo-classical style. Eventually I was playing harmonic arpeggios nobody'd done before. Octaves and thirds."

Atkins was in his office, seated in a rocking chair behind a desk that was covered with so many music cassettes that there was no room for his size nine-and-a-half brown loafers. They were propped on a desk drawer. Scattered across the rest of the room was an assortment of guitars. There were Gretsch guitars and Ramirez Classics. There were also Chet Atkins model Gibsons, which carry as much cachet among pickers as Ted Williams's signature Louisville Sluggers do for batters. There were some Japanese guitars with nylon strings and a twelve-string Martin. Beyond this were the guitar fetishes: a guitar clock, a guitar frog, and a picture-wire guitar. For Atkins, a guitar is as essential a part of his personal land-scape as worry beads are to an Arab. "I take one everywhere I go," he said. "I carry it on the plane—it'll go in the overhead. I only went on one trip when I didn't take one. It was a trip to Mexico City. I thought, hell, there'll be a guitar on every street corner, but I couldn't find one. Most of the time I don't play them. I just need it for comfort. It's like I forgot my teeth or my shorts."

He swung the shoes off the desk drawer—they flashed, he was wear-ing red socks—picked up a guitar that was close at hand, and settled back into the chair. His hunched-over performance posture hasn't changed in fifty years and seems as classic as Picasso's Old Guitarist. Slouching over the fretboard with his shoulders curved, his head cocked left, his brows drawn together, and his eyes looking off at terrain somewhere in the dis-tance beyond the knuckles of his left hand, he played a few bars of a melody straight with his ring finger. "Pure tone," he said. Then he began to work again, adding his thumb to make a syncopated rhythm and his fore and middle fingers to create a harmonic progression. The melody was still there, but sprinkled all around it now were supplementary noises. It nodded a greeting, said something cheerful, and finally it winked.

That was just a taste. Chet Atkins can make a guitar chortle and he can make it wince. He can pick out a waltz, a jitterbug, or a jitterbug waltz. He can also use it to banter like a butcher or brag like a senator. As a young man he was so diffident that, he says, "I'd get with a girl and I'd get all ner-vous. The blood goes to your arms and legs and that's just good for fight-ing." As a guitar player, however, he soon figured out how to flirt with dazzling subtlety and how even to say something bold. Naturally, if things weren't going his way, he could summon up some devastating blues. Lis-tening to Atkins play "A Taste of Honey" or "Yakety Axe" is like moving from a pulp mystery into some Raymond Chandler—same story, but in-vested now with such wit, intelligence, and inventive detail that it seems unlike anything you've encountered before. Name a few of the best ones—Merle Travis, B. B. King, Les Paul, Django Reinhardt, George Barnes, Hank Garland, Doc Watson, Andrés Segovia—you wouldn't say that Atkins sounds like any of them.

Atkins put the instrument down, placed his feet back up on his desk drawer, and took a sip of black tea from an Elvis Presley mug. (Atkins arranged and played on "Heartbreak Hotel" and several of Presley's other country hits.) While he held the mug I could see his beautifully smoothed and rounded fingernails. The moment Atkins notices that he has developed a nick or rough spot on a nail, he files it down. Sometimes, when he is caught with a shaggy nail and no emery board, Atkins will reach out and manicure himself on the side of a brick building or even stoop and use the sidewalk. He does not have many other obvious grooming idiosyncrasies. His clothing is natty—he has a penchant for checks. Today he was wearing a solid smalt-blue silk necktie over a checked shirt that had come untucked from his trousers. His neatly clipped hair had some silver in it—he is seventy-two—his waist was trim, and his face youthful and tanned. Atkins is still an eighteen-handicap golfer.

There is the matter of the red socks. Garrison Keillor started him on them. "The reason Garrison wears red socks is because when he was a bachelor he could fill up a drawer with them, "Atkins confided." Then he just reached in and never had an unmatched pair." Since 1982, Atkins has performed on Keillor's radio variety show, *A Prairie Home Companion,* where his droll humor and guitar-picking legerity are much admired by the host. "His playing is very seductive, very sensuous, and very appealing," says Keillor. "He plays things so that they can really swing. That's quite unlike using the guitar as a kind of hot rod."

The night before, Atkins had been celebrated for some of these qualities during a black-tie ceremony at Nashville's Vanderbilt Plaza hotel, where he was presented a Governor's Award. "I killed them," he exulted now, referring to his acceptance speech. "I told them how I remembered when I was born, my cradle wasn't painted, I had no clothes, no teeth, and no hair, but I did have a pick on my thumb. I told them about playing my ukulele and how when a string broke, I ripped a wire off the screen door. That's true. There was always one loose because a dog or a pig had run through and torn a hole. I told them when I got rich and successful I got a swimming pool shaped like a guitar amplifier." He grinned hugely. "I stole that line from Garrison Keillor," he said.

Atkins comes to work at a stone and wood house on Seventeenth Avenue South in central Nashville, a section of town that is known as Music Row. Since the 1950s, when Atkins first arrived in Nashville, the country music industry has operated out of a several-blocks-long strip of pretty cottages and foursquares that could easily be mistaken for fraternity houses. Country's recent boom has prompted a few of the larger record- and music-publishing companies to construct modern concrete and black-glass office buildings for themselves, boasting grand features like spavined atriums filled with ficus trees. Denizens of Music Row generally do not advertise their trade, but Atkins is particularly withdrawn. He keeps his front door locked, discourages visitors with a prim plaque that says "By Appointment Only," and pulls the blinds closed over the second-floor window behind his desk. Part of the reason for this discretion is that he is, he says, "naturally shy," and the rest is that besides becoming the most-recorded guitar player in history, for more than twenty years he moonlighted as the studio manager and director of artists and repertoire (A&R) for RCA Victor's Nashville division. That made him King of the Row. Along with his chief rival, Owen Bradley at Decca Records, Atkins was the most powerful man in country music. His residual authority is such that his desk is littered with all those demonstration tapes, even though he quit working as a recording executive fifteen years ago. "The word is out how I don't hanker to produce anymore," he said. "Too much stress. People still come with tapes, but I usually don't see 'em unless it's a shapely girl."

Atkins has been married for fifty years to a former duet singer named Leona Johnson, whom he met at a Cincinnati radio station, but matrimony has done nothing to interfere with his passion for lascivious badinage. He can work something mildly salacious into conversations with the same fluidity that his fingers climb over the hill in "Black Mountain Rag." Atkins is also an incorrigible connoisseur of profanity. He gets nostalgic recounting the many merry hours he and his friend, the country singer and comedian Archie Campbell, spent together refining their collection of Spoonerisms. "Pitch reople," explains Atkins. "Beepin' sleauty. Pee little thrigs. Mugly other. I'll huff and I'll puff and I'll how your blouse down. You got to learn to talk that way. You can cuss and everything! I'll meet a new girl or something and say "Do you live in a hood wouse or a hick brouse?" Which leads him to recall another old friend, Dolly Parton. "She grabbed me by the ass three times last year," he says proudly. "I was gonna sue her for sexual harassment, but only for fifty dollars 'cause I kind of enjoyed it, you know. Dolly grew up forty miles as a crow flies from me. She's from Sevierville east of Knoxville. Luttrell is north."

"**C**hester and I, we grew up here together," Buster Devault was saying. Buster still lives in the same nameless holler two and a half miles outside Luttrell, Tennessee, where he and Atkins were children together during the Depression. Buster always refers to Atkins as Chester. Atkins describes Buster, less kindly, as "a chubby guy as big as that cabinet. A butterball. A lardball." About the only pejorative thing Buster ever says about

Chester is that "he wouldn't have made a good farmer. He's just guitar." Buster doesn't mind the japes. Chester also calls him "my first true friend."

Buster is indeed a plump, pink-faced fellow whose tight white undershirt reveals the generously rounded contours beneath his blue overalls. There was a time, however, when he and Atkins had the same waistline and shared the one pair of decent trousers they owned between them. Chester was taller, and so when he had music auditions, Buster's wife Lorena would iron out the cuffs.

Today, Buster is seventy-five and a retired Tennessee Valley Authority draftsman. When he and Atkins were children, the holler population was seventeen and people were so poor that some days all they ate was bread and milk. There may be a few more people around the holler now; Buster isn't sure. Tucked on a threadbare hillside beneath House Mountain hard by Flat Creek, it's still a lonely little place. A freight train carrying coal from Kentucky rumbles by once a day. Sometimes the automobiles come less frequently than that. The holler didn't get electricity until the mid-1950s. Buster's first telephone was installed some ten years later, although he and Atkins did hang a wire between their houses as teenagers. "It's about the same here now as when we were growing up except that everybody had corn in the creek bottoms at that time," says Buster. "Now there's nothing but grass and cattle around here."

Until his mother died a few years ago, Atkins came back to the holler for a visit at least three times a year. These days, the two men mostly keep up by shortwave radio. As kids, Buster and Atkins built crystal sets together and searched on them for country music shows. "We were tickled to death when we picked up *The Grand Ole Opry,*" says Buster. Listening to the radio is how Atkins learned to play the guitar. He couldn't see what anybody was doing, of course, so he took his best guess and ended up using two more fingers than any other country picker had thought to.

Buster took me on a walk around the holler. The old Atkins house, barn, corn crib, and the spring house where the milk and butter were kept cool have all been torn down. All that's left of the four structures is the corn-crib door, and that remains only because Chester carved his three initials into it as a boy. The man who bought the Atkins property saved the CBA—the B is for Burton—door and had it fitted into his living-room wall. It's nailed into place right over the piano.

At sunset, Buster and I sat down in one of the five rocking chairs on his porch, and had a drink. The house is at the top of a rise, and so you can look down at the empty railroad track or over at House and Clinch mountains. "Way back, they used to have dances around here," Buster said. "Somebody'd have a barn dance at their home. They'd push the furniture back, somebody'd call the dance, and somebody'd fiddle. They'd have a guitar too, and people would dance. I reckon that's all anybody heard was string music. They'd have a big time. Wasn't really a barn dance at all. They had it inside the house. They don't have dances no more. Yeah, they don't do that around here no more. Everything's changed. All the people I knew when I was growing up, everybody's gone. Most of them are dead. Rest of them went into Knoxville to work. I'm glad we didn't move. You know how the cities are. Out here it's quiet."

Atkins is well aware of how unusual it is that a sickly farm boy from an Appalachian holler would grow up to become not just a great country guitar player, but something of a model of musical sophistication both as a musician and as a businessman, and he had promised that he would one day tell me more specifically how it had happened. He was wearing a

The holler outside Luttrell, Tennessee, in the mid-1930s, when Chet Atkins was growing up there. "I was no good on a farm. I hated it."

well-tailored, summer-weight gray suit the next time I stopped by his office. A man from Gibson was there too, showing Atkins some new guitars. When the Gibson man was finished, Atkins leaned back in his rocker.

Somewhere along the way he lost most of the East Tennessee from his speaking voice. It sounds light and dry, like good gin, unless he's saying something self-deprecating such as "I'm only a part-time singer," in which case his *i*'s become flat *a*'s and vowels are occasionally passed over so that "myself" becomes "m'self." If he employs a word like "risqué," a "hell" or a "damn" is coming soon. There is an insouciance to his conversation that matches the nonchalant brilliance of his arpeggios. Chet Atkins is a master of informality.

"My mother's name was Ida Ella Sharp," he said. "She played piano and sang. She was very emotional. To be a good musician you've got to be an emotional, melancholy sort of person. The music I play, anyway. I think horn players may be different. She always worried about her health and lived to be ninety-two. She became younger and younger and more childlike.

"I grew up in that holler," he went on. "Luttrell was two miles away. It was real hard times. Depression come along and my mother and dad parted. My dad, James Arley Atkins, was a music teacher. He taught voice and piano. He was away from home a lot. He didn't fall in love with another woman. He just left. He was an itinerant voice and piano teacher and choir director. He left when I was six. I had a brother, Jimmy Atkins. He left when my daddy left in 1930. Went to Nebraska. Before he left he'd play his guitar and sing to me. I'd play with his guitar. I used to fill it with dirt and drag it around the yard with a string. He didn't like that worth a damn. He went on to various things. He and Les Paul had a trio before World War II. He was on NBC for Chesterfield cigarettes. To me he was a big star. He was twelve or thirteen years older than me. I admired him.

"I played ukulele first. Once my mother told me to go to the spring and get some water. I didn't do it. I was into something heavy with my ukulele. She picked up that ukulele, knocked me over the head with it, and it split down the back. After that I graduated to the guitar, although I didn't learn anything until I was twelve or thirteen. Too small. When I got a little older and could play, I'd steal from everybody who came through town. When I got a crystal-set radio with an old-fashioned telephone earpiece I could hear good guitar players like Karl Farr from the Sons of the Pioneers. It was hard to learn because it's hard to learn when you can't see what somebody's doing.

He shifted in his chair and went on. "There were three houses in the holler, same as there still is. Up above us they'd rent it to various families. The Fraziers lived there. They had two girls. We wanted to score with the two girls bad, but we didn't know how to do it. They chewed gum. You could hear them comin', poppin' it. We'd yell, 'Hey, girls! How about a little?' They'd pop their gum and say, 'No thanks.' That's how we thought you scored."

When Atkins laughs, he giggles more than he guffaws. He can also compose himself quickly. He did that now and his mood seemed to shift. "My mother married a young farmer after my daddy left," he said. "In the fall we were clearing up the shucks and cornstalks. We were working down field, burning up the cornstalks. I saw some crabgrass. I thought, I wonder what would happen if I light that dead crabgrass afire. I put a shuck that was burning to it. It went up the side of the mountain like a streak. Men fought that fire all night. They probably whipped me.

"I was no good on a farm," he said. "I hated it. A train would go by and we'd wave at the hobos. That was the excitement. There were a lot of hobos during the Depression. We never had any money. We bought shoes for winter and went barefoot in the summer. We'd take jelly sandwiches and corn on the cob in a paper sack to school for lunch. I can still smell it."

Atkins suffered from severe asthma as a child. In 1935, when he was eleven, he was sent to live with his father in Hamilton, Georgia, north of Columbus, where it was hoped that the climate would be kinder to his gasping lungs. "He took me down to his farm, where he and his young wife Tommie lived," Atkins said. "She was his fourth wife. He married five times. She was twenty-two years old and worked in the cotton mill. She was so good to me. It takes a big person to be a good stepparent. I think she was so nice to me, my dad was a little jealous. [James Atkins was forty-seven at the time.] Eventually, my dad taught me the rudiments of music where I went to high school. He'd get on my ass. I was paying more attention to a fifteen-year-old girl than to what he did on the blackboard.

"In Georgia there wasn't all the killing and moonshining I'd been exposed to in East Tennessee. Somebody was always stabbing somebody in an argument there. I'd been in Georgia two or three days when my dad's wife took me to hear the blacks in the church. We were in a Model A Ford outside looking in the window. They'd preach, the women would faint, and I'd hear these spirituals. I'd never seen a black person. All those blue notes. The preacher had a brown suit. I could see his teeth flashing. The black people were so great. I still go down there, and they say, 'You're Mr. Atkins's boy!' like only a few years passed and hell, it's been fifty or more.

"I stayed in Georgia a year and a half and that's where I first heard Merle Travis play guitar on the radio. He played with his thumb and his first finger. He couldn't play a lot of notes, but he had a hell of a rhythm. I came back and lived with my sister in Tennessee for a year or so. I stayed with my sister because my stepdaddy chased me off. Those were hard times and that meant one less mouth to feed. Just ignorance. He was doing the best he could. I support him now. I don't carry a grudge. I went back to Georgia, then after the war started, I came back to Tennessee and I got a job at WNOX at Knoxville. I was seventeen. Oak Ridge went up overnight, but we didn't know what they were doing. I asked a friend at the radio station. He said, 'They're splitting the atom.' I didn't know what the hell he was talking about."

The classically trained Irish tenor James Atkins hadn't been entirely pleased with the prospects of a son who wanted to be a country-pop musician. That changed after he listened to Atkins play with The Dixieland Swingsters, the WNOX pop orchestra in Knoxville. "I saw him in the back of the auditorium afterward," Atkins says. "I greeted him. He had tears in his eyes. He was from that Victorian era when men never cried. He used to put down country music all the time, but I think he saw then I might amount to something. I thought, 'That's nice. Maybe he finally realizes I was right to follow what I wanted to do.'"

Atkins spent four years in Knoxville and then, in 1945, he left for the radio station in Cincinnati. His unconventional guitar-picking style got him fired there, as it did at several other stations around the country over the next three years. Atkins had been let go in three times zones by 1949, when he found himself back in Knoxville playing guitar behind Mother Maybelle Carter and her three singing daughters, Helen, Anita, and June. Perhaps because she was such a gifted musician herself, Mother Maybelle was more accepting of the young guitar player. "Maybelle was kind of like a second mama to me," Atkins said. "We never had a cross word. She was just a gentle soul. Very talented. And she could dance very well. Tap-dance." By 1950, they had all moved on to *The Grand Ole Opry*.

Atkins quickly established himself first as a versatile session player in Nashville—he played on several of Hank Williams's hits, including "Your Cheatin' Heart," and Everly Brothers numbers like "Wake Up Little Susie"—and then as a formidable solo performer whose polished country licks were abetted by his interest in classical, Latin, and pop gui-tar. Harlan Howard is right: Atkins liked anything with melody. That's why he was never terribly interested in modern improvisational jazz. It was his feeling that things got so complicated that the melody got lost and very few people could understand it. "I think they've played themselves into oblivion without a melody people can hear and love," he said to me. "A lot of modern jazz has a lot of hostility to it. They're mostly playing for each other."

If music executives admired his supple fingers, they also appreciated his quick wits. Steve Sholes, the RCA official who ran the country division out of New York, began to consult Atkins when he needed personnel for recording sessions. Sholes informally came to regard Atkins as his Nashville-based production liaison, and it wasn't long before Atkins was earning $7,500 a year as RCA's primary country producer, doing his best to revive country sales, which had been devastated by the rise of rock 'n' roll. Through the 1960s, Sholes sat back and watched as Atkins added strings, horn sections, vocal choruses, plenty of echo, and smooth tempos to Eddy Arnold's, Don Gibson's, and Jim Reeves's vocals. Soon, this fusion of country and pop was being called "the Nashville Sound," and the name for its wry impresario was "The King of Music Row." By the time Atkins quit producing, he had signed up a Texas hellcat named Waylon Jen-nings—Atkins instructed him to wash his hair—and Charley Pride, a black man who had learned to sing like Roy Acuff while listening to *The Grand Ole Opry* on the radio with his father in Sledge, Mississippi. Pride became country's first black singing star. Atkins describes signing Pride as "my greatest civic thing" and says, "The only problems Charley ever had were from black people—'What are you doing singing white man's music?' " (Pride's first three singles were released to radio stations and record shops without accompanying publicity photographs, so nobody knew what he looked like. When he walked out onstage in Detroit to per-form in his first concert, there was a great hush. Then Pride made a com-ment about his "natural tan" and everyone began clapping.) Along the way Atkins also acquired several lots of prime real estate around Music Row, not to mention a third of the RCA Building.

"Nashville was a terrible place for musicians until they allowed whiskey," he said. "It's been about thirty years now. The only place you could get it in the 1950s was Printer's Alley where they paid off the cops. I used to play jazz in there when the town was dry. I'd see cops come in for their payoff. Backstage we'd try to outplay each other. Standards like

'Honeysuckle Rose,' 'Lady Be Good,' 'Sweet Georgia Brown.' Most of my jamming was done with horn players and piano players. They knew more than I did. The jazz musicians in Knoxville used to make fun of me. Charlie Christian had been hot around then with Benny Goodman, and they were baffled that I didn't play with a pick the way he did. But I wanted to be different. I wanted to play like me. One alto sax player, he'd see a girl he'd want to dance with and he'd say, 'Play a few choruses, kid.' I can't dance. Still can't. Great way to meet girls, but I was too ignorant and too shy.

"I met my wife when she was singing duets at WLW in Cincinnati. I was sick quite a bit up there. Had asthma. Had the mumps. Very seriously ill. I was in the contagious ward, where only one person could come to see you. She'd come and bring me gifts. She's been being nice to me ever since." He sighed. "Everything happens for the best, I've always said. Been true in my case. Each time when I got fired I'd say, 'Well, maybe I'll get the respect I want somewhere else.'

"When I got here to Nashville, Hank Williams was at the height of his popularity. I went down to the *Opry,* and he was there. He had real dark eyes, very slender. Somebody introduced me and said, 'Chet can write a little.' He said, 'Let's get together.' We did once. I went out to his house and we tried a couple of things. I wish I had them now. He told me, 'Audrey [Williams's wife] is the judge of what's good that I write.' He was crazy about her.

"Nashville used to be known as the Athens of the South because there were so many colleges here," he said. "Back in those days, the music was not admired. When I first came here I was invited out to the Rotary Club and to parties in Belle Meade, the rich section of town. They liked me. I played standards. But the stars of *The Grand Ole Opry* were kind of looked down upon. Nashville was ashamed of the country boys. Some of the people at National Life, which owned *The Grand Ole Opry,* were ashamed of it, but they found out that all a salesman on the road had to do was mention that they owned the *Opry* and doors opened. Now the music is more palatable to city folks. The lyrics and melodies and chord changes and recording techniques are more sophisticated."

"That was you moving it uptown," I said. He nodded, and said, "Somebody interviewing me once asked me, 'What's the Nashville Sound?' I was stumbling around for an answer and he got out some coins and shook them and he was right. People were in it to make a living. The Nashville Sound is just a sales tag. If there is a Nashville Sound, it's the Southern accent. You speak with it, maybe you play with it, too. I don't know if there is such a thing as Nashville Sound. We took the twang out of it, Owen Bradley and I. What we did was we tried to make hit records. We wanted to keep our job. The way you make hit records is to incorporate a new rhythm feel or something lyrically different. In my case, it went more uptown. I'd take out the steel guitar and fiddle, which branded a song as strictly country. I tried to make songs for both markets."

He took a sip of tea from his Elvis mug and smiled. "The other morning, my guitar player called me. He said, 'I'm proud of you. I saw you on TV and you looked so extinguished.'" Atkins laughed. "That's it. Owen and I, we polished it. In my contract with RCA I insisted that any new equipment they added in New York that Nashville get the same. I never enforced it, I was so damn busy. But I did have it in my contract. Back in the 1950s, I never expected this." He meant country music's current prosperity. "Each year I'd think that the growth would stop. By the 1960s I thought, 'Well, maybe I won't get fired,' and I started demanding raises. Then one day I went to work and my shoes didn't match. I said, 'Fuck this, I'm working too hard,' and I made plans to quit."

That was in 1981. Since then Atkins has been a full-time musician, making records with the likes of the rock guitar whiz Mark Knopfler and the country chanteuse Suzy Boggus, playing some golf, and dropping in from time to time on his friend Keillor at *A Prairie Home Companion*. In recent years Atkins has sometimes expressed reservations about how far afield he took country music from the relatively unadorned prewar downhome sound, and he said now that he still has them. "I've said a lot of stuff, but we almost do lose our identity sometimes," he said. "We get so pop fans turn away. Then a good country singer comes along, a Ricky Skaggs, a Randy Travis, and gets us back to where we should be—making good, soulful country sounds. To young folks right now, country music just means some guy with a tight ass and a white hat. But to the older people— Johnny Cash, Merle Haggard, Bob Wills—they're important to the older people. But I'm not good at talking about that. I'm just a guitar player. Right now we're in a curve with everything sounding alike, but somebody'll come along and get us back where we need to be."

PART TWO

DEEP COUNTRY

Young girls at the post office, Nethers, Virginia, 1935.
"Men came first in country music," says Loretta Lynn. "Men dominated."

SARA CARTER, KITTY WELLS, *and* PATSY CLINE

THREE WOMEN

SARA CARTER

The great Virginia mountain singer Sara Carter was only three when her mother, Elizabeth Dougherty, died suddenly. To be a motherless Appalachian child in 1901 made you an orphan—nobody expected a man to raise a family on his own—and so Sara and her three brothers were sent off from their home in Flat Woods to live with scattered friends and relations. Sara was taken in by her aunt and uncle, Melinda and Milburn Nichols, farmers from Copper Creek, Virginia. Aunt Nick and Uncle Mil were warmhearted people who made a practice of welcoming strays. They kept the larder stocked, the table set at all hours, and always had several extra beds fitted with clean sheets ready to accommodate anyone who wandered by. Though it's not clear how Sara felt about growing up in a home that amounted to a boarding house amid a rotating crowd of unfortunates, people who knew her as an adult describe a diffident, sometimes remote person. "Sara didn't let people get close to her," her granddaughter Rita Forrester told me.

She turned out to be a ravishing young woman with long waves of black hair, a gracefully sloping forehead, and stunning dark brown eyes that seemed to her daughter Janette Carter to be dusted with a few fine grains of gold. Janette doesn't share many of these facial features, yet she says she is often told that "I favor my mother quite a bit." The resemblance has to do with a quality of grave reserve in both faces. "Aunt Sara was kind of majestic in a way, like a real thoroughbred," says Sara's niece,

June Carter Cash. It so happened, however, that A.P. Carter fell for Sara before he saw any of this. He'd already heard her sing.

It was probably on an early spring day in 1914 when he was twenty-three that Carter, a religious man with the heart of a dreamer, was out in the country moving through the hills on an errand that had taken him over Clinch Mountain and a fair distance from the tiny settlement of Maces Springs where he lived. In Copper Creek he overheard Sara singing an old train-wreck ballad, "Engine 143," on her uncle's porch. The stark, wistful voice moved him powerfully and he went to see who it was.

"She had a lot of strength in her voice," June Carter Cash says. "Like a man's. Real low. Sometimes when she talked to you on the telephone you had trouble telling whether it was Aunt Sara or some guy." Sara Carter was a natural alto who could sing high enough to handle soprano parts too, but it wasn't just vocal range or her craggy, hill-country vowels that made her a distinctive singer. She had a raw, somber tone that infused simply worded songs with intense layers of feeling. What got to A.P. Carter as he came upon this beautiful girl singing about the lonely, brutal death of a country railroad engineer was how sensual she sounded. In time, the unembellished emotional character in Sara Carter's singing would make The Carter Family immensely popular across the workingman's South. She took on tender subjects—orphaned children, worried men, abandoned women—and with them stirred something powerful in people. That was certainly A.P. Carter's response. He struck up a conversation.

The story of A.P. and Sara Carter's courtship is fresh news to nobody of a certain age in Maces Springs, Virginia: A.P. Carter was downright garrulous compared with his wife. Janette Carter says that it pleased her father to tell about that day he left Maces Springs on an entrepreneurial venture and returned a suddenly reluctant bachelor. "Daddy was out selling fruit trees," she said. "He heard her singing and he stopped. He tried to sell her uncle pear and apple trees. I imagine he bought some. Mommy was selling dishes and I think Daddy bought some from her. After that he found his way back pretty often." Sara Dougherty was sixteen when she married A.P. Carter and moved to the other side of the mountain. After that, A.P. liked to exult, "I got the dish and the girl!" Theirs was destined to be a fraught relationship.

In A.P. and Sara Carter's day, people in Maces Springs lived, according to Rita Forrester, "a secluded lifestyle. Growing up, they didn't see a lot of outsiders." Maces Springs is still pretty insular. It's on Route 614, a quiet spur off Route 421 that cuts through Poor Valley between Clinch Mountain and the north fork of the Holsten River. Except for a handful of houses along the road, most people live somewhere away from 614, up in the hills. There are no stores in Maces Springs, and only 200 residents, perhaps four times as many as in 1914, when A.P. Carter brought Sara Dougherty back to live in a cabin deep in a forest of oak, pine, and black gum trees.

Alvin Pleasant Delaney "Doc" Carter and his teenage bride were very different people. Sara Carter kept a spotless house, wore perfume scented with wild roses in her hair, knotted exquisite quilts, and was gritty enough to work with Kit and Maude, the family mules, hauling timber off the steep hillsides. Once the logs were down the mountain, she could also handle one side of a crosscut saw as the wood was turned into lumber for railroad ties. Her children describe Sara Carter as a devoted mother. Unlike her husband, she was someone you could depend upon.

"He was nervous," Janette Carter says of her father. "He was born thataway. He was always nervous and shaky." These tremors were palsy, a condition that A.P.'s mother, Mollie "Ma" Carter, told Janette had visited her son after she was badly frightened while pregnant with him. A bolt of lightning struck an apple tree and then shot a streak of fire across the ground close to where Ma Carter was gathering apples. "Back then they believed in people being marked," says Janette Carter. "His mother said that when he was born his hands trembled."

Janette Carter adored her father, yet she freely admits that there were curious things about him. He was intermittently distracted, a tall, handsome man who spent a lot of time daydreaming, liked to travel, and followed his impulses with such capricious ease that he could quite effortlessly withdraw from the thrum of one activity and engage himself headlong in another. "Daddy always seemed to have things on his mind," Janette said. "He tried out a lot of things. He had a sawmill. At one time he had a grist mill. He had a grocery store. He sold lumber. He sold fruit trees. He was a carpenter by trade. He walked up and down that railroad track a lot. He did. He walked a lot everywhere, like he was in a deep study."

A.P. had a weakness for sawmills and would buy them whenever he could. Once he came home from North Carolina with a sawmill on the back of his truck, unloaded it in a field, and never touched it again, leaving it there to rust. It wasn't just sawmills. As a child, Janette spent months saving up the thirteen dollars that an Autoharp cost. When she had it all, she gave her father the money and asked him to buy an instrument for her at a store in Bristol. Along the way he noticed fresh chickens that someone was selling and that's what he came home with. Janette says she wasn't angry with him. "I was just hurt," she says. "He would sometimes do things that were a little bit strange. But he was a very, very kind, good man."

The Carter Family's musical career was, at first, no more than this quixotic carpenter's latest burst of whimsy. Since their marriage, A.P. and Sara had sung together at church and social gatherings. Their successful professional experience was limited to a concert A.P. had hastily arranged outside Charlottesville, when one of the vagabond automobiles he always drove broke down. The impromptu show sold enough tickets to pay the garage man. Once they had auditioned for a record company, but the record executive insisted that A.P. play his fiddle and go by the name "Fiddlin' " Doc Carter. It was Ma Carter's belief—not uncommon in those parts—that a fiddle was a tool of the devil. She had, in fact, asked her husband to put aside his banjo and he had. Now, in deference to his mother, A.P. turned the record company down.

One day at the end of July 1927, A.P. came upon an article in the *Bristol News Bulletin* describing a man named Ralph Peer from the Victor Talking Machine Company in New York who had set up a makeshift studio in a building on State Street in Bristol and was paying local people $50 a side plus a modest royalty to make recordings of their singing. A.P. had earlier received some correspondence from Peer, and now he told his wife that they were going to Bristol to make a record. Her initial response was less than he might have hoped for: "Aw pshaw," she said. "Ain't nobody gonna pay that much money to hear us sing." When she gave in, she said it was "just for curiosity."

Sara would sing and play the Autoharp while A.P., who had a rich, sonorous voice, was "bassin' in." To add instrumental rhythm and melody, A.P. asked his mild-mannered brother Ezra if he could take along Ezra's teenage wife Maybelle, a gifted guitar player and a good singer as well. Maybelle was eight months pregnant and Ezra balked at the idea until A.P. coaxed him into it by promising to handle a nasty weeding project for Ezra. On July 30, A.P., the two women, seven-month-old Joe, whom Sara was still breast-feeding, and A.P. and Sara's oldest child, Gladys, along to babysit for Joe, squeezed into Ezra's Model A. Janette stayed home, which, in some ways, made her lucky.

Even today, when Route 421 has been smoothed with asphalt, it's not an easy road to drive. Gladys's daughter, Flo Wolfe, told me that she hates going into Bristol because climbing the steep grades and maneuvering around the many sharp curves makes her queasy. In 1927, when Route 421 was called Route 411, there was no bridge over that section of the Holsten, and so cars had to ford the river. After that, the twenty-five miles of travel between Maces Springs and Bristol were along a hilly, rock-strewn dirt trail that in low areas was sometimes interrupted by rushing streams. (Roads were so bad at the time that once, after A.P. had poured himself a concrete porch, Joe carefully rode his bicycle back and forth in the damp concrete because he thought that outdoor surfaces were *supposed* to be full of ruts). Enduring the beating July heat for hours inside the stifling car was torment for the passengers. It didn't help matters that the tires kept blowing out. Occasionally the engine would stall.

Bristol is a drowsy city now, but seventy years ago it was the urban center of the Appalachians, a thriving railroad town with shops, banks, and comfortable hotels. Joe Carter, who was, of course, too young to remember the trip, has heard that Bristol was "like the old West. That town was wide open. Muddy streets. Didn't know what paving looked like. State Street wasn't even rock. Just dirt. People still drove wagons and buggies."

The Carter Family: Maybelle, A.P., and Sara with her Autoharp.
"What it took to put it across was Sara's voice."

Some of this was true, but the really wild town was neighboring Johnson City, where bootleggers and gangsters had the place teeming with brothels and saloons. Peer chose Bristol in part because it was a fairly up-to-date town, a commodious place for a New York businessman to spend an extended visit. I asked Joe Carter what his parents made of Bristol when they arrived in town to meet Ralph Peer. "There wasn't ever much said about the first trip," he said. The Carters were rural people who used squirrel broth to cure fevers, applied raw turpentine to neck pains, and relied upon Ma Carter to midwife Sara's babies. They weren't accustomed to long drives followed by bustle and clamor, and it's clear that this expedition enervated all of them.

Bristol's principal thoroughfare was—and is—State Street, running along the Virginia-Tennessee border. Cross the street and you are in another state. The space Ralph Peer had rented was in an old furniture store on the Tennessee side. (It's gone now.) While Gladys spent all day with a squalling Joe outside by Beaver Creek—Mrs. Peer tried to help her out by buying the baby ice cream, which only gave him a bad bellyache—A.P. and the two women went to the furniture store. Peer responded to Sara Carter just the way A.P. had the first time he listened to her sing. "They wander in," Peer said later. "He's dressed in overalls and the women are country people from 'way back there. But as soon as I heard Sara's voice, that was it. I knew it was going to be wonderful."

Peer had come to the Appalachians because New York record-company executives had become convinced that the South was a ripe market for what was then known as hillbilly music. The first batch of songs the Carters chose, "The Poor Orphan Child," "The Wandering Boy," "Bury Me Under the Weeping Willow," were all notably melancholy numbers that showcased the clear, unrefined conviction in Sara's singing. When she sang about abandoned children who "Once had mother's hand to smooth their golden curls," her sincerity was obvious and even if you didn't know that she had been orphaned herself, the effect was very moving. As soon as Victor had the records available, many thousands of copies were quickly sold. The eager customers, who as a rule couldn't spare a nickel, were poor rural people as well as the increasing numbers of displaced farming families now living in the Southern cities.

Unlike the sprightly Jimmie Rodgers, whose style evolved significantly during the six years after Peer recorded him in Bristol, the Carter Family sound was fairly consistent over a career that lasted more than twice as long as Rodgers's did. Although they sang everything from gospel to old ballads to sentimental parlor songs, other than seeming a bit more polished, their later recordings are a lot like the early ones. Their appeal was their close, melodic, somewhat subdued sound, and they didn't vary it much. Chet Atkins has said that the Carter Family's singing was the apotheosis of the way his and other Appalachian families "used to sing sitting around at home." It was straightforward music filled with honest feeling; a template for what would be called country.

A.P. gathered the bulk of the material, putting his restless energies into protracted song-hunting forays. Sometimes he went off with no warning and stayed away for as long as a month, leaving his wife and three children behind without a dollar for groceries or a stick of firewood. Out on the road he looked in on trappers, miners, sawyers—anybody who could share interesting music with him. Some Carter Family songs came from the forgotten pieces of sheet music A.P. turned up inside people's piano benches. Many of the songs he heard and copied down, from "Little Darling Pal of Mine" to "Foggy Mountain Top" to "Worried Man Blues" to "Wabash Cannonball," became beloved classics, and Carter Family melodies have since been appropriated by scores of songwriters, from the *Grand Ole Opry* star Roy Acuff to the folksinger Woody Guthrie.

A.P. had an excellent ear for affecting music, but a poor memory for melody. To help him, sometimes he was accompanied on his trips by Lesley Riddle, a black blues singer and guitar player from Burnsville, North Carolina, whom A.P. met on a front porch in Kingsport, Tennessee. It was pretty unusual for a hill-country white man of A.P. Carter's generation to be keeping company with a black, but A.P. Carter went his own way in most respects. "Fine fellow," Joe Carter told me when I asked about Riddle. "He worked at a cement plant, where he lost his leg. Mother bought his first artificial leg for him. He went with Dad some, but not all the time. Dad went to the sawmills and Lesley went along for the ride. He'd come over to the house and stay all night."

"Very friendly, warm person," Janette Carter added. "Lesley was the only colored person I know Daddy was real close to."

"Played mean blues guitar," said Joe.

This was something Maybelle Carter also noticed. "The Carter Scratch," Maybelle's famously clear guitar style, involved picking out a tune's melody by applying her thumb to the bass strings and simultaneously brushing her fingers downward on the treble strings for rhythm. It became the early model for country guitar pickers. How much of this technique she learned from Riddle isn't clear—June Carter Cash says, "They gave something to each other"—but blues like "Cannonball Blues" and the powerful "Motherless Children" definitely came to the Carters courtesy of Riddle. Maybelle knew how to play bottleneck guitar—a style of playing also known as "slide," in which a finger on the fretting hand is slipped into a small tool traditionally made from the top of a beer, soda, or whiskey bottle and then pressed to the strings—and there, undoubtedly, she got a lot of help from Riddle, a slide master.

Janette Carter says, "What it took to put it across was the voice, and she's right." Sara was the real star of the show. In a world busy with recorded voices, you can't confuse Sara Carter's with any other. By 1929, the year she recorded the number that may be her most mournfully heartbreaking, "Motherless Children," the Depression was on and she was expressing the despair that had a lot of people suddenly feeling like the characters in the song: "Sister does the best she can but she really don't understand/ Orphaned children have a hard time in this world." From the first, country music encouraged faith and forbearance in struggling men and women; Sara Carter's voice brought a little sunshine to people in the shadows.

Discovered on the same day in the same place as Jimmie Rodgers, Sara Carter could have been as prominent a national star as Rodgers except, of course, that she was a woman. It was only because A.P. Carter fronted the group that it was possible for two Southern country women to have a public career in music at all. "If it hadn't been for A.P. they wouldn't have done those things," says Rita Forrester. "Women just didn't do those things then."

A.P. was careful to maintain proper appearances. When he tacked up posters advertising Carter Family concerts at schoolhouses and local gathering places in small Appalachian communities—the Carters lacked Jimmie Rodgers's dazzling performance skills and never played the big halls he did—the signs mentioned only A.P.'s name—twice—and assured people that "The Program Is Morally Good." In fact, Maybelle and Sara made most of the music. A.P. was always prone to distraction, and his behavior during rehearsals and even during concerts became increasingly erratic. "They'd be singing and he'd walk around, look out a window, come back, and put in a word now and then," June Carter Cash says. "He always reminded me of a musical instrument. Just came in when he felt like it." This wasn't the sort of man you could shame on such matters, either. "My daddy had a very bad temper," Janette says. A.P. didn't get angry often, but it wasn't pleasant when he did and nobody liked to push him.

Sara Carter was a pretty independent character herself. "Not the type of grandmother who was a little old lady with a bun standing in the kitchen cooking," says Rita Forrester. "She was very stately, very commanding. I guess some people would have thought she wasn't that approachable. She wore a lot of slacks. My grandmother was liberated before we knew what liberated women were." Sara Carter wrote and arranged music. (She and Maybelle composed the classic "You Are My Flower" together, and the music historian Charles Wolfe says he suspects that it was Sara who handled the arranging on a lot of the material A.P. brought home from the road.) She went big-game hunting and shot bears, she smoked cigarettes, and she took guff from nobody, including her absent-minded husband. In 1933, she left him and returned to Aunt Nick and Uncle Mil's place. Six years later, she went ahead and got divorced. "*Nobody* got divorced in the '30s, in that country anyway," says June Carter Cash. "There was a lot behind it."

No one in the Carter family has ever liked to talk specifically about the hard feelings between A.P. and Sara except to stress, Janette says, that "they *were* different." A measure of Sara's maverick mettle is that she continued to make music with her former husband until 1943, although, June Carter Cash says, "Sometimes it was kind of uncomfortable." The situation became even more strained when Sara married Coy Bayes, A.P. Carter's first cousin. They moved to California, where Coy became caretaker of the Calaveras County fairgrounds, a place made famous in Mark Twain's yarn about a fabled jumping frog. Until 1943, Sara came east to record. Otherwise she lived in a remote California countryside settlement called Angels Camp. The folksinger Mike Seeger visited Sara there twice and says, "It struck me as almost being a California version of Maces Springs, Virginia, in its feel." Seeger was intrigued by Sara. "I had the picture of a rural aristocrat," he says. "She was proud in a humble kind of way. So totally self-possessed. She seemed not to be impressed necessarily by her fame or the fame of others. She was quiet and somewhat independent, I would say. I've not met too many people like her. She was such a big person. Her bearing, I mean. It was almost like she was on another plane when she talked with you. She was seemingly very much at peace with herself in the world."

Sara kept house in Angels Camp and, except for a couple of brief reunion performances, didn't sing publicly anymore after the group broke up. "She wanted to be far away from people," says Sara and A.P.'s friend Bill Clifton. Each year or two Sara and Coy came east to visit Sara's three children. These were awkward times in Maces Springs. "A.P. wouldn't walk on the same side of the street as Coy," says June.

A.P. never remarried. "I think he probably loved her all his life," says Rita Forrester. "They remained jealous of one another. It was obvious they still had affection even though they were no longer together. There was still something between them." Knowing about this bond makes listening to their 1931 duet "Lonesome for You," in which A.P. sings, "I'd give all that I own just to have you back home," extremely poignant.

A.P. opened a general store in Maces Springs, where he sold buckets of loose lard, October and pinto soup beans, canned goods, and soda pop—mostly things that wouldn't spoil because, predictably, he kept irregular hours. At Christmastime he stocked dolls and other toys. People who had no money paid him with eggs. "The store done well," Flo Wolfe told me. "He was a thinkin' man. Liked to spend time by hisself quite a bit. When he ran the store in the summer he'd sleep in the store at night. Then in the morning he'd come up to Mother's for breakfast."

A.P. died in 1960. Toward the end of his life he'd sometimes hear a woman's voice and become confused, thinking Sara had come back to him at last. After her death in 1979, she nearly did. A.P. and Sara are both

A.P. and Sara Carter standing with their daughter Janette on the steps of his general store in Maces Springs, Virginia, in 1954, fifteen years after she divorced him. "There was still something between them."

buried, three graves apart, in the shady cemetery behind Mount Vernon Methodist Church in Maces Springs, a small white building where many years ago Ma Carter bowed her head and prayed that her menfolk, so interested in fiddles and banjos, would be spared damnation.

Today Route 614 has been renamed, somewhat grandly for a narrow, two-lane road, the A.P. Carter Highway. Twenty years ago, in honor of their parents, Joe and Janette opened The Carter Fold, a rough-hewn music hall on the Clinch Mountain side of the road in Maces Springs. "A gathering place, a refuge" is how Joe describes the Fold. Every Saturday night people from Virginia and neighboring states like North Carolina, Kentucky, and Tennessee find their way through the mountains into Poor Valley to listen to old-time country music not unlike what The Carter Family sang. (Only when June Carter's husband, Johnny Cash, plays at the Fold are the rules prohibiting electric instruments relaxed.) Janette Carter always begins the evening by accompanying herself on her Autoharp while singing a Carter Family song.

One night at the Fold, I asked the Carters why their mother gave up singing. Janette said, "I never did think Mother was all that interested in it."

"No, she wasn't wrapped up in music," said Joe. "Her heart wasn't in the music like his was. She wasn't out to be in the spotlight. She preferred to be a housewife."

KITTY WELLS

In the decade after Sara Carter retired, all the most popular American country music singers were men. The singer and songwriter Loretta Lynn says that when she listened to the radio while growing up in Butcher Holler, Kentucky, in the 1940s, "You didn't hear any women. I never thought anything about it. Men came first. Men dominated." After World War II, meanwhile, country songwriting began turning out a fantastic variety of songs on the theme that remains its most palpable: cryin' over you. With men singing them, invariably these songs featured decent fellows who'd been wronged by an array of flirts, heartbreakers, and slatterns. Real women didn't always recognize themselves in these accounts. When a retiring Tennessee matron named Kitty Wells offered a mild objection, she became country music's first great female star.

This change happened rather suddenly, in 1952. The Waco, Texas, belter Hank Thompson was enjoying an outsize hit, "The Wild Side of

Life," in which a scorned man sneers, "I didn't know God made honky-tonk angels/ I might have known you'd never make a wife." In a voice resonant with sincerity and a lightly bruised vibrato, Wells responded: "It wasn't God who made honky-tonk angels/As you said in the words of your song/Too many times married men think they're still single/That has caused many a good girl to go wrong."

"First time I heard it I thought there was an angel singing," Loretta Lynn told me. "I thought, 'Gee, here the women are starting to sing!' It was such a treat to hear a woman sing. I think with that song she touched in me what I was living and what I was going through and I knew there was a lot of women that lived like me. I thought, 'Here's a woman telling our point of view of everyday life.' You know, women staying home at night while the guy's going out for a card game. Game didn't last all night, but the men did. Men going out with the boys, but they're not out with the boys. It was something nobody else was writing or singing about. It really got to me. I thought, 'This is a great thing.' So I started writing songs."

Kitty Wells flanked by her husband, Johnny Wright, and his brother-in-law Jack Anglin in 1950. "There wasn't any women singing back then to amount to anything."

"It Wasn't God Who Made Honky-Tonk Angels" was the first of the Kitty Wells songs that over the years became a virtual medley about feminine romantic despair. "The Queen of Country Music" sang about a woman giving her wedding dress away because her fiancé has taken up with her younger sister, and she sang about men renouncing their girlfriends because they weren't virgins. Some lonely women in Kitty Wells songs get hopelessly stuck on men who don't love them; others worry that they will end up as spinsters. Wives don't have it any better. They marry either cold and sexless men who ignore them, rovers who telephone home from roadhouses swarming with other women, or roués who leave them after a few years for someone half their age. When a woman even briefly gives in to passion, however, she flays herself afterward. In Wells's world, inevitably it's the woman who stays home with the baby on her knee while her husband is out trolling the bars, and—less realistic—it's the man who wins custody of the children in the divorce settlement.

Like "Honky-Tonk Angels," many of these songs were so-called answer songs, lyrics written in response to a song performed by a male singer. By taking up the woman's point of view, Kitty Wells offered the first sustained feminine perspective in country music history. Although she didn't write her songs, she was the vehicle for them, and so they really became hers. She was much admired by women in a way that no other female singer before her had been, including Patsy Montana, whose 1935 hit "I Want to Be a Cowboy's Sweetheart" made her the first woman to sell a million records.

When I went out to Madison, Tennessee, to visit with Kitty Wells, I was hoping she would tell me how she had come to such a vivid understanding of feminine misery, but in contrast to someone like Sara Carter or Merle Haggard, she was quick to say that her life had been free of difficult or risqué experiences of the sort she sings about. "Well," she said, reconsidering. "I made some records with Red Foley in the 1950s. People thought I was running around with Red Foley." She frowned slightly. Then she said, "They found out different."

"They said you ought to be ashamed of yourself for running around with Red Foley," said Wells's husband, Johnny Wright. "They'd write to her. People are funny."

"I sang 'It Wasn't God Who Made Honky-Tonk Angels,' but it had nothing to do with my life at all," Wells said. "I was looking for a hit just like everybody else. I think one of the reasons it was a hit was that it was telling the menfolk. But it didn't have nothing to do with me. I just sang the song. It didn't pertain to me. I was just singing. Of course, I was feeling for the women that had been done wrong. There's always been that type of stuff going on."

Kitty Wells is all deference. The heart shape of her face makes her jaw seem set in a smile giving her away as someone who is sweet-natured and exceptionally amenable, which, by most accounts, she is. "Women always had been pushed back," says Kitty Wells's friend, the singer Martha Carson, whose song "Satisfied" was a country-gospel hit in 1951. "Country music was a man's world. The first ones like Kitty Wells and myself were determined." But Kitty Wells stayed jake with the good ol' boys and made it as a country singer in part because she seemed too placid to be much competition for anybody. She was a devoted wife and mother who didn't drink or smoke, took a Bible with her on the road, and carried herself, the popular Tennessee governor Frank Clement observed, in "the finest tradition of Southern womanhood." When the *Grand Ole Opry* comedienne Minnie Pearl was asked how it was that Kitty Wells became country music's first female star, she said, "Kitty is a lady . . . some tramp could never have done it."

Even her singing voice contributed to the image of a noble, yielding female. "Kitty had this little voice that had a certain quality to it that made it seem like it all might have been happening to her," her producer Owen Bradley told me. "There was no hardness to her. Later on, Loretta Lynn had the opposite quality—'You don't straighten up, I'll beat the hell out of you.' But with Kitty, it seemed possible that these things were happening to her—'I've really been hurt,' you know."

What Wells was saying, of course, turned out to have great interest for women. She drew crowds of them at her concerts, sold millions of records, and created scores of admirers in the two generations of female singers who have followed her, including the likes of Patsy Cline, Loretta Lynn, Dolly Parton, and Emmylou Harris. "She was my hero," Loretta Lynn says. "I started singing just like Kitty Wells. I got away from that one night when a drunk stumbled up to the stage and said to me, 'There's only one Kitty Wells. If you're gonna make it, you better quit singing like Kitty Wells.' That kind of registered with me."

"I appreciate the respect people have for me," Wells was saying now. "I know a lot of women had a hard road to travel to make it on their own. I've never felt myself to be a feminist. I've always traveled with my husband. I never traveled alone. Dolly and Loretta had to go out on their own. I always had somebody to look after me."

Johnny Wright smiled at that. We were sitting in an office at the souvenir-shop-cum-museum known as the Kitty Wells–Johnny Wright Country Junction. He was behind a desk and Wells and I were in chairs, facing him. Wright was a successful country singer well before his wife was. He sang with his brother-in-law Jack Anglin in a duo known as Johnny & Jack. Until the phenomenal success of "It Wasn't God Who Made Honky-Tonk Angels" changed everything, Kitty Wells appeared on his bill, the way Sara and Maybelle Carter appeared on A.P.'s.

Wright is an energetic man with bright eyes. The right one lazes half-shut, making him look like the shrewd businessman he is. He has been married to Kitty Wells for so long—fifty-nine years—that he talks about her life even more easily than she does herself. It is as though he considers her life his own. Which makes a kind of sense. Wright gave her both her stage name—she was born Ellen Muriel Deason—and the song "It Wasn't God Who Made Honky-Tonk Angels." Kitty and Johnny's devotion to each other is something that is talked about in Nashville with much admiration. At seventy-seven, Kitty Wells still spends as many as a hundred nights a year on the road, mostly because, it is said, her husband enjoys performing so much.

"I thought it was great for her to tell the women's side of the story," he was saying now. "There wasn't any women singing back then to amount to anything. It made you feel good to have people think so much of Kitty. But she didn't sing it to make people think a lot of her. She just sang it from the heart. It was just an accident she got ahold of that tune. I brought the song home and asked her if she liked it."

"There were a few women singing then," Kitty Wells said. "Martha Carson. The Carter Family. At that time I was just going to stay home and take care of the house, cook, have children. Then I got ahold of 'It Wasn't God Who Made Honky-Tonk Angels.' J.D. Miller, a boy from down in Louisiana, wrote the song and he'd sent it to [the Decca record executive] Paul Cohen. Paul sent it to Johnny to see if he liked it. When I went in to record it, I'd already recorded eight sides for RCA. They hadn't done much. We did the song and said, 'Well, it might not do much but at least we'll get paid for the session.' They released it in July 1952 and it became a hit. It was kind of the womenfolk getting back at the menfolk."

"She laid it on the menfolk," Johnny Wright said.

But that was just talk; Kitty Wells never laid anything on anybody. "She's so real," Martha Carson exclaimed when we were talking about Kitty. "I mean, she's the same way every time you see her."

Today Kitty Wells was wearing a purple track suit and low heels. Her hair was short and brown, there were a few lines around her mouth—but not many—and behind a pair of glasses her eyes had in them a sparkle of vigorous goodwill that you see in tranquil people who have never cultivated enemies. "I just sang the songs," she said. "You know, with feeling—like I thought people'd want to hear it. I feel for somebody if they're having problems. I feel like I'm one of them."

Wells is the rare country singer to be born in Nashville. Later her family moved a few miles outside town to a farm in McEwen, Tennessee. She was sixteen, working at a shirt factory in South Nashville and thinking about becoming a singer, when she met Johnny Wright in 1935. "I lived next door to Johnny's sister," she said. "Nashville used to be a country town. The music industry changed all that. It was small back then. People from the country would bring in their vegetables downtown to the courthouse. Beans, potatoes, watermelons. They'd park right on the square."

"They'd sleep under the car on the pavement with a blanket," Wright said. "You could buy a crate of tomatoes for fifty cents. One section of Nashville, they used to call it Varmint Town. There were possums, rabbits, even polecats. They'd get hit by cars. You were as liable to run over a rabbit as a possum. The old possum, he'd make out like he was asleep. Then he'd get up and take off if he wasn't dead. They'd call them *sull* possums. *Sulling* means playing dead. A lot of people got bit by them because they thought he was dead."

"If you made someone mad they'd sull," said Wells. "Just stand there not saying anything and looking at you like this." She made a face.

Her husband laughed, as much at the idea of Kitty Wells making someone mad as at her expression. He was a deliveryman when his sister introduced him to the quiet girl next door. In 1937, he married her.

Seven years later, Johnny & Jack had a job on a daily radio show in Knoxville, where Chet Atkins, not long out of high school, was their fiddle player. "Lowell Blanchard was the boss man," says Wright. "He was a wonderful guy. He says, 'Johnny, I like that girl's singing, but nobody can remember Muriel Deason. It's not a catchy name. If you get the right name for her I believe she could sell some records.' The old song 'Kitty Wells' went back to the Civil War. We used to sing it together around the house. 'Sweet Kitty Wells.' " He sang a few bars of it that involved songbirds, blooming myrtle, and a great deal of weeping. Then he went on: "I said to Lowell, 'What do you think about Kitty Wells?' He said, 'That's it! I guarantee people will remember Kitty Wells.' "

By 1949, Chet Atkins was playing with Maybelle Carter and her daughters while Kitty, Johnny, and Jack had moved on to Shreveport, where they were singing on *The Louisiana Hayride*—a sort of country cousin to *The Grand Ole Opry*. Hank Williams was on the *Hayride* too. "He was all right," Kitty Wells said. "Hank always enjoyed getting out and singing for the people. People loved him. He stood tall and lanky. You could always tell he meant the songs he was singing. Nowadays the songs they write don't have the feeling of the old songs. 'Cold, Cold Heart,' 'Your Cheatin' Heart'—he used to write good songs. Fred Rose helped him write, but Hank had the ideas. In country a lot of the songs are written because people have something happen to them and they write a song and other people have had it happen to them." Kitty Wells never wrote songs herself. "It was harder for women," she said. "They didn't write songs for women back then."

"Roy Acuff told me, 'You can't headline a show with a woman,' " Wright said. "I told him I didn't see why not."

"I didn't let it bother me," Kitty Wells said. "Johnny told him he'd try it anyway."

"Roy didn't want Kitty billed over Johnny & Jack," Wright said. "Roy didn't think Kitty would last. There never had been a girl popular like that. In the end he thought there never had been a girl like Kitty Wells." He looked delighted. "This was in 1952," he said. Then he got up from behind his desk and said, "Come on. I'll show you the museum."

The Kitty Wells–Johnny Wright museum is toward the rear of the Country Junction and, like most displays of this sort, consists of a large number of photographs, scrapbook items, and curios from a life in music. We passed pairs of each of Wright's parents' shoes and photographs of Kitty and Johnny standing with Roy Acuff, Ernest Tubb, and also Jack Anglin, who was killed in 1963 when he lost control of his car on the way to the Nashville memorial service for Patsy Cline. Sometimes there were several men in a photograph, but almost always Kitty was the only woman. "She was just one in a million," Wright said. There were invitations from presidents and commendations from just about everyone. "All those awards," Wright said. "For sixteen years she was the number-one woman in country music." He pointed to a lyric sheet from the song "Kitty Wells." "It's a sad song," he said. "Kitty, she's really happy. She's a country girl. Raised up like myself. Real hard."

The exhibition ends with a full-scale replica of the kitchen from the first house Wells and Wright shared in Nashville right after they were married in 1937. Wright explained that Kitty Wells is nearly as fine a cook as she is a singer. "Kitty cooked green beans, potatoes, squash, okra, candied yams, chicken," he said, smacking his lips. "She was a good cook. Her mother was, too. She got it natural." He produced a copy of the *Kitty Wells Country Cook Book*. On the cover was a photograph of Kitty in a large calico apron. Inside were recipes for corn-fried onions, apple fritters, jam cakes, and pork-chop casseroles. "Her flapjacks make you flap your uppers and lowers," said Wright.

Kitty Wells rejoined us. I asked her how a singer felt about being honored with a kitchen, and the way she responded made it clear that a woman wasn't wrong to look at Kitty Wells's life and conclude that she could do most anything she chose. In the least aggressive way possible, Kitty Wells said that her life proved that a woman could have it all. "I've always loved to cook," she said. "I don't cook so much anymore, but I always cook Christmas dinner. I still enjoy singing, too. I got to do both. Sure did. Not a thing I'd do any different. We always worked together, Johnny and I. I always let Johnny handle the business. He promoted me more than himself. We had lots of fun. We traveled on the road with the family and always had a good outlook on life. We've always been family people. We've always had a good home life. When we got married it was a lifetime contract. We never even thought about getting divorced. We never cared about going to honky-tonks and stuff like that."

PATSY CLINE

"Patsy grew up singing in honky-tonks," the sultry singer Patsy Cline's widower, Charlie Dick, was saying. "We were both crazy when we were kids. I'm sure we were a little wild. Today she'd fit right in with everybody, but back then women didn't do certain things."

Around other people, Cline was high-spirited and such a loud talker that, says Dick, "if she was in a room, you knew it." (Cline always claimed that her booming voice was the dividend from a childhood episode of rheumatic fever.) She preferred one brand of beer—Schlitz—and liked many kinds of bars, including the hardscrabble "skull orchards" she sang in along the roads outside her hometown of Winchester, Virginia, when she was a young woman struggling to make it as a singer. Her favorite Nashville saloon was the songwriters' haunt, Tootsie's Orchid Lounge, where she spent a lot of time swapping off-color stories with the wisecracking men who wrote sad love songs for her: Harlan Howard, Hank

Patsy and the boys. "She acted more like a man.
She could spit out some words and it didn't take her long."

Cochran, Mel Tillis, and Willie Nelson. "She could tell a joke just as raw as you could," says Tillis. "And boy, could she laugh. She bellered out." As tall as many men and completely comfortable in masculine company, Cline was one of the boys. "You'd never see Kitty Wells over at Tootsie's," says Dick. "In the old days, a wife's place was in the home."

Cline had been around male musicians since her early teens and their bearing appealed to her. "She acted more like a man," says Bud Armel, who led The Kountry Krackers, a Winchester band that Cline sometimes sat in with. "She could spit out some words and it didn't take her long." Cline swore like a bachelor, but her conversation also had an easy offhand swagger to it that instantly seemed credible to men, who looked up when they heard a woman say "howdy" followed by something saltier. She used colloquial language that was vivid and imaginative. Most everyone she liked was called "Hoss"; groups were addressed as "you doggies"—as in, "Well now, how in the hell are you doggies?"—and she always referred to herself as "The Cline."

Men appreciated a great deal about Patsy Cline, including the way she looked. "A big-built woman," Bud Armel says. "Not fat. Big. She was beautiful." To emphasize her luxurious figure, Cline wore knee-length, tight-waisted dresses, many of them sewn for her by her mother, a professional seamstress, and push-up brassieres fastened beneath snug sweaters. One of her front teeth was chipped, but she smiled wide anyway, burnished her full lips with bright red lipstick, and had gleaming eyes that seemed to promise what was, in fact, true: that very little inhibited her.

Cline was a bold flirt and willing to take matters further. "She wasn't above an evening of entertainment, but she was right picky," says James Kniceley, who grew up with her in Winchester. People often describe her as a misty romantic, but they've been listening to her music. Lusty and gleefully so was more like it. "Now Hoss, wasn't that the best fuck you ever had," is what her biographer, Ellis Nassour, reports she said to one man after she'd finished with him. A Royal Canadian Mounted policeman was astonished to hear her announce, "My name's Patsy Cline and I'm gonna screw the boots off you." Even while resisting she sounded a little brazen. Mel Tillis says he remembers her telling a roomful of men, "There ain't nobody getting none of this but my Charlie."

If she was coarse, it was only in the same way that the men she knew were. Her first husband, Gerald Cline, was the prodigal heir to a Frederick, Maryland, contracting business. Deciding that he was a hopeless boor, Cline was unfaithful to him. At least one of her lovers had a wife at home. After she and Gerald Cline were divorced, Cline put on spiked heels and a stunning white taffeta and dark velvet dress and danced for hours after getting married to a handsome, hard-drinking *Winchester Star* linotype operator with a little Bill Bailey in him—"Good-Time" Charlie Dick.

It was a lusty and sometimes intemperate union. In a dudgeon over his profligate ways, Cline might bait her husband by calling him "Mr. Cline," or sneer that she was stuck with a "no-good bastard." Dick is said to have responded on occasion with his fists. This is something that he mostly denies—"Smacked her one time," he says—and Bud Armel doubts as well. "She didn't let nobody run over her," Armel says. "She'd put them in their place real fast. Charlie Dick never beat her. If he had, she'd have killed him." During one scrap, it was Cline who supposedly wielded a tire iron. "These stories!" vexes Dick. "There's another one where I heard she pulled a gun on me. Didn't happen." When he describes his wife, he says, with approval, "She had balls."

Brassy, bigboned, and generous—"She had a dime, you needed it, she gave it to you," says James Kniceley—Patsy Cline was what men in her day called a wonderful broad. "She had no spiritual restrictions, let's put it that way," says Jack Fretwell, another Winchester bandleader who worked with her. "But she could sing 'Amazing Grace' or 'Just a Closer Walk with Thee' and make tears come to your eyes. Just a natural, loving person." When Loretta Lynn moved to Nashville, Cline took her out shopping for clothing and drapes and then paid for all of it. Harlan Howard says that a silver bracelet engraved with "Dear Harlan—Thanks for the Hit—Patsy" arrived when "I Fall to Pieces" became her first number-one single in August 1961. His co-writer, Hank Cochran, received a silver money clip. Howard was the hottest songwriter in the business in the 1960s. In all those years he says no other singer ever sent him a thing.

Behind a microphone, Cline was a different woman. All her life she took pleasure in describing herself as an "ol' hillbilly," but unlike traditional country singers like Sara Carter, Rose Maddox, or Kitty Wells, whose lack of polish was part of their appeal, Cline brought a mannered sophistication to country music. Patsy Cline was the first down-home torch singer. By living hard and singing smooth she fully inverted country's expectations of a woman, something that made it easier for Nashville to accept other unconventional types like Emmylou Harris when they came along.

She was born Virginia Patterson Hensley in 1932, six days after her father, a middle-aged sometime blacksmith named Sam Hensley, married sixteen-year-old Hilda Virginia Patterson. Sam Hensley was heir to a squandered fortune, a lifelong drifter, and nobody's idea of a stable parent. After he married Hilda, his family wandered with him, moving nineteen times in sixteen years. Cline gave friends the strong impression that, at least once, her father got drunk and made lewd advances to her. For much of her youth the Hensleys lived in and around Winchester in the northern Shenandoah Valley apple country, a few miles from the West Virginia border. That is where Hilda and her three children remained after her husband disappeared. "Patsy was through a lot when she was young," says Bud Armel. "Her father left the family and they had rough going. It was three kids."

Winchester was a staid old Virginia city of 15,000, where the railroad tracks really did separate the prosperous side of town from the shabby area that Cline grew up in. They still do. The five-and-dime closed not

Patsy Cline.
"I sing just like I hurt inside."

long ago and the population has increased, but generally it's a point of pride in Winchester that things haven't changed very much. The Civil War remains an active memory—for a while Stonewall Jackson made his headquarters in town—the annual Apple Blossom Festival abounds in old society traditions, and the weatherbeaten wooden house on South Kent Street that Cline lived in is still there too, its cramped quarters standing in bleak contrast to the amply orieled and belvedered manors that sprawl only a mile or so west of Washington Street.

Cline was sixteen and a sophomore in high school when her father walked out. Four people couldn't survive on what her mother earned sewing, and so Cline quit school and began a succession of jobs. She cut off chicken heads in a poultry plant, worked at the Greyhound bus station, and waitressed the soda-fountain booths in Hunter Gaunt's drugstore. After work she sang in talent shows, at fairs, in supper clubs, and in the dreary little joints out on the state roads. That she went to honkytonks, dated men she met there, and drank a little beer seemed wanton to the Winchester country-club set. For an uneducated woman living in chronic poverty, however, the moral views of people who regarded everyone on South Kent Street with easy contempt didn't have much bite. Charlie Dick says that Cline "didn't think a hell of a lot about how people in Winchester thought of her." There would be enough trouble without them. Cline had an abortion, married badly, was divorced, and then got involved with a drinker who describes himself as "hardheaded." Armel remembers, "When she came to sing with us, she'd be wiping the tears away."

Cline's development from a cowgirl singer in a Stetson hat to a pop vocalist who wore cashmere and sequins is well known, but in the retelling this tends to become more of a linear narrative than was really so. She was only thirteen when she introduced herself to Armel and the other members of the swing band he was playing with then. "She asked to sing and we let her," he says. "At that time she wanted to sing pop." Jack Fretwell remembers her renditions of Gershwin and Berlin a few years later. "She sang a little of everything," he says. "Just trying anything to make it."

When Cline finally did succeed, it was because her producer, Owen Bradley, thought to back her with a piano and soft strings, recording country songs as though they were standards. This was a controversial thing to do because many people believed its rustic sound gave country emotional authenticity. In contrast to "The Tennessee Plowboy," Eddy Arnold, who began as a country singer and then distanced himself from country when he went pop in the 1940s, Patsy Cline always made it clear how much she loved country music, something that's also audible in even her most polished renditions. Cline owned up to who she was, and it showed in her music. That "Crazy" is still the most requested song on American jukeboxes supports what Bradley suspected forty years ago: because their words and melodies are so true to basic human emotions, good country songs can have salon appeal. If Cline had lived longer, she would have been singing "I Can't Help It (If I'm Still in Love with You)" at Rainbow & Stars.

She had spectacular equipment. There was her artesian phrasing, the glorious range of keys, and her rich palette of sounds. She yelped, growled, made her voice flatten, ache, drift, catch—the famous "oh" in "Crazy"—throb, and swoon. She was also a master modulator. "Sweet Dreams" doesn't simply begin in a long rush. Within four words Cline has opened to a full-throttle crescendo and then pulled back toward more ruminative territories. She was a favorite with songwriters because she understood how they used syllables to achieve emphasis and knew how to showcase their choicer lines. When Cline sang, "I've got your memory or has it got me," in Hank Cochran's "She's Got You," she called attention to the revelation by slurring the "or." Cline handled sudden turns in a melody as an expensive sedan does a veer in the road—with such consummate control that you don't really notice the difficulty. In "Strange," "Half as Much," and her other best numbers, she pressed so much emotional energy into the songs that Charlie Dick says they seemed to him to be full-length movies distilled into three minutes of singing. This is by no means an uncommon reaction.

Those performances all came late in her career. Part of the reason was that in 1954, when Cline was twenty-two, Bill McCall, the crafty manager of a small California record company, signed her to what amounted to a six-year contract that limited her to recording only the musical pap he supplied. Yet it's also true that gathering control of her ability took Cline most of her twenties. Even though her hits date from 1960, when she recorded Cochran and Howard's "I Fall to Pieces," Cline was not a truly consistent singer until two years later, in 1962, the year before she died. Of the extant studio recordings she made after that January, there isn't a one that misses. Not one.

Every once in a while, in a certain mood, I put on a Patsy Cline record and listen to what heartache sounds like from the inside. Her songs don't wrench a listener the way George Jones's do, and they aren't as lonely as

Apple stand outside Winchester, Virginia. "Patsy didn't think a hell of a lot about how people in Winchester thought of her."

Ralph Stanley's are, but Patsy Cline's is troubling music just the same. Or rather, it is music about getting accustomed to trouble. Hers is the voice of a woman burdened with a few problems already and expecting more soon. Away from places like Tootsie's, that's really the way it was. "Patsy had a sad life," Jack Fretwell told me. "She could sure sing those sad songs. That's where the pain came in." Cline would have agreed with him. "Oh Lord," she once said, "I sing just like I hurt inside."

Cline and Dick married in 1957, and moved to Nashville two years later. They stayed broke or nearly so until summer 1961, when "I Fall to Pieces" went to number one on the *Billboard* country chart. Two months before that happened, Cline was in a bad car wreck that sent her through the windshield, crumpling her face and breaking her wrist. She began to have premonitions of death. June Carter Cash says that Cline came to her and told her how she wanted her children cared for when she died. Cline was twenty-nine at the time. In the next year, 1963, when she had replaced Kitty Wells as the biggest female star in country music, the private plane carrying Cline, her manager Randy Hughes, and the singers Cowboy Copas and Hawkshaw Hawkins home to Nashville from a benefit concert in Missouri went down in bad weather. When rescue workers got to the crash site, they saw one of Cline's red slips dangling up in the trees. She and everyone else had been killed. Cline was thirty years old.

Patsy Cline died young, beautiful, and in the bloom of success. Unlike Kitty Wells, secure in the comfort of home and family, Patsy Cline seems like a luminous, lonely figure striding out bravely in a man's world. Because her blue love songs made her seem as vulnerable as she turned out to be, like Marilyn Monroe, Cline has become even more popular in death than when she was alive. Compilations of her music have sold millions of copies, her face has appeared on a postage stamp, and Jessica Lange portrayed her in a film: *Sweet Dreams*. In Winchester, however, she remains a vaguely disreputable presence. It doesn't seem to be hostility so much as committed indifference. For a lot of people, just because she died young doesn't change what she was—a white-trash trollop who sang cracker music.

Doc Madagan isn't having any of it. "They never did treat her right," he said. "Makes me mad. They act like she's not even from here." Madagan owns Gaunt's Drug Store. He joined the pharmacy staff in 1958, a few years after Cline quit her job serving lime rickeys and cherry smashes to sing full time. She'd liked it there, though, and came by sometimes just to visit. Which is how she got to know the new druggist. "She'd flop in, hair up in curlers, dressed in blue jeans and a red bandanna," Madagan said. "She looked good. She always looked good in public, even in curlers."

Gaunt's soda fountain has been gone since the 1950s, but Madagan keeps one of the old wooden booths in the store and urges customers to "take a seat in my Patsy Cline booth" while they wait for him to fill their prescriptions. More often than not, Madagan has one of Cline's records playing as he works. Fastened to a nearby wall above shelves stocked with lemon glycerin swabsticks are a number of photographs of Cline that Madagan has collected over the years. Among them is a sequence showing her singing at the Lawton, Virginia, fire department's New Year's Eve party in 1957. In the last photograph, Charlie Dick has leaped onto the stage and he and Patsy are exchanging a luscious kiss.

Down the wall is a publicity still inscribed "To Mom, We finally made it." Hilda Hensley still lives on South Kent Street, across the road from her old house. She keeps a Cadillac that Cline bought for her parked out front, but she isn't seen much around Winchester anymore. "When Patsy got killed some of Hilda left too and she got kind of reclusive," Madagan said. He is an organized man with an owlish face and a carefully knotted necktie, and as he talked he prepared pills for a woman who had pains in her legs that were keeping her from sleeping. "Hilda and Patsy grew up kind of like sisters," he said. "She was only sixteen when she had her. It hurts. We're talking about enduring this pain for thirty-five years. She's had so much sadness I guess she doesn't want to talk about it anymore."

There are also a few shots on the wall of Cline riding in open cars during local parades, smiling radiantly as she passes crowds of people. If you look closely you can see that many spectators are standing with slack jaws and arms folded across their chests, scowling back at her. Next to the photographs, Madagan has tacked up a clipping from the *Richmond Times-Dispatch,* which describes Cline's funeral in Winchester. "Most of the mourners were from out of town," it says.

As the afternoon wore on, a number of customers came into the drug-store and joined the conversation. They all seemed to be working people with Patsy Cline stories of their own. One man who had gone to high school with Cline's younger sister Sylvia described Cline singing with a band during a Christmas party late in the 1950s. "Someone made a re-mark," he said, "and she jumped out into the crowd and started swinging. Spunky she was!" He said that Cline used to come back fairly often to Winchester from Nashville and sometimes when she did, she'd treat her friends to trips to the beauty shop and buy them new dresses afterward. (Charlie Dick says that on other occasions she made up their faces and fixed their hair herself.) "She cussed and she drank an occasional beer," the man at Gaunt's said. "She didn't do as much as they say she did. Lot of gossip."

The woman with sore legs agreed. "She was a good girl," she said.

Another man came into the store. He said he'd met Cline one night at a Winchester snack bar when they were both teenagers. "She asked me to walk her home," he said. "We just passed the time. Her mother was wait-ing for her at the front door. She was a nice girl."

Bill Monroe back at the old home, Rosine, Kentucky.

PART THREE

BLUEGRASS

*Bill Monroe and his Blue Grass Boys in the early 1940s: Chubby Wise,
Curly Bradshaw, Monroe, bass player Wilene "Sally Ann" Forrester,
Clyde Moody, David "Stringbean" Akeman. "They'd a probably
had to plowed a lot of furrows if they hadn't a been in
bluegrass music," said Monroe.*

BILL MONROE *and* RALPH STANLEY

FULL OF BEANS

Early on a Saturday night in Nashville at the end of a hot, sticky Southern summer, the twin pillars of traditional American string-band music were finding themselves a bit drawn. Seated in his dressing room at the Ryman Auditorium beneath a photograph of a grinning Minnie Pearl, Bill Monroe was all frowns. "The Father of Bluegrass Music" had just been presented four pints of fresh Vulcan, Missouri, mountain blackberry jam, homemade and hand-delivered by an admirer who knew that Monroe was soon to turn eighty-three. But just then Monroe didn't crave jam. He wanted a red pill. When his assistant whispered that there was a show to play and a red pill "might make Mr. Monroe drowsy," Monroe responded in a way that seemed only natural in someone whose sixty-eight years of nimble mandolin picking and Kentucky-style buck-and-wing dancing have at last worn tender on his joints, heart, and hips. "But it makes you feel so good," he said plaintively. There was some further discussion and finally it was decided that Father knows best.

Out on stage at about that moment, Ralph Stanley, whose raw, mournful tenor recalls the Appalachian hollers he grew up in, was saying, "I hope you'll enjoy what we have for you: some of the old-time mountain songs." Stanley was speaking from his heart and he was also speaking from his posterior. Only a few weeks earlier he had fallen off the back of a pickup truck he was unloading at home in Coeburn, Virginia. When he hit the ground, his sixty-seven-year-old femur had been badly broken.

"I've done a lot of suffering," he admitted later in private. "I really shouldn't travel. But I'm dedicated to the music."

Monroe grew up a wall-eyed Kentucky farmboy with bullying older brothers and a very limited wardrobe: each year he was given one pair of shoes and two pairs of overalls. As an adult, to distance himself from that plowboy persona, Monroe has always performed wearing a necktie and a crease in his trousers—unless, that is, he overlooks the latter in favor of a Kentucky gentleman's boots and riding breeches. Monroe is such a competitive man that when he was younger, if he shook hands with someone in the street, the situation often developed into an impromptu tug-of-war. This practice was reserved for men, of course. With women, Monroe's methods changed. He liked to show them he could sing higher than they could.

At the Ryman, he greeted me with a brawny handshake. Then we sat down and I saw that the trouser crease was still there too and so were four of his other trademarks: small Jesus and American-flag pins were attached to his blazer lapel; the Gibson mandolin he has played on for fifty years was in a battered brown leather case at his knee; and his conversation was as silent as the pines of old Kentucky.

That was to be expected. Monroe is, in fact, a notoriously reticent man. Chet Atkins likes to tell the story of the musicologist from an Ivy League university who traveled south to pay Monroe a visit. "He said he was gonna write a book about bluegrass," says Atkins. "He had on wedges and a sweater tied around his neck. He told Bill about the Andes and about Ireland and about Egypt. Told him about what music all over the world had to do with bluegrass. Then he asked Bill where bluegrass came from. Bill said, 'Down home.' Short interview."

Monroe can hold his peace—and a grudge—for a long time. In 1948, when the masterly guitar and banjo players Lester Flatt and Earl Scruggs left their positions as sidemen in Monroe's band, The Blue Grass Boys, and subsequently formed their own group, Monroe's response was twenty-one years of silence. When Monroe's record label, Columbia, signed up The Stanley Brothers in 1949, Monroe abandoned Columbia and made a deal with Decca. By some accounts, the Stanleys became his sworn enemies. Nobody could be absolutely certain, however, because Monroe was closemouthed on the subject.

If the feud with the Stanleys was real, then there Monroe has relented. At the Ryman he said he had nothing but affection for Ralph Stanley, although he expressed it succinctly, of course. "I enjoy playing with him," he said. "He's a good friend of mine. We like to get together and let the people see Bill Monroe and Ralph Stanley playing together."

Monroe performing a gospel song such as "Walking in Jerusalem" expresses deep faith. Yet even more than Monroe's, there is a washed-in-the-blood quality to Ralph Stanley's singing. If ever a man can sing high and sound sepulchral, it is he.

Because Bill Monroe is the Father of Bluegrass Music, and because some early Carter and Ralph Stanley recordings made in the late 1940s and early 1950s sound an awful lot like Bill Monroe's recordings from the same time, Ralph Stanley has been described as a Monroe acolyte. The Stanleys did cover several of Monroe's songs, but they wrote hundreds of their own, and whatever debts the early Stanley sound owed to Monroe's, it evolved into something distinct. This difference has become even clearer since Carter Stanley's death in 1966. If you know that the very name "bluegrass music" refers to Monroe, who comes from the "Bluegrass State," Kentucky, it comes as no surprise that in recent years Ralph Stanley has taken care to emphasize, as he did here at the Ryman, that what he sings is actually old-time mountain music—not bluegrass.

I talked this subject over with Ricky Skaggs, who grew up in Kentucky, spent three years as one of Stanley's Clinch Mountain Boys, has recorded with Monroe, and now counts himself as a good friend of both men. "They're singing two different things that complement each other," Skaggs told me. "Ralph doesn't refer to his music as bluegrass. I think Ralph was turned on to the music before he ever heard The Monroe Brothers. When you hear Bill Monroe you hear the fire of the music. When you hear Ralph Stanley you hear more of the high lonesome sound of the mountains." The nettlesome fact of the matter for Stanley is that people will always refer to what he does as bluegrass because that is the familiar musical genre it most closely resembles.

Bluegrass is a form of traditional acoustic string music that still sounds pretty much as it did in the 1940s, when people like Monroe and Stanley took it off the front porch and began playing it across the country, often at gatherings that looked like evangelical revival meetings. A typical bluegrass song employs only three or four chords, accompanying a series of verses linked by a chorus. An instrumental like "Blackberry Blossom" uses an "A" section and a "B" section, with the "A" played in, say, the key of G and the "B" section shifting to a minor key. A standard song with vocals, like "Roll in My Sweet Baby's Arms," has two distinctive melodies, one for the verses and one for the chorus. Sometimes there will be an eight-bar bridge as well. All this structure does not much distinguish bluegrass from country. What sets bluegrass apart is the restrictions.

Only with a very few string-powered instruments can a band play the sprinting breakdown arpeggios and lilting refrains that sound like bluegrass. This limited assembly includes banjo, fiddle, mandolin, guitar, bass fiddle, and dobro. You might well find a banjo in a country band, but if someone is using a piano, drums, or an electric guitar, he isn't playing bluegrass. Bluegrass places primacy on instrumental virtuosity and on the syncopation inspired by black dance music. Bluegrass sidemen take solo breaks as jazzmen do, and bluegrass fans can tell Earl Scruggs's banjo from Don Reno's as readily as jazz buffs can inform you that it's Lester Young blowing that sax, not Zoot Sims.

Even though it is only fifty years old, bluegrass has always styled itself venerable music. Just as the instruments are old-fashioned, the lyrical content of a bluegrass song is emphatically pre-Edison. These wistful songs of faith, family, love, loss, pain, and redemption are anchored in a distant rural past. There are no condominiums or shopping centers in bluegrass and, in Bill Monroe's words, "no filth" either. In bluegrass, not much good ever comes to anyone who leaves for the city, is feckless in love, or drinks whiskey from a fruit jar. Because bluegrass songs tend to be crowded with infidels who, in fact, do stray far from home, drown their lovers in rivers, and soak themselves in moonshine, bluegrass generally features high, keening vocal harmonies that singers summon by tamping down the backs of their throats, even if they don't come from the Appalachian hills where people grow up singing this way. (A persistent canard holds that all bluegrass musicians come from Appalachia.)

Perhaps because it has been so stubbornly resistant to stylistic change—and maybe because it is not nearly as remunerative as country—bluegrass's most admired practitioners remain the men who first popularized it. It's also true that Ralph Stanley and Bill Monroe possess the two most distinctive voices in bluegrass history. They keep on going both because they want to preserve the music and because nobody can sing it the way they can.

At the Ryman, Stanley had begun his performance of "the old songs," some of which, like "Shout Little Lulie," he said he still played "just like my mother taught me." Monroe could hear him through a speaker in his dressing room. "He's got a good voice. Sings like it should be sung," he said. "Keep it pure, you know." People were applauding loudly at every opportunity and Monroe heard that too. "You see the music really touching them, being sung like they want it to," he said. Some people believe that Stanley has sounded like an old man since he was young, and now sings better than ever because his age has finally caught up with his voice. Monroe couldn't be sure. "He's singing good now," he said. "He sang awful good when he was young. I think he sings awful good now, though." Then, after a long pause, suddenly he looked at me and for the first time he volunteered something. "Would you put something down for me?" he said. "Ralph and I are gonna be friends and help each other as long as we live."

As a young man, Bill Monroe stood six feet tall and weighed more than two hundred very solid pounds. He could jerk a baseball bat in half as he made contact with a fastball. Today he is stooped and frail, with only his stevedore's handshake left as a keepsake from the once formidable physical strength. To see Monroe sickly and attenuated, and to think of Stanley ailing too, makes you worry that bluegrass also is fragile.

When Monroe walked out onto the Ryman stage, however, he was a man transformed. Adopting his defiant performance posture, with legs set firm, upper torso thrust forward, head tilted slightly upward, eyes hooded, lips apart and turned down at the corners, he sent out vigorous renditions of "Muleskinner Blues" and "Blue Moon of Kentucky." He mugged with his banjo player and even danced the Kentucky backstep to "Uncle Pen," the song he wrote to honor his mother's brother, Pendleton Vandiver, a country fiddler whom Monroe calls "the fellow that I learned how to play from." For this number he received a standing ovation. Monroe looked so spry that when I encountered his assistant, I raised my eyebrows. She smiled. "He was just messin'," she said. "He didn't take any red pill. He's just got his own way of doing things. See all the attention he got?"

Out on the stage, Monroe doffed the large white Stetson hat he wears above his long white sideburns and called Stanley back out for an encore. Stanley reappeared, on crutches this time, to finish off his evening with "I'm on My Way to the Old Home." Monroe wrote the song about visiting "the fondest spot in my memory," the small light gray house outside the town of Rosine, where he was born beside a winding road "high up in the hills of old Kentucky." To hear Stanley applying his tenor to the song's mournful cadences, you would suspect that he too spent his youth listening to the foxhounds baying through the Kentucky dusk. As I watched him, it occurred to me that I had never before seen a singer performing while hunched over a pair of crutches, but a friend of mine who attended

the Ryman concert and who grew up not far from the Appalachian mining village of McClure, Virginia, where Stanley really did spend his childhood, explained them to me. "No way Ralph was gonna be seen out on
stage sitting down next to Bill Monroe," he said. "It's the code of the
mountains, and Ralph Stanley's a proud man."

Driving through the mountains of southwestern Virginia, on my way to
visit Ralph Stanley, I was thinking about something else Ricky Skaggs
had told me. "Ralph Stanley brings the lonesomeness, the hardness, the
poverty, the faith of Appalachia to his singing," he said. "He sounds exactly like where he comes from."

That would be Dickenson County, Virginia, where the hills swell up
close around the small villages. Through my windshield from a rise on the
blacktop, those hills looked soft, like plump green cotton balls, but there
is nothing forgiving about them. Within the hills is anthracite coal, and
alongside the roads that wind and twist through the mountains you can
see slag heaps, slash piles of clearcut timber, slopes that have been strip-
mined bare, and mean rows of identical shotgun houses put up years ago
by mining companies to house the help. It's the sort of place you might expect a man whose signature songs include "Man of Constant Sorrow" and
"All the Good Times Have Passed and Gone" to reside. Life here can be
very bleak.

"For us it was hard to believe there was any 'rest of the world,' and if
there should be such a thing, why, we trusted in the mountains to protect
us from it," is how the singer Jean Ritchie described growing up in the
Cumberland Mountains of Kentucky in the 1930s. In a similar sense, the
Virginia version of those hills still obscures places like Dickenson and
neighboring Wise County from the prosperity of the America beyond
them. It may be fashionable to say that people just don't suffer the way
they used to, but it isn't necessarily true. Appalachian Virginia still feels
like the hidden frontier. Towns named Poor Bottom and Big Lick suggest
this, as they do the marginal, hardscrabble quality of life that persists here.
On my radio, a discussion of black-lung benefits paused for an advertise-
ment that began, "When my child comes home with head lice . . ." Off the
truck routes, I could never drive too fast because the smaller roads leading to the hollers and ridges support a steady traffic of tractors, chickens,
and box turtles. There are trim subdivisions in larger towns like Norton,
but in an afterthought of a community like McClure, the cool valleys are
full of old wooden cabins and patched-up trailer homes resting at crazy

angles on blocks. In yards scattered with sagging corncribs and abandoned car chassis, people lash their rusted television antennas to tree
stumps because the roof won't support them.

Not that I would ever see anybody sitting around and complaining
about how rugged their lot was. There wasn't time. With automation and
closings making mine work scarce, men were traveling 100 miles for jobs
in the Clinchfield Coal Company's McClure #1 Mine, where a sign by the
gate says "First Class Miners Working Together with Success in Mind."
Bernard Rakes, the retired Dickenson County treasurer, told me that one
of his sons lives in the county and every day drives an hour and half each
way over "rough roads" to West Virginia to work at a strip mine. He said
his son was responding to the situation with equanimity because he likes
living in southwestern Virginia. "People here are friendly, everybody
speaks to everybody—people are awful friendly here," Rakes told me. "I
at one time could call 20,000 people by their first name." It's true that
nowhere in my travels were people kinder to me. "Places like this never
change," said Fran Meade, the waitress at the Kountry Kitchen in Coeburn, the next town over from McClure, as I ate a plate of Virginia ham.
"Just country people. That's good people, isn't it?"

Ralph Stanley's music is still popular here because it is old-time music
for a place that as much as anywhere in America is stuck in the Depression.
The pleasure that people take in "the old songs" comes with awareness that
those songs are from here and that they don't change. In 1949, James Ho-
bart Stanton, who produced The Stanley Brothers on his Rich-R-Tone
Record label, was consternated that he could sell Stanley Brothers records
by the thousands in Appalachia, "and not give one away in Georgia." Because people who live here have absorbed so many gibes about their lack of
sophistication, there is now grim resistance to the idea of acquiring it. Bill
Monroe says, "Keep it pure" because he knows that pride as much as listening pleasure is involved in appreciating old-time bluegrass and mountain music. That's one reason why, over the years, Ralph Stanley has
self-consciously sought to sound more and more traditional. The songs he
and Carter wrote mirror the sound and the sensibility of authentic traditionals like "Wild Bill Jones," which he learned as a child. Hubert Powers,
who has been a barber in Coeburn for thirty-two years, told me, "It's down-
to-earth music, just old hillbilly mountain music. It's still really down-to-
earth mountain people around here and I reckon they like it."

Stanley lives in a stone house he built six miles outside Coeburn. His
name is on the mailbox out front, which is the Appalachian equivalent

of Frank Sinatra putting his number in the Manhattan telephone book. "I don't reckon I'll take my name off it," Stanley said. "Sometimes you want people to find you anyway." That's modesty speaking, for Ralph Stanley is hardly the Rank Stranger who inhabits one of his best-loved songs. Around here, everybody knows where to find him, as they have for a long time.

He was born in 1927, in a holler along Big Spraddle Creek in McClure. When he was nine, his parents, Lee and Lucy Smith Stanley, moved the family three miles up onto Smith Ridge, six miles from where he lives today. "We didn't have any running water, didn't have any bathroom until the last part of my teens," Stanley told me. "There's things we'd liked to have that we didn't. We didn't have a change of clothes for every day. We didn't have electricity until later years. First electricity we had was powered by a Delco gasoline engine. Before that we used kerosene lamps and lanterns. But we didn't suffer. My mother washed on a washboard. I split the wood. We had horses to plow our garden. Always kept a milk cow. I have some cattle now and I always raise a garden. I guess I was just raised to do that and it's never left me. Take the boy out of the country, never take the country out of the boy."

One great pleasure in Stanley's youth was hunting up in the Clinch Mountains. ("Takes your mind off everything to see a big coon up in a tree.") The other was music. When someone had a garden full of beans to string, or thirty bushels of apples to be peeled for winter canning, the neighbors would turn out and help. "It's hard work, but people'd sing," says Stanley. "I have heard of people putting a half-gallon can of moonshine whiskey on the floor, piling twenty-five bushels of apples or beans over it, and saying they didn't get to drink until they got to the can. Me, I drank a little but I never did like the taste of whiskey."

What he did like was the singing, and so did his parents. All week, Lee Stanley operated a sawmill and raised a little corn and tobacco on the side. On Sundays he was a church singer. "My father had just an old-time lonesome voice, down to earth like he dug it right out of one of these mountains," says Stanley. The strict Primitive Baptist churches the Stanleys attended didn't permit instruments during services, and so all the music was a cappella singing. A male member of the congregation would lead a song, and everyone else blended in. When Stanley was five, he led a song for the first time. "There was a song my father wanted to sing," he says. "He couldn't remember how it went, so he asked me to sing. I was scared to death but I reckon I got him started on it. Probably forty people there. A little country church."

Carter and Ralph Stanley. "Ralph, you had to hunt him up. Carter, he'd just sit down and talk to you anywhere."

When Ralph Stanley performs a gospel song today, he sometimes chokes up and begins to cry. "That's when you're meaning what you're doing," he says. "People never mention it, but then I see lots of tears in the audience. Back years ago I'd see women get up and shout when I'd do a gospel song. I haven't seen any shoutin' for a while, but I see a lot of tears. I guess that's when you're feeling something, feeling the spirit. I believe it helped to sing a hymn in church when I was five years old."

Roughly half of Ralph Stanley's material consists of sacred songs like "Memories of Mother," "I'll Pass over Thee," and "Angel Band." Even in his so-called Saturday night selections an implicit catechism is at hand, in which faith, devotion, and decency are always rewarded. Scorn your true love, and you will live an unfulfilled life. If you kill someone, not only will you meet up with a surly sheriff and his cold prison cell, you will experience the greater discomforts of remorse. In a place where life is not easy and where, as Stanley says, "there's always been a lot of murder and a lot of heartache," his music is not just entertainment; it's consistent with a morality that steadies people through hard times. Old-time music brooks no changes because it is part of a broader moral system demanding that you keep right no matter what the temptation or the travail.

The young Ralph Stanley took a sociable drink or more and also wasn't immune to feminine charms—he met his wife while he was out on the road. These days, however, as he moves about the country singing gospel songs, Stanley conspicuously cultivates the aura of a gentle country pastor. He avoids bars, has been with the same woman for almost forty years, and can proselytize energetically. "I've had a lot of people write and tell me they've had a bottle in their pocket, they heard my gospel songs, and they'd throw the bottle away and go to church," he told me. He has white hair, a quiet manner of speaking, bright, friendly eyes, and a lean, solid jaw. "People tell me they've spent their payday on drinks, not got their family what it needed, and 'your songs changed that.' I think it makes better people out of worse people, according to that." For a time, while his band, The Clinch Mountain Boys, was on the road, Stanley played them tapes of mountain preachers on the bus, and then at night, with everyone assembled in his motel room, Stanley read the Bible aloud to sleepy-eyed guitar pickers. With evident glee, he told me about "one mandolin player who became a minister, and he says that's what got him interested." Stanley's contempt for rock 'n' roll music is as much predicated on men like Elvis Presley having nearly depleted the market for traditional country music in the late 1950s as it is grounded in moral suspicion. "It made the teenagers wild," he says dryly. "But I'm not sure it helped the country any." In recent years, Stanley has introduced a cappella religious singing to bluegrass festivals.

Besides singing in church, Lee Stanley also liked to sing around the house, which is where Ralph first heard some of the traditional songs, like "Man of Constant Sorrow," which he would later record. "Old-time singing, nobody learns it," he says. "I didn't have any lessons or any training. I just do it by ear, the way I feel it. I think it's born in you. It's here in Virginia, Kentucky, West Virginia, Tennessee, and western North Carolina. It's in the people. I believe that feeling comes natural if you've got it."

Lee Stanley didn't play an instrument, but Lucy Stanley did. She came from a family of twelve children, all agile-fingered banjo pickers, and Ralph learned his first licks from her. "Back before my mother was married, she'd play banjo at square dances, sometimes until daylight," he says. "She'd walk back home. Could have been five miles. Then she'd go right to work planting corn, hoeing corn, putting up hay—whatever needed to be done. She played the claw-hammer [brushing the strings with your index or middle finger and plucking the fifth string] a little different than I do. She dropped her thumb [plucked other strings besides the fifth]. I never did try drop-thumb. She taught me a couple of tunes—'Shout Little Lulie' and 'Cluck Old Hen'—and I liked them. When I do the claw-hammer I still think of her and nearly always mention her."

In the 1930s, well-known musicians barnstorming through the South would sometimes play a few miles from the Stanley home in the one-room schoolhouse at Pilot Knob. Stanley saw The Delmore Brothers there, and the dazzling Georgia fiddler Clayton McMichen. Yet it was only when the family moved to Smith Ridge and his father purchased that rural staple, a battery-operated Philco radio, that he began to hear professional music with any frequency. Entertainment options were few in the hills, and the Stanley brothers went through batteries as rapidly as young Abe Lincoln wore out chalk at night by the fireplace. As they listened to The Carter Family and The Mainer Brothers, Ralph and Carter Stanley played along with them, after a fashion. "We'd make fiddles or banjos with kindling sticks and beat on them like we had instruments," he says. On Saturday nights, neighbors would come from miles away to sit around the Stanley radio and listen.

When he was eleven, Stanley put away his kindling. At the time he was contemplating what he was going to do with his life and had come to a decision: he wanted to be a pig farmer. "I was liking the farm work," he says. "I liked the looks of hogs and pigs—thought they were pretty." Stanley

was due for a present, and Lucy Stanley's sister Rosie owned a fine sow
that had recently given birth to a litter of pigs. Rosie also owned a banjo.
Lucy was running a small grocery store at the time and she struck a deal
with Rosie: Ralph could choose either a pig or the banjo in exchange for
five dollars worth of provisions from the grocery. "That was the end of
raising pigs," says Stanley. Lee Stanley would have preferred the pig. "My
dad used to run me out of the house," says Stanley. "He couldn't concentrate on his paperwork. 'Get out of here,' he'd say." So Stanley would sit
for hours under an apple tree with his banjo. If a piece of fruit fell nearby,
"I'd eat it and go on picking."

Aunt Rosie's banjo wasn't much of an instrument—it suffered from a
tatty, fraying skin, for one thing—and when Stanley had saved up enough
money from cutting mine-shaft timber, he ordered a new one from a
mail-order catalogue. It was delivered to him by the local postman, who
sang and played the harmonica as he made his rounds on horseback.

With his catalogue banjo Stanley turned himself into a fine, fine picker,
but not a fancy one; these days he is quick to describe himself as "more of
a singer." Stanley just wants his banjo to accompany him. "If you put a slur
in a word, you put it in that instrument, if you can—make it sound just as
much like the way the sound goes," he told *Frets* in 1979. There are no at-
tempts at impressing listeners with a sunshower of rapid banjo notes.
Ralph Stanley's banjo imitates his vocal inflections as closely as possible.

After he finished high school in 1945, Stanley served a stretch with the
Army in occupied Germany. He rose to sergeant largely on the strength
of his superiors' enthusiasm for his banjo playing, but as soon as his time
was up, he resisted invitations to stay in the service and came home to Virginia to look for a job. "I had some brothers who worked in the mines, but
I never did," he says. "I never did think I could stand it. I had asthma and
I figured I'd smother in there. I had a little thinking of making a veteri-
narian of myself. I liked to help sick animals. But I soon got that out of my
mind." Soon meant exactly three months: it took that long for Stanley to
find himself in a Bristol, Virginia, radio studio making his debut performance on a new show, *Farm and Fun Time*. He played the banjo and sang
tenor behind his brother Carter. The response was good, as it usually
would be for The Stanley Brothers and The Clinch Mountain Boys over
the next twenty years.

By now, Stanley had set aside the claw-hammer and was picking with
three fingers as Bill Monroe's banjo player Earl Scruggs did. The Stanleys
stayed in Virginia until 1958, and then were lured to Live Oak, Florida,

by the prospects of a new audience. (They needed it, because rock 'n' roll was claiming a lot of their old one.) All this time, they were taking advantage of the publicity gained from their broadcasts by giving large numbers of live performances. They drove relentlessly from town to town around the South in a station wagon they called "The Old-Time Car," performing in schoolhouses, fairground barns, movie theaters, on the backs of flatbed trucks, and sometimes, to Stanley's displeasure, in saloons. "I don't like to play in a bar," he says. "People ain't themself. After they get a few drinks in them, you might sing 'em 'Pretty Polly' and then five minutes later they'll holler 'How about "Pretty Polly"!' "

He did like to drive, and could do so for ten hours at a stretch, day after day, while Carter wrote classics like "The White Dove" in the backseat. "I'd guess I've driven millions of miles," says Stanley. It was an exhausting way to live, however, and in 1952 the Stanleys quit music and went to work in the Ford factories in Detroit. Jesse McReynolds, a mandolin-playing Coeburn native who, with his brother Jim, performs in the bluegrass band Jim & Jesse, says that he too once had a brush with regular employment. "I applied for a cotton-mill job in Kingsport, Tennessee," he told me. "I got inside the gate, didn't like the looks of the place, and thought I'd rather go back home and pick my music a little bit." The Stanleys' hiatus from music didn't last much longer than Jesse McReynolds's did.

There were other brief interruptions in the 1950s. Carter sang with Monroe for part of 1951 — they'd become warm friends by this time. Ralph also briefly served as a Blue Grass Boy, until he was badly injured in a head-on collision while returning from a show. Mostly, the brothers were making music together. The cuts they recorded for Columbia and Mercury between 1949 and 1959 are full of American acoustic string band classics, from "The Fields Have Turned Brown," about a young sport who goes out to see the world and then finally comes home for a visit to find that his parents have been dead for years, to "A Vision of Mother," the story of a harried man who is buoyed by the idea that he will one day see his dead mother again in heaven. Carter's credo was to "sing a song with the best feeling you've got," and when the brothers did that, it was difficult not to be moved by them.

The relationship was not without its uneasy periods. Carter was a confident man, naturally hale and jocose, and during the twenty years the brothers performed together his charisma seemed to have a slightly dour and retiring effect upon Ralph, who was shy by nature. Hubert Powers has photographs of both brothers on the walls of his barbershop—Jim and Jesse McReynolds and Bill Monroe are there, too—and in those photographs, as in most portraits of the Stanleys, Carter looks expansive and handsome, a born emcee, while Ralph seems a little grave. Each Stanley spent a lot of hours in Powers's chair, and the barber's descriptions of them are telling. "Ralph, you had to hunt him up," Powers says. "Carter, he'd just sit down and talk to you anywhere."

But Carter was "a dram drinker," as they say in Dickenson County, and on December 1, 1966, he died at age forty-one, spitting up his insides as his liver gave out. Since then Stanley has gradually overcome "my backwardness. I wouldn't say I'm shy now," he says. "If I talk to you I'll talk, but I just never did like to push myself on anybody. Carter was more forward." Within five days of Carter's death, Stanley had taken over the band, found a new lead singer, and hit the road again. Two years later, he moved back to Virginia from Florida. At home in the mountains he began composing rafts of music. Much of it, like "I'll Answer the Call," is excellent material, but his voice is what makes Ralph Stanley special. After Carter's death, that eerie tenor became an incredible vessel of sadness.

Violent death was not exactly unheard of in Stanley country. From the murders of passion to the accidents in the mines to the cars that swerved off the steep mountain roads in Dickenson County, plunging people to deaths that might not be discovered for weeks, the southeastern hills were full of lurid demises. Many of them became, in turn, the grist for classic, traditional songs. "The Banks of the Ohio" tells of a man who drowns his sweetheart in the Ohio River when she refuses to marry him. "Omie Wise" is about a young woman whose faithless lover first lures her to sleep with him, then promises to marry her, only to drown her in a spring instead. Ralph and Carter Stanley knew a lot of these songs. Others they wrote on their own. After a bus full of children was wrecked in Floyd County, Kentucky, in 1957, Carter promptly came up with "No School Bus in Heaven." When Carter died, he left his brother to make a living on a repertoire stocked with murder, suicide, and sorrow. "I guess a lot of the old songs, 'Omie Wise,' 'Barbara Allen,' 'Banks of the Ohio,' actually happened," says Stanley. "People back in the country like this, when they have disputes and arguments, it often leads to a killin'. It's that way everywhere. In the cities you heard about it through newspapers. Here, back in the country, you heard about it through songs."

When an untimely end came to Carter, Ralph Stanley didn't respond by explicitly writing or singing about his brother's death. But after 1966, it was gradually apparent that Stanley had allowed a tragic timbre to sink into his voice. Fraternal tensions aside, he had loved Carter, and what you heard then, as now, in Ralph Stanley's tenor was grief.

Out on his own, Stanley grew less inhibited, and with that self-assurance came the competitive desire to be regarded as something other than another disciple of Bill Monroe. "I never wanted to sound like Bill," he was already telling Ralph Rinzler in 1974. He has employed two guitar players in his band—something Monroe would never do—and he distinguishes his music from Monroe's in a fashion similar to that of Ricky Skaggs, by saying, "I think the old-time mountain music has more of a down-to-earth feeling to it. Bluegrass is supposed to have a drive to it. I think my music has a different drive. It's played more simple." All that is true, and Stanley went to great lengths to apply a layer of dust to his music. He sometimes played the banjo in the claw-hammer style his mother had taught him, he wrote songs notable for their lyrical austerity, and he stripped down the Clinch Mountain sound so that his voice rang clean and spare above the strings. Stanley made it seem that his was the kind of traditional string music that Bill Monroe transformed into bluegrass. And it was, except that Stanley had emphasized his connection to it in response to Monroe's discovery of bluegrass.

Stanley is, naturally, used to being classified beneath the aegis of bluegrass, and the weekend bluegrass festival circuit that formed in the 1960s has been a relative sinecure for him. Still, he is hardly a wealthy man—not that he ever expected to become one. He traveled the rough roads for so many years because it was more of a pleasure to earn a wage making music than as a pig farmer or a coal miner. Ralph Stanley's songs eluded the jukebox, but there was something timeless in the music—it meant something to the people who loved it, and he says he has been proud to preserve it for them. "It's like 'Old Joe Clark,' that old fiddle tune," he says. "It was here yesterday, it'll be here tomorrow. These big hits'll be gone tomorrow. Garth Brooks—you'll never know he existed in forty-eight years. I've been in the business forty-eight years. I don't know why it is they make more in a month than bluegrass will in ten years. Don't have to last, I guess."

That is what fuels Ralph Stanley, keeps him traveling to dates seven hours with a shattered leg, keeps him making the old music. "There'll probably be some that'll sing it, but when people like Ralph Stanley and

Bill Monroe are gone it'll hurt," he says. "That's one of the reasons I still sing so often. I'd like to keep it going. I doubt if I can last as long as Bill Monroe. I doubt I'm as tough as he is. But I'll play as long as I can."

After that, Stanley will go up to The Hills of Home, the cemetery he built behind his grandfather Smith's old homeplace on Smith Ridge, a grassy slip of topland pasture surrounded by forest-covered mountains in McClure. Smith Ridge is where Lucy Smith Stanley spent her childhood, where she brought her children to live when Ralph Stanley was nine, and where she taught him to play the banjo. The six-room house she was born in is gone. Lucy Stanley was canning apples one day thirty-five years ago, when her old woodstove caught fire and burned it to the ground. Ralph built his mother one to replace it, and now it is occupied by another family. Out back, however, is Stanley's grazing land, and on it are his Charolais and Simmenthal cattle and his graveyard.

"Let Me Rest on a Peaceful Mountain" says the hand-lettered sign over the cemetery entrance. Inside are two pine trees and a lonesome locust shading stones marking generations of Smiths and Stanleys. All Ralph Stanley's dead kin are buried here: parents, grandparents, aunts, uncles, and cousins, right down to the small stone that says "Baby Girl Smith 1924." Most of the graves are flat, with only "Daddy" or "Mother" or "Father" chipped into the rock. At the rear of the small graveyard, however, is a large rectangular granite vault, about twenty feet wide and rising three feet above the ground. Stanley commissioned it for himself, his wife Jimmie, his mother, Carter, and Carter's wife Mary. Mary's and Jimmie's sections of the vault facing are filigreed with white doves. This is a reference to "The White Dove," Carter's song about a man's childhood in the Virginia hills and the sorrow that grips him because "Mother and Daddy are dead." Carter's portion of the tomb has a molded guitar on it. Ralph's is decorated with a banjo. Flat on the ground in front of Carter's grave is Carter's original gravestone, embossed with the phrase "Farewell Carter for a Little While." Death, generations of family, the old homeplace, these are the things Stanley has spent a lifetime singing and brooding about. "I still miss him," Ralph told me, speaking of Carter. "That's where we were mostly raised. If you stand up on that cemetery and look at all those hills there, you can get an idea where Carter wrote all those songs from."

There are two rank strangers in the cemetery. One day a group of men on Harley Davidson motorcycles drew up to Stanley's home in Coeburn.

The bikers said that a friend of theirs had died of a drug overdose. The dead man had told his wife that the Stanley family cemetery was the nicest place he'd ever seen and when he died, he said he hoped he could be buried there. "I gave them permission," Stanley says, explaining that the bikers then roared into the cemetery and had what Stanley calls "a get-together." At one point they opened the dead man's casket and, in a truly bizarre act of mourning, shot him full of dope. Then they drove his body around on their motorcycles. Finally—presumably when they realized there was no reviving him—they buried the body. "He had a son," says Stanley. "He done the same thing—died a year or so later of an overdose. He's buried there too."

I wondered at Stanley, a self-styled preacher, allowing such people to share his family sanctuary, and then I decided that their presence was a warning about going wrong, much as so many of Stanley's songs are. The untimely death of a father and his son must also have appealed to Stanley's lifelong fascination with tragedy and self-destruction. Stanley built The Hills of Home to honor his dead family, but he also uses it to savor the sorrows of his past. Stanley is more than just comfortable with sadness and death; he is attracted to them. Visiting the cemetery gives him the same bittersweet pleasure other people get from his music. "I go once a week," Stanley told me. "I look around and reminisce. In a way it makes me sad. In a way I like to go." As he said that, I was reminded of something he'd told me about his five-year-old granddaughter, Lucy Joy Stanley. "The other day when I walked in the door, she looked at me and said, 'Papaw, if you ever die, I want to lie right down with you.' Stuff like that, makes you feel good and bad, don't it?" Then he smiled his tight little smile.

"**N**ow it's beginning to look a bit more like Kentucky," Emmylou Harris was saying. We were half an hour north of Nashville and outside the car window everything was green and golden brown. Horses looked up at us from rolling pastures bordered by huckleberry and gum trees, thickets of blackberry brier flanked the dirt road, and split-rail fences held off the brier. Not so high up in the early evening sky was a pale moon that, if you used a little imagination, could seem blue. Tonight, everyone was looking at it in just that way, particularly people like Harris, who was on her way to pay respects to the man who wrote "Blue Moon of Kentucky," Bill Monroe. "Mr. Monroe" is an irascible retired gentleman farmer and he always stands on ceremony, particularly when a ceremonial occasion is involved. So it was that a few days earlier Harris had received this missive from him:

> *Come Help Me Celebrate My 83rd Birthday*
> *In a Powerful Pickin' and Picnickin' Way*
> *6:00 P.M. 'Til the Cows Come Home*
> *Monroe Farm, Goodlettsville, Tennessee*
> *Bring Your Instrument and Covered Dish*

Once, when I asked Monroe about his music, he had said, "It's for everybody," and now, as we approached the picnic tables crowded with food set up outside the unfinished wood cabin where Monroe has lived for forty years, I could see that some of everybody had come to share the evening with him. There were record producers, colonels down from Monroe's home state of Kentucky, farmers, fiddlers, mechanics, neighbors, neighbors' children, men named Hoss, and Porter Wagoner too, and they'd all cooked Monroe their country best. The security guard at the Ryman Auditorium, where Monroe performed for so many years on *The Grand Ole Opry,* had made ham and sweet-potato biscuits. Emmylou Harris brought a moist lemon poppyseed cake baked and lightly sugar-iced by her mother, Genie. There was some tender Tennessee barbecue, a tangy field pea salad, and somebody's prize butter dill pickles. One hapless soul, it's true, had shambled in with a covered dish filled with Kentucky Fried Chicken, but even that was fortunate; everyone else seemed to have brought beans. There were more beans than I have ever seen in one place—lima beans, navy beans, pinto beans, red kidney beans, green beans, and beans of uncertain pedigree hidden away in pies. Monroe, as he would put it, is powerful fond of beans.

At the moment, Monroe was not eating beans. He was receiving. Bob Dylan once described Bill and Charlie Monroe's music by saying, "That's what America's all about for me," and Monroe had certainly dressed the part. He sat in a rocking chair under an elm tree, wearing cufflinks, a white Stetson hat, his rhinestone Jesus and metal American-flag pins on his jacket lapel, both an American-flag tie and a necklace made of seashells around his neck, and a dark red birthday rose pinned to his breast. The Father of Bluegrass Music seemed pleased to see everyone, but it's true that he flushed with a special kind of pleasure when Emmylou

Harris stepped up to the rocking chair to pay her respects. With her aureole of silvery white hair and soft brown eyes, Harris could pass for Linda Lou, the gloriously pretty young woman Monroe wrote about in "I'm Going Back to Old Kentucky." "Happy Birthday, Mr. Monroe," Harris said to him, and Monroe looked up at her and informed "Miss Immy," in his high croon of a speaking voice, that he was sure glad she was here and hoped she would sing for him later. She said she would be happy to.

Everyone, of course, wanted to say hello, but sometimes the throng around Monroe dissipated. When that happened, he leaned over to the rocking chair next to his—only two of them were on the lawn—and whispered a few words to the elderly man sitting quietly beside him. This was Earl Scruggs, Monroe's old banjo player, old friend, old enemy, and old friend again. And what were they talking about? It turned out that this was Scruggs's first visit to Monroe Farm. "I was admiring it—real rustic," Scruggs said later. "People still think we're enemies. It's not true by any stretch." The sight of the two of them sitting there like that, however, created much discussion among party guests. They looked so congenial. Was Monroe mellowing? Most people were in agreement. They thought it was too early for Monroe to be mellowing. After all, he was only eighty-three.

Before it got dark, I had a look around. Now that it was mid-September, a lot of the buttercups and cornstalks were turning brown and the hens were plumper than in June. Just down the road was a little Baptist church. As for the air, though it was still too early to light the hearth, if autumn was here, a chill could not be far behind.

Monroe settled outside Nashville to be close to the *Opry,* but as Emmylou Harris had suggested, he chose a part of Tennessee where just about everything but the color of the sod looks like home. The land around Monroe Farm really does resemble the fields off the Bluegrass Turnpike in the Kentucky farming country thirty miles north of Bowling Green where Monroe grew up pushing a handheld plow behind a team of mules.

James and Melissa Monroe's light gray farmhouse, where their eighth and youngest child spent his youth, is still standing outside the Ohio County town of Rosine, Kentucky. On the way to Rosine, you can pass through Hartford, which greets visitors with a sign that says "Welcome to Hartford Kentucky Home of 2,000 Happy People & a Few Soreheads." Rosine's sign is similarly goodnatured—"Hi There. Welcome to Rosine—Home of Bluegrass Music," it says—and the town is as offhand as

Hartford about its population. The best anybody seemed to know was that somewhere between 100 and 200 farmers and coal miners live in Rosine.

To get to the house where Bill Monroe grew up, you have to pass a few cornfields and a former cornfield that is now a strip mine, cross a railroad track, drive up along a winding road about a mile beyond the sign that says "Coon Hunt," to a cable strung across the entrance to a trail cutting through the woods. The trail was filled with deep puddles the day I visited and frogs were leaping out of them in front of me as I walked. A couple of startled deer also bounded across the path, and a few rabbits. When I finally got to the house, it looked like it hadn't seen anybody in a while, either.

The glass in all the windows was gone and trees were bending in through the gaps. Plaster hung from the ceilings like old lace, a bees' nest filled a portion of one room, and the floor in another was covered with soft dirt. A skim of moss added a greenish patina to the roof. I knew that a Kentucky coal miner dying of black-lung disease had made a pilgrimage to the house and stripped it of one of its doors, which he turned into a mandolin. Yet the house did not have the aura of sorry dilapidation that comes over a property sullied by vandals. Instead, there was the sense that it was gradually being reclaimed by the forest. Bill Monroe, a notoriously taciturn man who sings notoriously wistful music, grew up in one of the loneliest places I have ever seen.

His Goodlettsville cabin differs from the house in Rosine. For one thing, in Kentucky there was never a mandolin-shaped clock or row of Stetson hats on the wall. For another, the Rosine house does not have a path of fifty stones cutting through the yard. At first glance, these are pretty banal as stepping stones go, but I had heard something about them that livened them up a bit. When Jason DeParle, a *New York Times* reporter, came to Goodlettsville, Monroe told him that each stone was from a different state in the Union. DeParle looked down and said, "Really?" Whereupon Monroe barked, "Why would I lie? I ain't a Yankee." (This, by the way, was quite a conversation. When DeParle asked about songwriting, Monroe fixed him a look and demanded to know how much DeParle had paid for his shoes.)

The pickin' portion of the picnic was set to begin and Monroe moved onto his front porch. He grew up learning to play music on porches with his fiddle-playing great-uncle Pendleton Vandiver—"Uncle Pen" in Monroe's song—and he was going to celebrate his eighty-third birthday in entirely familiar circumstances. Monroe likes to perform even better than he likes beans or women as fetching as Emmylou Harris. It is fair to say that he is obsessed with it to the point of recklessness. Three years earlier, Monroe had played his annual Indiana Bluegrass festival—it's in the town of Bean Blossom, naturally—in 100-degree heat three weeks after he was hospitalized for emergency triple-bypass surgery. At Bean Blossom, he played two full two-hour shows in a three-piece white wool suit with a paramedic posted just offstage. The paramedic never had to budge.

Tonight, lingering in the shadows of the porch, there were only friends. Earl Scruggs had gone home to bed and so too had the sun, leaving the front yard dark as pitch, but many other prominent pickers and grinners remained in the gloaming to tell the dozens of regular guests leaning against fences and seated on lawn chairs a little bit about Bill Monroe. The musicians all had nice things to say and different Bill Monroe songs to sing—no trick, given that Monroe has written more than five hundred of them. The banjo player, John Hartford, said that Monroe's music "carries a person forward." Ernest Tubb's son Justin remembered the moving way Monroe had sung at his father's funeral ten years earlier. Emmylou Harris described Monroe's triple-bypass Bean Blossom, commenting that "Mr. Monroe outplayed and outdressed all of us." Then, as promised, she sang "Kentucky Waltz" with him and they even danced a little. Monroe played "Uncle Pen" with astonishing speed, yodeled high during "Muleskinner Blues," and when Carl Smith wanted to sing a Bob Wills song, "Deep Water," Monroe picked that through without hesitation or complaint. "Bill Monroe can play anything!" a hefty man near me exulted.

Jesse McReynolds—the Jesse portion of the fraternal bluegrass tandem—got up. "Well, I'll try one," he said.

"Jesse, I appreciate your coming up," said Monroe.

"Glad to be here," returned McReynolds. "Sorry Jim couldn't be here. He's recovering from a tractor ride."

They sang "Rabbit in the Log," which is a meditation, of sorts, on how to capture a wild hare when you have no rabbit dog. Then Monroe went right into "Roll in My Sweet Baby's Arms," which deals with gentler matters. Monroe sang high with Peter Rowan and he picked fast with Sam Bush. He tore through the instrumental crowd-pleaser "Raw Hide," and didn't slow down much for "I'm Going Back to Old Kentucky." Also he talked, but briefly, of course. "I really appreciate everybody's friendship," he said at his most voluble moment. "I want y'all to pull for me. In fifty-three years on *The Grand Ole Opry* I was late only three times. I want y'all to pull for me and I'll keep pulling for you." Then he struck up "Bluegrass Breakdown," and an old woman sprang to her feet and danced a brief, impromptu jig.

As the evening wore on, it was clear that Monroe really would be playing until the cows came home. This performance was very much in character; Monroe's stamina is nearly as legendary as his music. "Bluegrass is competition," he once said, and for him, so too was everything else. Monroe's approach to life has been to clutter his path with obstacles and then tear through them, a vague sneer hanging at his lips. "He grew up in a mean period, the Depression," Monroe's fellow singing Kentuckian Don Everly of The Everly Brothers says. "Bill, he had to be tough. Right or wrong, you got to have some kind of leader. I had a hostile period too when I was younger. You were raised that way. You go somewhere and people treat you like a hillbilly if you're from Kentucky. But in Kentucky we're pretty tough." As a boy Monroe was taunted by older brothers who could be, by their own admission, "mean as snakes." His mother died when he was ten, and when his father was buried six years after that, Monroe moved in with his bachelor uncle Pen in a little two-room house up on Jerusalem Ridge in Rosine. Then he went north and joined his brothers in Whiting, Indiana, where he spent the next five years working for Sinclair Oil, fielding empty oil drums tossed to him from railroad boxcars and beating the dented ones back into shape. The drums were very heavy and Monroe taught himself to catch them as deftly as a shortstop taking a relay. After that, he reveled in displays of strength that went beyond his handshake duels. Who else even thinks of balancing a wooden plank across his shoulders with his entire band seated on it, much less goes ahead and does it?

After singing for four years with his brother Charlie, Monroe formed The Blue Grass Boys in 1939. If you worked for Monroe, you worked hard, and sometimes for trim wages. The eastern Kentucky fiddler Kenny Baker quit The Bluegrass Boys for short spells in 1958 and again in 1963, because he had a family to raise and could make more money working as a coal miner. When they left Monroe and went out on their own, Lester Flatt and Earl Scruggs's financial circumstances improved markedly. Monroe seemed to feel that his sidemen were rubes who should feel lucky to be working for him. His attitude was, as he put it, "They'd a probably had to plowed a lot of furrows if they hadn't a been in bluegrass music." He kept his band moving at a febrile pace on stage and off. The "Blue Grass Special," the band's car, covered as many as 150,000 miles a year, with the musicians sleeping on a mattress one night in seven. On those odd nights, sometimes they slept head to toe, three in a bed. Still, no band played as fast as Monroe's. If a bone-tired sideman slowed the music down, Monroe moved across the stage with furious strides to give him a shove. When Monroe hired a banjo player named Bill Keith, he became known as Brad, because Monroe could abide only one Bill in his band. Monroe did, however, name his favorite mule Bill.

Offstage, Monroe was another kind of terror, for he collected feuds as some men do coins. Before concerts he led his band in baseball games against local nines, and he played for blood. There is a famous photograph of The Blue Grass Boys in their baseball flannels. Four band members are gathered on the left, all smiles, and Monroe stands slightly apart from them, his hands on his hips, scowling. Because sometimes baseball is a sedate game, Monroe occasionally warmed up for a show in a new town by taking on—and generally thrashing—anybody who would box with him. This would have been bare-knuckle fighting. In pugilism, as in music and most everything else, Monroe cast himself as a stoic adherent to the old ways. Only late in his life did he consent to owning a telephone. His afternoons at home were spent raising horses, breeding fighting cocks, and walking in his garden behind Bill, who was rigged to a wooden plow. Monroe said that he liked cockfights because it pleased him to see what an animal would do to try and survive and become the best.

Fulfilling the dynamic of the sacred and profane, which holds that the pleasure of Saturday night makes for the passion of Sunday morning, Monroe was soothed in the usual way. After a performance filled with classic songs like "What Would You Give in Exchange for Your Soul" and "Wicked Path of Sin," Monroe became a rover, pursuing women with enthusiasm. Stories of Monroe the rake abound in Nashville, like the band audition he arranged in his hotel room for a young woman who fled after Monroe made a play of a decidedly nonmusical sort. Band members have said that in the old days with Monroe, as the Blue Grass Special—sometimes referred to as the Whorehouse Special—left a town, they would peer out the rear window to make sure no shotgun-wielding husbands were pursuing them.

Both of Monroe's marriages ended in divorce. Not long after the second one concluded in 1985, he came home to find his beloved Gibson mandolin smashed into almost two hundred pieces. It took a patient man at Gibson three months to put it back together with tweezers. Years earlier, Monroe had taken a knife to that same mandolin and scratched out

The Blue Grass Boys traveled the country in the Blue Grass Special.
As they drove through the night, Monroe taught his music to generations
of sleep-deprived fiddlers and guitar players.

When they arrived in a new town,
they all often suited up for a little baseball before taking the stage.
Monroe was pretty demanding on the diamond too.
"He liked to killed me playin' ball," a sideman once said.

the name Gibson after a business disagreement. The company did not charge him for restoring the mandolin.

The ferocious drive that made Monroe a sometimes truculent person also inspired music of sensitive beauty. "It's played from my heart to your heart and it will touch you," he said once. As I watched him now, working his Gibson, I was thinking how much this Kentucky farmboy who never made it out of grammar school had done with himself. His songs might be filled with nostalgic memories of Mother, the old home, and the weathered brown barn, but the bluegrass sound was extremely progressive, influenced not just by the fiddle shuffle perfected by early country bands like The Skillet Lickers, but also by the jazz musicians he listened to on records, by gospel hymns, and particularly by Arnold Schultz, the black freight hauler and blues guitar player whom Monroe met at a dance near Rosine. It was through Schultz that Monroe, the product of an insular backwoods Kentucky community, was first musically exposed to the external world and to many of the exotic licks that make his music something beyond down-home entertainment. "Rocky Road Blues," a jumping blues with a walking bass line, is rollicking performance music. "People can tell my music is from Kentucky," Monroe had told me when I asked him about it. "People know I'm from the state of Kentucky and, you see, there's feeling for Kentucky in it, the Methodists and Baptists, the old blues, the old fiddle and guitar. That's how the music has been going on there for a long time." The truth is that Monroe took music that had been going on for a long time and transformed it. The syncopated licks he learned from Schultz helped him to make old-time string-band music into something livelier and more complex, shaping his notes into sophisticated rhythm structures that experts will be hashing over for generations.

Just about every prominent musician who ever played with Monroe says that the experience changed his life. "From the day I met him, I was always just about trembling around him," says Jim Rooney, a Nashville producer who played with and wrote about Monroe. "You knew you were around somebody unique and special. I felt that way around Duke Ellington and Muddy Waters too. Everybody felt that way around Bill Monroe." Monroe was a bear to work for, but he was also something close to a savant, a man whose head was full of music nobody else could hear. He willed it into generations of sleep-deprived fiddlers and banjo players, rehearsing them in the backseat and in the hotel room night after night until the fellows had it tight as a jar. And though these *were* poor country boys—Kenny Baker was a miner, Lester Flatt and Earl Scruggs had been mill hands—they were also gifted musicians. They had to be to handle the demands of what Monroe was fond of referring to as his "hillbilly version of jazz." The fiddler Vassar Clements traveled from Florida to audition for Monroe with less than a dollar in his pocket. Monroe looked him over and knew just what to do with Clements's brisk bow. When he placed it amid his own muscular mandolin and Curtis McPeake's rippling banjo in numbers like "I'm Going Back to Old Kentucky," the effect was a delicate interlacing of sound. The Blue Grass Boys always played much faster than anyone else, and they spiced a slap-that-bass swinging rhythm with whimsical bursts of harmonic expression that took the music far beyond country string-band terrain. Monroe's bands never just churned through a melody. He experimented with keys—B flat and B natural, among others—and syncopation. Rather than simply featuring one instrument as his lead and deploying the rest as rhythmic support, Monroe wrote music that assigned each string a place in a musical conversation. When the banjo said something hot-tempered, the fiddle responded cheekily and then the mandolin rolled his eyes and tweaked them both. The surprised bursts of applause you hear on old live recordings come because nobody had ever heard country musicians play with such speed and precision, or with such personality. Monroe hired excellent musicians and he let them show what they had; he left room for Earl Scruggs to approach a banjo break differently from the way Rudy Lyle might try it. Monroe made a band speak, and in as many voices as there were instruments. Couple that with high vocal harmonies that sometimes had Monroe singing above another tenor and you know why he's been packing them in since 1936. "Bill used the old music, but he invented bluegrass with it," says the Kentucky singer Jean Ritchie. "In that day it was Punk, it was Hip-Hop. He took the old music and he made it new."

And that wasn't all. He danced. Monroe could shimmy with a mixture of vigor and élan. As a musician, not only did Monroe master the mandolin, he made it into a lead instrument, insisting that the usual lead—the fiddle—follow him, and daring it across sixty years to keep up. The mandolin was his riding crop, and he used it to goad his band into a perfectly ordered frenzy. As a singer, no tenor went higher than Monroe, and though you might prefer to listen to Ralph Stanley's voice, you'd never say it was better—only different.

For all of it, on this night as I watched Monroe and his guests sweep through song after song, the thing that struck me most was what a gifted writer he is. For Monroe, the air was full of songs. His good material alone would get the porch players through the whole night, with plenty more left over if they cared to stay past breakfast. Love songs, tragedies, gospels, and the breakdown instrumental classics—so much that Monroe wrote stuck in the ear and tugged at your chest. He shouldered his way through life with a gruff swagger, and yet many of his songs are delicate and tender, the work of a man who admits only in song that he has spent his life mourning the parents who died when he was young.

Everyone has his favorite Bill Monroe tune. If you like instrumental bluegrass, it doesn't get much better than the banjo and mandolin spree "Bluegrass Breakdown" or the fiddle showcase "Roanoke." When he writes lyrics to go with this joyful, torrid music, Monroe is stripped down, straightforward, and usually melancholy. "Uncle Pen" is an economical portrait of Monroe's fiddling uncle, whose bow was always "ready to go" until, after a life of making people happy, "it was time for him to go." In "On and On," Monroe describes the pallor of life when there are only "Memories of how we once loved each other/And now you are saying goodbye." With "Blue Moon of Kentucky," his biggest hit, Monroe expressed forlorn love by fastening on one of those memorable imagined natural images that are found only in great songwriting. But it is in the autobiographical "I'm on My Way to the Old Home" where you can actually see the personal turbulence taking musical form. Monroe had arranged with his brothers to meet in Rosine for a visit. When he got there, he discovered that they had already left. He channeled his rage and disappointment into a song in which he describes coming upon the old gray house tucked deep in the woods. He hopes to see a light in the window, only to find that the house is empty and dark. He thinks back upon the quiet nights in the hills with his father, listening to the foxhounds, and of how alone in the world he was after his parents died. Since then, no matter who was inside, the house has always been dark for him. Monroe's lead vocals are supported by banjos and fiddles. It all adds up to pathos. "His music brings back my younger days," Frances Johnson Harvey of Rosine told me. "Sometimes I wish I could go back in those days. But, you know, there's a good sad and a bad sad. Bill Monroe's music is good sad."

On the way back to Nashville from the birthday party, Emmylou Harris was talking about Monroe with stories that came at an up-tempo pace. "When he had hip-replacement surgery, I called him in the hospital and asked him how long he would be in there," she said. " 'Oh, 'bout two or three days,' he said." Then she was describing Monroe at a formal White

House dinner honoring Roy Acuff. "He's really an elegant man—he dresses beautifully," she said. "He was wearing a tuxedo and his white hat. He's in the receiving line and then suddenly he leaves the line. They had a band at the dinner and Bill goes over to talk to the musicians. He comes back and sighs. 'Well,' he says. 'They don't know "Blue Moon of Kentucky." ' He loves his music and he's consumed by it." She stopped talking, and all you could hear were the crickets. Then she shook her head and said, "I never saw so many beans." Back on the porch, Monroe was still playing.

Bill Monroe died on September 9, 1996, in Springfield, Tennessee, four days before his eighty-fifth birthday.

Carolina banjo picker. "Most good banjos were sold in North and South Carolina," says Earl Scruggs. "I don't know why that is. Some parts of the country you go to, the woods are full of good fiddle players."

EARL SCRUGGS

THREE FAST FINGERS

Everybody was saying, "What is happening? What is that chord?
How can he play so fast? What is happening in this music?"
It created an unbelievable sensation. . . .

—The French Jazz critic Hugues Panassié, describing the scene
at the Rue Chaptal in 1948, when the first Charlie Parker
saxophone records reached Paris

The roads that lead into Boiling Spring, North Carolina, are lined with mossy gray Confederate memorials, Baptist church spires, and less sober institutions where strapping farmers compete in "Tuff Man" contests. There is always a tractor traveling along Highway 18 to slow up traffic, and a ramshackle building just around the curve selling pit-smoked pork barbecue tasty enough to stop it cold. Here in Cleveland County on the western fringe of the Piedmont, larger towns like Shelby are shady and peaceful and smaller ones can be even calmer. When I pulled in to a filling station to ask how much farther it was to Boiling Spring, a smiling man told me, "You're in the middle of it." It's a quiet place in a quiet part of the state, which makes it not terribly different from the way it was sixty years ago when a quiet local farmboy named Earl Scruggs spent his evenings teaching himself to play a banjo better than anybody ever had.

Scruggs lived his childhood in Flint Hill, a small community of wooden frame houses lying three miles south of the one stoplight in Boiling Spring. "It's really grown," Gretel Anthony, who has lived in Flint Hill for fifty-three years, told me. We were seated in her kitchen, which is two kitchens away from the one in the house where Scruggs lived from the time he was about seven. "His house and the one between it was the only ones," she said. "Well, there were three really. Now, well, there's about nine."

Flint Hill is folded into an angular ripple of hills and meadows dappled with cornflowers, and it's well tucked away on most other levels as well. The houses are scattered, the woods are silent, and unless you have lots of time and terribly strong legs—or access to a vehicle—your horizon is two or three houses down the road. Though I'd been in Nashville in the morning, as soon as I got out to Flint Hill I had a sense of being very far from other people, a kind of bucolic seclusion, so even the sight of a license plate from one state west immediately seemed exotic.

Almost every one of the nine houses in Flint Hill still has a garden full of squash, okra, butter beans, and cucumbers. Scruggs's father, George Elam Scruggs, was a cotton farmer. These days, the closest most people in the region get to bolls is down at the mill where they turn them into socks or blue jeans. The weather here is, of course, the same as it ever was. "Gets a little foggy at times," Gretel Anthony said. "Between early spring and summer, that's the worst of it. I've had it so bad I've had to stop driving and pull over." When Earl Scruggs named his famous band The Foggy Mountain Boys, it was as much a tip of his hat to the old home as it was to A.P. Carter's song "Foggy Mountain Top."

Across the road from Earl Scruggs's former house is a forest of Carolina pines. Behind it is, Gretel Anthony says, "a big old tiny pear tree." Inside is twelve-year-old Tywaina Kennedy. Tywaina's mother and stepfather are textile-mill workers, just as Earl Scruggs was until it occurred to him that he could make a living doing something that pleased him more. Tywaina is thinking along the same lines. "I want to get me a real job," she said. "I couldn't work in a mill all my life." Tywaina hopes to become "a lawyer or a model." She asked me if there really were tall buildings in New York City. Later, I mailed her a packet with postcards of the Manhattan skyline and a tape of Earl Scruggs's music enclosed—he isn't played on the radio stations she hears—but the post office sent it back, making me wonder if perhaps they hadn't been able to find the house. Flint Hill is pretty isolated.

Earl Scruggs taught himself to play a banjo in part because he wanted the company. "I didn't have access to radio or cars," he said. "Maybe you could see another house or two. I played whenever I got a chance. In the wintertime I'd build fires in the cookstove for my mother to cook breakfast. I took that job so I could play while the stove heated up and Mother cooked."

The banjo came easily to him, especially after he experienced one of those rare, charged moments when a great musician discovers something for himself that will forever change the way other people think about an instrument. Many string musicians are precocious in acquiring their skills, but even by that standard Earl Scruggs was a quick study. He was ten, he thinks, when one day he and his brother Horace quarreled. Their mother sent them to opposite ends of the house. "I was sitting playing a tune called 'Reuben,' " said Scruggs. "Ever sit around daydreaming? Nobody knows the thoughts you are having. That's what I was doing. During that time I was suddenly playing that tune the way I do now. It sounds like a made-up story, but it's not. It actually happened that way. I was sitting in the living-room part of the house by myself. It turned me loose to play many different tunes because you can play a song like the words go. People can tell what I'm playing because it sounds like the words are said. You can pick out the syllables of the words."

What Scruggs had done was to begin playing a five-string banjo with three fingers. His thumb, middle, and index fingers were all picking, creating two strands of harmony to buttress the melody. In a sense, he could function as a trio all by himself. Because he alternated three fingers, Scruggs could play one note after another in rapid succession, giving the impression that he was playing his banjo at terrific speed. Later, when he joined Bill Monroe's band, Scruggs was introduced as "the boy who can make a banjo talk."

He needed a companion. "I grew up in Depression days with nothing much for enjoyment and that helped me enjoy music more," he said. "I didn't have television or other distractions. Playing was something that made me feel good. Like my daddy. He had an old banjo, probably wasn't worth three dollars. He could play for himself. It makes me feel better so I'd think it made him feel better." Scruggs said that he came to depend upon the music, that it made him feel he had something to cheer him constantly even though he liked living in a place that he thinks first to describe by saying, "There were a lot of trees." Scruggs's father died when he was four. "I remember him, but not very well," Scruggs said. "I remember when he was sick. It really used to bother me growing up an awful lot."

◆ ◆ ◆

The banjo became a staple on the American blackface minstrel-show circuit beginning early in the 1800s. For a brief time at the end of the century, it also enjoyed a vogue among well-to-do urban northeasterners, who played it in plush New York parlors and oak-paneled Philadelphia club rooms. Jazz bands like the New Orleans Rhythm Kings included a banjo, but it was strictly relegated to providing cadence. For rural working-class, twentieth-century Southern white Americans, the banjo served the function that it probably did for the Africans who invented its gourd prototype: it was used for entertainment and ceremony. In all cases there was a recreational, casual attitude toward the banjo, a feeling that serious musicians could find something more versatile and challenging.

Up through the early 1940s, most country banjo players picked out songs by striking the strings of the instrument with a fingernail in a strum, note, strum, note rhythmic pattern. This downward motion was variously referred to as rapping, frailing, stroke, drop-thumb, and, as Ralph Stanley's mother played it, claw-hammer. Though you could certainly strum a tune on the ol' banjo, through World War II professional country musicians regarded the instrument primarily as a vaudeville prop. Famous banjo players like Dewitt "Snuffy" Jenkins, Marshall "Grandpa" Jones, David "Stringbean" Akeman, and especially "Uncle" Dave Macon earned their wages by cracking wise. They might be skilled banjo pickers and bright men, but they were also comedians, and their instrument was, like Grandpa Jones's suspenders and knee boots, just another part of a hillbilly clown's wardrobe. It's not hard to see why. The clear, boinging tone you got when you plucked down on a chord punctuated a performer's slapstick hayseed stand-up, much as a drummer's rimshot might for a Borscht Belt comic or a sheet whistle does for a circus clown.

Earl Scruggs never could tell jokes. He is a sober man, diffident when he is fresh to a situation and sweet-natured when he gets comfortable. Though his conversation is engaging, it is never witty. From the first he was much too serious about his music to pass as a clown and he knew it. "I didn't know whether I'd be able to make it or not," he said. "I wasn't comedy oriented. Just didn't know whether I'd be accepted working for somebody when the only talent I had was playing the banjo."

Early in the 1940s, when he was a teenager, Scruggs played his banjo in local groups, like The Morris Brothers band across the South Carolina border in Spartanburg. In his late teens he worked as a spare hand in a

Shelby mill that made strong thread for sewing parachute cloth. "One reason I didn't leave the mill—it was only paying forty cents an hour—was I didn't want to leave home," he said. "The other was I didn't feel right leaving a job making thread for the Army during the war. They needed more help. A lot of guys were away fighting. After the war, that's when I left the mill."

By the time Scruggs turned twenty-one in 1945, his musical tastes were already well-defined. Back when he was fourteen or so, he'd been trying out some up-tempo boogie-woogie numbers on his banjo and his mother overheard him. "She said to me, 'Earl, if you're gonna play something, play something that has a tune to it,' " he says. "That stuck in my mind. She'd heard me play from the time I was five. I thought, my goodness! If she can't tell what I'm playing nobody else can. That got me interested in trying to play the tune. I'd hate to waste it, have nobody know what I'm playing. I have played with people like King Curtis, the great jazz saxophone man, and I do like to play around a tune—it's fun. But I don't like to play around a tune as much. I have to make it recognizable. So I've always tried to keep what would be the vocal a little louder than the rest."

Scruggs talks in a quiet, self-effacing way. He said now that he learned church songs from his neighbors in Flint Hill and through them he also picked up what he calls "the old songs": "Sally Goodin," "Cripple Creek," "Cumberland Gap," "John Henry," and the like. Many of them were Scotch, Irish, or English tunes that were now more popular in the southeastern American mountain country than they were in Britain. The Scruggs family acquired a Victrola when Scruggs was very young, and then a radio several years later. Scruggs listened carefully to the records made by The Carter Family. "Simple" is Scruggs's word for Mother Maybelle's guitar playing, and he says that with admiration. After a while, he could play a melody on a banjo as clearly as she did it on her Gibson. The difference was that for all his love of melody, he simply couldn't contain his supernal fingers.

Late in 1945, Scruggs was working for a bandleader named Lost John Miller. Miller was based in Knoxville, but he traveled to Nashville every Friday night to do a Saturday-morning radio show. When in Nashville, the band stayed at the Tulane Hotel, and in the hotel coffee shop one Saturday, Scruggs met Jim Shumate, a North Carolina fiddle player who played with Bill Monroe's Blue Grass Boys. The Blue Grass Boys were in town for their weekly performance on *The Grand Ole Opry*. Shumate told Scruggs he thought he would make a fine addition to Monroe's band.

Scruggs was happy in East Tennessee, but Shumate was persuasive; this would be a wonderful opportunity, he said, and offered to set up a time when Monroe might stop by Scruggs's room and listen to him play. Scruggs allowed himself to be cajoled into showing Monroe what he had.

Shumate knew that Bill Monroe could use a new lead musician. Until then Monroe was running what amounted to a traveling carny show, a revue of sorts, which over the years had blended string music with a succession of novelty acts. When he breezed into town, besides a bass, guitar, and fiddle, under the tent with him he might have an accordion player, a jug blower, a harmonica player, an electric-guitar player, or a banjo player. Many of these men were comedians. Monroe had no problem with that. He was a showman with profit on his mind and he was always eager to bring variety to his entertainment. It was leading a fast band that won him both professional satisfaction and cachet, however, and Monroe was therefore always eager to find musicians who could keep pace with his boiling mandolin. (Monroe went so fast that the guitar player, Lester Flatt, took to clamping his middle fingers on the first and sixth strings of his guitar to begin his famous time-setting scissors "G run," a syncopated riff that quietly accelerated until Flatt was on the third string in the key of G and cruising when he opened up and rejoined the others at full volume.) Monroe was skeptical about the idea of Scruggs, but not at all opposed to seeing if a man could play alongside him on a banjo. He agreed to meet Scruggs in his room at the Tulane.

On the appointed day, Monroe knocked on Scruggs's door at the hotel, came in, and sat down. Scruggs began to play. "When Bill came to my room to listen to me I played two tunes, something familiar, 'Sally Goodin,' and something fast, 'Dear Old Dixie,' " said Scruggs. "He seemed very interested, but he seemed confused." Monroe didn't say much before he left other than to tell Scruggs that he should come over to the *Opry* later and play a little with The Blue Grass Boys. Scruggs did that, and in just a few minutes he turned backstage at the *Opry* into the Rue Chaptal.

Monroe had mentioned Scruggs to Lester Flatt, and Flatt told Monroe that as far as he was concerned the kid could "leave the damn banjo in the case." A sharecropper's son and a former silk-mill hand from the central Tennessee town of Sparta, Flatt had been singing lead and playing guitar with Monroe for nearly a year. When "Stringbean" Akeman had been a Blue Grass Boy, he had vexed the other members of the band because they wanted to play fast and he couldn't keep up with them on his banjo. Flatt knew all about banjos. They were sand in the gears and he didn't want them in any band that he was in. "Lester's whole way of thinking changed after we struck up a tune," says Scruggs.

"I was just dumbfounded," Flatt told a friend many years later. "I had never heard anybody pick a banjo like he did. He could go all over the neck and do things you couldn't hardly believe." Flatt had just seen a soft-eyed, bashful twenty-one-year-old kid transform the banjo into a different kind of instrument. Instead of the pluck, strum, pluck of the claw-hammer, here was real melody. Scruggs played at a terpsichorean pace but with impeccable smoothness as he lent rich layers of texture to the songs. It was a little bit like watching a Model T take flight right in front of you. Monroe asked Flatt what he thought. Flatt said, "If you can hire him, get him, whatever it costs."

Another person sitting in on the *Opry* audition was a chubby old man who had stenciled "World's Greatest Banjoist" on the side of his instrument case. "Uncle" Dave Macon, "The Dixie Dewdrop," wore expensive suits, had fillets of gold in his teeth, a goatee, a thick watch chain, an infectious cackle, and a repertoire of songs with titles like "Keep My Skillet Good and Greasy," "Chewing Gum," and "Rabbit in the Pea Patch." He liked to announce that "Uncle Dave handles a banjo like a monkey handles a peanut," but that wasn't so. Uncle Dave was a beloved singer and a master sight-gag comedian. On a banjo, however, he was no more than a capable professional entertainer. Which he knew. "Shucks," Macon said when Scruggs finished the two songs. "He maybe can play in a band but I bet he can't sing a lick."

"He also said I wasn't a bit funny," says Scruggs. "He said that. I liked him. He was a proud old man. In essence he was saying that all I could do was pick. He had a lot going for him. He was funny and he could sing. I did sing, but I wasn't a featured singer. I wasn't trying to do what he was doing."

Scruggs wasn't sure he wanted to be a Blue Grass Boy. "I'd got enough of show business with the band I was with and I wanted to go back home," he said. "By nature I was a homeboy. I missed Carolina, missed my mother. I was tired of living in hotels. But at the time I didn't have a job back in the mill at Shelby, so I thought I'd try it for a few months and see. I was at the age when I enjoyed trying new things."

Soon after Scruggs joined Monroe, the tenor singer Curly Sechler paid a visit back to his home in China Grove, North Carolina. When he got there he found that "everybody was saying, 'What happened to Bill Monroe's music?' " What happened, Lester Flatt reflected later, was that with the inclusion of Scruggs, Monroe's band had moved their playing into a new realm. "When we got Earl, it was really the first time a sound like that had been heard," Flatt said. "There had been maybe a similar sound, but we then had what was to become known as bluegrass music."

Strictly speaking, Scruggs didn't invent a banjo technique so much as he refined a new style. Almost nothing in music comes straight out of the air. There had been men before him who could play banjo arpeggios with three fingers. Oddly enough, most of them came from the Carolinas. "After I left the Carolinas I learned that most good banjos were sold in North and South Carolina," says Scruggs. "I don't know why that is. Some parts of the country you go to, the woods are full of good fiddle players." Capable as men like Snuffy Jenkins, Hoke Jenkins, Johnny Whisnant, Don Reno, Wiley Birchfield, Charlie Poole, Smith Hammett, Rex Brooks, and Scruggs's own older brother, Junie, were with a five-string, the speed, agility, and personality with which Scruggs could play a banjo were beyond what anyone else was doing.

The banjo as a serious musical instrument was a source of incredulity in country music circles. People had to see and hear Scruggs for themselves. Once they did, most simply came away enthralled. "People really accepted it," Scruggs told me. "They'd come backstage and try to get me to explain what I was doing, ask me questions. Everything was fitting so well. He [Monroe] played a type of music that fit in for me."

Other banjo players immediately began to imitate Scruggs. When he was working with Monroe, The Stanley Brothers were playing a show on a radio station in Bristol, Virginia, and they sounded a lot like The Blue Grass Boys, in part because Ralph Stanley had taken up Scruggs-style banjo picking. "That was the greatest thing to happen in my career; that I could be playing well enough for somebody else to like it," says Scruggs. Monroe didn't respond as gracefully. When he ran into the Stanleys, he accused them of ripping off his sound and stopped talking to them for a while.

Lester Flatt and Earl Scruggs were together with Monroe from 1945 to 1948, and many people consider that version of The Blue Grass Boys to be the seminal bluegrass band. The classic song of the period that reveals how much verve and grace Scruggs's picking brought to Monroe is the instrumental "Bluegrass Breakdown," in which Monroe on his mandolin, the fiddler, Chubby Wise, and Scruggs take turns speeding through an instrumental number that sounds a little like a bird being pursued by a pair of quick, eager dogs. Monroe, the bird, bursts out of the brush, madly fluttering his wings. Scruggs and then Wise each take a turn making a run at him, Monroe soaring away from them each time on his mandolin. Because Monroe takes the last break, it is fair to say that Scruggs and Wise don't catch him, but that they make a nice chase of it.

That was the way it was when you worked for Monroe: he was always out in front. The exception is "Molly and Tenbrooks (The Race Horse Song)," in which Scruggs has three solo breaks and sets the galloping pace for this musical account of a match race between two champion thoroughbreds. Generally Scruggs did not dominate the breaks in a tune any more than Chubby Wise did. In other words, with Monroe, Scruggs played the role of sideman, subordinating himself to his bandleader. All things being equal, for a time that was fine with him. Scruggs was only in his early twenties and he knew that everyone in Monroe's band was an unusually talented musician. Further, Scruggs happens to have been born with a sideman's disposition. Saying that Scruggs is modest is an understatement. He is humble; it comes naturally to him.

"You just get into a way of doing something," is how he describes his approach to music. "I don't have anything else to do. I'm concentrating quite a bit when I'm playing with somebody that's singing or a fiddle player. I spend most of my time trying to think of something to make him sound better. That's what I'm doing a lot of the time."

The fine young banjo player Alison Brown tells a story about Scruggs's self-effacing qualities. "I met Earl in the summer of 1990 with five Japanese banjo players," she said. "It was a big deal for me going to the master's house. The five Japanese guys had been to the Gibson banjo factory to buy five Scruggs model banjos and now they were on their way to Scruggs's house so that he could christen their banjos, so to speak. When we got there, I sat down in a corner and watched. Here's these five Japanese guys and a couple of other players and Earl. We all had our banjos. We go around and kick off 'Fireball Mail,' one of those old Scruggs tunes. He played backup while everybody else took a solo. He didn't need to take a solo. It was such a selfless thing. He's the father figure for all banjo players. It's impossible to play bluegrass banjo without learning Earl Scruggs. People spend hours poring over the old recordings to get it right—just like Earl did it. Here, with us, he had nothing to prove. He was content to play backup in a style everybody knows he invented. He's kind of the opposite of Bill Monroe in that way."

Scruggs has received many compliments over the years for his playing, but the most resonant one is Robert Shelton's observation in his *New York Times* review of the 1959 Newport Folk Festival that Scruggs "bears about the same relationship to the banjo that Paganini does to the violin." Niccolò Paganini of Genoa was the great virtuoso of the nineteenth-century classical violin, a brilliant showman who could play a new concerto on sight, was a master of left-hand pizzicato, and specialized in pyrotechnic bowing, in which he ricocheted through a succession of notes on a single stroke. Paganini so thrilled to impress people that he would produce a scissors and cut every string on his violin but one and then proceed through a piece working on that string while his audience gasped and applauded. Many people swore he was possessed, that "he had dedicated himself to the Evil One," as Franz Liszt excitedly said. When I asked Scruggs about Shelton's praise he said, "Everybody likes a pat on the back, I guess," and looked like he wanted to crawl under his easy chair.

Not only did The Blue Grass Boys travel a relentless schedule of one-night stands across the South, they sped through the night in a converted limousine, taking turns driving and trying to sleep sitting up while the car passed over crooked, two-lane country roads. When they arrived in a town, they threw a baseball around to feel human again. "Monroe carried two or three baseball gloves and a ball with us," said Scruggs. "We'd be in the '41 Chevrolet all night and all day and we couldn't shift our legs, so we'd go out and play catch to loosen up our legs and have something to do until showtime."

Monroe's twin obsessions on the road appear to have been musical perfection and punctuality, as his salute to life with The Blue Grass Boys, "Heavy Traffic Ahead," makes clear. "We worked everything from coal camps in Kentucky and West Virginia, to farmland from Florida across the southeast," Scruggs said. "In those days they were all acquainted with the music." Besides playing his instrument, Scruggs was the Blue Grass Boy who sold tickets at shows and kept the books for Monroe. What he saw was that, given the daily take, Monroe was paying the band scantily. Flatt's biographer, Jake Lambert, says this income disparity bothered Flatt and Scruggs. Scruggs says not. He told Monroe's biographer, Jim Rooney, "I loved Bill like a brother and he was always good to me."

Of course Scruggs spoke to Rooney well after 1948, the year he and

Scruggs with Lester Flatt and The Foggy Mountain Boys.
"I grew up with it. It's just an everyday thing to me."

Flatt gave their notice to Monroe and left him to form their own band. Flatt and Scruggs always publicly insisted that it was coincidence that they left at the same time. They claimed they had no plans to continue in music together. This account has been difficult for many people to believe—Jake Lambert says Flatt told him in confidence that it wasn't accurate—but Scruggs still adheres to it. "It's untrue," he protests whenever the more skeptical version of the events is presented to him. Scruggs is a civil man and has obvious distaste for unseemly behavior, which he would consider leaving his first employer in the lurch to be. Monroe asked him to stay on for an additional two weeks and Scruggs readily agreed. He tried to please people. Still, he wanted out.

"I had got enough of music," Scruggs said. "With his [Monroe's] methods of operation we were traveling so much I was hardly going to bed. I had intended to go back to Shelby into a mill. When my notice was filled Lester turned in his notice; he was gonna leave. Lester called me and said he'd been thinking about it and we wouldn't be happy back in the mill. He suggested we get a job at a radio station in Carolina, closer to home. We put a five-piece group together within a few weeks and we went to WCBY in Bristol, Virginia, and started making a living real quick. I've heard he [Monroe] felt we formed up to start a show, but that wasn't it.

He went several years without speaking to us. That all went away. I consider Bill as my friend now."

It was precisely twenty-one years before they had a conversation. Monroe used his influence to keep Flatt and Scruggs off the *Opry* stage for several years, and even into the 1970s, whenever he talked about what he clearly considered this betrayal, Monroe seethed. Not that he lacked for a banjo player. Ralph Stanley was only one of many banjo players who quickly embraced Scruggs-style picking. Just as many distance runners began to complete a mile in less than four minutes once Roger Bannister had done it, banjo players began to play leads at warp speed as soon as Scruggs showed them how. Don Reno and later Rudy Lyle followed Scruggs in The Blue Grass Boys, and they handled Scruggs's old breaks with aplomb. Largely because of Scruggs, the banjo was now being accepted as an indispensable lead instrument in a bluegrass band. Meanwhile, Earl Scruggs and Lester Flatt thrived on their own.

Between 1948 and 1969, the two former mill hands made bluegrass music of exceptional range and beauty. Pointedly, they referred to themselves as country musicians, eschewing Monroe's label. In 1948, Scruggs married a Tennessee woman he'd fallen in love with named Louise Certain and went back to live in a house he owned in Shelby. He didn't see it much because Flatt, Scruggs, and The Foggy Mountain Boys were mostly on the road, traversing the South. At first they played short stints as the in-studio band on radio shows in places like Danville and Bristol, Virginia, Lexington, Kentucky, Knoxville, Tampa, Roanoke, Raleigh, and, finally, in 1953, in Nashville. By 1955, they were covering 2,500 miles a week, hawking Martha White biscuit flour, and forcing the *Opry* to take them on despite Monroe.

Flatt's mellow, Saturday-afternoon stroll of a singing voice contrasted with Scruggs's prancing banjo, meaning that they could offer their listeners fast instrumentals like "Earl's Breakdown" and "Foggy Mountain Chimes," mid-tempo, crooning heart songs such as "Your Love Is Like a Flower" and "My Darling's Last Goodbye," and bittersweet, longing numbers like "Someday We'll Meet Again Sweetheart" and "Cabin in Caroline." It's bracing to hear Scruggs twinkling alongside as Flatt ambles his way through another lugubrious portrait of pain and hardship; the good songs are all about sorrow. Though a fiercely Christian morality is always implicit, Flatt and Scruggs hardly saw life as uncomplicated. They liked to make up vignettes of people grappling with disconcerting or intractable situations: a good man who loves a promiscuous drunkard; a worried man who finds himself separated from his love because he has to go to the city for work, or he has to serve time on a prison farm, or—a favorite dilemma—he has been called off to heaven. The details are always kept sketchy so that while Flatt and Scruggs are outlining the idea, the listener imagines the specifics. Flatt and Scruggs were workingmen who had working people in mind when they made their music, but these songs spoke to Americans of all kinds, from the New Yorkers who sold out their concert at Carnegie Hall to the Tennessee farmer named "Poodler" who rode a mule twenty miles to see them play.

Shortly after Scruggs left Monroe in 1948, he began composing banjo music. He wrote fairly steadily over the next few years at home, on the road, and even in a hospital bed while recovering from surgery to repair severe leg injuries he sustained in a 1955 car accident. Scruggs was hurrying back to Flint Hill to visit his sick mother when another driver pulled out from a side road and ran a stop sign directly into his path. Scruggs's femur never quite healed properly and he has since walked with a limp.

Most of the breakdowns—rapidly played instrumentals—are very distinct. "Foggy Mountain Breakdown," later to become the theme song for the film *Bonnie and Clyde,* was the first full-length banjo vehicle Scruggs wrote. With its classic whoomph every few measures, this tune embodies what the musicologist Alan Lomax meant when he defined bluegrass as "folk music in overdrive." "Foggy Mountain Breakdown" sounds the way a mountain brook looks as it plunges down the grade, skipping around rocks and then pouring right over them, rushing faster and faster, moving, moving, *moving.* "Earl's Breakdown" is cooking country jazz, with the banjo stating the melody and then trading riffs with a fiddle above a driving beat. "Earl's Breakdown" features a plunging sound as Scruggs suddenly shifts pitch. He did this by clamping specially modified tuners to his second and third strings. They worked, in effect, like gear shifts on a racing bicycle, so that Scruggs could be certain that when he wanted to change from B to A and G to F sharp, he could do so in perfect pitch every time.

Another classic instrumental piece in which Scruggs used the modified tuners is "Flint Hill Special," which was written shortly after "Earl's Breakdown," and bears some similarities, although "Flint Hill Special" is a more interesting tune. Scruggs begins with a casual introduction before he lifts things a register and takes off. He jumps a bit with Benny Martin on fiddle, slows—listeners often roar and madly applaud here—has another encounter with the fiddle, and then serves up a final portion of particularly molten banjo. This arrangement, like the others, is highly sophisticated, but there is an insouciant quality to Scruggs's delivery, a "we're jes' hillbillies messin' around with these here syncopations and harmonics" motif. Scruggs has a way of ending his fastest, most complicated instrumentals, like "Flint Hill Special," by slowing way down to plunk out the last eight or nine notes, a "weren't nothin' " dénouement that works like a sly wink.

A different kind of instrumental is Scruggs's "Nashville Blues." Not to be confused with The Delmore Brothers' mellow close-harmony song that shares the title, Scruggs's "Nashville Blues" is a wistful, melodic instrumental that is a complete departure from the breakdowns. Scruggs calms his pace and modulates his tone in creating something that has all the dolorous features of a Flatt-Scruggs lyric. "Nashville Blues" sounds like a man riding in a car along some far-flung road, looking out the window and missing home. Given all this imagery, the tune might well have been called "Flint Hill Blues," had anything specific inspired Scruggs's instrumentals. But Scruggs was not a narrative writer. Instead, he was a cubist with his banjo, using it to dismantle and examine qualities of human feeling—or "moods," as he called them. He liked to think about how sounds fit together rather than how events did. "When you write a tune like 'Foggy Mountain Breakdown' you don't have anything in mind," he said. "It just comes together and plays good. You can put anything into a tune. It's the mood you're in. When you write an instrumental there's not much to go on to give it a title. 'Flint Hill Special,' I named it because I was born in Flint Hill, North Carolina."

These tunes made Scruggs's name so synonymous with his instrument that young musicians like John Hartford sat in their homes and learned them note for note off the record. Each breakdown is a two-to-three-minute, rapid instrumental. Scruggs has weathered criticism for making the bluegrass sound generic, and if there is any truth in that, it's the fault of his skill. His technical virtuosity is such that it can distract a listener from paying attention to the sound of the music. Scruggs is sometimes playing at such a rapid pace that notes flash by like boxcars on a highballing freight; you want to look at each one and guess what's in it but you can't because the next one is already upon you. "Sometimes we'd play terribly fast," Scruggs said. "It wasn't intentional. Accidentally you got started that way. Speed was something we never did go for. That may not sound true, but I feel you can get it too fast and you lose the flavor of the gum, so to speak."

In 1969, Flatt and Scruggs disbanded The Foggy Mountain Boys. Scruggs had begun to feel stifled by playing only bluegrass tunes. "I was playing the same numbers night after night that I had been playing for years," he said in a press release from the time. "It reached the point of becoming extremely monotonous. The banjo was locked into a category and I could see no reason why it wouldn't be accepted in other forms of music. I wanted the chance to give the banjo and myself freedom to breathe."

Scruggs continued to play his classic instrumentals, but now he also sat in with other country musicians and with popular folksingers like Joan Baez and Bob Dylan and folk rockers like the Byrds. Flatt's sensibilities were more conservative. He began to feel that Scruggs was giving him the high hat, and they parted gruffly. Speaking of his old partner, who died in 1979, Scruggs told me, "We went a long way together. He was a brother to me. We talked about that; he felt the same way about me. I still have moments when I think about him and the old days in the past, but I was happy to be making a new sound with my boys."

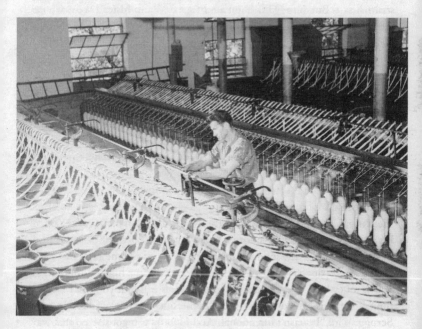

Textile factory, Greene County, Georgia. "We wouldn't be happy back in the mill," Flatt said to Scruggs.

With his sons Gary, Randy, and Steve, Scruggs founded The Earl Scruggs Revue. The Revue was a country rock band, replete with drums, electricity, and long hair, which led to stinging remarks from fans who guarded the church of bluegrass with great care and now treated Scruggs like a wayward parson. He was accused of gettin' above his raisin' and of heresy for consorting with the demon electricity. Scruggs says he was too happy to care about such carping. He allowed his hair to creep below his ears, played some guitar in addition to the banjo—he was always a fine guitar player—and had himself a lot of fun with his sons. "My feelings toward them wanting to be in music were that it was strictly left up to them," he said. "They chose it by their choice. But it really made me feel good to work with them on the road. That was a treat for me. When my boys were growing up I was on the road a lot. I'd go out just about every day. Playing with them was the highlight of my musical career."

Musicians who push themselves in a new direction are always encountering the reservations of fans who grow attached to the material that made their reputation. This happened repeatedly to Miles Davis, whose mantra was "Don't play what's there, play what's not there," and famously to Bob Dylan, who walked onto the stage at the Newport Folk Festival carrying an electric guitar, to a barrage of contumely. That's an understandable response, and yet a perverse one because it is precisely their innovative impulses that make musicians like Davis, Dylan, and Scruggs compelling to begin with. "These people who are real purists and insist on playing the music just like Earl did are missing his spirit," Alison Brown said. "It's evolving all the time." Of his days with Monroe, Scruggs told me that "we were expanding what we were raised upon." Today's expansion is tomorrow's standard.

That Earl Scruggs has found himself involved in two of country music's most famous feuds is astonishing because he is a person whose antipathy for calling attention to himself is legendary in the business. Part of this trouble is the consequence of being a talent; both Bill Monroe and Lester Flatt lost something when they no longer had Scruggs to play with them. It's also the function of a personal feature common in kind men—they so much don't wish to hurt people that when they have to disappoint someone, it feels worse coming from them. Scruggs himself feels that all the tales of his breaches with Monroe and Flatt have been distressingly exaggerated. "It's like a snowball," he protested in his living room. "We've never been on the outs with anybody. But you can't defend yourself on stuff like that. It's not true, but it's my word against theirs." By constantly distancing himself from these disagreements, Scruggs puts them on some-body else—not a bad strategy.

Scruggs told me that he isn't "playing much these days." He looks frail—he has been in poor health for years—and it did nothing for his spirits when word came on a day three years ago that his son Steve and Steve's wife had both tragically died. Scruggs has always relied on the counsel of his wife more than most other performers, but now Louise Scruggs appears to watch him with more concern than ever. But Scruggs smiled when I asked to see his famous banjo, and he went to get it. Coun-try musicians are loyal to the instrument they grew up with, refusing to exchange it for a new one, and Scruggs with his Grenada banjo is no dif-ferent from Bill Monroe with his Gibson mandolin. "I've been playing the same one since 1949," he said. "I traded banjos with Don Reno. He had it. It was an old banjo then." The banjo is probably a 1934 model, and Gib-son—who manufactures three different "Scruggs Model" banjos—has kept it sleek for him. The maple back of the instrument is a handsome burnished brown, and his name has been set into the neck. The neck and fingerboard are decorated with mother-of-pearl inlays of hearts and flow-ers. "I've had the outside repaired and cleaned up," said Scruggs. "But as far as the banjo itself, I've never let anybody do any altering. That's where the tone comes from. This banjo cost $37," Scruggs said, fingering it. "It was in a pawnshop in Greenville, South Carolina. They were asking $50. Each time Snuffy Jenkins came through town, he'd offer $25 for it. Finally they split the difference." Reno then got it from Jenkins, and Scruggs, finally, traded with Reno for it. This is a banjo that has kept some good company.

Sitting in his living room, Scruggs started playing and the mood in the room abruptly shifted. Where his conversation is often terse, once the banjo is doing the talking, Scruggs becomes expansive. He began with two fingers. Then, with a nod, he switched to three. The banjo sparkled. After a few phrases Scruggs paused. A look of mild concern furrowed his brow. "A lot of well-intentioned people interpret things you never thought you were doing," he said. "I grew up with it. It's just an everyday thing to me." He began playing, again with three fingers. The room filled with a rush of notes. "See," Scruggs said. "It's more of a flow this way."

PART FOUR

THAT OLD-TIME COUNTRY

*Baptism in the river. "I think my brother Ira was tortured by religion,"
says Charlie Louvin.*

THE LOUVIN BROTHERS

HELL'S HALF ACRE

I don't know nowhere to go, any ole place will do
I'm leaving old Sand Mountain, just getting away from here
You're gonna be sorry for breaking my heart.

—ALTON AND RABON DELMORE, "Sand Mountain Blues"

Sand Mountain is a massive twenty-mile-wide, steep-sided plateau that rises like a broad steeple beyond the northwest Georgia flatlands, makes a blunt seventy-five-mile cut across northern Alabama, and then pitches straight back down again. As I drove through its tiny communities with names like Jay Bird and Hustleville, I passed great clumps of churches. There were Baptist churches, Primitive Baptist churches, Free Will Baptist churches, Missionary Baptist churches, Assembly of God churches, Methodist churches, Churches of Christ, and the occasional Catholic church. If you knew where to look, there were also Holiness churches, where some people express their faith in Jesus by speaking in tongues, drinking strychnine, and clutching timber rattlesnakes to their breasts. "A Jesus-haunted country," Walker Percy called the South, and the profusion of places of worship made it clear that people in rural northern Alabama do take their salvation seriously. So too did a sign outside one of the churches: "Welcome Visitors—Members Expected."

When I reached the gnarled little farming town of Henagar and walked into one of its stores, I fell into a brief conversation with a woman who told me that "murder's fresh on everybody's mind, I reckon." The day before, it turned out, an elderly woman and her grown daughter had been the victims in a gruesome twin killing. Someone shot the mother once in the head and then stabbed her through the heart with a home-made spear. Her daughter was shot three times in the head and stabbed all the way through the neck with a large butcher knife. Then a spear was plunged through her heart for good measure. Because fewer than 2,000 people live in Henagar, that meant a sizable portion of the town had died.

I also heard about a woman who received a telephone call informing her that the automatic feeder in her chickenhouse was empty. When she went out to replenish it, someone who was waiting for her hidden inside the chickenhouse nearly beat her to death before she escaped.

Henagar's chief of police, Robert Trotman, said that from Henagar north to the Georgia line, Sand Mountain had something of a reputation for violence. Happy Holler, an unincorporated backwoods community outside Henagar, was, the chief said, notorious for murders, shootings, and "raisin' Cain." When I wondered how this could be in such a conspicuously religious community, he said, "It's hard to understand people. I don't know why it is. Pride could be part of it."

That and stricken poverty, which has long been a lethal combination in the rural white South. (Blacks generally stay away from northern Sand Mountain.) "Most of them around here, they're pretty good country people until they start drinking," Robert Trotman's brother, Buford, retired pastor of the Sand Mountain Holiness Church, told me. "Then the worst comes out. I guess a lot of it's poverty. I don't know. They lose their self-control. Most of them they can't do enough for you, but if you make 'em too mad they're liable to kill you."

Henagar is a crossroads Alabama community of farms and saw-mills, but farming has declined in recent years and so a lot of people are now driving down off the mountain to work for somebody else in places like Scottsboro and Chattanooga. From the number of discarded appliances stacked on front porches, junked cars rusting in fields of wild-flowers, and sagging barn roofs, you can tell that there isn't a lot of money in these parts. (The per-capita income for DeKalb County, which includes Henagar, is $12,579.) Nor has there ever been, which leads people, somewhat defensively, to bring conversations around to Kentucky. "There," you will be informed, is a place with "real" and "horrifying" poverty.

Isolated both by geography and economics, Sand Mountain has long been a place where people took ardent refuge in the sacred or expressed their frustration in violence and debauchery. Sometimes they did both. Early in the century, not far from Henagar, at a so-called Buckeye Baptist church called Hell's Half Acre, people prayed until midnight and then drank and fought until dawn.

"It ain't changed," Charlie Louvin, who grew up in Henagar during the 1930s, was saying. "It's a very, very small place. They had a post office and a cotton gin. Now they don't have a gin anymore. They've quit raising cotton." So too has Charlie. His father, Colonel Monero Allen Loudermilk, planted his five-acre government allotment in the sandy loam and also grew vegetables and sorghum cane, which he milled into syrup. (The sorghum was hauled down into Chattanooga and sold for 25 cents a bucket. The vegetables were picked in the afternoon and loaded onto the family wagon for a night-time trip into Fort Payne, where they were sold promptly at 7:00 A.M. when shops opened.) Colonel was his given name; he never served in the military. Instead of a tractor, which he couldn't afford, Colonel Loudermilk had seven children. Their father's life wasn't one Charlie and his older brother Ira wanted for themselves, and so together they found a way off the farm. "I guess I was twelve and Ira was fifteen when we saw Roy Acuff pass by in an aircooled Franklin," says Charlie. "A long car. A limousine. We knew where he was going to perform. At the Spring Hill schoolhouse. We'd heard it over the radio. We went that night. We didn't have the money to get in. We stood outside in the yard with three or four hundred other people and listened and thought, 'That's what we want to do.'"

While they hoed and plowed, The Louvin Brothers, as they would eventually call themselves, devised possibly the most beautiful and sophisticated harmony arrangements in country music. Their duets succeeded because of the way they sounded together, of course, but the brother with the extraordinary vocal gifts was Ira. An untutored singer who couldn't read music, he sang high enough that he was sometimes mistaken for a woman, and then he slid down into lower keys with such consonant ease that Bill Monroe's older brother, Charlie, once hired him to sing bass for The Kentucky Pardners. When Ira sang about unfulfilled longing and desire in songs he'd written, like "When I Stop Dreaming," his crystalline tenor wound around his brother's steady lead with a fluid, easy grace.

If his gorgeous voice and songs of heart, hearth, Mother, and Savior made him seem blessed, Ira's corrosive temperament lurked in turbid contrast. He was, in many ways, the stereotypical cracker—a fiery, God-fearing son of the dirt-poor lower Appalachian hill country who could not control himself around women or drink. To cross him was to release a sharp scythe of anger that cut through friendships—Elvis Presley idolized him until the day Ira humiliated him with vile invective—destroyed several marriages, and wrecked his relationship with his brother. He never stuck a spear into anyone's chest, but he did try to strangle his wife with a telephone cord. There was a profane pride and a violent misery in Ira Louvin that was as grim as the insular place he came from.

Three years ago, Charlie Louvin left Henagar for good. He had gone back and spent eight years living on the family homeplace, but for a number of reasons—that the Baptist church let a preacher go because parishioners disliked his wife was one of them, he says—Louvin never felt comfortable in Henagar. And so he came down off the mountain and bought a home in the Tennessee horse-country town of Wartrace. Louvin still sings on *The Grand Ole Opry,* and Wartrace—locals sometimes pronounce it "wart race"—is two hours closer by car to Nashville than Henagar was.

Wartrace once was home to Strolling Jim, a walking horse who brought distinction to the area by winning a world championship. Strolling Jim is long gone, buried behind the boarded-up Walking Horse Hotel, and Wartrace too is a little down at the hooves. Perhaps for that reason, Louvin often finds himself heading one town over to the thriving hamlet of Bell Buckle. Were Bell Buckle a seven-year-old child, she would have freckles, red curls, and a pink dress. The buildings that once housed the bank, the drugstore, and the stables have been renovated into quaint antique and gift shops with names like the Daffodilly and Traditions. If the gilt price tags Louvin spots in Main Street shop windows haven't got him too agitated, he can sometimes be urged into sitting in for a few songs behind the mike at the Bell Buckle Café. Either way, he usually ends up at the café. For one thing, the hickory-smoked ribs are tender and plentiful. For another, Louvin's photograph is on the wall. It's a place he can relax in.

There is glee in the way Louvin brandishes his opinions. He doesn't like taxes and he can't abide welfare, which he thinks will be the ruin of the Republic. He is, he says, "old school," and for that reason he believes in "frying" criminals and in calling scrub pine trees what he's always called them: "nigger pines." "I don't mean nothing by that," he says. Louvin likes guns, but he isn't very keen on men with long hair, such as the one who had just served him a plate of ribs at the Bell Buckle Café. "If you read the Good Book, it says that long hair on men is an abomination," he says loudly. "I don't care how good a man plays, I wouldn't hire him with long hair. 'Course that don't mean anything. I have a son forty-one years old and he has a ponytail." Louvin can't stand a scraggly lawn, either, and that he can do something about. When the grassy patch across from the café got a little ragged, the citizens of Bell Buckle were treated to the sight of Louvin pulling into town with his lawn mower in tow and setting things right. "It looked tacky," he says. On the matter of food, Louvin is fond of ribs and Moon Pies, but fried crawfish leaves him cold. "Ditch-critters," he says. "When I grew up we ate only what we could grow. The only things we bought at the grocery store were salt, pepper, sugar, and flour. A Moon Pie would have been expensive for us. Or a soda cracker with peanut butter would have been expensive.

"We were both raised rough," he says. "Daddy told you to do something one time. If you didn't do it he was all over your ass and I don't mean verbally. Farming is hard work. Extremely hard work. You clear the fields, plow the fields, plant it, thin it, keep the grass out of it—work it with hoes. You don't do your evening chores until it's too dark to see in the fields. On Sundays we didn't have to wonder if we was going to church. Our daddy took us. He didn't send us. He hitched up the wagon with the mules and he took us. When Daddy had time, he hired himself out to other people at fifty cents a day. A day meant daybreak to dark. In summertime that can be fourteen hours. He walked six miles each way, too. That's what made him rough. He wanted to push us to do something else. He convinced us that farming with mules and a hoe in your hand wasn't any way to make a living."

Louvin, who never drinks alcohol, takes a swallow of lemonade and goes on talking. "I guess Ira was raised rougher. First one always gets more whippings than the second one. My father mellowed. He got to see he'd been too rough and he backed off. Ira married, I believe, to get away from home. He was married at seventeen, a daddy at eighteen, and grandpa by the time he was thirty-one. There's no doubt in my mind he did it to get out from under my daddy's roof. And then, of course, in those days it was hard to make a living. He had an eighth-grade education. That's as far as our school went. You got out of there and you figured that's all there was. So it was hard for him to find work. He moved to Rome, Georgia. All my mother's people were from Rome, Georgia. He worked in cotton mills. Once he pushed an ice-cream cart. He'd push it through the neighborhood ringing a bell. Maybe that job paid a dollar an hour. No more."

Louvin decides to order some dessert. There aren't many restaurants that have hot Moon Pies on the menu, but the Bell Buckle Café is one of them, and the tasty prospect of warm chocolate and marshmallow reminds Louvin that it was his weakness for sweets that prevented him from learning how to read the shaped notes in a gospel hymnbook. "We were supposed to go to school for that," he says. "Where we were raised, Sacred Harp singing was famous. This singing teacher had been bugging my daddy—he'd seen us singing at cakewalks and ice-cream suppers. 'Colonel,' he said, 'you better send those boys to school so they'll know what they're doing.' We had absolutely no cash flow, but Daddy gave us $12 for two weeks."

Louvin sometimes will explain things with the aid of an aphorism. When I ask why, if his father was broke, he would put his money into singing lessons, he says, "Our family was too poor to paint and too proud to whitewash." You can tell when somebody's been using whitewash because as soon as it rains the whitewash begins to fade. Louvin meant that by pressing him so often, the singing teacher had played upon Colonel Loudermilk's pride. You could only put off a singing-school teacher for so long. After a while you had to paint or say you couldn't.

"We were to take the money and give it to the singing-school teacher," Louvin goes on. "Instead, Ira and I and two or three other boys we were raised with went by the store a quarter mile from our house and we bought Moon Pies, RC Colas, Baby Ruths, and cigarettes. Then we drifted off into the woods and played all day. We knew what time singing school let out. At about that time we went back home. It was about the fourth day we done this that my daddy ran into the singing-school teacher. He said, 'Colonel, I thought you was gonna send those boys to singing school!' My daddy said, 'Well, you know how everything is.' He sure was laying for us when we got home from the woods that evening. First he said, 'Are you learning anything at the singing school?' and we said, 'Everything is great!' Then he had us for lying *and* for not going to school. Unless you've been whipped . . . Well, we got a real one. Today that's called child abuse. Back then it's called raising children. I don't guess it taught us very much. We picked and sang by ear. I still say that's the best way a person can do it."

Charlie and Ira Louvin grew up during a thriving period for so-called country brother groups, something they knew all about because Colonel Loudermilk liked buying records. The pairs of brothers whose music Charlie and Ira listened to most carefully were Rabon and Alton Delmore and Bill and Earl Bolick, who called themselves The Blue Sky Boys. The Delmores were the sons of a hired man who farmed and operated a cotton gin on Brown's Ferry Road, in rural Limestone County, Alabama, about sixty miles from Henagar. In songs like "Southern Moon," "Blues Stay Away from Me," and the irrepressible "Brown's Ferry Blues," the Delmores sang about soft rains, hard labor, and chewing tobacco in a distinctive soft, mellow, exceptionally clear tone that featured harmonies of more careful construction than country was accustomed to. The Bolicks, whose parents were cotton-mill workers from Hickory, North Carolina, sought a more sober and intimate sound. They sang religious songs such as "Dust on the Bible" and "The Cross on the Hill," and secular parables, including "The Last Letter" and "Banks of the Ohio"—moral songs that gave country people spiritual encouragement. Their harmonies were even more closely meshed than the Delmores', in part because where both Delmores played a nippy guitar, The Blue Sky Boys regarded their instruments strictly as complements to the singing. Bill Bolick played a mandolin, on which he liked to unleash high, plaintive runs above his brother's stolid guitar so that the instrumental sounds blended perfectly with their voices.

"The Delmores and The Blue Sky Boys both had unbelievably close harmonies," says Louvin. "Their phrasing was perfect. Ira and I strived for perfect phrasing. We could do that because we were brothers. There's no way to meet a stranger and get as close as brothers can get. The tenor singer has to have a lead singer he knows. Ira and I had the advantage of singing while we were working. We sang the old songs and a lot of gospel. 'The Knoxville Girl,' 'I'll Be All Smiles Tonight,' and a song that was going good when we were children called 'Little Mary Phagan.' She worked in a pencil factory in Marietta, Georgia. We'd always pick a medium-paced song. Our motto was songs that tell a story. If you can't hear the words, you can't tell a story. Sometimes I mess around and pick with some people here in Bell Buckle. They'll start at ninety miles an hour and I'll say, 'Guys, I can't sing that fast. I'll just stand over here and watch you.' "

On July 4, 1941, when Ira was seventeen and Charlie about to turn fourteen, the brothers had their first paying job as singers. "We worked in a place called Flat Rock, Alabama, eight miles from where I was raised," says Louvin. "We worked on a flying jenny. Today you'd call it a merry-go-round. You made it move with mules. We'd sing two songs and they'd make the people get off. Tickets cost five cents. We got two dollars each for the day. We must have been up there six or eight hours. The four dollars we made was as much as my daddy could make working eight days, daylight to dark."

A year later, Ira had a job in the Peerless Woolen Mill in Chattanooga when he heard about a local singing contest. The prize was a predawn live radio show. He sent for Charlie and they entered and won. For the next decade and a half they were country gospel singers, playing gigs all over the South. "We'd always gotten along good," says Louvin. "It was better in the early years. We were pretty good friends. I was the only one he knew who could sing lead the way he wanted it sung. He was the only tenor I knew who could sing tenor the way I wanted it sung. We had a great common cause."

Although Ira's voice could climb much higher than Charlie's, The Louvin Brothers employed the same drawling vocal inflections when they spoke—Ira's name came out "Iree"—and when they sang, *when* was "whin" and *lie* sounded like "laah." Otherwise they didn't look much like brothers. Ira was significantly taller, with a face that was dominated by the large whites of his eyes. His glowing pupils always made Ira appear just a little unhinged. Shorter, with reddish hair, cups for ears, freckles, and a boyish grin, Charlie Louvin looked like a game kid brother. These days the grin is still ready, but his hair has thinned and so too has his chin; some of it was left behind when he fell off a ladder. Louvin seems far more discomfited by the $900 the injury cost him in hospital bills than the damage to his face.

For most of the Louvin Brothers' musical career, money was tight and often Ira was too. Ira showed Charlie what he knew about playing the guitar and then he taught himself the mandolin by listening to Bill Monroe, Bill Bolick, and The Bailes Brothers records. A mandolin can be a tricky instrument to tune for some people, and there were times when Ira didn't bother. If he didn't like what he was hearing, he'd smash it on the stage and walk off. He was always threatening to quit show business and get a full-time job, "so," he'd explain, "we can live like white people."

In 1947, a promoter named Smilin' Eddie Hill hired the Louvins to work his *High Noon Roundup* radio show in Memphis. They spent three years singing hymns there, and grew so popular that by 1950, in one week they received 10,000 fan letters. Besides their radio show, they played concerts in the Delta towns surrounding Memphis. Before a show at a school in Dyess, Arkansas, Charlie asked a local boy to direct him to the toilet. "He was a poor kid," he says. "Overalls. No shirt. It was the end of hot weather and he was almost as tan as a Moon Pie. Bet he could have walked on nails. I was the same way when I was his age. Walking back from the bathroom I pulled out a pack of soda crackers and the kid asked why I was eating a cracker. I said, 'To keep from starving to death.' " Charlie let the boy into the show for nothing. Which explains why, when he grew up and started singing himself, for years Johnny Cash ate soda crackers before every show.

Smilin' Eddie Hill moved on to Nashville in 1950, and soon Charlie had enrolled in barber school in Memphis. Ira got a job across the state in a Knoxville grocery. A little while later both Louvins were working the graveyard shift in the Memphis post office and making their music on weekends. For a time they even broke up the singing team. Not until 1955 were they welcomed onto *The Grand Ole Opry,* where people would listen to them sing songs Ira had written, like "I Wish You Knew," "If I Could Only Win Your Love," and "You're Learning," and marvel at the harmonies.

Ira liked to write on the toilet—"he did most of his best writing on the throne," says Charlie—but even his nonsacred lyrics were clean enough from what vitiates to please a talcum-dusted deacon. Still, until 1955, when they recorded "When I Stop Dreaming" and joined *The Grand Ole Opry,* they weren't allowed to record anything but gospel. There was worry at Capitol Records that if religious singers took on nonsacred material their fans would scorn them as hypocrites.

Ira had worked hard to lend the group a moral persona. Typical of his gospel compositions was "Broadminded," a screed against gamblers and drinkers that also censors good-time mamas who go out drinking and dancing all week and then show up in church on Sunday. Ira liked to fold

The Louvin Brothers, Ira and Charlie, on stage.
"I felt we really had something. I guess we did."

brief spoken sermons into a song, and here at the end of a crackling condemnation of carnal life he intones: " 'Broadminded' means sin if you'll read."

It was the harmonies that made the music special, the way the brothers separated a song into minute vocal sections, so that they were constantly shifting between lead and tenor, singing in different octaves, merging their voices, and then branching off again. In "Weapon of Prayer," they switch parts so often and so smoothly that the effect is similar to watching a fine doubles tennis team at play, with the two players moving fluidly amid each other, deferring to each other's strengths, and executing challenging shots with little apparent motion or exertion.

In 1960, they recorded a complete album of songs made famous by The Delmore Brothers. The Louvins' versions of songs like "Sand Mountain Blues," "Nashville Blues," and especially "Southern Moon" were so beautiful that the Delmores' old guitar player Merle Travis, who watched the Louvins record them, said they "sing like a dream."

"A lot of stuff we did came natural because of our raising—our closeness," Louvin says. "I knew early on what my limitations were and what Ira's abilities were. I could sing high, but not nearly as high as Ira. He had unlimited range in the tenor. We knew when to switch when something came along that was too high for me, how to switch to high and low harmonies. In one line of a song we'd sometimes change parts twice. We could change parts in the middle of a phrase. Other people could take the song apart and learn how we did it, but we did it instinctively."

After the large midday meal, Louvin decides a walk around Bell Buckle might be refreshing. The prices being asked for the birdhouses, quilts, and curios in the Main Street shops are not small, and when Louvin notices what an old but otherwise unremarkable section of fence will fetch, he sets his teeth. Then he spots a battered banjo that somebody has priced at $125. "I wouldn't give two bucks for it," he says. "It's totally broke. The neck's broke and it doesn't even have a resonator." He considers the instrument for a moment. As a boy, Ira Louvin built what was, in effect, a four-string banjo out of a syrup bucket, cornstalks, and beeswax-coated sewing thread. "Ira could got have got ahold and fixed that," Louvin says, gazing balefully at the banjo. "He'd stomp his mandolins and then he'd put them back together. 'Course if he stomped them on the road he'd have to call his wife and have her send one to the next date."

Ira became increasingly bellicose through the 1950s. "He would fly off the handle easily, get upset with other musicians and his brother," says Chet Atkins, who knew and recorded him then. "When he'd sing, he'd sing so high the veins would pop out on his forehead. He was different." The Louvins had top billing in 1955, when they began a 105-day tour with young Elvis Presley. By the time they hit Wilson, North Carolina, in the fall of 1956, Presley was a hipshaking phenomenon and Ira was laying for him. "Elvis does his show and comes back afterwards," says Louvin. "He sits down at a piano, hits a few chords, says 'Here's what I like,' and sings a gospel song, an old hymn. Ira says, 'You fuckin' white nigger. If that's the kind of music you like, why don't you do that out there instead of that shit you do?' Elvis just kind of looked at him—that was before his karate—and he said, 'When I'm out there I do what they want to hear. When I'm back here, I do what I want to do.' That was the end of that conversation. After that time, after Elvis was real hot, he'd say The Louvin Brothers were his all-time favorite country gospel singers. Yet he never recorded a Louvin Brothers song. If a guy said that to me, I'd ignore his best songs too."

Presley devastated traditional country music. Once they heard The King, people wanted their popular music to grind and bounce. Eventually the Louvins' producer at Capitol Records, Ken Nelson, said that he believed the mandolin might be harming the sale of their records. "From that day on after Nelson said that, Ira hated the mandolin and drank twenty-five times more," says Louvin. "He went through his second wife, his third wife, became ungodly nasty to disc jockeys and Capitol Records people. He'd just as soon cuss you out as look at you. He had put in fifteen years of slavery to learn the mandolin and he was as good as you'd find. It crushed him. Now he'd get to drinking and say, 'If I'd learned to blow a French harp we'd still be selling records.' I'm sure his drinking problems broke up his marriages and eventually the duet. Beyond his meanness, he made the act undependable. You can't do nothing when you're messed up."

I asked Charlie how this scabrous behavior squared with songs like "Broadminded," and he said, "A lot of people said Ira was called to be a preacher. Evidently he didn't want to do that so he rebelled." He also said, somewhat cryptically, "Just because we were Bible Belt didn't mean we were good guys."

Ira seemed inexorably driven to the very pleasures he railed against in song. He'd sing in a honky-tonk, revile himself for being there, and booze himself into a stupor in the car afterward to forget it. When he stayed straight, he liked to flirt, and to more than flirt. His drinking, his tantrums, and his infidelities made for volatile marriages. At home in Nashville, Ira and his third wife, Faye Cunningham, were an especially toxic combination. "I had to move a fair piece from them," says Louvin. "There's always somebody locked up in the bathroom with the other one trying to get in and kill them. Once she cracked an iron skillet on his head and ran to the bedroom. He tried to choke her with the telephone cord and she remembered he had a pistol loaded with .22 short shells. She didn't shoot him once. She emptied the pistol. The hospital wouldn't admit him until I drove 100 miles to Nashville to guarantee the bill. Ira asked me to have her committed. I was trying to do him a favor. He asked me once, he asked me two dozen times. Then afterwards, I had to get Roy Acuff to help me get her out of there." In the newspaper article that reported the incident, Faye was quoted as saying, "If the son of a bitch don't die, I'll shoot him again."

In fact, he lived—for a while. The doctors decided it was safer not to remove the five bullets, and so Ira carried them around with him for four years until 1965, when he was killed in a head-on automobile collision. By then, the brothers had parted ways. "Two things happened before we broke up," Louvin says. "He'd say, 'When we get home after this date, you can count me out of this fucking business.' After he'd sobered up he'd call me and I'd say, 'Thought you quit.' He'd say, 'It was that whiskey talking.' Well, the next to last date we worked was at an Air Force base outside Kansas City. There was free whiskey. They had lots of people there who couldn't give it to him fast enough. He attracted a real George Jones following. I don't think he had any sober friends. The next morning he and I were going to Watseka, Illinois, to work with Ray Price. It was drizzling rain. I packed all the stuff. He wanted his mandolin packed on top of the other stuff, so I had set it by the car. He told me, 'Don't you ever touch my fucking mandolin again.' I said, 'Don't worry. I was trying to do you a favor.' He said, 'This is the last day I work in this fucking business.' He cussed me all the way to Watseka. Told me, 'Without me, you'd be doing nothing. Maybe working in a service station.'" The next time Ira called, Charlie said, "You convinced me," and that was it.

Charlie embarked upon a moderately successful solo career. He would, among other things, record some nice duets with Melba Montgomery. Ira went out on his own too, but his resolve wavered. He moved back to Alabama and told a minister there that he was going to sing one last show in Missouri, and then he was going to buy a tent and start preaching. "After that, he came to Nashville," says Charlie. "Roy Acuff and some of his other drinking buddies saw him there. I didn't. Then he went out to Kansas City and on the way home he got killed. My mother thought for an absolute fact he'd be a preacher when he got back. A week later I worked in Kansas City. I stopped on the road where he wrecked and saw the car. Ira wasn't drinking that day, but the two people who hit him were nine times drunk. It happened at the break of day, June 20, 1965. Father's Day. Two weeks later, a state trooper came to my door in Hendersonville, Tennessee. They wanted him for a DUI in Nashville. I showed the trooper a newspaper with Ira's death in it."

Buford Trotman, retired pastor of the Sand Mountain Holiness Church, describes Charlie Louvin as "a slow man—by that I mean easygoing." To me he seemed to have a fair amount of bitterness in him. In the car, heading toward Wartrace, he bristles some more about the living a man can make in the antiques business. Pointing to a fence bordering a pasture, he says, "You take a piece of that fence, soak it in salt water, get it good and rusty, and then you can sell it in Bell Buckle for a pile of money." Louvin has been married forty-nine years to a patient woman named Betty who was born in Meridian, Mississippi, where Jimmie Rodgers held her infant self in his lap. As we drive, Betty's dog barks at cows while Louvin alternately complains about "welfare Cadillacs" and points out the pieces of farmland he wishes he owned. His two acres are, he says, too close to the side of Highway 64. "But," he adds, "it's a good house except I miss a tin roof. My wife hates them. I grew up with them. On our off days we used to lie in the hayloft and listen to that rain on the tin roof and I'd drift off. Can't stay awake long under a tin roof in the rain."

I say he sounds like someone who misses Alabama. "At the time, I hated it," he replies. "I really looked forward to getting away from it. Once I was away from it—well, a guy spends the first twenty-five years of his life trying to get off the farm and he spends the next twenty-five trying to save up enough money to buy one. Our harmonies came from there, you know. Ira and I stayed in it twenty-three years," he says. "I've been in it thirty years without him. I don't think my friends have problems getting along with me. If you hate people and you hate traveling you certainly ought to get in another business. You ought to get you a job pumping gas."

We're all quiet for a moment and then Louvin says, "I think Ira was tortured by religion. I never was able to get into his head—he told other people, he never told me. I couldn't handle the drinking. Today they call it an illness. In those days it was bein' mean. They want you to feel sorry for a drunk. I guess I could have. But you're part of a team. If I ain't there, you might call the hospital and ask how I am—I've always prided myself on my punctuality. Ira was a totally different person. Nobody individualizes you, you know. It's always, 'The Louvin Brothers cussed somebody out.' But I never did. He cussed record people, he cussed disc jockeys, he'd cuss anybody. But I didn't want the team to break up. I felt we really had something. I guess we did. It's been thirty years since we were separated and still, if I'm playing a Louvin Brothers song, when I get to the harmony part, I move off to one side of the mike. It's a habit I can't break."

*Doc (left) and Merle Watson—seated—on the front porch in Deep Gap,
North Carolina. "Doc was hurt over his son, but Rosa Lee,
she couldn't control it."*

DOC WATSON

JUST ONE OF
THE PEOPLE

Shortly after he was born, the flat-pick guitar player and singer Doc Watson's corneas became so raw with infection that the sight of the morning light was agony for him. Blind before his first birthday, Watson just vaguely remembers seeing anything. He has a sense of what a full moon looks like, but he doesn't recall colors or shapes. To sign his name, he makes an X. To tell the time, he touches his Braille pocket watch. When he wants to go anywhere outside his hometown of Deep Gap, North Carolina, he needs someone to guide him.

Yet Watson, seventy-two, is what his old friend, a welder and singer–guitar player named Clint Howard, calls "kind of an outstanding blind man." Beyond the fact that Watson has no use for the familiar accessories of his handicap, such as dark glasses, white canes, or trained dogs, what Howard means is that Watson often appears to live his life as though he can see. On their outings together to buy dresses for their wives, Howard has noticed that "Doc can pick out one just as pretty as I can. He can't tell you the color, but he can tell you more about how each dress is made than I can." Watson has also rewired his entire house, tuned pianos, taken apart and repaired motel air conditioners, unstopped pipes, and built the large utility shed in which he stores, among other things, his lawn mower and his axe. He can tell what's wrong with a car's engine just by listening to it, and he then can go ahead and fix it.

Watson cuts his own grass, and for years he also chopped enough firewood to heat his house through the winter, never so much as grazing himself. During the time he was building the utility shed, however, he did once strike his thumb with a hammer. "See where it's all purple and torn," he would say afterward when relating the mishap to friends, and the thumb was just as he described it. Watson's conversation is, in fact, strewn with precise observations, and when he mentions someone's smile, or refers to the illustration on the front of a seed packet, the details are so true that people tend to forget they are hearing about what flowers look like from a blind man. Then, with a start, they begin to wonder how he does it.

"Doc fascinates me," says Earl Scruggs. "We went to his house one time years ago and Doc was sitting on the couch. Somebody had brought me out a banjo and we were sitting and picking. Afterwards, I didn't want to tell Doc to put it away, so I went into the bedroom and there were two open cases. I began to put it in one of them, and from the couch Doc says, 'That goes in the other one, Earl.' I don't know how he knew." The public-relations agent Penny Parsons recalls a similar experience. "Once," she says, "he asked a woman, 'You aren't by any chance a redhead, are you?' and she was."

Watson is not as impressed by all this as other people tend to be. Calling attention to his handling the same household chores as anybody else in Deep Gap casts him as an exception, which is precisely what he wants to avoid. And so it is with slight impatience that he explains that he knew Scruggs had the wrong banjo case by the way the latches sounded when they clicked open. The redheaded woman's personality, he says, made him confident of her hair color. What some people have taken to calling his "sixth sense," Watson dismisses as no more than a combination of good memory, sensitive ears, and a capacity for shrewd guesswork.

Watson can—and occasionally does—play a guitar as fast as you can hear it, and naturally people are prone to make ecstatic pronouncements after seeing him do it. Watson doesn't enjoy them. The appellation he likes least is "artist," and he is quick to shuck off such praise. Sometimes he does so indirectly, by referring to his instrument as "the old flog box." For him, guitar playing is just another skill, no different in its way from overhauling a transmission or building a table. He is so resolute in this conviction that after spending a little time around Watson you expect him to be wearing a dark green button-front work shirt with "Doc" in red embroidered script in a white oval over the left breast. (In fact, he usually favors brown trousers and broadcloth shirts.)

Watson has a chunky, well-mottled face and a shock of brown hair that he pummels into order with a thick comb. Because he speaks in a warm, mild, extremely resonant baritone voice and talks about things in a lightly expressive, thoroughly distinctive way, other people like to repeat even his mundane remarks. When, for example, Watson catches himself referring to someone by the wrong name, he may say, "I keep calling him Jim. I hope he don't despise that name much."

Watson is more than just a gifted fellow with a humble streak. He is a rugged-looking man with such a strong belief in modesty that it pervades everything he does, not least his views on how music should sound. As a rule, Watson has a distaste for decorative flourishes. He has no use for musicians who seek to please a crowd with novelty—or "flash," as he puts it—and he particularly dislikes the thought of an audience so enthralled with his fancy flat-picking that it doesn't notice the strong feelings lodged in the songs he performs. For this reason, no matter how quickly Watson's left hand is moving, there is always a cleanness to his guitar playing. It might be said that when he plays music, Watson considers it his obligation to make people see.

He puts his voice to the same purpose. Watson is an attractive, plain-spoken singer, and because his baritone is so clear and versatile, it is an ideal way of enlivening images for other people that he has, of course, never glimpsed himself. Of the 1,500 songs he knows, not a few are train songs, and Watson says that it's really no trick at all to sing about boxcars and locomotives without ever having looked at one. "I've climbed all over train cars," he told me. "I've been on engines and I've heard them. When I was a boy playing in the yard, a train would come up at Deep Gap depot. I *knew* trains." Watson can fill something like The Delmore Brothers' "Blue Railroad Train" with just the right forlorn clickety-clack of melancholy motion and then turn around and steam merrily across A.P. Carter's "Wabash Cannonball."

"The talent for music is a God-given thing," he says. "You have a box and usually there are three or four talents in there—whatever life deals you. When I was a little boy they handed me a box and music was in it." Watson says that had he been able to see, "music would have been a hobby" and he would have been a mechanic or a carpenter or an electrician. "I'm not as bright as people make me out to be," he says. "I'm just one of the people."

In 1960, when a part-time folklorist from New York City named Ralph Rinzler was making a pass through Appalachia in search of regular people who had grown up playing old-time music, the world beyond the Blue Ridge Mountains came to know Doc Watson. At a fiddlers' convention in

Galax, Virginia, Rinzler had met Clarence "Tom" Ashley, a legendary banjo-picking ballad singer and comedian. By hawking tonics, soaps, and salves on the traveling medicine-show circuit in the 1920s and 1930s, Ashley had become popular enough to win himself record contracts from Columbia and Victor. But he had long since faded into obscurity and now thought of himself as part of "a group of farmers who play, pick, and sing a little in the old country way." Ashley may have been keeping time with farmers who played string music, but he had not plucked a banjo for many years when Rinzler encountered him. "The reason Tom Ashley quit is that people wouldn't listen to him," says Clint Howard, who was Ashley's friend and neighbor in the hamlet of Shouns, just across the North Carolina border from Mountain City, Tennessee. "He would put on a show and couldn't draw twenty flies, much less people. Then Ralph Rinzler brought the music back. The music was just something we been living with. We was used to it and didn't have no thoughts of what it was."

Ashley had told Rinzler that he could come down to Shouns and record him and the farmers, but he asked for some time to get his voice and banjo back up to speed. When Rinzler and a colleague arrived with their tape recorder a few months later, in the group of musicians Ashley had assembled to accompany him was a blind electric-guitar player. Rinzler was after something a little more homespun and he asked Doc Watson to switch to an acoustic guitar. Watson had been earning money by playing in a local rockabilly dance band, and the electric guitar was the only instrument he owned. He could tell, however, that Rinzler seemed disappointed at the sight of a country boy holding a Gibson Les Paul.

The next day, Ashley arranged for a group of his friends and neighbors to meet and play for Rinzler at a house in Saltville, Virginia, two hours away. He said he would take Rinzler there. Rinzler settled into the bed of a pickup truck and began to amuse himself by playing hoedowns on a five-string banjo he had with him. After a few minutes, the truck suddenly stopped and Watson climbed out of the cab. "Let me see that banjo, son," he said, and Rinzler handed it over. Whereupon Watson, Rinzler remembered, "ripped off some of the best pure mountain picking imaginable." Rinzler would write later, "Here was the context of the folk music I had heard in recorded and concert performances for twenty of my twenty-six years."

The Watsons fled Scotland at the beginning of the nineteenth century when the lairds began enclosing their farmland and renting it in vast tracts to English sheep farmers. Eventually, Great-Great-Grandfather Watson settled beyond the Piedmont country in northwestern North Carolina, which, with its profusion of oak and chestnut forests, wildflower-covered hillsides, and steep rocky crags, looked to him a lot like the Highlands. Today, people Doc Watson refers to as "outsiders" have bull-dozed huge gouges in the old hardwood forests around Deep Gap and re-sown them with upscale housing developments and Christmas-tree plantations. But early in the 1960s, when Rinzler showed up there, Deep Gap was still no more than a well-shaded wide spot in the road, a community of perhaps two hundred farmers and woodsmen living without electricity in small, weatherbeaten wooden houses tucked into the valleys and ridges ten miles from the county seat at Boone. Doc Watson grew up sharing a bed with two of his brothers. There was a weeping willow tree right outside the house, and a grove of white pines.

One of the things Great-Great-Grandfather Watson liked to do in his spare time was make music. "Their music was very much integrated into the lives of the original mountain people," says Nancy Watson, Doc's daughter. "It's like it's in our blood. It was passed down through generations and that's how it got to Daddy." Doc Watson came from a family full of casual fiddlers and pickers. The Watsons and their kin had unusual names—Watson's father's given name was General Dixon Watson, his father-in-law was Gaither Wiley Carlton, and Watson himself had been christened Arthel. Their children ran around barefoot all summer, their pantries were filled with fruits and vegetables canned from the garden, and they all talked down-home. Watson addressed men as "son," and when he wanted to refer to a man in conversation, he was "that ol' boy over yonder." He was always saying things like "I reckon that suits their notion," or "I guess I might tell you a little fun tale." And when he sang and accompanied himself on the "git-tar," he sounded, as he would put it, so country you would swear you could smell the frost on the sweet-potato vines.

The problem was that Watson didn't sing many of the songs he had grown up with anymore. Instead, on his weekends he was taking the bus to Johnson City and slinging "Tutti Frutti," "Blue Suede Shoes," and "Tea for Two" at VFW halls on his electric guitar. For seven years he had made steady money playing Saturday-night dances with the pianist Jack Williams in a popular local country swing band, The Country Gentlemen. Watson may have grown up hearing sacred songs sung from shaped-note hymnals in church and listening to his father croon doggerel with lines like "Here comes Sal with a snicker and a grin, the groundhog gravy all over her chin," but his family owned both a radio and a phonograph, meaning that he also knew everything from "The Sheik of Araby" to "Heartbreak Hotel." He was, one of his friends told me, "never some hick from Deep Gap."

Meanwhile, as the 1950s ended, up north they were clamoring for the old mountain songs. On college campuses and in cities like New York, San Francisco, Chicago, and Boston, interest had suddenly surged in traditional American string music—old Delta blues, acoustic country, and pre-Depression airs. At the vanguard of this so-called Folk Revival were middle-class performers like Pete Seeger, Joan Baez, and The Kingston Trio, which had a surprise hit in 1958 with the old Appalachian murder ballad "Tom Dooley." Ashley found these urban folkies somewhat lacking. "A lot of people in the city are playing old-time music these days," he observed dryly. "But country people play their feeling and feel their playing. That's the big difference." It was Rinzler's surmise that audiences might agree, and he was right. Just as it is important to the whites who buy three of every four gangsta-rap records sold today that the music come from authentic inner-city blacks—preferably with violent lives—1960s revival audiences were eager to hear songs like "Tom Dooley" from people who really did live in the pastoral places where the music came from.

After listening to him play and sing, Rinzler convinced Watson— whose grandparents knew Tom Dooley's parents—that a market was burgeoning for the old songs. It wasn't that difficult to bring him around. There weren't many ways for a blind country boy to earn a living, and singing the music he'd always loved beat them all. And so Watson began to revisit his childhood.

People in the tiny mountain communities across western North Carolina and Virginia, eastern West Virginia, Tennessee, and Kentucky lived remarkably self-contained lives during the Depression and, superficially, remarkably similar ones. Their houses, gardens, and clothing looked alike, they prayed in white frame country church houses, listened to the same radio shows, and played the same string instruments. When Doc Watson met the singer and hammered dulcimer player Jean Ritchie at a party at the musicologist Alan Lomax's home in New York in the early 1960s, she says they understood each other instantly. And why not? They might as well have grown up together. In *Singing Family of the Cumberlands,* her sprightly memoir of Viper, Kentucky, Ritchie writes that her family felt so isolated in their mountain home that singing together in the evenings became an anodyne, helping them stave off gloom. "People," she says, "could get lonely looking at the hillsides."

As someone who lived in a sparsely populated holler and couldn't see, growing up with singing around him was perhaps even more important to Doc Watson. His was a religious family—Free Will Baptist—and a musical one. Watson says his earliest memory is of "sitting on Mama's lap hearing them sing 'The Lone Pilgrim,' in the little frame church. I must have been about three or four years old." At home, while she churned butter or patched her husband's overalls, Annie Watson would sing the traditional songs, like "The House Carpenter," which came across the Atlantic from the British Isles with the early Appalachian settlers. Her voice is a lonesome wail in the recordings that Rinzler made of her. "Mama knew a few of the old ballads," says Watson. "I don't know how many. Somebody asked me once if she played a guitar. There was no time for her to learn. She was too busy raising nine brats."

General Dixon Watson was a farmer and the upright scion his name portends. Before the Civil War, hill-country farmers had compensated for the short growing season by renting their pastures to cattle ranchers, who fattened their stock in the fertile glades and meadows before selling them off. When railroads made the long cattle drives obsolete, the Appalachian farmers had a hard time of it. Many of them packed up and moved to mill or mining towns. Others, like General Dixon, took on "public" work—repairing roads, building bridges—and stayed where they were. "He was barely fit to read a Bible, but he had a head crammed with horse sense," is how Watson describes his father. General Dixon was a good shot, an able carpenter, "grew" his own pork, and knew his way around a fiddle. Not that he played it much. Instead, every evening he assembled the family and led it in readings from Scripture and in singing sacred songs like "When I Die" out of the *Christian Harmony* hymnal.

As much as all the Watsons enjoyed the music—and they enjoyed it very much—none of them responded to it with quite the zeal that the sixth child did. (Watson's brothers and sisters mostly stayed around Deep Gap, working as farmers, carpenters, and timber cutters.) "If something had a tune, I liked to hear it rattle," says Doc Watson. "I'd be beating on something, playing on little bells or the bottom of a tin can." Even as a "little thing," Watson says he was fascinated by the slight variations in sound that came from cow and sheep bells when you tapped them with a stick. He could sit on the porch for hours listening carefully to the wind blow through the grove of white pine trees near the house. Not long ago, a logging company cut the trees down. "Doc misses hearing the timber more than we do looking at it," says Clint Howard. "I've heard him talk about those trees. He sure misses that great big field of pines. Sounds and shapes mean a lot to him."

His father noticed. When he was five, Watson received a harmonica in the toe of his Christmas stocking. The next Christmas he got a new one. As he did the Christmas after that, and after that. Sometimes it was that Watson had spent so much time "harp tootin'" that he'd worn out the reeds. In other years, he says, "I'd either let my brother play it and he'd lose it, or I'd lose it or get it full of dirt. When you're a kid you don't realize the value of a thing. Then you lose it and you cry."

When Watson was six, his father spent a week working at a relative's sawmill. As part of his payment he accepted a windup gramophone and fifty or sixty 78-rpm records. Later he brought home a radio. It was mainly with these two machines that Doc Watson made a musician of himself. "Ninety percent of the music I learned was absolutely self-taught," Watson says. "I learned half a thimble from other musicians, but most of it was from listening to the old records." One explanation for Watson's refined sound is that records and the radio exposed him to a precision and expertise in both singing and playing that he never would have encountered had his teachers been casual local musicians teaching him melodies on the front porch.

Over the years the family added to its record collection, and Watson wore them all out. His favorite singer was Jimmie Rodgers, whose lazy-river sweet singing made the hint of tragedy in his rough and rowdy songs all the more poignant. Jimmie Rodgers was nobody's idea of a dazzling guitar player, and so Watson listened to others. He liked Merle Travis's agile but never garish picking well enough to name his son after him. Travis mixed a little jazz, blues, and ragtime in with his country finger-picking, and Watson learned to do the same with a flat-pick. He listened to Rodgers's and Travis's music so much that after a while he says he felt he knew both men.

One of the fascinating qualities in Watson's music is how he quietly manages to make old songs sound fresh. He can sing and play somebody else's song straight—with all their inflections and filigrees—or he can play an independent version that he's decorated with ornaments chosen from a drawer stuffed with the music he likes. "That's the gift the Good Lord gave him," says Clint Howard. "He'll play a Delmore Brothers song note to note, exactly like they did, and then he'll put a few Doc Watson licks to it."

From the first, he took something from almost everyone he listened to. Mother Maybelle Carter set him an early example of affecting guitar playing that avoided gratuitous embellishments, and by the time he was eight, Watson knew several of the more lilting Carter Family melodies, like "Little Darling Pal of Mine." Doc Watson often sounds like a lullaby singer when he sings, and he honed this comforting, unadorned tone on the plaintive melodies A.P. Carter gathered when he went song hunting around southwestern Virginia in the 1920s. Watson also liked the banjo-charged comic "foolishness" of "Uncle" Dave Macon, and the mellow harmonies of Alton Delmore and his brother Rabon, who sang forlorn and gentle, got sick up north, and went home to Athens, Alabama, where he died young of lung cancer. Like so many country musicians, Watson was heavily influenced by black music. At an early age he heard the Memphis jug-band master Gus Cannon, the happy blues guitar of Mississippi John Hurt, and the more brooding Delta blues of Skip James, and liked them all. But it was another blind man, the mysterious country guitar player from Couchman, Texas, "Blind" Lemon Jefferson, who sang the blues that really spoke to Watson. "With him blues is not just music, it's a feeling," he says. "The soul of lonesomeness."

By the time Watson was ten, the harmonica wasn't enough instrument for him. Because nobody in his family owned a guitar or a mandolin, he began to improvise. "I remember once stringing a wire from the granary door," he says. "Got me a good bass tone. I'd play 'Home Sweet Home,' and a couple of slow songs and old hymns. You can imagine what a bagpipe sounded like playing 'Home Sweet Home,' and that's the way my wire sounded. I think my dad did laugh at me. 'Son,' he said, 'what do you think you're doing?' I said, 'I'm playing pretty music.' "

That year his father sent him to Raleigh for the first of the four years he would spend at the School for the Blind. Watson read a lot there, listened to jazz records, and learned a few guitar chords from "a little old boy" who had one. Yet somehow from the start it was an unpleasant experience, so much so that Watson never talks about it. When he came home to Deep Gap for a visit right before springtime, his father looked him over and said, "Son, I used to pick a banjo a little and I've a good mind to make you one this summer."

In June he began. The fretless neck was carved from maple, and had maple friction tuning pegs similar to those on a dulcimer. After boiling a piece of hickory in water, General Dixon bent it into a hoop. For the head, he tried stretching a groundhog skin across the hoop, but groundhog hide was too stiff and muffled the ring. And so he found something better. "My grandmother Watson lived a hundred yards away from us and she had an old cat," says Watson. "It was about twenty years old by that time. When they're twenty, they're getting pretty decrepit. It couldn't see. It couldn't hear. It couldn't walk. It was in miserable condition. My brother Linny was carrying up wash water for my mother. My grandmother asks him, 'Do me a favor. I'll give you a quarter or maybe fifty cents if you put my cat out of its misery.'

" 'I don't like to hurt anything,' my brother said.

"She said, 'I know you won't make it suffer, and you do shoot things when you hunt.' She put the cat in a tow sack. Dad was splitting stove wood. My brother came along with that little sack with a cat in it in one hand and a heavy bucket of water in the other.

" 'What do you have, son?' Dad said, and my brother told him. Then Dad said, 'You boys skin it and I'll make you a banjo.' " He scraped the hair off the skin and tanned it, and then he stretched it tight across the hoop. "The catskin made a great head and a beautiful sound," says Watson. When General Dixon had it tuned up, he picked out "Rambling Hobo" and several other songs. Watson learned them all so quickly that one day his father said to him, "Here, son. Take this and learn to play it good. You might need it in this world. It's yours now." That was it. As Watson told *Frets* magazine, "He never would pick no more after he got me started."

He learned the guitar just as fast. After he'd learned those first few chords at school, Watson came home on another vacation to find that one of his brothers had borrowed a guitar. His father was eating breakfast one day while Watson was plucking at it. General Dixon asked Watson how much money he had saved in his piggy bank. "I had about seven or eight dollars," he says. "People were always giving me fifty cents because they wanted to. I used to think I could dance when I was little. 'Dance me a tune and I'll give you a quarter,' they'd say."

"Son," his father said, "if you can learn to play and sing a tune by the time I get back from work, we'll go to town Saturday and buy you a guitar." Watson likes to describe himself as "a slow learner" on the guitar, someone who requires at least a week to get a tune down, but he didn't begin that way. When his father got back from work, Watson played him The Carter Family's "When the Roses Bloom in Dixieland" straight through. "Son," his father said, "I guess I'll have to keep my word." They drove thirty miles to Wilkesboro in his uncle's truck and selected a Stella flat-top. Watson paid over what had been in his piggy bank and his father added the balance. Then Watson finished the job of teaching himself to play guitar.

That's what his father expected of him. General Dixon's attitude was that his blind son should be able to handle the same tasks as his other children, from working a crosscut saw to hoisting a shovel. "You can't take that young 'un out there, he'll get hurt," Annie Watson used to say to her husband.

"He's got to learn like the rest of us," he would reply. "I'm gonna take him out and put him to work." And so, like any other hill kid—and incidentally like Ray Charles, who grew up blind in a small Florida town—Doc Watson did the family chores. He shucked corn, dug up roots and stumps, cut kindling, and fed and tended the cattle. Annie Watson might raise her eyebrows if he banged into something and came home with blood trickling down his face, but his father kept sending him out. What came of it was that a few years later, when Watson wanted a better guitar than the Stella, he bought it for himself with money he earned cutting down dead chestnut trees. People like Clint Howard and another guitar player who has toured the country with Watson, Jack Lawrence, say that Watson succeeded as a professional musician because he had a father who pushed him.

As a teenager, Watson began setting out with his guitar to play individual dates. At a furniture store in Lenoir, North Carolina, his performance was to be broadcast live on the radio. The announcer mused that the name Arthel might be too cumbersome for his listeners. "Call him Doc," shouted a girl in the audience, and after that everyone did. (Jean Ritchie has heard another version of this. "They called him Doc because he was smarter than everybody else," she says.) If he didn't have a job, he went out busking for change. He'd set up near a produce stall or a taxi stand in Bristol, Tennessee, with a cup hanging from a tuning peg on his guitar and take requests. He took them for the better part of seven years. "Somebody asked me once if I was ashamed," he says. "No. I was selling something same as I do now." Later he met up with Jack Williams and joined his band. In between he was introduced to his "curly-headed baby."

"The first time I saw Rosa Lee she was a little girl nine or ten years old," he says. "She and her sister sang a few old-time country songs like Molly

O'Day used to do on the radio. I don't know if Rosa Lee noticed me. I thought, 'Why, she's got a pretty voice.' A few years later her family moved into the county. Me and my cousin were unpacking dishes. She turned around and said 'Hello,' and you might as well have hit me with a brick. I didn't have a lick of sense. I thought, 'Well, if it'll be, that's the girl for me.' Sometimes that doesn't happen. I guess I was lucky." Doc Watson married his third cousin, Rosa Lee Carlton, when he was twenty-three and she was fifteen. Three years later, in 1949, Merle was born. Their daughter, Nancy, came two years after that.

They only just scraped by. Watson received state aid for the blind, he tuned pianos, and he played dances at local schools. "I used to try to play fiddle some," he says. "It went like a hungry pig. Finally I came up with a few fiddle parts on my guitar." To this day, one of the more impressive sights in country guitar picking is Doc Watson playing fiddle tunes. Before him, nobody had tried to flat-pick something so fast on a guitar.

When Watson met Ralph Rinzler and began to polish renditions of the older regional music, it took some doing because much of the material that became his repertoire Watson didn't know at the time, and the rest of it he hadn't played in years. Nobody he knew had wanted to hear it. "Coming into the folk music boom was a real effort for Doc," says Jack Lawrence. "He went back to relatives, to Cecil Sharp's book of Appalachian folksongs. Cecil Sharp came through the mountains when Doc's mother was a young woman. Doc went back and studied the old songs. Portions he remembered, portions he didn't. Doc really had to do some studying and recollecting. He asked relatives for the words to songs. Ralph told him to play the folk revival for what it was worth. Play the old songs first, he said, and then you can do what you want to."

It worked. In 1961, Watson, Ashley, "Fiddlin'" Fred Price, and Howard went up to New York and played together at folk clubs in Greenwich Village. Watson performed old ballads of love and heartbreak, wistful songs that—you can see it in their eyes—make people all over think of things that have been gone from their minds for a while. Listening to the applause, Watson said, "I believe they like that music."

"No," Clint Howard told him. "They just feel sorry for us old mountain people."

"No," said Watson. "I do believe they like this old-time music." At home he traded in his Les Paul and got himself an acoustic guitar.

A year later they played Carnegie Hall. "Clint, I'm a little nervous," Watson told Howard on the way out to the stage.

"I said, 'Son, you've done waited too late,' " says Howard. "It was unusual for us uneducated mountain people to play in Carnegie Hall. I got through eighth grade."

Watson was obviously something special, and soon he was accepting invitations to play on his own. "Doc told me the happiest day of his life was the day he made so much money that the government would have to stop his check for the blind," says Howard. "He grabbed me around my neck and said he could support his family."

Watson was "discovered" during a time when people were eager to hear old songs, but as Ralph Rinzler urged him to do, he built a career merging a few mountain traditionals with blues and some of the more mainstream country music of the 1920s, 30s, and 40s. Anybody who can handle such a range of material has a versatile voice, and that is certainly true of Watson. His singing is warm, straightforward, and comforting as a favorite sweater. It also features perfect enunciation, something Watson considers a matter of obligation. "One thing that bothers me bad is the way modern singers, when they sing, it sounds like they have mush in their mouths," he says. Watson has saved his own life more than once by sensing the hollowing vibrations his footsteps made as he approached a precipice. As a singer that kind of magnificent hearing means that he never cheats a melody. Though the hues he can color it with aren't anything like those available to a great vocal stylist, when Watson sings you always feel there is a large heart behind the words.

Watson tends to favor songs loaded with enough natural emotion that a dazzling voice isn't required to deliver them. Another element is tone. All those years of listening to the pines left a slightly plaintive tremor in his voice. It would be difficult to find anyone who could deliver a more poignant rendition of "Omie Wise," the classic North Carolina ballad about a beautiful nineteen-year-old pregnant orphan from Asheboro, whose feckless lover lured her to a spring, then drowned her. Watson likes songs about life's sorrows almost as well as those about life's pleasures, but either way, when he sings a song it may have a tinge of nostalgia drifting through it. That's as true of songs of obvious regret like "Bright Sunny South," "Country Blues," and "My Rough and Rowdy Ways," in which men look back upon their younger days, as it is of "Roll in My Sweet Baby's Arms," the carefree Flatt and Scruggs standard that Watson turns into something more wistful. "Anything you sing about, you should feel, and the emotion should come through and the scene should come through," is Watson's way of thinking about singing, and he never interferes with what a song has to say.

That's also true of his guitar playing, which is as warm and sweet and clear as chimes. Watson has large, beautiful hands with long, supple fingers, and he can whip them into heat across a guitar string without ever so much as one smudged note. With a guitar in his hand, however, as Clint Howard implied, Watson doesn't feel as bound to the letter of a song as he does with his voice. His additions are subtle and can amount to slipping in a blues riff, a hint of Dixieland at the bridge, or a little country counterpoint for a classic blues like John Hurt's "Make Me a Pallet on Your Floor." Either way, it always swings. To listen to him keeping pace with Bill Monroe's racehorse mandolin on their 1964 recording of the fiddle standard "Soldiers' Joy" is to hear the very limits of the instrument expanding. Other guitar players hadn't thought it possible to maintain such a pace while exploiting so many varied resources with a flat-pick until they heard him.

Now, says the fiddle player Mark O'Connor, "everybody's doing it. I think of Doc Watson's flat-picking the way I do George Jones's singing. You can't imagine not having it. He's put so many influences together. Earl Scruggs is like that, too. All those notes in a row! Nobody else could do it. But he also molded it and shaped it so he could make classic records that have shaped a generation. Same with Bill Monroe, when he mixed blues and Appalachian stuff. It scared people. Bill and Doc are as progressive as anybody I've ever heard of."

Through the years, Watson has always traveled with another country guitar player. He spent his early days on the road with Clint Howard. They came home from one trip to learn that Watson's son Merle Watson had taught himself to fingerpick a guitar. Merle was a large man whom Watson sometimes referred to as "a tall drink o' water." Everybody who heard him play said he was a natural. By 1965, when he was seventeen, he had replaced Howard. People say that he and Watson seemed more like brothers than father and son. It was Watson's belief that he wasn't the great guitar picker his son was.

One night in 1985, when he was thirty-six, and already a grandfather, Merle was living in Caldwell County, North Carolina, and working late in his shop making staircase banisters with a bandsaw. The blade caught in a knot and kicked up a chunk of wood that embedded itself in his arm. There was a lot of blood and Merle decided to go to neighbors for help. He got up on his tractor and rode down a steep dirt road to their house,

Father and son. "The talent for music is a God-given thing."

where they gave him some wine for the pain and bandaged him up. The tractor was old, and Merle often had trouble with it. On the way back, at a curve in the road, the brakes locked and the tractor skidded off the embankment. As it rolled over, it trapped Merle and crushed him to death. Merle had recently purchased a new car, and many people think he didn't take it because he was worried about getting blood all over the seat.

"Doc Watson was hurt over his son, but Rosa Lee, she couldn't control it," Clint Howard was telling me. We were taking his truck from his home in Mountain City for a ride through Deep Gap. "She couldn't control it as much as he could," Howard said. "She didn't know how to whup it the way he did. Some people can't stand trouble, can't agree with it the way other people can. Doc hated it just as bad as she did, but he knowed how to control it better, it seemed like. It was something anybody would be tore all to hell about." As Howard talked, we passed steep hillsides. It was early fall and most of the leaves were already down.

Near Howard's house was a small church. Howard said that an old-time revival service was in the works there. Watson, he said, had promised to come over and sing. As we approached Boone, which Howard calls "a wheelhoss of a town," he said, "It's a cold place here in wintertime. About the worst thing that can happen to a man is to live through winter in Boone and die in springtime."

Appalachian State University is in Boone, and the school's expanding presence has meant that the town looks very different from the days when Doc Watson and Clint Howard used to come in to buy dresses for their wives and overalls for themselves. It has rock-climbing outfitters, vegetarian restaurants, young men with their hair in dreadlocks, young women wearing skin-tight Lycra, and cars with FEMINAZI bumper stickers. The old tractor dealership is now a building contractor's office.

Some people call Boone "The Dixie-fried Boulder." It certainly doesn't seem like Doc Watson country. "Everything grows," said Howard. "This road is getting more like New York. More houses, more roads. Thicker and thicker every year." We were getting close to Deep Gap. "There will always be people and there won't ever be more land," he said. "People from Florida. They come up here and build houses on these damn mountains, places I wouldn't think of building a house, and they love it. There's houses hanging all over these woods back in yonder. I can't blame them. I ain't never noticed how beautiful these mountains are because I was born and raised here. Only when I got into this music business and people started asking me did I start to pay attention to it. I just love these mountains. About all I can say is they prove to me there is a Lord Jesus Christ. I think we all sound like these mountains. That's something we've inherited. It's born and bred in us. What Bill Monroe or Chet Atkins did, we couldn't sound like them, and we didn't try. Doc Watson and I sound like ourselves. As far as I'm concerned, we sound like the mountains. That's where it comes from. No way you can change it."

We drove around for a while, looked at Merle Watson's grave on a lawn behind the green house Merle helped build for his father up the road from the old brown one where Watson grew up—Doc wasn't at home, Howard said, and we didn't want to bother Rosa Lee—and then we headed back toward Tennessee.

Howard likes to sing, but for him it is a hobby. He owns enough farmland in Mountain City to keep a hundred beef cattle. His wife still cans her own pickles and sausage. When Howard's nose gets stuffed up, he takes a dose of "country Nyquil" from the jar of white lightning out in the barn. "I been a welder all my life," he was saying. "I know how to weld better than play music. I did this music on the side. I'm a welder because they don't pay a farmer enough money in this country to survive."

This was exactly the way Doc Watson had told me he would live if he could see: working a job and playing his guitar casually with friends on the side. This image made me think of something Jack Lawrence had told me about Watson. "You ask Doc what he wants to be remembered for and he couldn't give two shits in a bucket how good a guitar player he was," Lawrence had said. "He wants to be remembered as a pretty good old boy. He doesn't put the fact that he plays guitar as more than a skill. To Doc, there's no difference in him being a great guitar player than there is in old Joe down the road being a great auto mechanic. To him it's an acquired skill—something he has a knack for. The best thing you can be remembered for is being a decent human being. As well as I know him, Doc would say that's the whole thing. Live your life, don't make a great deal of enemies, and if people miss you when you're gone, you've probably lived a pretty good life."

I asked Howard if this reading seemed right to him. "Son," he said, "yes, it does."

Boy with the family guitar. Describing his childhood on the Arkansas Delta, Johnny Cash said, "The last thing I remember before going to sleep was my mother beating time on the old Sears Roebuck guitar, singing 'What Would You Give in Exchange for Your Soul?' My mother's guitar brought a closeness and comfort that couldn't be found any other way.
By the time I was four I was singing along with her."

PART FIVE

TWO REAL COUNTRY STARS

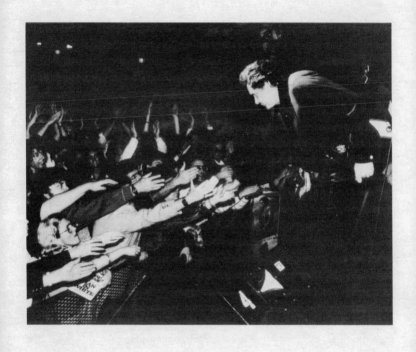

Cash and the people. "I want everybody of every age or walk of life or race to hear that song I'm going to record and say 'I love that.'"

FADE TO BLACK

orty years in music have made "The Man in Black," Johnny Cash, as much a piece of Americana as John Wayne's pistol, Frederick Remington's cowboy sculptures, Buddy Holly's motorcycle, and Al Capone's chair, which are just a few of the objects on display in Cash's private museum, the House of Cash, on Johnny Cash Parkway in Hendersonville, Tennessee. Most of the museum's collection consists of possessions that have assumed a luster simply because they belong to Cash, including the bedroom furniture that the singer and his second wife, June Carter, used when they were first married, and some of their wedding photos (in which Cash, of course, is dressed in black).

Through a door adjoining the museum is the House of Cash gift shop, and on a Saturday morning in spring 1995, a hundred or so members of the Johnny Cash Fan Club are lingering there, carefully examining the Johnny Cash belt buckles, Johnny Cash train whistles, Johnny Cash keychains, the Mama Cash recipe books, and the faux-parchment broadsheets on which the lyrics to Cash's great anthem to fidelity, "I Walk the Line," are printed. The fan-club members could continue on to the rest of the museum, but Cash has invited them to Hendersonville, and they have come from all over the country—indeed, from all over the world—to share a ham-and-biscuits breakfast in this room, and nobody wants to chance missing a minute with him.

Cash, who lives on a 165-acre estate a mile away, finally arrives, an hour late. He has long, spindly legs and lank hips supporting a robust trunk that has lately taken on extra bulk. His face looks pale and drawn. "How y'all doin'?" he says, over and over, in the familiar river-bottom bass-baritone, as he moves through the crowd, shaking hands. Purses begin un-snapping as people reach quickly for their Instamatics.

Country music fans like to describe their favorite singers as one of their own, and the singers are only too glad to go along with the image of down-home solidarity. Which explains why Johnny Cash, who spent his youth picking cotton in northeastern Arkansas, is sharing one of his rare mornings at home in Tennessee with a group of strangers wearing over-alls and synthetic knits. He wants to make sure they know that he is still one of them.

But whether Cash is on stage in Hollywood, crossing through an air-line terminal, playing a set at the White House, or mingling with the faithful here in Hendersonville, the Man in Black does not work a room so much as it works him. In his long black swallowtail coats, Cash resem-bles an old Southern preacher, and that's how people treat him. They come up and tell him about themselves, establish a connection so that in the future they can say they are old friends.

Country music is, in fact, full of rituals adapted from Christian reli-gion, and one of them holds that worshipers show their devotion to their favorite performers not only by purchasing records or concert tickets, but by lavishing presents upon them—offerings of sorts. During his career, Cash has received everything from a desk that belonged to Chiang Kai-shek and one of Abraham Lincoln's beds to an automobile assembled from three decades' worth of vagabond Cadillac parts by a retired Okla-homa coal miner, who offered the vehicle as homage to Cash's 1976 hit about an assembly-line worker who pilfers parts to make his own car, "One Piece at a Time." When Johnny and June spend a few days at the Carter family homestead in rural Virginia, jars and baskets of food are left for them outside the door.

Today, after Cash and June take a seat, the fan club conducts a brief ceremony during which the singer is presented with a check for $2,025—a sum collected in $5, $10, and $20 increments from individual mem-bers—earmarked to buy some shrubs for Cash's garden. After a toddler steps up and sings one of Cash's songs, Cash gets to his feet and gives a little speech. "I really love you folks," he says.

At the moment, Cash is in the midst of reviving a career that had ebbed so far that he spent most of the late 1980s and early 1990s trudging along on the county-fair circuit. Then, in April 1994, he released his most acclaimed album in decades: *American Recordings,* produced by the erstwhile rap impresario Rick Rubin. The album spawned a video (featuring Cash and the model Kate Moss) that was shown on MTV; it earned Cash his eighth Grammy Award (for Best Contemporary Folk Album), and it exposed him to a hip young alternative-music audience that came in throngs to see his shows at venues like Johnny Depp's Viper Room, in Los Angeles, and the downtown club Fez, in New York. Cash has sold more than fifty million records and has produced more *Billboard* hits than Billy Joel, Michael Jackson, Elton John, The Supremes, and Barbra Streisand. (Only a handful of pop-music acts—Elvis, The Beatles, and Julio Iglesias—have kept record shops busier than Johnny Cash.) This time out, however, the cash registers were relatively quiet. In a day when country was the fastest-growing music in the United States—record sales more than quadrupled from 1989 to 1996, pushing annual revenue past $2 billion—sales for *American Recordings* have leveled off at less than 300,000 copies.

With *American Recordings,* Cash had succeeded in reminding the music world that he was still capable of making distinctive music. The album stripped away the frilly pop crinolines of string sections, background singers, and puerile titles like "Dirty Old Egg Sucking Dog" that have swaddled so many of his past records. Left alone with his guitar, Cash executed a spare self-portrait of someone struggling with his attraction to sin. The eerie collection of songs by Tom Waits, Nick Lowe, Leonard Cohen, Louden Wainwright III, and Kris Kristofferson, among others, was deftly chosen to take advantage of the singer's brooding voice, his self-destructive reputation, and his cravings for redemption. Songs like Lowe's "The Beast in Me" and Glen Danzig's "Thirteen" become the disturbing confessions of a man whose sense of the holy is overwhelmed by his knowledge that "I was born to bring trouble to wherever I'm at."

There is also a vague strain of self-parody coursing through *American Recordings,* giving rise to the suspicion that the Man in Black is, as he sometimes puts it, "burlesquing myself." Cash embodies all the dilemmas of an artist subsumed by his own image, and part of the intrigue—and the excitement—of his music has always been that you're never sure whether art is imitating life or vice versa. Cash himself wrote four new songs for *American Recordings,* but these meditations on his "evils and abuses" are modest offerings that fall short of the other songwriters' work. The truth is that *American Recordings* is a fine vocalist's album, nothing more.

His next record, *Unchained,* was more of the same. From Jude Johnstone's title track—which broods, "I've been restless/I've been unwise . . .

I am weak/I am vain/Take this weight from me/Let my spirit be unchained"—on through spirituals, old country songs, and new rockers previously recorded by the likes of Jimmie Rodgers, Dean Martin, Tom Petty, Beck and Soundgarden, the long dark shadow of Cash's past again makes it seem as though each song was written for him. A couple of them really are his: a slightly retooled version of "Mean Eyed Cat," the delightfully spiteful number he wrote in 1959 to which he has added, alas, a happy ending; "Country Boy," a treat dating back to 1957; and one new song, "Meet Me in Heaven." This is the spiritual he'd mentioned over the summer, and it seems callow and also a little banal next to the vigorous 1950s songs. *Unchained* is a good record, one that again displays Cash's unforgettable voice—it wavers more here than in the past—his affinity for a broad range of American popular song—and his troubling inability to add anything new himself to the canon.

Long ago, however, Johnny Cash was a great songwriter. In the mid-1950s, at Sun Studios in Memphis, both Cash and Elvis Presley recorded songs that infused white popular music with a parboiled emotional intensity. Unlike Elvis, Cash wrote most of his best material himself. He didn't have the frenzied delivery—and gyrating hips—that drove Presley's audience into hysterics. Cash wrote instead about what got people all shook up, and why men who'd already been jumped by life still headed down the same dark alleys.

From 1955 to 1957, Cash was prolific. He wrote in cars, at rest stops, in waiting rooms, and in time those songs have come to be one of the most influential bodies of work in both country and rock history, remaining an enduring fillip to songwriters from Bob Dylan to Bruce Springsteen. Over the next several years, Cash finished a few more fine songs—he wrote "Tennessee Flat-Top Box" in 1961—but somewhere the powerful lyrics stopped coming and Cash became less an artist than a personality. Night after night, decade after decade, when he sang "Folsom Prison Blues," "Big River," and his other early masterpieces, he relied upon those songs as the core of his set list and the fundament of his public persona. He remained a national icon, a stirring, compelling entertainer, and his fame grew, but he had forsaken his art for his image.

"The Man in Black" originated as a composite grafted from the tough, doomed characters galloping through his early songs. By the mid-1960s, however, Cash was buttressing this persona, not with fresh musical ideas, but with his own lurid and well-publicized personal travails. It says as much about the evolution of Cash's personality as it does the nature of

American musical celebrity that he put aside what made him most original so that he could live his life as a star, as the Man in Black. And now,
the more I saw of Johnny Cash, whose career started at the same time and
place as Elvis Presley's, the more likely it seemed that he was on his way
to ending up like The King—a spent talent coasting on mystique and
fueling himself with drugs.

On his way out the door of the Hendersonville gift shop, Cash clasps a
few more hands and tells a local newspaper reporter that "it's been a great
year for me, a great year." Meanwhile, twenty miles away in downtown
Nashville, the word on the street is that the Man in Black is dying. Without question, he is in terrible shape. The layers of black clothing he buttons snug around his torso give him a puffy, overstuffed appearance, and
the thick moss of makeup he wears for performances can't obscure a face
that looks sallow, bloated, and vaguely corrupt. "Whopperjawed" is how
June Carter refers to her husband's visage, but now he is all jowls, sagging
from cheek to waist.

He is in chronic pain, and has been for years. In 1990, an oral surgeon
sliced into Cash's left cheek to remove a cyst and the impacted wisdom
tooth beneath it. A few days later, Cash bit into a piece of steak and his
jawbone broke—"It popped like a firecracker," the singer tells me. His
next five years were a farrago of infection, surgery, and nerve damage that
defied every doctor he visited. Through all of it Cash lived with the constant sensation that someone was holding a blowtorch to his chin. "It hon-
estly felt like my face was gonna explode," he says.

And still, night after night somewhere Johnny Cash was singing. For
forty years he has lived a peripatetic existence, moving relentlessly from
city to city, from ovation to ovation, and he kept up the pace even now. Arriving at a fresh hotel, he would wait there, restless as a tawny cat in the
local zoo, until dusk, when he opened a garment bag full of black ensem-
bles and put one on. Then he would appear, striding across another stage,
left leg splaying out like a loose screen door, guitar slung casually across
his back, to greet the latest town with the same superfluous words he had
flung at the last one: "Hello, I'm Johnny Cash."

He sang what the people came to hear: "I Still Miss Someone," "Get
Rhythm," "I Walk the Line"—the songs he wrote thirty-five to forty years
ago. Cash has performed each one tens of thousands of times. I recently
asked Bob Dylan if he thinks it might become boring for Cash to sing the
same songs every night for so long, and he scoffed at the notion. "They're

just so automatically perpetual," Dylan says. "They always existed and they always will exist. Who would get bored singing those?"

In January 1995, Cash sang at the Pantages Theatre, an old art deco film palace on Hollywood Boulevard in Los Angeles. When he finished his first song, "Folsom Prison Blues," the hipsters in capes and black leather, the skinheads, the women wearing silver lamé and fox fur, the portly men with cowboy hats, and the old ladies favoring sensible brown shoes all sprang cheering to their feet. At a post-concert party backstage, celebrities like Sheryl Crow shyly shook hands with him. When it was my turn, I could see that there were double bags under his eyes. "I gave it the best I had," he said. Twenty minutes later he was gone, on his way to Phoenix.

That March, after he endured more unsuccessful jaw surgery, I met Cash in New Orleans, where he was performing at The House of Blues. A few minutes before the show, he invited me onto his bus, which was parked outside the stage door. "I'm dead tired on my feet" were his first words, and he seemed jittery and nervous. "They've got me all shot up with painkillers," he said.

I asked him about his hometown, Dyess, Arkansas. "I haven't been there in years," he said. Through the window I could see a crush of fans outside the bus; somebody was waving a 1969 issue of *Life* magazine with Cash on the cover. In the photograph, he looked lean and wickedly handsome. I didn't stay on the bus long.

Over the next few weeks, Cash found himself waking up in the middle of the night sobbing from the pain in his jaw. After a concert in Cincinnati, he finally checked into a hospital there, where the surgeon snipped off most of a nerve. Right away, Cash was back on the road, but soon he was calling family members to say he felt so poorly that sometimes he was scared to perform. Occasionally I too received dire messages, passed along by his staff. "I've just been trying to survive," one of them said.

On May Day, not long after the breakfast at the gift shop in Hendersonville, and still only a few weeks after the nerve surgery, Cash flew up to New York to appear on *The Late Show with David Letterman* with Willie Nelson, Waylon Jennings, and Kris Kristofferson; they are all old friends, and sometimes record and perform together as The Highwaymen. Cash was in a foul mood. When one of Letterman's producers wondered if, as a gag, he would come out dressed in a flannel shirt—"The Man in Plaid!"—he was not amused. In the elevator he glared at everyone who looked at him. I decided to steer clear and talked instead with Kristofferson and Nelson, who were sitting in a dressing room. Both men met Cash in the 1960s, when he was gobbling fistfuls of amphetamines and barbiturates every day. "Johnny seemed to epitomize the driven, self-destructive artist," said Kristofferson. "At some point or another, that was really appealing to male artists."

Nelson agreed enthusiastically. "We all like the old Bob Wills, George Jones, Hank Williams stories," he said. "Johnny's had more lives than a cat."

Kristofferson shook his head. "When I first went to Nashville he was skinny as a snake and just as impossible to predict," he said. "Everybody was afraid of him. He'd probably eaten so many pills he was flying, but he was exciting to watch." He shook his head again. "Boy!"

After the Letterman taping, Cash boarded a plane to London, where he was to begin a three-week European tour with a concert at the Royal Albert Hall. He spent several hours in the flight passed out in the first-class toilet. When the crew finally succeeded in rousing him, the pilot informed Cash that he would be turned over to the police when they landed in London. Cash talked him out of it.

The next night, he sang at the Royal Albert Hall as scheduled, and a sellout crowd gave him a prolonged standing ovation. Cash doesn't remember much of the show. What he does recall is finding himself gazing out of a hotel window at the city of London at four in the morning and confronting the irony of a sixty-four-year-old American hero who debases himself behind locked doors only to receive ovations when he staggers out in public. He decided to cancel the rest of the tour, flew back to the United States, and checked himself into the drug-rehabilitation center at the Loma Linda Community Medical Center, in California.

No one, it turned out, had injected Cash with painkillers in New Orleans, or anywhere else. "I had me shot up full of pills," he told me. It was July, eight weeks after he'd passed out on the plane to England, and I had come back to Hendersonville to visit Cash and June. We were in one of his Mercedes sedans speeding along the highway west of Nashville and Cash was explaining to me that over the first several months in 1995, he had developed too much of a taste for Percodan, a synthetic opiate derivative. He began with four a day—the maximum daily prescribed adult dosage—and soon was helping himself to two or three an hour. Cash has endured many struggles with drugs, and when he describes them, he does so with epic flourishes. Moments of baroque drama—"I wrestled with an angel"—were punctuated by admissions of vulnerability—"I was edgy, I was scared"—which, in turn, gave way to graver revelations: "June was so embarrassed and so hurt," he said. "I had a guilt trip about that too, that I got over. I don't feel guilty about a thing. Nothing. I've been through it. I paid for it. God has forgiven me. Man doesn't always do that. I really don't care. Seems so long ago now."

Even though I knew that Cash's life had been studded by a succession of lethal addictions followed by remarkable recoveries, I was astonished to see how vigorous he was looking. There was a hale flush to his cheeks, his eyes were clear and friendly, and where previously he had been truculent and terribly restive, now he was in warm, even puckish spirits.

He was still a touch fidgety. Back at the house the day before, June said that Cash found it nearly impossible to stay in one place. "We'll come home for one or two days and he'll say, 'Let's go to the cabin, let's go to Jamaica, let's go to the farm, let's go to Florida,' " she said.

Cash had, in fact, slipped off somewhere, leaving June and me in the kitchen, where she was minding a pot of long green beans—"Kentucky Wonders," she called them. June, sixty-six, married Cash on March 1, 1968, after he had spent most of the previous eight years hooked on amphetamines. She did so with some reservations—she had been close to Hank Williams, whom she had watched kill himself with pills and booze—but ultimately she couldn't help herself. "I felt God's hand was in it more than mine," she says.

June is the middle-born of Maybelle Carter's three daughters, which makes her a country music Brahmin. During her childhood, June often sang and performed slapstick routines with her mother and her sisters, Helen and Anita. As a young woman, June lived with Elia Kazan and his wife in their New York apartment while she studied at The Actor's Studio. She is prone to making blithe remarks like, "I have upgraded my emeralds down through the years." And yet, June still favors long white muslin dresses and a vivid backwoods patois she learned growing up in Maces Springs, Virginia. When she offers to give me a tour of the large house she has shared with Cash since they married, she calls it a "big old lumbersome house," and warns that much of it is "anniegoglin," or "kind of long and slumindicular," by which, she says, she means that "nothing is rectangular here."

Built in the mid-1960s of local fieldstone and reclaimed Tennessee barn timber, the house is a sprawling manse set above Old Hickory Lake on a sheer cliff, off which an amphetamine-blurred Cash twice drove Jeeps in 1967. Inside, it is a pastiche of the rustic and the cosmopolitan. There are wings rounded to resemble pagodas, massive baby-blue vaulted ceilings, and some gold-leaf wainscoting. June says that she has a "penchant for side-boards," and in every hallway is another Jacobean cabinet brimming with silver services, china, crystal, and lace. By no means is all of the Cashes' furniture on display. Although they have only seven bedrooms, June tells me that she and Cash are the rare nonhoteliers who own 226 beds.

I was in a hallway looking at a photograph of Elizabeth Barrett Browning—the Cashes' Jamaica home was built on a sugar plantation that belonged to the poet's father—when Cash reappeared. He and June led me up to see the third floor. Cash says that he "stopped arguing over furnishings many years ago," but here is a slender alcove that Cash calls "my room." He has decorated the space with a cot for his daily nap, a tape deck for listening to the demonstration tapes of new songs sent him by writers who hope he will record them, a domino set, a Yo-Yo, the skull of a 500-pound crocodile named One-Eyed Jack that Cash killed in Florida, editions of Tennyson, Burns, Darwin, and Faulkner, and several husky history books about religion and the American Indian. (Cash is a big reader.) On the wall, Cash has hung a photograph of June in a loopy clown costume and one of Faye Dunaway in something a little more snug. "I just like Faye Dunaway," he explains.

Next day, Cash offers to show me his western Tennessee farm, and we head off toward Memphis in the Mercedes. When we get to the farm, Cash says, "I'm home!" The spread consists of 107 acres with a log farm-house that was built in 1847 by an old Tennessee farmer named Weems. According to local lore, during the Civil War Weems shot two Union soldiers who tried to requisition his cow. "Old Weems is buried over there in that field," Cash says, pointing out toward some plump haystacks. Closer to the farmhouse are fig and magnolia trees and a grape arbor. A caretaker looks after the place, but Cash enjoys feeding the cardinals and the black-birds and watering his grapes. "This is my hideout," he tells me. "I love this place." But within a half an hour, he is done with these chores, and we're on our way back to Hendersonville.

Bob Dylan told me that Cash is "the kind of person you'd turn around and he'd be gone." I have the feeling that appointments and destinations don't matter to Cash as much as the going. He is someone who travels for the sensation of motion. "There is a restlessness there," Cash admits. "I've always found a need to control that restlessness. That I inherited from my father. He was always on to the next job. That desire and need to do something led me to use stimulants, and then sedation to make me stop for a while." Cash has been off the road for twelve days now, and he says he is eager to get back on tour again. "Home life's nice and quiet," he says. "But I love the road because I get to do that show every night. I like my bus. A daily fleeting anonymous existence. I go into a city. I see the city out the hotel window. I stay in the nicest hotel they've got. Then I'm gone."

Not only is Cash unwilling to slow down, he is also probably afraid to. Taking the stage every night is a salve for whatever ails him. Cash kept performing in March and April, even when his wounded jaw kept him in excruciating pain, because, he says, "When I was singing on stage I'd get into the songs and the pain would go away and I'd forget about it." The last time I saw him, late in 1996 before a show at Irving Plaza in New York, he told me he was taking two new kinds of "non-mind-altering medication," that the daily "level of pain is a five or a six on a scale of one to ten," and that "I've been to all the doctors I want to see for now. *Working* is good for me." He looked dreadful, and he sounded pretty awful too when he first walked out onstage. But by the time the show was done, his voice was restored, the crowd was ecstatic, and Cash was glowing. "He's like a vampire," someone near me marveled as he finished up. Staying on the move and singing to adoring audiences serve to insulate Cash from the beasts inside him. But the story of his life is that no matter how desperately he dodges them, the demons are always gaining on him.

When he was growing up in Dyess, Arkansas, J.R. Cash's closest friend was his brother Jack, who was two years older. (Cash, who was born February 26, 1932, in Kingsland, Arkansas, was christened J.R., and only in the Air Force did people call him John. Then, when Sam Phillips, owner of Sun Records, gave him his stage name, he became Johnny Cash.) Jack and J.R. fished for eels and crawfish in the drainage ditches, and Jack taught J.R. how to kill snakes with a hoe blade. They rode each other everywhere on the handlebars of their bicycle, and they worked side by side in the cotton fields. In many ways, Jack was J.R.'s foil, tow-headed and sober where Cash was dark and raffish. Jack carried a Bible with him to the fields, and when he was eleven he told his mother that he had been called to preach. As for J.R., he was small-town bored and restless. "I broke fruit jars just for meanness," he says. But if you asked him what kind of mischief he'd been making, J.R. would own up to everything.

One Saturday when J.R. was twelve, he was walking down a road carrying a fishing pole when his father and the Baptist preacher came roaring up in a Ford. "Get in," Ray Cash said. "Jack's been hurt awfully bad."

Picking the cotton. "The land and the work were unforgiving."

When they got home—a five-room house and twenty acres of cotton fields—Ray Cash got out of the car carrying a blood-soaked paper bag. "I want to show you," he told J.R., leading him into the smokehouse. There, among the curing hog carcasses, he opened the bag and removed a shredded shirt, a pair of trousers torn open down to the crotch, and a thick leather belt that had been chopped in two. Cash had seen his mother cry, but never his father. "We're gonna lose him, J.R.," he said, and he wept. Cash ran out of the smokehouse.

It was goodness that killed Jack Cash. On weekends he sometimes earned three dollars for his mother by cutting fenceposts with a table saw. On the day he died, J.R. had tried to persuade him to go fishing, but Jack said he felt he had to work. That morning, he somehow stumbled into the whirring saw blade, and it carved him open from chest to thigh. He lived for a week. Cash came to visit his brother at the hospital twice. Both times Jack ignored him. Just before Jack died he asked his mother if she could hear the angels singing. She said she couldn't. "What a beautiful city," Jack said. "And the angels singing. Oh, Mama, I wish you could hear the angels singing." Then he was gone.

Dyess is a small—population 466—Mississippi Delta farming community forty miles northwest of Memphis. These days, there is a forlorn quality to the place. The black dirt fields are groomed neat as clay tennis courts, but the trailer homes and the faded wooden houses set along roads radiating in spokes from the center of town have dusty front yards strewn with rusty barrels, discarded tires, and broken toys.

It's difficult to imagine Dyess as the once thriving locus of the American Dream, but in 1935, when Ray and Carrie Cash arrived there from southern Arkansas in a truck stacked high with furniture and children, Dyess Colony was the most promising-looking mudhole they'd ever seen. In the depths of the Depression, the New Deal government had offered a few busted sharecroppers twenty acres of land and a mule. All they had to do in exchange was to grow cotton.

Johnny Cash was not yet three when the family drew up at House 266 on Road Three in January 1935, yet he says he remembers peering out from beneath a tarpaulin in the back of the truck that had brought him there. The trees were frosted with ice. The land was a cypress swamp, and Joe the mule and Ray Cash, who wore high boots to protect himself from water moccasins, drained and plowed it into flatland. By summer 1936, J.R. was toting drinking water out to the fields where his father was growing cotton, corn, alfalfa, and sorghum.

Carrie Cash was a gentle disciplinarian, a devout woman who baked "Scripture cakes," which used only ingredients found in her Bible. (When she wrote down her recipes, instead of simply naming each ingredient, she listed only the citation from a verse where, say, salt appeared so that bakers who didn't know the holy book as well as Carrie felt they should had to look them all up.) Ray Cash may have been the son of a Baptist pastor, but he was more lighthearted than his wife—"a pixie," one friend calls him. At the end of the day he liked to hoist his children—Cash had three brothers and three sisters—onto his lap and bounce them there as he sang marching songs he'd learned as one of Pershing's doughboys during World War I. Carrie Cash never once tasted alcohol, but Nat Winston, Cash's friend and former psychiatrist, says that Ray was not above sneaking off for a quick sniff of moonshine. His wife never knew.

Dyess was, of course, a Bible Belt town—Sunday-school attendance figures were published in the weekly newspaper, the *Colony Herald*—and Carrie and Ray Cash went to church Sunday morning, Sunday night, and again Wednesday evening. Carrie liked to sing, and sometimes in the evenings on the porch at home she would lead the family in gospel standards like "What Would You Give in Exchange for Your Soul" while beating out a rhythm on her old Sears Roebuck guitar. The woods were still full of panthers, and when one of them screamed, Carrie just sang louder. Cash was thinking about those days when he made *American Recordings.* In the liner notes he recalled "the closeness and comfort" that his mother's music brought him.

By the time he was ten, Cash was walking a furrow behind Joe in the spring planting season, and then dragging a seven-foot cotton sack along those same rows when it was late summer and time to pick. The land and the work were, he says, "unforgiving," and to take himself away from the beating heat and the dirt and the bugs, while he worked he sang gospel songs in a high tenor that carried across the fields.

Cash was saved when he was twelve, but it was seven years earlier that he first really believed. In January 1937, hard rains swelled the Mississippi over the levees at Wilson, Arkansas, and brought it rushing toward Dyess. "The water kept rising," says Cash. "Flooded our whole land, come up and started rising on the house." The National Guard came around and ordered the family to higher ground. (In 1959, Cash wrote and recorded a song based on the flood, "Five Feet High and Rising," which, at one minute and forty-six seconds, is one of the shortest singles in country music history.) Two weeks later, the waters subsided. When Carrie Cash opened the door of her house, she found a foot of mud inside. "My mama sat down there and cried," Cash says. "Everything was gone, floated away. But the next spring, black river dirt covered the land and we had the best crop we ever had. The cotton was twice as tall. That incident was the foundation for a great faith. I remember my mother saying, 'Commit your ways to the Lord and something good will come out of every evil thing.' That's what came out of that flood—a good cotton crop. We were in better shape than before the flood. Bought us two cows instead of one. So we were rich. A two-cow family."

But after Jack died, in 1944, the tragedy hung over them like humid weather. "Death was something that just wasn't talked about," says Cash's sister Reba. J.R. distracted himself with the country music he heard on the family's battery-powered mail-order radio. Sometimes Cash could hear Hank Williams singing out of Shreveport on the weekly *Louisiana Hayride.* (A few years before, over XERA, a powerful Mexican station just across the border from Del Rio, Texas, he picked up Mother Maybelle Carter singing with Anita, Helen, and ten-year-old June.) The most prominent live radio show was *The Grand Ole Opry,* broadcast over the powerful wattage of WSM Nashville on Saturday nights. J.R. would tune in to hear Ernest Tubb and Bill Monroe on the *Opry,* and then spend his nickels at the Dyess Café jukebox, playing their songs over and again.

In summer 1947, Cash was hired as waterboy for a crew of workmen clearing the banks of the Tyronza River not far from his house. At lunchtime, while the workmen talked, Cash would sit in their cars, eating biscuits and sausage and listening to Charlie and Ira Louvin singing their lush harmonies on their segment of *The Noontime Roundup,* a radio show in nearby Memphis. When a car's battery wore down and the radio grew faint, Cash switched cars.

Late that summer the Louvins came to Dyess to give a concert at the high school. Before the show Charlie Louvin happened to ask Cash where a bathroom was. Cash showed him to one. Walking back to the auditorium, Louvin chatted with Cash about soda crackers and then let him into the show for nothing. Many years later Cash returned the favor. When Louvin was $1,200 behind on his debts, Cash heard about it, approached him, reached into his pocket, and gave him the money. A month later, when Louvin tried to pay him back, Cash said, "You don't owe me anything," and walked away.

Country music gave the teenaged Cash a view beyond Dyess. The Arkansas horizon of endless flat cotton fields created a corresponding sense of personal limits. As far as Cash looked, all he could see were dirt farms. Even today there is a pressing isolation in all that open space, a feeling of solitude that makes people linger at the only store in Dyess even when there's nothing new to talk about. J.R. could be a taciturn kid, and as he grew older he would sometimes feel as low as his voice had suddenly become. He would never be able to be good like his saintly dead brother, and he didn't want to stay and be a cotton farmer like his daddy.

Sam Phillips is telling me what it felt like to hear Johnny Cash sing rockabilly for the first time. This performance happened forty years ago, in 1955, but as he talks, Phillips is getting very excited. "Nobody I'd heard sounded like him," he says. "Even if you didn't like that voice, it got your attention."

It still does. Cash's untrained voice has a natural ability to express suffering. The deep, affectless bass-baritone that struggles to keep up with even a medium tempo has no burnish about it, and no verve, either. Lodged somewhere between talk and music, his singing is flat and artless and grim, the way the white poverty-stricken South was flat, artless, and grim.

As soon as he graduated from Dyess High School, in spring 1950, Cash headed north for the auto plants in Michigan. He lasted three weeks, working on a punch press making hoods for 1951 Pontiacs. Then Cash hitchhiked back to Arkansas and took a job he couldn't quit. He joined the Air Force, trained to be a radio intercept operator, and was shipped to Landsberg, Germany. He was gone for three years.

While Cash was away, the radio back home around Memphis suddenly began to bounce. The man who was as responsible for this change as any-one else was Phillips, a redheaded country boy who had grown up chop-ping cotton outside Florence, Alabama. Phillips had been powerfully affected by the way the blacks who worked in Alabama cotton fields could sing, and he established Sun Studios in Memphis with the idea of record-ing "unknowns who were different." Phillips pursued Memphis street singers, field hands up from Mississippi, and convicts out on one-day fur-loughs. Howlin' Wolf and B. B. King set down some of their first blues tracks for him. It was a succession of white hillbilly singers who melded the blues into a driving country hybrid—rockabilly—who gave Phillips his reputation as the man who discovered rock 'n' roll.

In 1954, Phillips began to work with a young white truck driver who spiced his taste for country ballads with the juke-joint jive he'd heard growing up near Shake Rag, the black quarter in Tupelo, Mississippi. When *Billboard* reviewed Elvis Presley's "Good Rockin' Tonight" late in the year, it said, "His style is both country and R&B, and he can appeal to pop." Phillips's other rockabilly protégés were nearly as potent. They in-cluded Carl Perkins, a Tennessee cotton farmer's son whose first guitar was made of a cigar box, a broom handle, and strands of baling wire; Jerry Lee Lewis, a piano-thumping Louisiana bootlegger's boy who sold eggs to pay for his trip to Memphis; Roy Orbison, a small-town kid from the West Texas prairie with an improbably high voice; and a local secondhand appliance salesman lately returned from military service named John Cash.

Cash had spent three years intercepting high-speed Soviet Morse Code transmissions as an Air Force Security Service cryptanalyst. He was good at it—in 1953 he passed on the word that Stalin had died—but he had grown homesick. Sometimes he dealt with his anomie by hanging out in German beer halls, trying out a few guitar chords on a rowdy group of sol-diers who called themselves the Barbarians. He also spent a lot of time writing letters to someone he'd met at a San Antonio roller-skating rink when the Air Force sent him to Texas for basic training. Vivian Liberto had full lips and dark features, and she was a faithful correspondent. After eighteen months in Germany, Cash proposed over the telephone.

When he got back to the South in 1954, Cash decided to settle with Vivian in Memphis. His brother Roy met him at the bus station. Roy was a mechanic, and on the way to his apartment the Cash brothers bumped into Marshall Grant, who worked with Roy. When things were slow around the garage, Grant and a chary mechanic with bashful eyes named Luther Perkins would pull out their guitars and play. For some time, Roy Cash had been telling them both about his brother in Germany who sang like Hank Snow. "Roy came up and introduced me to this long tall drink o' water," says Grant. "I said, 'Roy tells me you play and sing a little bit. Let's get together.'"

They did, and they liked what they heard. The three men agreed that it didn't make sense for everyone to play rhythm guitar, and so they improvised. Grant bought himself a doghouse bass fiddle and learned to slap it by marking his notes with pieces of tape. Perkins borrowed an electric guitar and "played it strange," as Cash liked to tell him—one note at a time. Cash, never much of a musician, limited himself to three chords. When they wanted some extra beat, Cash slipped a piece of wax paper between his guitar frets and the strings, making it sound like a snare drum. They were, quite literally, a garage band. And yet anyone with formal training would have had to strive to make music so spare. "The first four bars we played together, the sound was there," Grant told me. "You're talking about two mechanics and a soldier who were not musicians. The only thing all three of us could do was what we did."

Married now, and with Rosanne, the first of four daughters, on the way, Cash took a job selling appliances door-to-door in a black neighborhood of shotgun shacks around the Orange Mound section of Memphis. "I was the worst," he says. "Never sold anything. I didn't want them to buy anything." Two or three days into the job, he encountered a retired Memphis street sweeper lounging on his porch with a guitar. It was the banjo picker Gus Cannon, whose band, The Jug Stompers, had been the toast of Beale Street in the 1920s. Soon Cash was returning regularly to Cannon's porch and bringing his guitar with him. "Oh, I loved it, yeah," he says. "I wound up spending most of my days sitting in the car listening to country music on the radio or sitting on the porch with the black people."

In May 1955, when the latest loan from Vivian's father was about gone, Cash went to see Sam Phillips. Cash told Phillips he was a gospel singer, and Phillips, after hearing two hymns, brushed him off, saying, "Come back when you've got something different." The next time around, Cash brought him "Hey Porter," a song he'd written in Germany about a homesick Southerner whose spirits lift as the train he's riding steams into Tennessee. Cash sang the tune, and was apologizing for having only Perkins and Grant along with him for the audition—the rest of the band, he said, couldn't make it—when Phillips grinned and told him he had a contract.

Cash's sound was too dour and too minimal for anyone to mistake him for a classic crooner, though, and that was probably a good thing because traditional country was in trouble. Hank Williams had recently died, at twenty-nine, and the careers of other country stars like Ernest Tubb and Hank Snow were suddenly flagging. "Why do you do that nigger trash out there?" Ira Louvin screamed at Presley, and the answer was that country music audiences weren't as interested in lilting songs about the old home when they could hear a white man go below the belt like Big Boy Crudup. Within a matter of months, Presley had gone from driving a delivery van to appearing on *The Ed Sullivan Show.* As for Cash, he had been singing in theaters with dirt floors until "Cry, Cry, Cry," his first single, nearly made it into the *Billboard* top ten, whereupon he found himself on *The Louisiana Hayride,* sharing the bill with Elvis.

Cash, Grant, and Perkins crossed and recrossed the country in a 1954 Plymouth, and while the two ex-mechanics kept the engine running, Cash was busy with his notepad. "Get Rhythm" came to him in the backseat of the Plymouth near College Station, Texas. Sitting backstage in Brisbane, California, in 1956, within sight of San Quentin Prison, Cash says he "started thinking about the men in there," and the result was "Give My Love to Rose." Backstage in White Plains, New York, Cash imagined the story of a broken-hearted man following a woman he met "accidentally in St. Paul" all the way down the Mississippi to New Orleans. "Big River" begins:

> *I taught the weeping willow how to cry*
> *And I showed the clouds how to cover up a clear blue sky*
> *And the tears that I cried for that woman*
> *Are gonna flood you big river*
> *And I'm gonna sit right here until I die.*

Bob Dylan told me he heard those lines on his radio when he was a teenager in Hibbing, Minnesota, and he says they seemed to him "just words that turned into bone."

As a performer, Cash aroused an audience, not in the overtly sexual way that Elvis did, but with something darker and more disturbing. For all his songs about a man being wronged by a scarlet woman, there was also always the suspicion that Cash had been into something malevolent, and deserved his pain. What kind of person, after all, bragged about shooting strangers just for sport ("I shot a man in Reno/Just to watch him die"), as the singer does in "Folsom Prison Blues," his second hit single? Elvis was pretty. Cash was the first punk rocker. June Carter puts it, "He's always been a sneerer."

He dressed like an outcast, too. When they played one of their first shows, at a Memphis church in 1955, Cash and The Tennessee Two, as Grant and Perkins were known, had wanted to appear in matching stage clothes. They found that the only uniform costume their three closets could produce was black trousers and shirts. Although it wasn't until the 1960s that he wore black exclusively, from then on Cash was The Man in Black.

Backstage in Gladewater, Texas, Cash and Carl Perkins got to talking about what it was like to be away from your wife for much of the year, with pretty young women everywhere you looked. A man might give in to temptation, Perkins said.

"Not me," said Cash. "I walk the line."

Perkins replied, "You've got to write that." Cash did, and in April 1956, "I Walk the Line" became a number-one country single and crossed over onto the pop charts, where it went to number seventeen. In time, it has become Cash's most beloved song. (Cash returned the favor in Amory, Mississippi, telling Perkins about an Air Force buddy who warned him, "Don't step on my blue suede shoes, John," as he pranced off for a night on the town.)

More than a hundred singers have recorded "I Walk the Line," but Cash's lean, unembellished version is the one people know. The spare sound came from Dyess. Growing up in such an austere place formed Johnny Cash as a songwriter as well as a singer. The most persistent theme in Cash's good songs is the feelings of a man who is trapped. The convict sitting inside Folsom Prison listening to a train going by outside imagines the rich folks in the dining car drinking coffee and smoking fat cigars. He doesn't begrudge them their pleasures so much as he envies their motion: "Those people keep a movin'," he sings, "and that's what tortures me." Other songs feature different nooses—a work-gang ball-and-chain, a two-timing woman, a bad deal, a glowering cat. Cash knew what it felt like to feel cornered by circumstance or by an evil impulse, and what it was like to lash out with a small act of meanness and get back much worse than you gave.

In a 1956 article about Cash, the *Memphis Press-Scimitar* said, "There are those who see him as the logical successor to the tremendous popularity of the late Hank Williams." If this was a particularly prescient opinion, it also cut two ways. Williams was the most gifted songwriter in the history of country music. But whatever lurked in Williams, compelling him to write songs like "I'm So Lonesome I Could Cry" and "Your Cheatin' Heart," also made him reach for the jars and bottles that would kill him before he was thirty. Johnny Cash, at his best, possessed that same dark power and those same dark impulses. And his listeners could sense them.

One of them was Gary Gilmore, the convicted murderer who spent his life in and out of prison and was executed at his own request by a Utah firing squad in 1977. Gilmore was such a devoted Johnny Cash fan that once, when he was released from prison, he spent his entire first day of freedom listening to Cash records. Gilmore's brother Gaylen, an alcoholic petty thief who would die of complications resulting from vicious stab wounds he sustained in Chicago, couldn't get enough of Cash's music either.

"He was the family's pop-culture patron saint," says Gary and Gaylen's younger brother, Mikal Gilmore, the journalist and author of the memoir *Shot in the Heart*. "Our mother loved him too. They saw the bad-guy outlaw image, and the side of Cash who understood outsiders and heartbroken people. My brothers also responded strongly to the idea that this person had been in jail. Even if it had only been for a few days, it meant a lot to my brothers. It became inflated in their imagination. He'd had some of the same experiences they'd had and therefore he could be trusted as their voice."

In 1957, Cash too began to yield to things that did him no good. He recorded cloying pop songs like Jack Clement's "Ballad of a Teenage Queen," which with its "Twinkle, Twinkle, Little Star" melody and soprano descant in the background was about as far from "Folsom Prison Blues" as a man could travel. Things only grew worse in the following year when Cash left Sun for the lucre Columbia Records was offering him. His songwriting faltered badly.

After signing with Columbia, Cash recorded a great many songs whose titles—"The Shamrock Doesn't Grow in California," "Flushed from the Bathroom of Your Heart"—suggest how slight they were. Cash also continued to sing about prisoners, gunfighters, working stiffs, and tearstained losers, but his writing wasn't as convincing as it had been on the Sun recordings. Still, the topics he chose were well suited to his grave, weatherbeaten voice, and whether he sang his own songs or covered tunes by other writers, he could make campy, even maudlin material stirring. "Don't Take Your Guns to Town" (a particular favorite of Gary Gilmore's), "I Got Stripes," Peter LaFarge's "The Ballad of Ira Hayes," Harlan Howard's "Busted," and "Ring of Fire," which June Carter wrote with Merle Kilgore, were all hits for him.

Cash kept up a grueling schedule of recording and touring, and in 1958 he began taking speed to help him through it. The pills made him so wired that he went days without sleeping or eating, his weight fell from 220 to 140 pounds, his skin turned a sullen gray, and his eyes burned out of his wasted face like black marbles.

Inside, he was seething, and his rages were legendary. Cash liked to destroy hotel rooms, smashing up the toilet, throwing furniture out the window just to watch it crumple, smashing bottles against walls, and, in a final spasm of hostility, pissing on the hot radiator right before he checked out. He wrecked every car he owned. "I always thought somebody was trailing me," Cash says. "They might have been, too. Just because I was paranoid doesn't mean they weren't trailing me." To make himself sleep, he began taking barbiturates, and soon he was hooked on those too.

Cash had moved his family to California in 1959, but he was rarely home, and by 1965, with his children afraid of him and his marriage imploding, he was spending most of his time in Nashville. One night, he ended a performance at *The Grand Ole Opry* by shattering sixty footlights. The *Opry* told him not to come back. On the way home, Cash cried until the tears blinded him and bashed his car into a tree, fracturing two bones in his face. Cash and Vivian were divorced in 1967.

Waylon Jennings's marriage was also breaking up, and he too was using amphetamines. For a while, Cash shared an apartment with him outside Nashville. Cash wasn't a very good roommate. He would tear apart the apartment looking for Jennings's stash of pills, and then sprawl on the couch, throwing his Bowie knife at the living-room wall again and again. On the road together in Buffalo, Jennings and Cash were driven around the city in the back of a new Cadillac by a local man who'd promised to get them pills and introduce them to women. When things were slow to develop, Jennings recalls, Cash began to compliment the man, in rather extravagant terms, on this beautiful car he had bought himself. As he spoke, Cash was using his pocket knife to make long gashes in the car's leather upholstery. "The thing was in shreds," Jennings says. "A lot of that shit was mean."

Cash has been jailed seven times in his life. Each time, it was for just one night. In 1965, after he bought more than a thousand pills from a pusher in Juarez, security officers across the border at the El Paso airport found them in his baggage. The next day, a wire-service photograph of Cash in handcuffs was published by newspapers all over the country. A year later, the Starkville, Mississippi, police locked him up when they caught him picking daisies in someone's front garden at two in the morning. In Carson City, Nevada, the police found Cash passed out naked in his car. (He says he'd fallen into a flooded creek and taken off his clothes so they would dry.) Cash was put in a cell there with a drunken lumberjack who was a lot bigger than he was. The lumberjack wanted to fight. Cash didn't know what to do, and so he began singing. He sang the man "Folsom Prison Blues" and he sang him a spiritual. "Me and you are a couple of drunks," the man said, "but you sure sound like Johnny Cash." He lay down on his bunk and went to sleep.

No matter how frazzled he was, Cash could almost always perform. Marshall Grant came upon him passed out on the floor one morning in Toronto with a mouthful of raw onion and a paring knife in his hand. Grant thought Cash was dead. A few hours later Cash did a show in up-state New York and received a five-minute standing ovation.

"People sort of expected him to screw up," Grant says. He was a fascinating combination of self-destruction and compassion, and his ruinous lifestyle lent credibility to his music. Cash thrilled people and he also made them feel that, as a fan put it to me, "he could understand the prisoner in all of us."

Perhaps because of his own evil streak, Cash felt a special affinity for real convicts, and beginning in 1956, when he sang at a penitentiary in Huntsville, Texas, he gave jailhouse concerts with some frequency. (Among the cons in the crowd at a 1958 show in San Quentin was a tough young man from Bakersfield doing two years and nine months for armed robbery: Merle Haggard.) When he visited California prisons in 1968, and again in 1969, Cash brought along a recording crew. What they came away with were the two most exciting albums of his career.

Live at Folsom Prison begins with the singer introducing himself by saying, "Hello, I'm Johnny Cash." The greeting went over so well that Cash has begun every concert since then with those words. He had stoked himself with amphetamines before he hit the stage at Folsom, and if the drugs made his voice raspy and limited its range, they added a rebellious glint to his demeanor—something that was apparent from the nasty way he curled his lip and spouted profanity throughout the show. "Convicts feel that I am one of their own," Cash said once, and at both Folsom and San Quentin he made it obvious whose side he was on. He alluded to his own time in jail, referred to prison wardens as "mean bastards," took requests, and sang his raunchiest lines with unmistakable glee. The audience responded with raucous cheers, just as it did after hymns of redemption like "Peace in the Valley."

During the following year's San Quentin concert, Cash nearly goaded the prisoners too far. On the flight out to California, he wrote "San Quentin," more a rant than a song, which begins "San Quentin, you've been living hell to me," and continues apace in a vivid screed against life behind bars:

> *San Quentin what good do you think you do?*
> *Do you think I'll be different when you're through?*
> *You bend my heart and mind and you warp my soul*
> *Your stone walls turn my blood a little cold.*

The response was electric. Prisoners began screaming. Some of them leaped up on tables. Above, on catwalks, the guards "looked awfully tense," Cash recalls. "Somebody later told me, 'If you'd said "Break," they'd have broken. They'd have rioted, torn the place up.' I was a little on edge myself. I knew when to stop pushing it."

Nothing violent happened, except on the charts. In 1969, the prison records were selling 250,000 copies a month. (Each of them eventually sold six million copies.) For more than two decades, *Johnny Cash at San Quentin* was the best-selling album in the history of country music.

With her long brown hair, iridescent blue eyes, and thick lashes, there is a beatific air about June Carter. June had been singing with Cash since 1961, and for nearly as long she took it upon herself to try to wean him from drugs, much as she had tried to help Hank Williams in the early 1950s. "With Hank Williams we'd shove water and food down him to get him on stage," she told me. "With John, I'd steal his pills. I'd get a key to his room. I'd steal them and throw them away. I was afraid he was gonna die. Hank had died and I didn't want John to die. I felt responsible in a way. I don't think I should have, but I did. The thing about it was that he was the one who straightened himself out. I didn't do it. He just had to reach down in himself."

June refused to marry Cash until he sought drug counseling, and so he spent thirty days in 1967 sweating out detoxification under the supervision of Nat Winston, the banjo-strumming Tennessee state director of mental health services. June married Cash six months later.

Cash wouldn't really put aside the amphetamines until 1970, when John Carter Cash, his only child with June, was born. That was also the year when he humiliated himself by going to Vietnam to play for the troops and getting so stoned that he was practically incoherent on stage. But in 1969, Cash was mostly clean, born again, and selling more records than even The Beatles. At San Quentin he'd recorded "A Boy Named Sue," Shel Silverstein's novelty song about a man who gives his son a girl's name to make

Johnny Cash and June Carter. "I'd steal his pills," she says.
"I was afraid he was gonna die."

him tough, and it became the biggest hit of Cash's life. (Cash now finds the song so insipid he can hardly bear to sing it.) At a time when the kind of music Americans listened to tended to reflect their feelings on the defining social issues of the day—the Vietnam War, civil rights, the sexual revolution, and drugs—everyone was listening to Johnny Cash.

"For old people over thirty," *Life* magazine wrote in its cover story, "he sounds a note of sanity in a mixed-up musical world." But Cash was also one of the original rockers, and people who were partial to Janis Joplin and Jim Morrison liked his wild side as much as country fans valued his genuine sincerity. Cash also proved nimble at linking himself with the progressive music of the time—in this case, protest folk. When Bob Dylan came to town in 1969 to record *Nashville Skyline,* he and Cash spent hours together in a studio singing duets of each other's songs. Dylan included one of them—"Girl from the North Country"—in the album. Cash had established himself as the ultimate crossover singer, a huge star whose broad popularity was proof that country could appeal to every sort of audience. Johnny Cash's country wasn't hillbilly music anymore; it was American music.

In that year, Cash became the host of an immensely popular ABC weekly television music-variety show, *The Johnny Cash Show.* The program showcased Cash's charisma—he remains the sort of magnetic person who stills any room he enters—and his sympathy with dissent. Although the show was filmed in the Ryman Auditorium, the home of *The Grand Ole Opry* and the cradle of conservative Nashville culture, he insisted that Dylan and the antiwar activist Pete Seeger be among his first guests. The show lasted two seasons, and included everything from Americana segments, to hymns that Cash sang with The Statler Brothers, to guest performances by a spectrum of popular musicians from Joni Mitchell to The Who to Louis Armstrong.

Then, just as amphetamines had once consumed him, Cash began to embrace religion with single-minded intensity. For a time he carried a copy of Foxe's *Book of Martyrs* everywhere he went, and he cultivated a close friendship with Billy Graham. In 1973, Cash took it upon himself to produce, narrate, and record a sound-track album for *The Gospel Road,* a film about the life of Christ. Some of his old friends were appalled. One of them was Waylon Jennings, who in 1974 told the journalist Peter Guralnick that Cash had "sold out to religion." Others criticized June, saying that Cash tried so hard to be pure around her that he wasn't himself.

For all the acclaim and profit that came to him around 1970, Cash was a show-business rather than a creative success. His hits were mostly written by other people, and his own work became increasingly lank and solipsistic, dependent as it was on his public image. In 1971, Cash wrote "Man in Black," a song that went to number three on the country charts:

> *I wear the black for the poor and the beaten down*
> *Living in the hopeless, hungry side of town*
> *I wear it for the prisoner who has long paid for his crime*
> *But is there because he is a victim of the times.*

He took the self-mythologizing to a further extreme in 1975, when he published an autobiography, also called *Man in Black*. The book is really a morality tale in which Cash progresses from life as a drug-crazed "sick man" to that of a gentled-down "happy man."

If that sounded facile, so too did his records. By the late 1970s and early 1980s, Cash's career was accelerating along an arc of protracted decline. Back in 1969, when he'd called Dylan one of his favorite country singers and covered the drug songs of a longhaired Rhodes Scholar–turned–Nashville janitor—Kris Kristofferson—Cash had broadened the borders of country music. Now he was recording songs by The Rolling Stones and Bruce Springsteen. This was material that couldn't possibly become his, and the charm of listening to Johnny Cash sing "No Expectations" wore thin for anyone who had heard Mick Jagger do it. Columbia decided in 1986 not to renew Cash's contract, and though it was no trick for Cash to find a new deal at Mercury, the only limits he was pushing anymore were emotional.

He wasn't the happy man he said he was. For all the platitudes about the pious life, the world found out that Cash couldn't control himself, and Cash learned that the world didn't really want him to. The Man in Black was *supposed* to show his outlaw edge. When he told a Nashville trade publication in 1987, "I'll never be free of temptation, never free of my carnality," by then he knew just how delicious that sounded to Cash fans.

For years Cash has vacillated between Saturday night and Sunday morning, between debauchery and devotion, and so he has kept the tabloids and the talk shows well fed. This pattern has resulted in some rather peculiar episodes. In 1983, for example, Cash took a swing at his eight-foot-tall pet ostrich with a two-by-four. The bird responded by kicking him in the chest, breaking three of Cash's ribs. The pain was too much for him, and he took Demerol and then amphetamines to help him tolerate it, resulting in the headline "CASH TIES DRUG BOUT TO OSTRICH." He spent some time in the Betty Ford clinic after that, and referred to it later as "the best forty-three days of my life." In 1986, he wrote a novel, *Man in White,* about the conversion of Paul. By 1989, he was back on the other side and checking into a Tennessee alcohol and drug treatment center.

Through it all Cash kept to the road. He would play anywhere. In 1989, he found himself singing in a 175-acre alfalfa field in Regal (population 30), Minnesota. Over the next few years there were Johnny Cash concerts in New Hampshire hockey rinks, in a Tasmanian velodrome, at the Knox County Fair, and at North Dakota rodeos. Cash's performances are almost always stirring, and he says they give him great pleasure, but as he admits, there is also something manic about the constant touring—as though if he stopped, he wouldn't trust himself with the free time. "Sometimes," he writes in his album notes for *Unchained,* "at night, when I hear the wind, I wish I was crazy again."

Cash's oldest child, the country-punk singer Rosanne Cash, says of her father, "The road is as natural to him as breathing. He wouldn't know how to do without it. If I were on a bus for forty years I'd kill myself. That's his life. He functions very well as a public figure. He's never rude. He's unfailingly kind to every person who approaches him. In the spotlight he's his true self. That's where he's most in his body. He's home.

"It's weird," she went on. "He's so comfortable living this public life for forty years that it's part of his private life. Real life tends to be disappointing for him a lot. I see him trying to get away from it. His impulses for healing and spirituality are constantly pulled on by his impulses of self-destruction. They're the same thing. One is a warped attempt to do the other. The constant travel, the spiritual seeking, the drugs. It's too much to sit still and be on this planet." As a girl, Rosanne Cash used to dread the rare days when her father was at home. She remembers him as "so wired you would almost break down in tears to be in the same room with him. He'd set fires. He seemed so miserable."

The protean behavior, the life lived behind the black mask of celebrity, the conflicting impulses toward preacher and hellion, all make Cash seem tormented. He still behaves like a man with something weighing on him, and when I began to talk with people close to him about what it might be, they pointed to the same thing. June Carter, who Cash says is the one person "who really knows me," believes her husband has been troubled ever since his brother was killed. "I think Jack's death was very painful and had something to do with it," she says. "I don't think John was a very happy man in his first marriage. I think he hoped marriage would take away the pain from his brother's death, and it didn't."

Nat Winston, the psychiatrist who worked with Cash in 1968, came to much the same conclusion. He believes that Cash's repeated spasms of self-destructive behavior are grounded in the memory of being the prodigal brother. People in Dyess today complain that Cash never comes back, but for all his fitful movements, Cash still seems to be struggling to get away from the colorless place where he went off fishing while Jack Cash died for three dollars. "He's not one you can sit down and talk with, so we'd walk through the woods and talk," Winston says. "We'd talk about his childhood. The biggest problem was the death of his older brother. He talked about that a lot. He had a severe amount of guilt."

Rosanne Cash says she has concluded that Cash is the classic loner in the crowded room. "It's very hard for people to get close to him and vice versa," she says. "His enigmatic, restless, constant seeking and self-destruction all goes back to that defining moment when he lost his brother. There's tremendous grief and guilt. All these things carved tremendous crevices in his soul. I don't know if he himself sees the ways he's still working it out."

When Cash's music became popular, it was often said of his singing that it sounded lonesome, the voice of a man who had lost a brother. Cash has long resisted that description, as he did during our drive across western Tennessee for the half-hour visit to his farm. He said that in 1983, during his stay at the Betty Ford clinic, he mentioned Jack in a counseling session. "They told me I had some unresolved grief over my brother's death, which would be thirty-nine years of unresolved grief if that were true," he says. "They put me in a group twice a week called Grief Group, where you go to shake off the grief, to dump it, get rid of it, like garbage. They got me to talk about my brother. Then they realized there was no unresolved grief over my brother's death. It was joy over the influence he had on my life. So I didn't go to Grief Group but twice. I haven't grieved over him since I was a kid."

The day before, however, Cash had said something different. We were standing in his room, on the top floor of the house in Hendersonville. Cash pointed to an old framed black-and-white photograph of a slim, sweet-looking boy with pale hair. It was Jack. "That was not long before he died," Cash said, looking at it. "I probably never did get over it. We were so close. It was like, you know, I've never been that close to anybody since."

Cash says he wrote his new song "Meet Me in Heaven" for June, but this happens to be the phrase carved on Jack Cash's tombstone.

People of great talent leading dissipated lives is a familiar story in country music. Merle Haggard, whose father died when Haggard was a child, spent years in jail as a young man, later lost control of his drinking, and has been married five times. George Jones, the other of Johnny Cash's most gifted contemporaries, is the son of an abusive drunkard and grew up himself to be an alcohol and cocaine fiend who flushed thousands of dollars down toilets, fired a pistol at a close friend, and was briefly committed to a padded cell. Jones is working on his fourth marriage. Like Cash, Jones and Haggard were raised in pressing poverty and perhaps they found wealth and fame overwhelming.

It seems just as likely that it was the angst they already had that prompted the music and the dissolute behavior. Country music is sometimes called the white man's blues, and though it may rely upon simple diction and honeysuckle melodies, the best of it—Jones calls it "hard country"—is strong stuff. It takes a dark side to sing about people whose lives are blasted by misery, gin, and faithlessness with the kind of pathos you hear in the voices of Johnny Cash, George Jones, and Merle Haggard. Certainly you don't hear it in Garth Brooks, Tracy Lawrence, Alan Jackson, and the other hat acts. "As rootless as country music is right now," says the country singer Marty Stuart, "it sure needs Johnny Cash."

It's not likely to get him back. *American Recordings,* Cash's best album since the Sun recordings, was classified as alternative rather than country music, a telling marketing decision, for the record happens to be full of songs that are variations on the bruised and stoic themes that have attracted country singers from Jimmie Rodgers to Hank Williams. One of them is "Delia's Gone," an old levee-camp holler that Cash first recorded in a different form early in the 1960s. In 1955, Cash transformed Gordon Jenkins's five-line "Crescent City Blues" into "Folsom Prison Blues." He followed the same approach with "Delia's Gone," substantially reworking the lyrics into a song about a violent misogynist who ties his wife to a par-

lor chair and shoots her to death. As Cash explains in one of the new
verses, the man feels justified because:

> *She was low down and trifling*
> *And she was cold and mean*
> *Kind of evil make me want to*
> *Grab my submachine.*

Later, in jail, Cash has the man reflect:

> *So if your woman's devilish*
> *You can let her run*
> *Or you can bring her down*
> *And do her*
> *Like Delia got done.*

It's a gritty, vivid song, one that seemed to promise that Cash was getting
interested in words again.

No such luck. Cash's response to the critical acclaim and modest sales
of *American Recordings* has been to fret. While he was at work on *Un-chained,* he said that he wanted "to reach the general population, not just
a few alternative listeners. If record sales are the thing that we're going
for, I guess I want to be a top record seller. I want everybody of every age
or walk of life or race to hear that song I'm going to record on the radio
and to say 'I love that.' " A classic conundrum of popular music is that hits
are not always good songs, and the best music doesn't always sell briskly.
Cash once told me that he was writing several new songs for *Unchained,*
but it turned out that the only fresh one on the record was "Meet Me in
Heaven."

Cash isn't terribly reflective about why he no longer writes great
songs—"It's just what happens in life," he said—but it's a void that other
songwriters think about. His life presents a poignant artistic dilemma:
that is, how you continue to see the world in original ways when you are
also a successful performer. Bob Dylan has written songs with Cash,
stayed at the house in Hendersonville, and corresponded with him. Dylan
implies that he thinks the trappings of Cash's fame have hindered him as
a writer, but he warns that he doesn't feel he knows Cash very well and
that he finds him almost impossible to figure. "His movements are unpre-

dictable," Dylan says. "He can make himself scarce at the drop of a hat." Dylan is a great admirer of Cash's songs, calling them "as imaginative as can be, really." When he begins to muse about what happened to that imagination, Dylan sounds as though he is talking with one eye inward. "As a person gets successful you tend to lose the focus of the early kind of imprint you made," he says. "It seems like the stuff you did when nobody was around has more lasting quality than the stuff you do when 'it's time to make a record.' Other entities get in the way of a person's development. It's like Tennessee Williams's plays. The later ones you've never heard about."

Like Bob Dylan, Bruce Springsteen is a great admirer of the Sun recordings. At Johnny Cash's induction to the Rock 'n' Roll Hall of Fame—Cash is the only living member of both the Country and the Rock Halls of Fame—Springsteen made the introductory remarks, and after a recent concert in Philadelphia he told me that "the influence of the Sun recordings was even in the songs I did tonight."

In some ways a Rust Belt version of the Man in Black, "The Boss" has plotted his life very differently from Cash. Although he is a fabled performer, Springsteen rarely commits to concert tours or makes public appearances. Instead, he spends a lot of time with his wife and young children. He continues to write in great volume, and there are always songs like "Youngstown" which reflect his prodigious talents. Springsteen says that as he became successful, "My world expanded. I had to try not to think of myself as The Boss. But the truth is that it always seemed ridiculous to me. It seemed silly. You draw your music from experiences and by staying attentive to the world around you. Just because my world expanded didn't mean I left the rest of my life behind me. You can get lost, but those are choices people make. I'd seen people who came before me, like Elvis. People who'd drifted into the isolation of rock-star success. I had to go through the very same woods, strive to reach an audience, and set my own limits."

Then Springsteen mentioned a Jerry Lee Lewis song, "End of the Road." "Great, great song," he said. "Fantastic song. Almost the last one he wrote. I asked him, 'Jerry Lee, why didn't you write another one?' He said, 'It took too much out of me.' Me, I never felt it took too much out of me. I've been writing even on this tour."

The new scraps of "Delia's Gone" to the contrary, it is possible that Johnny Cash is someone who flashed the early promise of a Bruce Springsteen or a Paul Simon, but lacked the imaginative wherewithal to keep it up. It's also possible that he has been done in by a disease: addiction. Either way, it's clear that life as The Man in Black has distracted him. With all his time spent in hotels, airports, and buses, he can't be (Springsteen's phrase) attentive to a world he doesn't see. Further, most songwriters will tell you that it is almost impossible to write something new and good when you are performing your old material every day. "If I was on the road a lot I don't know how I'd write new things," says Paul Simon. When Cash and I talked about what had happened to his songwriting, he admitted that his itinerant lifestyle is "interfering" with it. Since, as he also says, he lives for "that show every night," he's not likely to cut back.

For a period in his life, Johnny Cash made his miseries into great music that expressed elements of common suffering. His self-destructive behavior began in 1958, a time when his fame was building and when his best writing was behind him. Those bitter early songs seem like verbal expressions of the same febrile temperament which has kept him from ever getting too close to anyone since his brother died, which makes him flee the room, and which keeps him shifting back and forth between bingeing on drugs and religion. No one can say why he became attracted to ways of living that damped down his roiling imagination. His greatest sadness may turn out to be that he couldn't do anything more with his sadness. Ultimately, as with his Memphis contemporary Jerry Lee Lewis, writing may take too much out of Cash. Existing behind the elaborate black screen where he can sing those old songs with all the raw feeling he's got might just be more palatable for him than sitting alone with his pencil and stirring around among things he'd rather forget.

George Jones. "Me, I'm a ballad singer."

GEORGE JONES

JUST PUT THAT SAD BACK
IN THE BOTTLE

It was a perfectly ordinary spring day outside the town of Franklin in the rolling middle Tennessee hills, which is just the sort of day that George Jones prizes. He had awakened at his customary 6:00 A.M., and soon thereafter was aboard his tractor cutting the grass, as he does every morning that he is at home. Jones strongly believes that a man should treat his lawn as he treats himself, and so it followed that after the mowing was done, he had submitted his locks to their own daily landscaping session with his longtime barber, Ray Gregory. Then Jones had slipped behind the wheel of one of the seven vehicles he owns that sport "NOSHOW" license plates—today it was the NOSHOW2 BMW sedan—and zipped into town to purchase the taco that he eats every day for lunch. At some point he had also managed to exchange endearments with his wife, Nancy—he calls her "Legs," she calls him "Possum"—and pleasantries with Pee Wee Johnson, his faithful Man Friday, who addresses Jones as "Bossman" and favors "IDOSHOW" license plates on his car. Later, Jones would settle down for a little television before crawling into bed by 10:00 P.M. "I am," he said, "a TV nut."

Just now, however, he was seated poolside out on the patio behind the four-bedroom, seven-bathroom, twelve-column tan brick manse, discussing George Jones Country Gold dog food. For the noncanine, dog food is generally something less than a freshet for conversation that is absorbing, but those are dog-food conversations that do not involve George Jones. "It's doin' fantastic," he began, and his guests were rapt. "I think it has the same nutrition and ingredients that are in other pet foods for a lot less price," he went on, and the effect of his words was mesmerizing.

It was the voice, of course. Jones calls himself "a simple man," and until he opens his mouth, he really is your average short, potbellied fellow with a beyond-kempt head of hair and beady dark eyes set possum-close together. But hearing the man Frank Sinatra calls "the second best male singer in America" talk about anything in his sonorous, marinated-to-tender-perfection baritone is a pleasure similar to waking up in Tuscany. Listening to Jones sing a mournful country ballad is something beyond that. "If we could all sound like we wanted to, we'd all sound like George Jones," wrote the country singer Waylon Jennings, and Jennings has never endured much argument. If you listen to too much of George Jones on a gray day, you'll understand why from the time he was a teenager singing to the ship flangers and the roughnecks in East Texas honky-tonks, Jones has been able to reduce just about anyone to one drink, just one more, and then another.

The sad songs got to him, too. In country music, Jones is nearly as legendary for drinking whiskey as he is for singing about it. By the late 1970s, he was bombed so often that, as the old George Jones song goes, with the blood from his body he could have started his own still. For Jones, drinking was always part of the territory, and at first that territory was East Texas.

Born with a broken arm in 1931, Jones grew up in the hardscrabble settlements north of Beaumont around the Big Thicket, a gloomy expanse of hedges, baygalls, and dense piney woods scattered with pump jacks heaving oil out of the undergrowth. Early in the nineteenth century the area had been a popular refuge for criminals because, David Baker, who works for the Big Thicket National Preserve, told me, "If you weren't a fairly desperate person you wouldn't go out there. It's full of mosquitoes, it's hard to farm, and it's humid. But it made an excellent hideout." Saratoga, where Jones was born, is in Hardin County, named for men who settled there after fleeing a murder warrant in Tennessee. Around 1900, when oil was discovered in Saratoga, many more scoundrels poured into East Texas. "There was no planning, no law—it was just chaos," said Baker. "In Batson there were murders all the time. Crime was high because there was so much speculation. Fortunes changed hands in a day. There were tremendous numbers of saloons. Prostitution was open. A very lawless time."

In the decade when Jones lived there, the Big Thicket was still attracting a throng of dismal characters—hustlers, infidels, and no-accounts who took cover in the oil fields, the logging camps, and the saloons. One of them was his father. George Washington Jones worked, at times, as an ice hauler, a woodsman, a moonshiner, and a shipyard pipefitter. The only regular thing about him was his drinking. His favorite child, Ethel, caught a chill and died at seven, a loss that Jones says made a raging drunkard of his father. Late at night, George Washington Jones would come home, scuffed from brawling and reeking of raw whiskey, to rouse his son and slap him around until he sang for him. "He was a hardworking man and he liked to let steam off," Jones said. "He'd get me and my sister Doris up. He'd want us to sing Roy Acuff songs."

In a neatly symmetrical marriage of the profane and the sacred, Jones's mother, Clara, was a devoted Christian, and like so many great country singers, her son learned to use his voice by singing verse-chorus-verse "specials" in a Pentecostal church. It was also at church that Jones's Sunday-school teacher showed him his first guitar chords. Listening to Acuff, Lefty Frizzell, and Hank Williams on the radio taught him to sing country. "I wanted to sound like Hank Williams but I phrased like Lefty," he said. "I made five syllables out of one. You put them all together and your own heart and soul. Well, I thank them three people every day. You find out what you love the most growing up and you don't lose it."

By his early teens, the family had moved into Beaumont, and Jones was singing in the streets for change. (A photograph of him at twelve, dressed in sagging socks and rolled-up jeans, striding along the sidewalk with his guitar, is similar to the famous shot of a teenaged Hank Williams hustling pennies on the streets of Montgomery, Alabama.) For a man who talks about leavening his music with heart and soul, Jones can seem blandly detached while he discusses his life, but as he began to describe his youthful adventures in Beaumont, he suddenly sounded engaged. "One time I was playing at the entrance of a penny arcade on a Sunday afternoon," he said. "I was sitting on a shoeshine stand playing my guitar just to entertain my own self. Pretty soon there was eight or ten or maybe a dozen people stopped to listen. Afterwards they throwed nickels, quarters, and dollar bills at me. I added it all up. It was $24. I never seen that much money in my life. I gave those pinball machines hell that day. I carried my guitar [he pronounces it *git*-tar] everywhere. I had a string on it. All the bus drivers knew me. I'd go to the rear and they'd say 'sing,' and I'd ride for free."

Jones was twenty-four, had been singing in gutbucket bars for years, and was already a twice-married former housepainter, shoe shiner, and soda-truck driver when the up-tempo "Why Baby Why" became his first top-five country hit. He has since recorded plenty of other brisk numbers, from the whimsical "Who Shot Sam" to the sublimely clever "The Race Is On," but the slow songs, wrenching ballads of disintegrating love like "The Door," "A Good Year for the Roses," "The Window Up Above," and "The Grand Tour," serve him best. It's the way he lingers on a word, kneading it for a sadness you didn't know was there, which transforms ordinary, even trite lyrics into something intensely moving. Couple such phrasing with the sprawling registers and pellucid sound of a voice that lost some of its nasal timbre as it deepened with age, and you have a formidable instrument for expressing despair.

Jones is a turbulent man with a casual exterior. He was wearing blue jeans, running shoes, and a red and white zipper-front shirt the day I visited his home. It is the same way with his music. Absolutely crushing songs come dressed down in simple phrases. Jones says that for sentimental reasons, his early hit "The Window Up Above" remains his favorite George Jones song. There is nothing sentimental about it.

He was living in Vidor, Texas, in 1959, and one morning just after he'd returned from a concert tour, something in the smell of frying bacon got to him. "It was around 7:00 A.M. and my wife was cooking breakfast," he said. "It just hit me. I was in the den. I reached over and picked up my guitar. I wrote it in fifteen or twenty minutes."

That, and a lifetime, as country songwriters are always saying. The song is a two-and-a-half-minutes-long sketch of a cuckold. A husband sees his wife embracing somebody else, and from her serene expression and her obvious physical familiarity with her new lover he knows that he is finished. "I thought we belonged together, hearts fit like a glove," he says, and then he listens to his wife assure her new lover that her marriage "was all wrong."

Jones hasn't written many songs, and none of them are lyrically remarkable. What Jones would call "my phrasing" is what elevates the material. Words for him are interesting both for their actual meaning and for the meaning he gives to them. Jones can sing the word "love" in a dozen songs, make it sound a dozen different ways, and have it mean a dozen different things. Here, when he sings "How I wish I could be dreaming and wake up to a love that's true," the word is dispatched with a speed-quick intake of breath. That tells you the man's conception of romance has been devastated. Now, when he thinks about true love, he instantly associates it with betrayal. He can't even get the word out without flinching.

Jones has scored his singing in "A Window Up Above" so that you can concentrate on the sound, ignore the words, and still understand what the song is about. In the first lines, his tone is smooth and tender as Jones lets you know that the husband is basically a good enough sort, an honest Joe who aspires to give a measured account of an unhappy situation. But as the infidelity is revealed, he can't do it. The somber, heavyhearted lament spins into darker, more unsettling territory midway through the first verse. Jones makes that happen by placing emphasis on phrases like "he held you tightly," turning the word "tightly" into a sudden long wail of realization. Then the emotions begin fluctuating frantically. First incredulity and then bitterness—Jones sings through clenched teeth. At one moment the husband is scrambling for his dignity and the voice quivers. At the next he is seized with vindictiveness and Jones burnishes the phrase "I hope he makes you happy" with a nasty glint. Then he strips away the bravado, moves down a register, and the broken man has only despair. When Jones sings "I thought that we belonged together, hearts fit like a glove," he stretches "together" across several extra syllables, moving through two octaves so that you think he's about to lose it himself. But he doesn't. George Jones is a master at employing total vocal control to express emotions that are swinging wildly *out* of control. By the time he gets to the glove, he has the man emotionally spent. There Jones softens and lowers his voice. He is smooth and tender again. A glove becomes a sigh.

In 1970, Jones released the song that may be his finest, "A Good Year for the Roses," a three-minute ballad written for him by the Harlan County, Kentucky, songwriter Jerry Chesnut. Once again Jones is singing about a broken marriage. This time, however, the emotions belong to a man who is long past the initial impact of the failure, has thought everything through, still loves his wife, but realizes he can't make life with her work. "A Good Year for the Roses" is about confronting grief and anticipating depression. It's artfully written, not in the least because the images—lipstick on half-smoked cigarettes in the ashtray, lip prints on an abandoned cup of coffee—are both intimate and mundane so that they have immediate domestic resonance. A singer like Jones doesn't want clever, sophisticated lyrics. He does best with spare lines that leave him to do all the decorating.

The song begins with regret as a man surveys the house out of which his wife has just walked for the last time. The man finds himself suddenly feeling choked up about banal objects as they trigger memories of his marriage. For this first section, Jones's voice is clear, somber, and low, with a lone exception. When he describes the cigarette "*there* in the ashtray," "there" has a hint of a sob in it.

Then comes the chorus and the man's guts come pouring out. Jones can calibrate his voice during choruses in such a way that the sound rises and grows louder, like a symphony accelerating into a climactic crescendo of notes. (Jones's longtime producers, Pappy Dailey, and especially Billy Sherrill, liked to emphasize this technique by pairing Jones's singing with gushy background vocals and orchestral instrumental arrangements during the chorus in many of his hits.) "When you turn to walk away, as the door behind you closes," he sings, and what's artful is the way Jones handles his breathing on words like "turn," "away," and "closes," keeping enough air in reserve that he can hold his voice there as though he doesn't ever want to move on. The vocal effect is like a human bagpipe—the slow release of a deep, mournful sound. He gives you the picture of a man who senses that he is about to be unhappier than he has ever been, and will be for a long time. Someone who understood no English could hear Jones sing this song and would know instantly what it was about.

What sets Jones's voice apart is the hesitations and catches that complement his soaring tones. When he describes the "half-filled cup of coffee that you poured and didn't drink," he lingers on "drink." Later, when the man says he doesn't "care" about doing the yard work, Jones lowers and then raises his voice with a tremor all on the one word. The man cares more than is good for him.

The same morose impulses that imbued his music with lush, sorrowful feeling could plunge Jones into real despondency that he found difficult to shake. His description of what it was like for him to sing a Hank Williams song—he recorded two full albums of them—applies to most of his repertoire: "It makes you sad because you're singin' all those sad words, about how a man can do a woman and a woman can do a man, until you're just like the people in the song, and you're living it and their problems become your problems, until you're lost in the songs and it just takes everything out of you," he said. When the club or recording studio was shut for the night and he was alone with these song-inflicted woes, Jones was not graceful in his methods of venting the bad feelings.

To see him now, suntanned, short-sleeved, and obliging beneath the well-groomed lacquer of hair, it's nearly impossible to imagine that during the 1960s, 70s and early 80s, Jones put himself through a succession of indignities that included being arrested, filing for bankruptcy, threatening people he loved with pistols, and finding himself committed to a padded cell. He took his first drink of whiskey as a teenager in a Jasper, Texas, cow pasture, and didn't stop that day until he'd passed out in a pile of manure. It would be a recurrent pattern. Jones drank as obsessively as he now cuts his hair. For years he woke up in the morning to a Bloody Mary and then spent the afternoon and evening guzzling bourbon. With drink in him, Jones turned brazen, spiteful, and dangerous. The simple man became a master of baroque indiscretion. In hazes of booze and cocaine he flung wads of cash into the toilet, was accused of beating women, and was even spotted sitting in the backseat of a Cadillac talking like Donald Duck, slurping whiskey, and clutching a picture of Hank Williams.

Williams, perhaps the greatest and most troubled songwriter country music has ever known, had drunk himself to death by age twenty-nine, and Jones, who was twenty-two at the time, began to regard "Ol' Hank" as something of a tragic muse. "Lord, he drove me crazy," he once confided to his friend, the British New Wave rock star Elvis Costello. "He kept my head all messed up." Now he said to me, "I think people like that, the good Lord puts 'em here to make us happy and then to open our eyes towards certain things when they're gone."

With many singers, self-destructive drinking is a function of spending so much of their lives in bars around liquor, and also from allowing their celebrity to give them a feeling that they are impervious to what injures other people. "Everybody says George Jones, he's an alcoholic," Waylon Jennings told me. "George Jones likes to get drunk. With all of us it's 'Who's gonna tell me what to do?' " It didn't help Jones in this respect that some of his greatest songs were recorded when he could scarcely stand up.

Jones's chronic urge for whiskey was born of the same deep melancholy that gives such character to his singing. No cheerful man could have sung sad songs the way George Jones did. But even as his preoccupation with misery made for such moving music, it was also more than he could handle. And so, in a pattern of behavior that pervades country music, he kept drinking.

The great passion of Jones's life was his third wife and still occasional duet partner, the bleached-blond former Mississippi cotton picker and Alabama beautician Tammy Wynette. Wynette described him as "one of those people who can't tolerate happiness."

"She's called me a lot of things, I've heard say," Jones rejoined now, amiably enough, but through much of his career "Miss Tammy" did have a point.

From the time Jones interrupted an argument in the kitchen between Wynette and her husband, Don Chapel, to upset a table, declare his love, and then spirit her and her three children off to Georgia in his car, their relationship was always somewhat over the top. Married from 1969 to 1975, they recorded a string of duets together, including the classics "We're Gonna Hold On," and "Two-Story House," and kitsch like "The Ceremony," a mawkish musical reprise of their wedding day. Wynette helped persuade Jones to forgo the most famous skint-possum flattop crew cut in popular music. (Jones was amenable, he said now, because "as I grew older my ears grew bigger and I got a complex about them.") She had less success weaning him from booze.

Such was Jones's stubborn craving for alcohol that once, after Wynette had emptied the liquor closet and hidden the keys to all twenty-seven vehicles at the couple's house, Jones responded by hot-wiring the lawn tractor and driving it down the road to a package store. Jones says that Wynette has appropriated this incident and that it actually happened during his marriage to Shirley Corley. Nobody in Nashville pays atten-

George Jones and Tammy Wynette. "I guess where I really started feeling down was when I got my divorce from Tammy."

tion to such cavils. Wynette swears it is true, but says she doesn't doubt it happened with Corley as well. Another time, Jones menaced Wynette with a pistol. She wasn't the only one. When Jones's friend and former drinking partner, the songwriter Earl "Peanut" Montgomery, found the Lord and began urging Jones to do the same, Jones hauled out a .38, blurted, "See if your God can save you now," and pulled the trigger. He missed. Barely.

Eventually, this man who had formerly slept in a twelve-bedroom, fifteen-bathroom house and driven a garish Pontiac Bonneville studded with Texas steer horns and four thousand real silver dollars, weighed less than a hundred pounds, was homeless, and subsisted on sardines and beef jerky. In 1979, he missed more than fifty concert dates, earning himself the moniker "No-Show Jones." Gamblers made book on whether he'd appear for concerts or not. When he did show up, he was often so strung out that his staff had to prop him up, like "a mummy," in his words, through the performance. He spent a few weeks of 1979 in an Alabama mental hospital. It was not his first stay in an alcoholic ward, nor would it be his last. When he got out that time, he celebrated by hurrying to a store and buying himself some beer.

These recurrent struggles make Jones seem a lot like Johnny Cash, but the differences between them are considerable. Cash is a highly intelligent and witty man, a gifted artist struggling with demons, who turns to narcotics in an effort to distract himself from the very keenness of his worried mind. Jones clearly had plenty of demons too, but the truth was that he was dynamic only when he was drunk or stuffing his anger and misery into a microphone. Johnny Cash knows all about the extent of his talent, and it may bother him that he can't do more with it. With George Jones, everything—his singing, his cravings—comes from his guts. He is not a reflective person and doesn't ever seem to think much about his musical ability. It's just something he has. By chance, he is the consummate professional country singer, but he was never professional in the brain. At the time I met him, he was just finishing his autobiography, *I Lived to Tell It All.* The book turned out to be a massive chronicle of vile behavior related with brutal candor. If you picked it up without knowing that Jones was a famous singer, however, the book could be read as the confessions of almost anyone who spent much of his life throwing drinks in other people's faces. Next to nothing revealing is said about the art of singing. As Jones presents it, his life is the story of a nuisance.

"I guess where I really started feeling down was when I got my divorce from Tammy," he said now, taking a sip of ice water. Jones is said to dislike talking about his more sordid travails, but here in the spring sunshine he was calm and frank. "When we were first married and all it was a lot of fun," he said. "When we were onstage we were like in our own little heaven." As the relationship fell apart, he became inconsolably unhappy. "It seemed like I started drinking real, real heavy," he said. "I got down so low I started missing dates. My manager at the time introduced me to cocaine in the back room of the Possum Holler Club in Nashville when I was down and it gave me energy, got me through a show, made me feel good. Of course it also makes you want more of it. I got on it so bad I thought everything happening around me was in a science-fiction theater. You saw things that weren't there. People in Halloween costumes."

It was Nancy Sepulvado, whom Jones met in 1981 and married two years later, who Jones and many others say rescued him from reaching for the bottle. "When I met her I was really down," he said. "When you think it's the end of the road you don't give a damn. Whether you live or carry on don't make no difference. She came along and friends like Johnny Cash and Waylon Jennings started calling. They made me see things different. I did a lot of Bible reading in the hospital, got my thinking cap back on. My doctor told me when I came in my IQ was about 72. I couldn't have lived two months longer." Jones said he hasn't had a drink in eleven years.

Out on the lawn in Franklin, Nancy Jones shouts, "Smile, Possum! Show 'em those teeth." Nancy is a slender, informal woman who addresses guests as "Bub" and dresses in sneakers, black denim, and smallish diamonds. Down the hill from where she is standing is a small throng of people surrounding her husband, who is keeping a promise by giving some local children suffering from muscular dystrophy a quick spin in his motorcycle and sidecar.

Nancy, the motorcycle, and the sidecar became part of the prodigal Jones legend soon after Jones met her in 1981. Texas newspapers described them roaring away from a concert together. "It wasn't with tequila into the sunset the way they said it was," she said dryly. "Of course, I didn't know he was as messed up as he was. He hit it pretty good. I still look at myself and wonder what did I do?"

It is this cheerful directness that seems to suit her husband. "We've never got into any bad arguments," he will say later. "I don't know, she more or less understands me. She knows my problems and she helped me get my life back straight. She has a lot of patience with me when I flare off. She's more or less nursed me back into a life worth living."

Wynette had been a finger curled against the trigger of his frazzled emotions. Nancy offered something more peaceful: steady, unshakable affection. Jones could hit her, rip her clothing off, even kick her off his bus, leaving her stranded on a lonely stretch of highway—he did all that—and she remained devoted. And after a while, he gave up the whiskey.

Some compulsive habits, however, do persist. Throughout his life Jones has kept car salesmen hopping with his habit of divesting himself of recently acquired sedans in favor of something a few weeks newer and shinier. The current Jones family garage has room for eleven cars, a spatial allotment that can seem austere, given Jones's propensity for accumulating vehicles. At Christmas, Nancy selected a white Dodge truck for him, and when Jones went to the dealer to pick up the gift, the sight of it so delighted him that he pointed to a green version of the same truck and said, "I'll take that one, too." The BMW he had driven to the taco stand for his lunch turned out to have been in the family for less than thirty-six hours. When I visited, there were also three golf carts parked in the garage, a generous collection for a man who doesn't play the game.

Jones's home has many rooms, including an office for Nancy, a hallway with a full rack of shotguns, a game room featuring a handsome pool table, and a bar stocked with a solitary jar of coffee creamer. Jones is rarely glimpsed in any of these places. He is a two-chair man. In front of the Texas-sized television set in the living room is the large green easy chair, which, Nancy points out, Jones burned with a cigar butt, possibly because he isn't comfortable in completely spotless places. Through the kitchen is a cushiony black chair set in the center of a fully appointed home barbershop, where Jones has his daily rendezvous with Ray Gregory.

The George Jones barbershop is one of the few places in the house with evidence that a great singer resides here. Scattered amid the bottles of Sculpt Moist hairspray are souvenirs and awards, including an honorary key to the Nashville City Jail and the first printed ticket to Jones Country, the country theme park he operated from 1983 to 1989, in Colmesneil, Texas. There too is a signed copy of the lyrics to "He Stopped Loving Her Today," a campy dirge to unrequited love that, in Jones's hands, becomes the song that many consider country music's greatest. Among the gifts from fans that are on display is a letter from Supreme Court Justice

Clarence Thomas. It hangs in a frame just outside the door and describes how the song "Wine Colored Roses" helped him through a rough patch during courtship of his wife.

That song, unlike most of the material on Jones's recent recordings, is a forlorn ballad. In an effort to make him compatible with Hot Country's fast-paced, heavy guitar-laced sound, Jones's producers have mostly been shunning the slower stuff. That's because Hot Country sells like hotcakes to kids, although not, alas, when Jones is singing it. The situation has Jones none too pleased. He loathes what has become of mainstream country music. Not long before I met him, when he was asked about it, Jones had blurted, "Nowadays, if you're not twenty-three years old and got a cute butt in blue jeans and a black hat on or something, you don't have a prayer." Today, he was softer. "I say this is not George Jones," he told me. "I'm a ballad singer." Then the singer of "Same Ole Me" elaborated, a bit: "I still prefer the same type of songs. In my heart and mind I pretty well stay the same. I guess the best way to say it is I'm hard-core country."

Jones might be coaxed into recording something with the vapid bounce of Byron Hill and Zack Turner's "High Tech Redneck," but his recordings that will endure are about the permutations of sorrow: the ways people adjust their hopes as time grows shorter; how you get through a life that you never planned on; the way abiding misfortune feels and how you get used to it; what it's like to be left behind. This is not music for swinging teens. It's raw stuff for grown-up people who aren't getting any younger and know something about disappointment. When George Jones sings it, country music is about bad love. And what he means when he says of record companies, "They've taken the heart and soul out of country music," is that they've removed the pain.

Jones is still on the road 165 days a year, traveling from stage to stage. Not many country singers savor the relentless bus trips that punctuate one-night visits to Tupelo, Mississippi, and Wheeling, West Virginia, but in his dotage Jones seems particularly enamored of staying home. He has moved often and fitfully in his life, occupying, at various times, an assortment of houses in East Texas, several more in middle Tennessee, the large one he shared with Wynette in Lakeland, Florida, not to mention the scatter of refuges across several states in which he smoked his brain. It's impossible to say—and Jones doesn't—how harmful it was to persist in returning to East Texas, as he did throughout the 1950s, and then again twenty years later. One of the prominent features in the landscape there was George Washington Jones. No doubt Jones felt both a strong sympathetic kinship and an equally powerful aversion to his tortured father, who drank himself into the alcoholic ward of a Texas mental hospital and, on several occasions, humiliated his son by begging for spare change outside the places where Jones was performing. But if Texas was always an ambivalent experience, it wasn't as though his other addresses were any more soothing. In a conversation with a reporter Jones once said, "All my life it seems I've been running away from something . . . If I knew what it was, maybe I could run in the right direction. But I always seem to end up going the other way." And so the likely explanation for Jones's peripatetic life is his own: so distraught was he that he couldn't rest anywhere for long. This unhappiness brought unusual feeling to his singing voice, but it made for a torrid, miserable existence.

That seems finally to be over with. Some people fear old age. George Jones loves it. When he's on the road, he gazes out the bus window at ribbons of highway, thinking about all the things he likes to do back in Franklin. In "A Good Year for the Roses," Jones sings, "The lawn could stand another mowin', funny I don't even care," but these days life definitely does not imitate art.

Out on the grass, Nancy was attempting to explain the excitation Jones derives from lawn care. Shaking her head, she said, "He's a tractor nut. I've never seen anyone liked to mow as much as George Jones. We were gonna go to Tunica, Mississippi, to the new casino this weekend. He wouldn't go because he wanted to stay home and mow. He loves the beauty of something. It's something he can do. All he can do is pick and sing, but here he can look back and see how beautiful it all is."

"On the road I don't ever get a lot of quietness or peace of mind," Jones said. "You don't eat and sleep like you should bouncing around on a bus. So I relax at home trying to cut all this grass. I'm not no night owl like I used to be. I'm just a homebody now. I'm really enjoying life for the first time in sixty-three years."

*Oklahomans reach the San Joaquin Valley, California, in 1938.
"We were fruit tramps," says Buck Owens. "Those were terrible times.
I don't remember 'em very good and I'm glad I don't."*

PART SIX

THE
WEST COAST SOUND

The Maddox Family: Cal, Henry, Rose, Don, and Fred.
*"My brothers kept me too busy to get tired. We were having a good time
making the people have a good time."*

SISTER ROSE MADDOX

STILL KICKING

Not many miles north of grizzled former California gold-mining outposts like Black Butte, Weed, Guy's Gulch, and Yreka is the fresh-faced town of Ashland, a southern Oregon enclave of vegetarian pizza parlors, native western art-and-craft galleries, espresso bars, bagel, bead, and tofu shops, and skilled New—and Old—Age craftsmen who turn out everything from solar-heated homes to fully functional suits of medieval armor. People also come to Ashland for the (lithia) waters, the pears and grapes, and the acclaimed Shakespeare festival in the retired Chautauqua tabernacle. Ashland does not, however, have many dimly lit roadhouses thick with blue smoke, cheap whiskey, and loud, loud music, which makes it a surprising place to turn up country music's "Queen of the California Honky-Tonks," Sister Rose Maddox. But, in fact, you can't miss her.

Or her barn, anyway. It's a bright red one just off I-5, and has "Maddox Revolution Angus" painted on the side in large, bold white letters. "A Revolution Angus is a prize bull my brother Don had, so that's what he put on the barn," Maddox was saying in a voice that, at seventy-one, still seemed capable of filling spaces many times the size of the living room we were sitting in. She is a tall woman with feisty hazel eyes and a steep arbor of gray hair. Her blue jeans, faded blue-denim shirt, and white sneakers gave her the look of a wrangler in repose, but she soon cleared up *that* illusion.

"How much cattle do you all own?" I asked her.

"It's not you all," she said. "They belong to my brother Don. I just live here. I have no idea how many he has."

I said that it seemed surprising to find her in a place like Ashland.

"I don't live in town," Maddox snapped, as if the very idea threatened to wither her a little. "I live out in the country."

"How did you get here?" I asked.

"Drove," she replied. Outside, a skinny dog barked.

"I've been here since 1958," she said with a now-that-we-understand-each-other look. "Then I got stuck with it when my brother Cal died in 1968 and left his share of it to me. When my marriage broke up in 1969, I came back up here to look after my mother. I like the quietness and the solitude. Usually I live alone and don't have this mess around." She gestured toward a scatter of toys on the living-room floor. Her grandson Donnie, his wife, and their seventeen-month-old baby were staying with her for a while. "They ain't got no place else to go," she said. "Donnie plays bass with me sometimes. He just turned twenty-four. I love Donnie better than anybody in the world, but I could kill him sometimes. He irritates me and me and him fusses." She sighed and explained, "It don't take much to irritate me. I'm just very independent. I don't like to have to depend on somebody else for something. I don't like people depending on me. But they do."

"So you don't enjoy being a grandmother?" I asked.

"I don't." The response was prompt and decisive. "I always said that I'd never be called Grandma." Then she said, "That's all they call me."

Maddox isn't much for Shakespeare, either, by the way. "I hate reading," she said. "It's boring. You're not doing anything but settin' there. I'd rather be out there singing."

Rose Maddox has been out there singing for sixty years. In the 1930s, 40s, and 50s, she and her five older brothers, Cliff, Fred, Don, Cal, and Henry, called themselves "The Most Colorful Hillbilly Band in America," and they weren't simply referring to their gaudy array of rhinestone-spangled sateen costumes made for them by the Hollywood haberdasher Nathan Turk. The Maddox Brothers and Rose's repertoire included hymns, weepers, moaners, and novelty and cowboy songs, but what they did best were raw, driving numbers like "Move It On Over," "Hangover Blues," "Honky-Tonkin'," and "Water Baby Boogie." "Have you ever seen anything like that?" they would yell during the instrumental break, and the point was well taken—nobody had. It was a brand of foot-stomping music that anticipated rockabilly and packed roadhouses and dance halls all over the West Coast.

Rose usually sang lead in her blazing bawl of a voice that sounded like it came straight out of a coke furnace. It was full, clear, muscular, devoid of nuance, and thrilling with energy. Her brothers backed her with guitars, mandolins, fiddles, bass, harmonica, and a salty brand of vocal harmony that featured yips, yells, giggles, caterwauls, hoots, and naughty asides; in case anyone missed them, they were prone to repeating bawdy lyrics at the top of their lungs. No Maddox caused more of an uproar than Fred. He wasn't much of a bass player, but he found ways to compensate. "He was playing upright bass and acting like he was screwing it," Harlan Howard told me. "He hunched over it like a dog over a bone." Once someone from the audience approached Fred and said, "Fred, I notice you don't play any notes on that bass." "Maybe not," Fred replied. "But I've got the job!" He was, the singer Tommy Collins told me, "A showman, and a good one."

Fred might tell of an adventure checking out of a motel room: " 'How much do I owe you?' I asked the manager. He told me, 'Fifty dollars.' I said, 'Fifty dollars for that little ole room?' The manager said, 'That included your meal.' I told him that I didn't eat no meal. He said, 'Well, it was there for you, and if you didn't git it, I don't care.' So I gave him ten dollars and said, 'I'm chargin' you forty dollars for makin' love to my wife.' He says, 'I didn't make love to your wife!' I told him, 'Well, it was there for you. If you didn't git it, I don't care.' "

"Yes, we were having a good time," Rose Maddox said. "We had a *show* going on every time. Just hollering, cutting up, having a good time making the people have a good time. My brothers kept me too busy to get tired. They were energetic people who loved what they were doing. After the war we got some amplifiers so we could be heard over the people. A lot of country bands did that. We were just louder. We wanted to get the public's mind off their problems and their worries. When my brothers yelled, the people yelled back. They were all working people laughing, hollering, and cutting up with us." Large portions of their audience were displaced Southern farming families like themselves who were trying to make a new start in California. As her biographer, Jonny Whiteside, writes, "They offered the music of home for people who no longer had a home."

The Maddoxes might sing about wild nights of sex and booze, but with the exception of Fred, singing was as close as they came to the high life. Their mother didn't allow carousing—or much of anything else—and well into their thirties, The Maddox Brothers and Rose remained under her firm command. (Fred had some offstage fun because he was so good at climbing out of motel windows.) The provocative qualities of their performances were fueled by the tensions of their repressed existence. Rose was the only daughter, the youngest child at that, and the biggest star among them, so she received more of her mother's scrutiny than anyone. "I went in to the honky-tonks to entertain, not to have a good time," Maddox said. "Nobody was wild off the stage. We saved it all for the stage. We never drank. I still don't. Mama would have killed us. Well, Fred was a little wild. He frolicked and had a good time when Mama didn't catch him. Mama always caught me." Singing became so crucial to Rose Maddox because it was, in a sense, the only time she was free to assert herself. "Singing is my way of expressing everything," she told me. "My sorrow and everything else."

Buck Owens, who got to know Rose when the band came through Bakersfield, California, says that she was hard for anyone to miss: "In Rose Maddox's day all the girls ran from her. She was a great singer, she had unending energy, and she was *good-looking*."

Maddox was also eleven years old when she began performing with her brothers in places where the patrons all had to be at least eighteen. It wasn't just her youth that made her unusual. "There was no women when I started in country music," she said. "But I was treated fine and the reason was I had four big brothers to look after me. And Mama."

Lula Maddox stood less than five feet tall, but she was a stocky matriarch of such mettle that for twenty years she steered her brood in and out of the toughest joints across the San Joaquin Valley, facing down the honky-tonk dross of wastrels, crooks, thugs, and lechers when they came anywhere near them. She was something of a legend, both for the shoulder bag stuffed with cash that she carried with her everywhere—she once walked into a Cadillac showroom and pulled out enough to pay for seven cars—and for her combative nature. Men who'd ball their fists over an idle glance were ductile before Mama Maddox's resolute gaze. When the crowds pressed too close to the stage, she'd bellow, "I paid $50,000 for those uniforms. Now move back so people can see them."

"I remember seeing the Maddoxes at a dance hall in Tracy, in Northern California up by Modesto," Buck Owens told me. "They all got up on stage tuning up. Then Rose walks across the dance floor to get a Coca-Cola and Mama Maddox walked right with her. If Rose went to the bathroom, Mama went with her. Can you imagine her with all those kids?"

"We were her *kids,*" Maddox said. "Back then you didn't do what your mother told you not to do. My mother never let men near me and I never tried to get near them. She was a very dominant woman. Slightly heavy-set, not as tall as I am, dark hair, brown eyes. She grabbed your elbow, you felt it. She said 'Don't,' you didn't. She wasn't afraid of anybody. She didn't do cussin', but the sound of her voice was enough to scare the living daylights out of people. She was a demanding person. You did what she said—everybody did. She was the boss of the whole thing. She kept us together twenty years. That's tough to do. Any family fusses and fights. Don't yours? If it hadn't been for her we'd a had no career. She kept us in line. We knew better than to say 'No.' "

Hank Williams was one of the many people who wondered at the sight of Lula Maddox marching into dance halls with all her children trailing behind. Speaking to the independent record executive Don Pierce, Williams said, "Don, I tell you the act you've got that's really something is that Rose Maddox. I've got a song for that broad. I wrote this ["How Can You Refuse Him Now?"] with Rose in mind and I'll tell you why: when she sings songs like 'Tramp on the Street' and 'Gathering Flowers,' she sounds as pure as the drifted snow, then she'll turn around and sing my 'Honky-Tonkin'' and sound just like a gal that's straight out of a cathouse! What's she like, anyways?"

"Well," said Pierce. "Straight out of a boxcar."

"I was a sharecropper's daughter," Maddox said. "I grew up in Boaz, Alabama. That's twenty miles out of Gadsden on Sand Mountain. When they were married my daddy played a five-string banjo. My mother played mandolin. They just played barn dances was all. They grew cotton and everything else until everything went under in 1933. Cotton prices failed in Alabama. So we left for California, the Land of Milk and Honey." She laughed. It sounded like a snort. It was from reading paperback western novels that Mama Maddox got the idea that even the trees were hung with silver in California. "We only had $35 when we left there and a dream of going to California," Maddox said. "That was my mother's dream. Hitchhikin'. All of us. Five kids. We got as far as Meridian, Mississippi. They told us there how to get on the freights. We rode the rails the rest of the way. I was seven." They had walked for three days to get to Birmingham, and then hitched rides with truckers, sometimes sharing space with farm animals, until they reached Meridian. Then it was hopping the freights, sleeping in hobo jungles, and begging for food all the way to California. Rose says that they didn't spend more than a few dollars of their $35 cache the whole way out.

I said that her life sounded like a Merle Haggard song. "It does," she agreed. "I wouldn't trade it. Merle's my hero, you know. I sang at his last wedding. It was great. I sang at his third wedding and his fifth, to Theresa. Theresa seems like a pretty good woman and I don't say that about many women. But if it don't last, I'm next in line." She laughed and then she coughed (she had been suffering from bronchitis). "I think it will," she said. "He seems very happy."

Then she said, "None of us played or sang when we was back there in Alabama except my oldest brother, Cliff. He stayed behind—he was grown and married. My sister Alta, she stayed too. They came out later. I remember the brakemen were always good to us. We were the only family traveling. The rest was migrant workers, all men, heading for California. The brakemen helped us get on the right trains and they got us food from the caboose. Sometimes the brakemen locked us in the boxcars and told us to be quiet. Especially in Texas, where the railroad bulls were so bad. They were real bad. You could hear their guns going off, shootin' at all the other hobos, and they would be running from the bulls. The bulls couldn't go out of town, so as soon as the train was out of town the hobos'd swing onto the boxcars laughing at what they'd run into like barbed-wire fences—their clothing all torn up. When things were clear the brakemen would let us out. Inside the cars it was quiet. Normal people trying to get to California where there was some work during the Depression.

"We got to Los Angeles, California, in 1933. The Salvation Army heard there was a family coming. They didn't have enough room there, though, so Dad and Cal slept in jail. At least it was a place to stay. We went from L.A. up to Oakland on the freights. We lived in Pipe City. There were these huge culvert pipes and all the migrants were living inside the culverts. The mayor of Pipe City gave us his pipe to stay in. My mother got tired of asking for food every day. That's when we hit the front page of the *Oakland Tribune* as a family come west on the freights looking for work."

"Family Roams U.S. for Work," headlined the April 11, 1933, edition of the newspaper. In the accompanying photograph, the five Maddox children surround their parents, with Rose sitting between her father and mother wearing overalls and bangs. Charles Maddox is unshaven and, like his sons, he is slumped with an ashen expression on his face. Not Mama. Clearly in command, her eyes are steady, her posture erect, and she

FAMILY ROAMS U.S. FOR WORK

*Straight out of a boxcar. The Maddox family arrives in California
and makes the* Oakland Tribune, *April 11, 1933.*

looks fresh. There was no article in the *Tribune,* but the photograph looks like it was meant to rest alongside one of John Steinbeck's 1936 *San Francisco News* dispatches about migrant workers, the journalism that inspired the novelist to write *The Grapes of Wrath.* On October 5, 1936, he wrote, "They arrive bewildered and beaten and usually in a state of semi-starvation, with only one necessity to face immediately, and that is to find work at any wage in order that the family may eat."

Rose Maddox said that Steinbeck probably had it about right. "Sorrowful-looking bunch, ain't it?" she said, looking at the photograph. "Mama brought us out there. Papa, he wanted to stay behind in Alabama."

"Well, we didn't find any work in Oakland," she went on. "That's a city. My dad was a farmer and we rode another freight to the end of the line in Tuolumne, California. My dad and my brother Cal left on a Monday morning, caught the freights to work in the fruit fields in the San Joaquin Valley. They picked peaches and everything else. You got twenty-five or fifty cents an hour for peaches or apricots. They worked in the canneries in Modesto. They'd come back on Friday night and then they'd do it all over again the next week."

They tried quicker ways to make money around Tuolumne, but these didn't go well. "Mama knew there was gold up there," says Maddox.

"They panned for gold and didn't get much more than dust. The mother lode had played out. So in Tuolumne my mama gave me away."

She said this somewhat casually and I thought I'd misheard. "They *gave* you away?" I said.

She nodded. "They couldn't afford to feed me," she said. "They gave me to the postmaster to be a companion to his little girl. She was my friend until then. I hated it. All I wanted to do was to get back to my family. I was seven. I was a bitch. I was a mean little kid. My daddy finally got a steady job in Modesto and we lived in a tent in the fruit-ranch fields. Talbot's Ranch. We were all back together. I started school in Modesto. We finally got a cabin when I was about eight or nine. A two-bedroom cabin. Not a house, a cabin. We was all together. I went to the fields but I didn't work. I was too little and skinny. I let Mama get her cotton sack half full and then I got on it and let her pull me down the row. I always went to the fields to be with Mama. I never worked the fields.

"Then my brother Cal got a mail-order guitar for $8, I believe, from Sears and Roebuck. He learned to play it. My older brother Cliff had come to California and he taught him to play it. Nobody else played anything. We pitched tents down at the cotton fields in the migrant camps and sang around the campfires at night, but nobody talked about a band. One day we was in the cotton fields and my brother Fred had seen a group get $100 to play a rodeo in Modesto. He just decided we would become a band. We was in a cotton field down around Chowchilla. He got way behind. Mama hollered at him and he said"—Maddox exaggerated the Alabama in Fred's voice—" 'I'm a thankin' we should go back to Modesto and git a job on the radio, git a sponsor, git us a job in the music business.'

"The sponsor Fred got was the owner of a furniture store. Fred talked to him for thirty minutes. Fred only played a Jew's harp. He had no musical experience at all, but he had a long line of bull. The owner didn't say a word. He just let him talk. Then he said, 'I'll sponsor you if you emcee it and if you get a girl singer.' Fred said, 'We've got a girl singer.' " Rose Maddox chortled. "I was trying to sing then," she said. "Fred said to me he didn't know if I could sing or not, but he could hear me a mile away belting out them songs while I'd do the dishes. They had no intention of me bein' in the band. I was just a kid. Eleven."

It was 1937, when Rice's Furniture Store began backing the family on KTRB, Modesto. At first it was just Cal on the guitar and harmonica, and Fred on his bass fiddle, accompanying Rose's singing. Eventually, Cliff was there too—on the days he was getting along with his mother. During the war, Don learned to fiddle, and Henry chipped in with his mandolin. A steel-guitar player named Bud Duncan was hired and the band also took on a lead guitar player. At one time this was Roy Nichols, who would later become a stalwart member of Merle Haggard's band, The Strangers.

"It was a family affair," says Maddox. "We started on the radio in Modesto and got to be the most popular thing in the whole country. We started as The Alabama Outlaws and from that we became The Maddox Family. Then we finally settled on The Maddox Brothers and Rose. We entered a hillbilly contest in Sacramento in 1939, and we won the contest over fifteen other bands, and the prize was a radio show in Sacramento. So we worked out of there. I never started school again. I couldn't sing all night long and go to school, too. I got halfway through the eighth grade."

She was always known as Sister Rose, following the unwritten country music decree that said if you wanted to have a woman in your band, you'd better make it clear that she was family so that you wouldn't offend anyone's imagination. "When we first started, we followed the rodeos," she said. "In each town we got to, we picked out a bar and asked the manager if we could play for tips. They always said, 'Sure.' Right across the street from us would always be Woody Guthrie, who was doing the same thing. I met him, but that was the extent of it. I don't remember much about him. I was a kid. He looked tall and skinny. The Maddox Brothers and Rose was one of the first people that ever recorded a song of Woody Guthrie's. 'Philadelphia Lawyer.' I like Merle Haggard and Woody best. I like the way they write songs. You go through Woody and Merle's songs, you'll get me."

Her brothers went into military service during the war, and Maddox says she had a terrible time finding work because, until Kitty Wells came along, women didn't headline country acts. "They didn't use girl singers," Maddox said. "Then Carolina Cotton quit Bob Wills's band and I figured he could use me. He was up and down the Valley, and every night I'd ask him for an audition and he'd say, 'I don't have time tonight.' I followed him for a month and never did get an audition. Finally he said, 'I'll be in Hollywood. Meet me there.' I went all the way down there and he had no time and that made me mad. I told him, 'You wait. When my brothers get back from the service I'm gonna put you out of business.' Later on he played the Bostonia Ballroom outside San Diego. We'd been there the night before, now he was there the next. He was talking to the owner and the owner was telling him what a big crowd we drew. He was drawing well, but we drew more. He looked around and he said, 'She said she'd put me out of business and, you know, she damn near did.' "

The band lasted twenty years, making a lively reputation for themselves across the West with their eight-to-the-bar boogies. After a time, the family made a pretty fancy impression as they drove into town for a show. Each Maddox brother had his own black Cadillac and a trunk full of bright western suits festooned with hearts, flowers, wagon wheels, cactus, grape vines, and anything else Nathan Turk dreamed up to embroider on them. Noisy crowds of sailors, cowboys and fruit tramps came to hear "Do-Re-Mi (Dust Bowl Blues)," the "New Step It Up and Go," and the "New Muleskinner Blues." Woody Guthrie watched these raucous scenes many times and reported, "The boys in the crowds got even louder in their cheers at the sight and the sound of Sister Rose." Women who came to see the Maddoxes liked Rose's "(Pay Me) Alimony," "I Wish I Was Single Again," and her best-known number—which she wrote herself with Fred—"Sally Let Your Bangs Hang Down." The song is the story of a "love 'em leave 'em Sally." That wasn't Rose. During the war, at her mother's urging, she had married a man named E.B. Hale, who got her pregnant and then suddenly began insisting the baby wasn't his. He sent her home to her mother. They never lived together again. "I was all of sixteen," she says. "Mama thought I should get married. It was the war and Mama thought somebody should take care of me. He's dead and I'd just as soon not talk about him."

The end of the band in the late 1950s was less of a surprise. Rock 'n' roll was bad for the large dance halls on the western honky-tonk circuit that the Maddox family played, and Lula's kids were increasingly resistant to the kind of strict control she imposed upon them. "I had seen the breakup coming for quite some time," says Rose. "Fred, Don, and Henry were all married and their wives didn't like staying behind. Mama wouldn't let them go with us. Times were changing. Nightclubs were using house bands instead of guest stars. We weren't working as much. I found out I could make as much money as the whole family by myself. I had a son to support. I got married to a man in Oceanside, California. That one lasted six years. Jimmy Brogdon. He still lives in Oceanside. When I married him he was a nightclub owner. Now he owns half of Oceanside."

As for Rose Maddox, she's practically broke, with a hacking cough and a bad heart, living in a worn brown house. There were some good years in the late 1950s and early 1960s. She recorded a series of duets with Buck Owens, and a fine bluegrass album that Bill Monroe, who delighted in her yodeling, had long urged her to make. She shared the property in Oregon with Cal, Lula, and her son Donnie for years, but she says her mother made her life unbearable by monitoring her telephone calls, her visitors, her mail—everything she did. I asked her why she didn't resist, and she said, "I was raised that way and I never questioned it. It had to be that way if I was gonna be around her." When Rose did leave to marry Jimmy Brogdon, Lula told her she never wanted to see her again. But she would, especially after Cal, who had been taking care of Lula, died in 1968. With her marriage finished, Rose moved from California back up to Oregon and nursed her mother until she died in 1969. Lula Maddox's last words to her daughter were cast at Rose as she walked out of the house on her way to a job. Mama Maddox was begging her not to go off and sing.

After that, Rose continued to earn a respectable living as a solo performer for a while. Then her son Donnie died of a stroke in 1982, which hurt her badly. "I do miss him," she said. "Not as much as I used to. Time changes everything. But it takes time. It didn't hurt me when my mother and father passed away. That didn't hurt me like my son passing away. I'll probably never get over it, but it gets easier as time goes by."

A few years later her heart began to give out. Maddox has endured numerous heart attacks. Half her stomach was removed in the 1960s. She spent three months in a coma in 1988, and has received seven separate bypass heart operations. The hospital bills cost her almost everything she had, leaving her now, at seventy-one, where she began—singing for her supper. Her voice has some fraction of the volume that she once could summon, which is a lot of volume. There is still plenty of personality left in her voice, too. A man who owns a small room doesn't lose anything when he hires Rose Maddox, and the people go home feeling better than she does.

"After I had my open-heart surgery I had to learn to sing all over again," she said. "I had to learn my breathing and phrasing all over again. I just belted it out. I don't kick as high as I used to since that operation. I was unconscious for three months. When I got out I had to learn to walk and learn everything else all over again. I've never been the same since, physically."

It was quiet in her Oregon living room. The skinny dog wasn't growling anymore and neither was Maddox. For just a moment she seemed a little wistful. "I miss the good times," she said. "The traveling. The music. The crowds. It's just good memories." Then the cloud blew over and she brightened. "This past weekend I worked at a lodge out in the mountains," she said. "Big K Ranch with Johnny Cash's piano player. I don't go all night anymore, but I could."

Nashville West. In the 1930s, downtown Bakersfield was full of cheap hotels where Dust Bowl refugees flopped when they pulled into town.

BUCK OWENS

HONKY-TONK MAN

"I named myself after a horse or a mule, one of the two," the great honky-tonk singer and guitar player Alvis Edgar Owens, Jr., was saying. "My dad said mule. My mom said horse. My dad said I came in one day when I was three or four years old and said, 'Call me Buck.' He said I wouldn't answer if they didn't."

Buck Owens has, of course, kept mulishly to that promise. Right from the first, he explained, he has been an implacable sort. "Somebody said to me, 'I heard you were born in the backseat of a car on the way to the damn hospital,' " he said. "Somebody else said, 'I heard it was in the front seat.' I said, 'Yeah, but have you heard the part where my mother was driving?' " He laughed easily. Then he said, "I'll do my best to lie to you, but I'll tell you I'm lying. You've got to have some fun in this life. People are too damn serious."

Owens was sitting in the conference room of a modern white-concrete and black-glass two-story office building. Outside the door, people wearing ties and dresses moved in and out of meetings, answered telephones, and strode purposefully along carpeted hallways. Owens, however, was dressed for play. He wore a battered pair of white golf shoes, putty-colored golf slacks, a black sportshirt, and a black baseball cap. Every few minutes he pulled off the cap and slammed his fingers through a head of hair that was decidedly less ruly than the smooth bob he sported in the mid-1960s. Down the hall in a large corner office filled with several Fender Stratocaster guitars, a grand piano, some cowboy sculpture, a working fireplace, plush couches and chaise longues, a pistol that once belonged to John Wayne, a great number of photographs, and some gleaming exercise equipment, he'd left the television on. Nobody went in to turn it off. It was as though he owned the place. Which he does. There was, in fact, a time when people liked to say that he owned the whole danged town.

Buck Owens lives in Bakersfield, California, as he has since 1951. (He moved away to a suburb of Tacoma, Washington, in 1958, and then hurried back two years later.) His current holdings, centered in Bakersfield and in Phoenix, Arizona, include several radio and television stations, a syndicated radio-program package, and a pair of consumer newspapers. "Shit, he's rich," says Owens's former songwriting partner, Harlan Howard. "He's a tycoon!" Owens has some land in and outside Bakersfield as well, but people didn't begin referring to this oil-and-cotton town at the foot of the San Joaquin Valley as Buckersfield because he was another Okie who found gold in California. It was the music.

In the early 1960s, when much of the country coming out of Nashville was being cosseted with brass, strings, and background vocal arrangements, Buck Owens made music that sounded like a broken beer bottle. Every night in Bakersfield the cotton workers, the fruit pickers, and the oil-field roughnecks paraded into the honky-tonks and dance halls along old Highway 99. They came to talk, to dance, to drink, and sometimes to mix it up a little. Owens gave them songs you could do all that to. It was jerk-the-jukebox country, vigorous music spiked by difficult experience played loud enough to be heard above the clamor of a late night in a crowded room.

Owens himself was no hell-raiser. He didn't drink alcohol because he saw that liquor made men relax their judgment, and Owens always had his career in mind. This was, after all, a man shrewd enough to position himself to the far left of the photographer in group shots so that his name would appear first on the caption line in the newspaper. In his office now, he pointed to a framed poster of a fetching woman dressed in fox-hunting clothes standing beside a Rolls-Royce. "Poverty Sucks," it read. "My favorite poster," Owens said. "I believe that."

Buck Owens came to make hard-hitting songs for hard-bitten people by growing up with nothing in his secondhand pockets. He visited Bakersfield first as a child, working beside his parents as a seasonal fruit and cotton picker, an experience that he found so unpleasant he could remember almost nothing about the place when he came back years later to

*Buck Owens. "I'm one of those
turn-on-the-damn-thing-and-here-we-go folks."*

sing in the honky-tonks. From the stage in tough dance bars like The Blackboard, he would stare out at the crowds and know exactly what they'd been doing all day, and it repelled him. He didn't want that life again. When he'd first started playing, music had been a way, he once put it, "to avoid dealing with how hard we worked and how little we got paid for it." Eventually, he saw that his guitar could keep him forever out of the fields if he taught himself to play it well enough. That was all the incentive he needed.

The singer Bonnie Owens was married first to Buck Owens (from 1948 to 1953) and later to Merle Haggard (from 1965 to 1978). Aside from each man's having spent much of his life in Bakersfield, she says they couldn't be more different. "Buck has a business head on his shoulders," she told me. "He knows how to make things work for him. Merle's creating all the time. He could care less if the rent's paid. Money don't mean that much to him."

Money was dear to Owens, and his country music made him plenty of it. For a prolific period in the 1960s, every three months he had something new waiting when his latest hit began to relax. Owens doesn't write autobiographical music about the hard life as Haggard does. His songs, with their deft hooks and catchy titles, like "Under Your Spell Again" and "My Heart Skips a Beat," seemed calculated to distract people from their lot, to make them forget their bad times as he was resisting his own. It was commercial music, and perhaps a little bloodless, but the way Owens played it was always raw and exciting, and the crooning sound of his voice moved people. He might claim he didn't think about his past, and perhaps he didn't, and yet he couldn't pry it out of that voice so easily. It was so full of soul that people liked to say they could hear the Red River in it.

Then, in 1968, at the height of his recording career, Owens made a cynical decision. He signed on with *Hee Haw,* a new country comedy television show. "Did I know television was going to hurt my record career?" he said to me. "Yes. I saw what it did to Perry Como, Andy Williams, and Johnny Cash. No more mystique." Beyond this influence, it recast a serious singer as a hillbilly clown. To many people, Buck Owens, the man who'd invented the "Bakersfield Sound" and made country music hip by playing it loud and raw, became "That fool guy on *Hee Haw.*"

Music had made him a wealthy man. Still, Owens says money attracted him to television and kept him at it even as it transformed his reputation. In this way he was like the sizable number of Dust Bowl refugees still living around Bakersfield, who have made themselves rich but continue to live watchfully, searching the horizon for a new blight of the sort that wiped out their fathers sixty years ago. The entire year's worth of *Hee Haw* shows were recorded during a week-long session in June and another one in November. Owens says that at the end of each session he was paid a spectacular sum of money: "I'd leave and they'd hand me $200,000, and that was twenty-five years ago." He was a member of the *Hee Haw* troupe until 1986. His last number-one single, the treacly "Made in Japan," came in 1972. "Would I do it again?" he said. "Absolutely."

Buck Owens thinks like his music. His thoughts tend to come out in brief surges, and though they don't exactly sound pat or canned—he rarely consents to be interviewed—they aren't terribly vivid, either. He says he isn't reluctant to talk about his very interesting life, but the details of what is, after all, a kind of triumphant immigrant success story appear to have been compressed in his mind. He seemed to me more an active person than a meditative one, someone with plans and ambitions who wanted to get at the thrust of something and then to move on. More often than not, when Owens said something I felt sure he could tell a great deal more. Not that I thought it was ever a calculated decision to hold back. This was his nature. For someone who spent a considerable portion of his life in loud bars where you had to shout into someone's ear to be heard, succinctness is a virtue.

He was born in the Dust Bowl in 1929. "We lived in Sherman, Texas, just across the Red River from Oklahoma," he told me. "Sherman looked like a lot of little southwestern towns. It had red-brick streets, a little square—the courthouse was there—big trees. A typical little Texas town. We lived a short distance from the center of town. Two or three miles. Maybe less."

Earlier generations of Owens's family had pushed west from Appalachia. (His maternal grandmother came from North Carolina.) His father, Alvis Edgar Owens, was a Texas sharecropper married to an Arkansas girl named Maicie Azel Owens. Alvis Owens farmed his rented acres and sometimes also hired himself out to work on other men's dairy farms, which meant he was up milking cows before dawn and then going back to do it again after dark. For all his efforts, he couldn't beat the drought cycle. By the early 1930s, with dust storms blowing the rich topsoil off the land, the family gave up on Texas and joined the thousands of other people creeping west in overstuffed Fords, Hudsons, and La Salles.

"We left when I was seven," Owens said. "Ten of us in the old '33 Ford coupé. Five adults and five kids. My sister was two years old. She didn't take up much room. It took us a few days. Some days we made only 200 miles. We had a big old trailer on the back that my dad built. We tried to put all the heavy stuff in it so it wasn't too hard on the poor old Ford. We'd always stop to find stuff to build a fire with. You know *that* was our job, us kids. We had mattresses on top of the car. My brother and I slept on a cot. Regular army cot. He was on one end, me on the other. We overlapped on each other considerable. We went because we were looking for a better way of life. There were, if you recall from *The Grapes of Wrath,* circulars they put out. People thought they put them out here in California, but they actually came from Arizona. The circulars said 'Wanted: Fruit Pickers.' "

That was in 1937, the crest of a four-year arc of southwestern diaspora that saw as many as 500,000 people from Louisiana, Texas, Arkansas, Missouri, and Oklahoma cross into California. Regardless of which state they came from, when the Dust Bowl refugees got to California, they discovered that they were all just "Okies" to the locals, who regarded them with mixed fear and hostility. The Okies moved in anonymous packs with no obligations to the communities they passed through. They were said to be stupid, feckless, lice-infested, thieving, and indecent. Children were warned to avoid their encampments. "There was things where you weren't welcome," Owens said. "I remember my dad saying when we got into New Mexico that people would make disparaging talk about where we were going. You know, 'So-called people taking so-called jobs.' " The neat placards in shop windows that said "No Niggers/No Okies" did not exactly spawn brotherly feeling between poor whites and blacks. There was nobody left to look down upon.

The Owenses didn't make it to California. In Phoenix, the trailer hitch snapped, and because they had family in nearby Mesa, Arizona, they wattled what they had into a home right there. Most of the year, Alvis Owens worked as a manual laborer, hiring himself out to dairy farms, driving trucks, and digging ditches. He still barely made it from year to year. Buck Owens grew up in homes that sometimes had no electricity. Because the house in Mesa didn't have running water, Alvis Owens strapped a thirty-gallon barrel to the car and filled it at a local well. There were entire years when Owens slept head to foot in the same cot with his brother—his sisters did the same thing—and wore shoes he laced up with twine. When harvest season came, all the Owenses got into the car and drove to California, where they lived a bedouin existence, scurrying up and down the San Joaquin and Sacramento valleys, from cotton country to tomato country, trying to keep up with the harvest.

Owens is a large man with a stout trunk, outsize earlobes, creases where his cheeks furl into his chin, and long, thick fingers that are rarely still when he talks. Farmboy hands. "We were fruit tramps," Owens said. "The whole family worked. You got paid for how much you produced. After we got to Arizona they'd take us out of school two or three weeks early and we'd come out here to California to take up potatoes, then grapes, carrots, peaches. We spent most of our time picking cotton. I picked a lot of cotton. That's mostly what I did. You'd get back to Arizona two or three weeks late to start school. But nobody wasn't in your hair if your grades were good. Moving around was a hassle. A huge hassle. You start school, move somewhere else. Go to another school. Then another, another, then back to the first school. My daddy was always looking for something better. He was easily offended."

"How do you mean?" I asked. But Owens didn't mean to tell about specific flashes of temper. "He had four kids and a wife and he didn't know how he was gonna feed them," he said. "Lots of times as a kid I went to bed hungry. We'd had only cornbread and milk."

One of the places they passed through during those summers was Bakersfield. "We started coming out this way when I was eight, nine, or ten," he said. "I remember it as being like most other towns I ever saw. Hot and dusty. It looked like Arizona and Texas. It looked like . . ." he paused. "I guess the thing I remember best about Bakersfield then was they had a big old clock tower. Also, I remember they had some kind of a priest down at the traffic circle." He spread his big hands. "I really didn't care," he said. "Everything always seemed to look the same. They had labor camps and we'd stay in them for a few days. We always lived in tents, or we lived in some old house. Wherever. When you went to the labor camps they had rows of little old cabins with bathrooms down at the end and some of them actually had showers. Of course they didn't have any hot water." The interior walls, he said, were covered with newspaper. So too were the windows.

The camps were full of music. The black, white, and Mexican workers kept to themselves in the fields, each group claiming its own six or eight rows. As they worked, the Mexicans sang Mexican folksongs, the blacks sang blues and spirituals, and the white people sang country gospel and Jimmie Rodgers songs. On Sundays, wherever they were, Owens's family searched out a church. "My mother played piano," he said. "Let me tell you my mother could *shred* a piano. We always found a church to go to, and my mother played every church we ever went to. They were always looking for somebody to play a piano like that."

It was in Arizona that he first saw poor people coming into town on Saturday to blow the week's earnings on a big time. Not Owens—he was thrifty by nature. "After we got to Arizona on Saturdays you'd work in the morning and then in the afternoon we went to town," he says. "You had a dime to go to the picture show, a nickel for popcorn, and also a nickel for a cold drink. They always had a cowboy show for all the young people. I looked for length for my dime. How long was it? Most often I stayed twice. Then you roamed the streets of Mesa until dark, until the sun started to go down and you'd get your tail over to the car. I went to one of two theaters in Mesa," he went on. "One Saturday in 1940, I remember one theater had a cowboy movie, the other, The Ritz, had a three-hour movie called *The Grapes of Wrath*. I felt robbed after *The Grapes of Wrath*. I thought they'd duped me. Took my dime. I didn't need to see that. I'd done it."

Then Owens said that *The Grapes of Wrath* has become his favorite movie. I asked him why he too, like John Steinbeck or Merle Haggard, didn't try to write about the bedraggled people he saw out West in the 1930s and 1940s. The reply came fast. "In our world," he told me, "music is always dependent on the economic times. If times were bad, how were there going to be any happy songs? Those were terrible times. I don't remember 'em very good and I'm glad I don't."

Owens quit school after finishing the eighth grade in 1942. He was thirteen, but already taller than most men, and found it easy to get jobs. In the next couple of years, his parents gave him both a guitar and a mandolin, and the instruments led Owens into the Mesa honky-tonks. This didn't please his parents, teetotalers who had stood by just a short time before as a fundamentalist preacher baptized Owens in a river in Chandler, Arizona. "I was still learning to play music," Owens said. "My dad would tell me, 'Stay out of the damn honky-tonks. Nothing good ever happened in a honky-tonk.' But I hung around the honky-tonks, at the back doors if they wouldn't let you in."

He wanted to see and hear professional musicians, and a bar was, he says, the only place you could listen to good country music. "You could hear a little Sons of the Pioneers on the radio, but there were no country music stations like today," he said. "No rock stations. No Mexican stations. A lot of the radio was taken up by big band, but not too many of us hillbillies enjoyed that too much." He took off his cap, shot his hand through his hair, and then put it back on. "There were classical stations, but what did anybody with an eighth-grade education know about classical music?"

People told Owens he was some singer, but he didn't like to think of himself in that way. "All I wanted then," he said, "was to be the greatest guitar player there ever was." He'd bought himself a steel guitar by the time he met an enterprising Mesa filling-station owner named Mac MacAtee, who installed Owens as the steel player in his band, Mac's Skillet Lickers. There were some promising young singers around Phoenix at the time. One of them was Martin Robertson, a harmonica player's son who changed his name to Marty Robbins so that his parents wouldn't know what he was doing for a living. Owens knew him a little. A singer he got better acquainted with was Bonnie Campbell, a Blanchard, Oklahoma, dirt farmer's daughter who changed her name to Bonnie Owens when she was fifteen years old, four months pregnant, and just married to Buck Owens.

People who knew Owens in his younger days describe him as a good-looking woman-in-every-port scamp. He says as much himself. "I met a lot of women," Owens said. "Every chance I got, I went out with them. I loved women. I first got married in January 1948. Bonnie and I went together for about a year and a half and never had sex. I had done some things from the time I was thirteen or fourteen, but the belief in those days was there's girls to have sex with, but don't have sex with your best girl. Bonnie and I were boyfriend and girlfriend and the other reason why we didn't—we was so afraid we'd get pregnant. On my eighteenth birthday we decided to. Later on we counted and it was nine months to the day my son Buddy was born."

They had another son almost immediately. "After we got married, Buck worked all night in the honky-tonks, then he went out to pick oranges or pick cotton," Bonnie Owens told me. "He hated it. He kept getting kicked out of the nightclubs, you know. He was too young to play in them and he'd lie about his age. He'd get found out and get fired." Owens hadn't liked Bakersfield at all as a kid, but in 1951 he went there to live. It was a practical decision. Bakersfield had more bars than Mesa did, and was getting a reputation as a good place to hear country music. "For some reason, as opposed to Fresno or L.A., Bakersfield had the truest form of hard country music," the singer Tommy Collins, who lived there for much of the 1950s and 1960s, told me. "It was more like a town in the Midwest. I came from Oklahoma and I felt at home there right away."

Bakersfield then was a small city of 65,000 people, many of them Dust Bowl migrants from Texas and Oklahoma who were working in the oil fields or on farms. At night they came into town and went to the Clover Club—where Bonnie Owens took a job waitressing and singing when she and Owens first got to town—Jimbo's, Tex's Barrel House, The Blackboard, The Lucky Spot, and half a dozen more. Owens treated them all as a young painter with his sketchbook does the galleries in a museum. He looked at what other people did, tried doing it himself, and then began to work out his own ideas.

Not long after they got to California, Bonnie left him for good. Like a weak roof, gradually and then all at once, the marriage had collapsed. Owens told me he was "too young" for a family and Bonnie Owens agrees. "He liked to stay out all night," she said. "You know how that goes. Sometimes he didn't come home for two days." The way Owens talks about himself in those days, he makes it sound as though he was single-minded about his life both because he knew he had special talent and because "I wanted to be warm in winter, cool in summer, and not ever be hungry."

"I got in a band as soon as I got here," he said. "It was out at The Round Up. The place is gone. There were four other guys in the band. Forty bucks a night. We got eight bucks apiece. I thought, 'This ain't bad.' Not long after that I got a job at a place called The Blackboard. Great big place. Held 500 people. Chairs, tables, big dance floor. You came in there to drink, dance, meet somebody. Guy hired me away from the other band for $12.50 a night. I made enough money to pay my bills for the first time in my life."

The Blackboard—"Dancing Six Nites a Week"—was the biggest joint in Bakersfield, a rough, exciting nightspot where, says Bonnie Owens, "they'd fight and drink in that order." It was a long night at The Blackboard that inspired the songwriter Joe Maphis to write the honky-tonk classic "Dim Lights, Thick Smoke, and Loud, Loud Music." Owens was there for nearly a decade, working for a bandleader named Bill Woods. When the regular singer didn't show up one day, Woods told his new guitar player that he wanted him to handle the vocals. Right away it was obvious that Owens had just the sort of ringing, spacious voice that carried to the corners of a noisy room. "He sang," says Tommy Collins, "with a lot of confidence."

Harlan Howard says he used to rib Owens in those days because "Bill Woods was up there smoking a pipe and flirting with girls while Buck was working his ass off getting a menial wage."

Owens has a different perspective. "I was at The Blackboard seven years, six nights a week," he said. "The way I saw it, I was getting paid to

Dim lights, thick smoke, and loud, loud music: the classic
Bakersfield honky-tonk, inside and out.

learn my trade. When you pick cotton you're down like this." He stooped and bent his neck. "You don't look up. Once I got it going in music I never looked up. I was afraid if I looked up, when I looked back down the opportunity would have escaped."

Honky-tonks like The Blackboard were places people went to for pleasure. Yet when Owens describes the windowless concrete sheds where he spent his twenties, he makes them sound dreary and grim. "The typical honky-tonk held 100 people," he said. "There were different kinds of tables and chairs. Some of them might match. There was a long old bar that had been there for years. There were old mirrors at the back of the bar, a jukebox, a long shuffleboard table. The floor was wood—well used. The bathrooms would barely be passable. One stall, maybe. The bar was always wet—the bartenders would wipe it off with a wet rag. The bandstand might be three or four feet high, or it might be just standing over in the corner. I played those places," he said.

Then Owens began talking about who he saw in the honky-tonks. He didn't speak of anyone in particular. Like his songs, the spoken portraits were brief, fleshed out with a minimum of detail as though he was leaving it to you to fill in the faces. "They were places to go for the people to get out of the cold or the heat," he said. "It was women, if you were a man, and it was whiskey. Some could only forget when they drank. Some could only remember when they drank. I never drank. I saw what it made other people look like. Damn fools. I saw people get drunk, get out of control, and spend their week's pay in one night. Lots of drinking. I saw people's lives break apart, wives go crazy, men go nuts. I saw people spend the rent money. I always looked at it that it's better if they do it where I'm playing than down the street where somebody else was singing." Sometimes after people say something like this they laugh, to take the edge off it. Owens didn't laugh.

By the mid-1950s, The Blackboard was a popular redoubt for touring country musicians. Rose Maddox, Tex Ritter, and Patsy Cline all sang there, and any musician who was in town was bound to turn up at the bar. Among those who passed through for short or lengthy periods were Tommy Collins, Dallas Frazier, Ferlin Husky, Jean Shepard, Spade Cooley—until he was sent to prison for kicking his wife to death—Tommy Duncan, and Wynn Stewart. Stewart lived in Los Angeles, where he knew Harlan Howard. One day at The Blackboard in 1956, Stewart introduced Owens to the young songwriter. Before long, Howard was coming up to Bakersfield on weekends to collaborate with Owens. "Harlan and I, we'd go out to the honky-tonks and get home at 2:00 A.M. and sit up the rest of the damn night trying to write songs," Owens said. "Easiest thing in the world writing with him." Owens lived in a two-bedroom shack that had many features in common with a farmworker's cabin. When Howard stayed over he slept in a bed that had a cinder block where one of the legs should have been.

Popular as Owens became in Bakersfield, the records he made for Capitol in Los Angeles didn't sell. No longer confident about his future, when he was offered a job at a small Tacoma, Washington, radio station he took it. He was running a televised talent show in 1960, at a club called The Britannia, when he met Loretta Lynn. "In walks this girl in a blue suit with white fringe and her pant legs stuck in these white boots," he said. "She wins the talent contest. We give her a watch. Two hours later they have a talent contest at another place. They give her a watch too. She told me neither one of them worked."

"They broke all to pieces," Loretta Lynn told me. "I said, 'Buck, these watches fell apart.' He said, 'What do you expect. It's a three-dollar watch.' Buck was wild and rowdy, playing the clubs. The music was loud—too loud for me. He said, 'You'll never see nobody leave if the music's loud. If it's soft, people'll walk out.' So after that I played loud the way he did. When I got to the fourth or fifth song, if a fight didn't break out in Texas I'd think I was doing something wrong."

Another person he met in Washington was a pink-faced sixteen-year-old fiddle player named Don Rich. Rich was too young to work the honky-tonks, but he and Owens began playing at dance halls together, and when Owens drove to Los Angeles to cut more records, Rich went with him. "On the way down, I'm driving and singing, and Don starts singing harmony with me. I said, 'Hey!' He sounded like me. One of those guys who could read your mind a little bit. I don't know what it was. If you listen to all the cuts you'll think he's singing melody and I'm singing harmony. You can't tell. There are some people it just happens like that with. I never knew what made Don and I meld so much." Rich and Owens sang duets of a different kind from the acrobatic harmonies of The Louvin Brothers. There was something almost clairvoyant about the way they joined their voices together, so that in songs like "Hello Trouble" and "Cryin' Time" the effect is one sound coming from two men.

Rich turned out to be a wonderful guitar player as well. When "Under Your Spell Again" became Owens's first top-ten hit in 1960, he moved back to Bakersfield and shortly afterward Rich joined him there. For the next few years the two of them drove all over the country in a Ford, singing together at honky-tonks and often flopping in the same room at budget motels. Rich became the de facto leader of The Buckaroos, which is the name Merle Haggard dreamed up for Owens's band during the brief stint he worked as Owens's bass player in 1962.

Beginning with "You're for Me," in 1961, Owens and Rich made music that hit people clean, clear, and, Owens liked to say, hard as a freight train. Their vocals were always up front, shoved along in two-by-four rhythm by regular doses of steel, nervy electric guitar runs, and more drums than anybody else in country music was using. The "Bakersfield Sound" was stripped-down, no-chaser bar music that was livelier than the mainstream music coming out of Nashville. It was destined to bring Bakersfield fame as the locus of alternative country.

"There was no thought put into it," Owens said. "The sound just came about. I had a big old Fender Telecaster guitar, the walls of the buildings were hard, the dance floor was cement, the roof was sheet metal. There was considerable echo in there. You have to remember that you had a dance floor with 120 or 130 people on it. It was just the sound people wanted. In Nashville they were producing things with softer, more syrupy sound." He grinned wide and said, "I'm one of those turn-on-the-damn-thing-and-here-we-go folks."

On Owens's records from that time you hear a lot of treble and hardly any echo. "It was very raw so you could feel like you could reach out and touch it," says Bonnie Owens, who toured as a backup singer with her ex-husband in the 1960s. "To me the music was pure voice and everything else was behind. To me that's what the Bakersfield sound was. The voice was most important and the band was just accompanying, adding to the purity and rawness of it."

In his prime, Owens had a voice that all but pulled people toward it. In contrast to the coarse, jagged feel of the guitar runs, Owens's vocals displayed luxurious range and some of the bruised smoothness that you hear in another Texas-born singer, George Jones—not surprising because Owens listened to a lot of Jones's records in the 1950s and then spent time touring the country with him in the 1960s. Owens moved through a song like "My Heart Skips a Beat" more quickly than Jones would have, but the way he swooped up and down an octave and rested on his hard vowels gave his singing the same gusts of feeling that you hear in Jones. There is so much natural emotion to it, in fact, that the pattern and sound of the songs is as important as their meaning.

Owens sang mostly love and cheating songs that relied on snappy wordplay and smart turns of phrase. "I Don't Care (Just as Long as You Love Me)" is rife with lines like "Let it rain, let it snow, let the cold north wind blow, just as long as you love me/North or south, east or west, you know I will stand the test, just as long as you love me." When Owens wrote with Harlan Howard, the usual pattern was that Howard handled the lyrics and Owens wrote the melodies. The words for the song that is perhaps Owens's most powerful, "Excuse Me (I Think I've Got a Heartache)," came to Howard when he visited his friend, the singer and disc jockey "Texas" Bill Strength. It quickly became clear to Howard that Strength's wife was leaving him, an awkward situation that Strength finally resolved by telling Howard, "You'll have to excuse me, Harlan. I think I've got a heartache." Howard hastened out of the house and immediately began scheming about how to make a song out of the situation. It was music that came out of the air rather than from the heart.

Howard had left California in 1960, but he and Owens kept in touch. In 1964, they met up in Texas. "He and his wife Jan came down and spent a week with me," Owens said. "They drove down in a big Cadillac sedan. Jan was driving and I was sitting up there with her. I had a guitar. We were headed for Amarillo. Gonna be at the Cow Palace that night." Every Esso gas station they passed had a picture of the Esso tiger roaring "Put a Tiger in Your Tank." "I'd been moaning about writing a song about getting a tiger by the tail," Owens said. "Seems like the safest place to be and then he'll turn around and eat you. I'd been thinking about the old Dixieland song 'Hold That Tiger' ["Tiger Rag"]. We was riding along and all of a sudden Harlan wasn't talking. Took him all of ten minutes to write. Then he pitches me the lyric. 'There's your damn tiger by the tail,' he says. 'Where's the music? Put the Hydromatic to it.' He called my music that because it was considerably more frantic—more drums, more drive and zing to it."

"I've Got a Tiger by the Tail" was one of the fifteen number-one hits Owens had between 1963 and 1967. During one week in 1964, "My Heart Skips a Beat" and "Together Again" were the number-one and number-two hits in the country. The following week they exchanged places. A week later, they switched back again. Instead of honky-tonks, Owens was playing a night at Carnegie Hall and arriving for extended runs in Las Vegas. Owens took to using a red, white, and blue guitar in 1966, and for a time it was as familiar to music fans as Johnny Cash's black suit. Then, in 1968, he signed on with *Hee Haw*.

Five years later Owens was awakened by an early morning telephone call telling him that Don Rich had been killed in a motorcycle accident. Owens said that the tragedy thrust him into a malaise that lasted the better part of a decade. "How can I tell you how I felt in those years?" he said. "It was the most miserable time of my life. This guy, this person, this being that was always right here." He paused and thought for a long moment. "Musicians have got this great fear of hell," he said, finally. "What most musicians hate most of all is a drummer who drags the tempo. That's what we think hell will be for us. I've spoken about it with different entertainers. Hell is playing the same gig over and over with the same dragging drummer. That's what it was like for me. Nothing was fun. There were people who wanted Don to make records. He'd say to me, 'You know, Chief'—he called me Chief—'I don't want to get more famous. I like it like this.' I thought of Don Rich as my son and I thought of him as my brother. We were so totally . . ." He halted. "Well, we been together all those years in the old Ford, just him and I. I've never lost a son. I have three. I could not imagine." He stopped again, briefly. "We were closer than father and son. We were there, at times, twenty-four hours a day. We didn't have money for two rooms. We had money for one room. We'd be out playing every little place. Like Sam's Place. The quintessential honky-tonk. It's in Richmond, California. It held eighty to a hundred people. My first time there the owner tried to drive a car through the front door. The next time he got into an argument. He pulls out a .45 and shoots two or three shots through the ceiling. Big old gun."

As a young man during his first few years with Owens, Rich had been slender, with a crisp, cheerful look about him. His hair was short, his smile always wide, friendly, and carefree. He looked freshly laundered. Later, as he put on weight, his face sagged. Around Owens's office were photographs of Rich only as a young man. Some of the other pictures are of Owens's wife, Jennifer, and of Dwight Yoakam standing beside a bright red 1959 Cadillac. Yoakam is a young country singer who grew up listening to Buck Owens and opened his own first album with the line "I'm a honky-tonk man." He introduced himself to Owens in 1987, and their friendship seems to have eased some of the misery Owens felt over Rich's death. It was Owens who gave Yoakam the Cadillac. He also presented him with a song, Homer Joy's "Streets of Bakersfield," which Owens had recorded himself in 1972. Yoakam and Owens sang it as a duet in 1988, and it became a number-one hit for Yoakam. Owens's favorite line in the

*Buck Owens and The Buckaroos (Doyle Holly, Willie Cantu, Owens,
Don Rich, and Tom Brumley). "I thought of Don Rich as my son
and I thought of him as my brother."*

song is the first one: "You don't know me but you don't like me." When people come to Bakersfield, look around a little, and ask him why he lives there, that line comes to his mind.

Kern County, California, of which Bakersfield is the seat, produces more oil than all but three of the world's *countries*. Only two other American counties grow more crops. Despite all the revenue, Bakersfield looks gritty. It is a tough town, with its share of lean dogs, cheap Mexican and barbecue joints, used-car lots, car washes, and surly gentlemen slouching down North Chester Avenue in cowboy boots. Young men in pickup trucks like to scream past the blocks of low-slung houses. Boys always drive too fast in towns where there's nowhere to go.

For Buck Owens, staying in Bakersfield is a point of pride. "The people here in Bakersfield are my kind of folks," he said. "Nashville used to call Bakersfield Nashville West. I called Nashville Bakersfield East. I know everybody else left and went away and that nobody ever comes back here. I stayed here because these are my kind of people. The kind of people who come over to offer help because they see help's needed before you have to ask."

Owens is adding to the Bakersfield skyline. He's conceived a country music theater and museum to be called Buck Owens's Crystal Palace. There will be dining, shopping, and dancing. Hanging from the ceiling will be the Buckmobile, a silver-dollar-studded white Pontiac convertible with longhorns on the grillwork, a six-shooter gearshift lever, more pistols serving as door handles, and a horn that makes the sound of stampeding hooves. The house band will be none other than Buck Owens and his Buckaroos. "This is a five-million-dollar installation," he said. "My money. Money I made. I could have built it a lot of places. Here's where it all happened. Here's where it belongs."

The Crystal Palace will open in a town that is quite different from the one Buck Owens made famous in the 1950s and 1960s. Bakersfield has evolved in some of the ways that many places change and in one that is unique: all the great Bakersfield honky-tonks have vanished. The Blackboard building is still there, but these days it smells of oregano instead of stale beer; it is now home to a pizza parlor. On the former Tex's Barrel House site is an adult-entertainment shop. The place that most closely resembles one of the old joints is Trout's, which has many of the right touches, including no windows, a dance floor, and a reasonably hostile clientele. Somehow, Kenny G's lite jazz is on the jukebox.

"When I came here in 1951, there was three places that had bands six nights a week," Owens said. "Today the place is three times bigger and there's no place with a full-time band. I'm sad. Where's the music gonna come from? Where are people gonna learn? That's where you learn."

I asked him if he would play the Crystal Palace six nights a week. "I ain't that sad," he said.

Merle Haggard spoke the lines to his new songs aloud and Bonnie Owens wrote them down. "He'd say to me later, 'Bonnie, I don't ever remember saying those words.' I knew he said them. I was there."

MERLE HAGGARD *and* **IRIS DEMENT**

GOING TO GET
A SANDWICH

Merle Haggard is not the first person anyone notices when they walk into even an uncrowded room. He is much smaller than he appears on stage and, despite his well-known face, he has the ability, common in elusive men, to make people look right past him. When eventually you do locate Haggard, you are likely to find him gazing at you in a way that makes it clear he has been taking your measure for some time. I was a bit taken aback when I first found him studying me, but Haggard is a genuinely warmhearted man who doesn't mean any harm. He just wants to be sure you aren't the type to block the exits. Haggard escaped from correctional institutions seventeen times before he turned twenty-one, and though he gave up the rogue's life long ago, he has never shaken his need to flee.

Seven of us were in the console room of the recording studio at Shade Tree Manor, Haggard's Northern California compound. Hanging along the wall in the hallway outside the room were photographs of Haggard beside shots of people in the country music business he has known and admired, and the framed citations Haggard is always receiving from foundations thanking him for his support for hungry children. In photographs, Haggard tends to look somewhat like a peevish young Warren Beatty, his gonna-break-every-heart-I-can blue eyes glaring out from beneath dark eyebrows, which in turn are set below a bold plateau of forehead. The camera is invariably so taken with the energy in his face that it obscures Haggard's compact build, something I was reminded of when I finally found him slouched deep in an easy chair beneath a photograph of the legendary Texas fiddler and bandleader Bob Wills. Bundled up in a windbreaker that he wore over a rumpled green shirt, Haggard seemed reduced. His eyes had some red at the sockets, and though lines have been sketched on his face for years, as he approaches sixty they have deepened into shallow ditches. A Gas Processing cap was jammed onto his head. He hadn't shaved in a while, or possibly he was beginning a beard—it was hard to tell. "Set wherever you want," he said in such a way that you couldn't miss the Oklahoma in his voice.

The other people in the room included Norman Hamlet, Abe Manuel, Jr., and his brother Joe Manuel, who are all members of Haggard's band, The Strangers, a record producer named Lou Bradley, the young singer-songwriter Iris DeMent, and her husband, Elmer McCall. Iris DeMent has firm, intelligent blue eyes and straight, dusky blond hair that she wears at shoulder length, just a little shorter than Elmer keeps his pony-tail. The couple was on hand because Haggard had decided to record two of DeMent's songs, "The Shores of Jordan" and "No Time to Cry," and he had asked her to help him learn them. Like everyone else in the room, she is a devoted Merle Haggard fan.

At the moment they were working on "No Time to Cry," a song about a woman who has spent a year repressing the grief she feels over her fa-ther's death. Haggard asked DeMent to sing it for him. She has a raw voice that is also pretty and especially affecting in jut-jawed songs about troubled times, such as this one. As she went through lines like "If the feelin' starts to comin', I've learned to stop 'em fast/'Cause I don't know, if I let them go, they might not wanna pass," everyone looked a little weepy. When DeMent finished, Haggard said to her, "Iris, when you sing your eyes do exactly what Jimmie Rodgers's did." (Later, when Haggard was asked what he meant by this, he said, "They both look lost in the song, like they love it so much that they're *living* the song. That seldom hap-pens.") Haggard leaned forward in his chair and thought for a moment. "I'm trying to decide how to sing this," he said, finally. "It's not really sor-row. It's a kind of emptiness that comes on when you know the dearly de-parted are really gone. It's real hard to describe it without being morbid or unpleasing. Some songs, great songs, you can't bear to hear them because they make you cry."

Then he began to sing the song himself, and his slight frame seemed to expand. Haggard's voice is rich and supple, mixing melisma with the un-expected wrinkles of feeling that put the ache in his sad songs. His father died when he was nine, and many people who know him say the loss helped mold Haggard into the contradictory person he is—a mercurial loner who surrounds himself with wives, friends, children, and obligations. As he passed through the mournful lines, "And there's just so many people trying to get me on the phone/And there's bills to pay and songs to play and a house to make a home," Haggard might as well have been singing about himself. When he got to the refrain—"I guess I'm older now and I've got no time to cry"—he let his voice break a little on the word "older," and for a moment Haggard seemed shaky and vulnerable. You wanted to do something for him. But Bradley and The Strangers just nodded. They are used to watching him work. DeMent is not. "Boy," she whispered. "He makes everything sound like a poem."

She and Elmer—who travels everywhere with her—were enjoying themselves. Despite a placard that reads "Your Beer on My Console Is Your Invitation to Leave," the room felt welcoming. There were old Merle Haggard records lying around, song lyrics spattered with brown stains— Haggard is a big tea drinker—and the dusty stash of whiskey and vodka bottles that Lewis Talley, Haggard's first producer, didn't get around to drinking before he died in 1985. A toy railroad train was parked on a shelf not far from one of Bob Wills's cigar butts, the latter carefully preserved under glass. Through a window, an old photograph of Jimmie Rodgers giving the high sign was visible in the studio chamber. Another light-hearted notice, courtesy of the songwriter Roger Miller, advised that "We Shall Over Dub."

As the morning wore on, though, the most jovial spirits in the room belonged to Haggard, who relishes the informal company of musicians. More than most great performers, he is a devotee of other people's music, especially Jimmie Rodgers's, Bob Wills's, and Lefty Frizzell's. They make such frequent appearances in his conversation that it is clear he considers the details of their lives the touchstones of his own. He would work for a while on "No Time to Cry," and then, somehow, he would find himself describing the day in Dallas when the songwriter Cindy Walker, "a beautiful blonde," according to Haggard, presented the song "Goin'-Away Party" to Bob Wills at Wills's famous final recording session. "He'd already had his stroke," said Haggard. "Wills was nearly dead. She brought this song into the session and I got sort of suspicious." Haggard put his version of the song on the stereo and we listened to him sing "I'm throwing a goin'-away party/A party for a dream of mine/Nobody's coming but a heartache/And some tears will drop in most anytime/Don't worry, it won't be a loud party/Dreams don't make any noise when they die/It's just a sad goin'-away party/For a dream I'm telling goodbye." "That's a good song," said Haggard. " 'Dreams don't make any noise when they die.' That's good, man. That is a song about Cindy Walker and Bob Wills. It's her goodbye to Bob Wills."

(When reached by telephone in Texas, Cindy Walker said that "Goin'-Away Party" had first been recorded in 1972 by Jim Ed Brown. Later, after Wills heard Don Cherry's version on the radio, he wanted to record it. Only then did Wills learn that Walker had written it. When I recounted Haggard's story, she chuckled and said, "Bless his sweet heart if he thought that. That's not the way it was, but if he thought that, that's all right. He's got to have a wonderful imagination. I was never romantically involved with Bob Wills. Bob Wills and his wife Betty named their youngest daughter for me.")

Melancholy music makes Haggard very happy. If he'd seemed listless while buried in the depths of his chair, Iris DeMent, Bob Wills, and Cindy Walker now had him full of vigor. Bounding out of the seat, he moved across the room, his feet splaying out in quick little steps as he walked. He stopped beside the framed cover of "Seashores of Old Mexico," a record he made with his good friend Willie Nelson, and began singing: "I feel so good and then I feel so bad/I wonder what I ought to do." Then he skipped ahead in the song—it is called "If I Could Only Fly"—and sang, almost to himself, "Just dismal thinking on a dismal day/And sad songs for us to bear." "Willie could sing the *hell* out of this," he said. To prove it, he put the song on the stereo and stared at us hard as we listened. Yes, Willie could. Next he was telling a story about the day Hank Snow fired the fiddler Chubby Wise for knocking Snow's toupé sideways with his bow. Then he was addressing DeMent. "I think you're gonna do really good with your songs, Iris," he said earnestly. "I've never seen material that good miss. If it goes over people's heads or between their legs, fuck 'em. Either it's good or it ain't." His hat was now on backward and he was beaming. He sang "No Time to Cry" again. "Better all the time," he hummed. "This album," he went on. "I'm gonna do it for me, for me to listen to. I'm in no rush. We got time to learn, and the desire. That's what it takes, the desire. Or a lot of dope, and I quit dope." A moment later he was excusing himself. "I'm just gonna go get a sandwich," he said.

DeMent looked over at me. "He won't come back," she said. She was right. We didn't see Haggard again all day.

◆ ◆ ◆

Merle Haggard has always been a person of strong enthusiasms. After his father died, he pursued them somewhat recklessly. That is to say, if he wanted something, it was often his policy just to take it. He was poor and poverty made him resentful. "I grew up in an oil town but my gusher never came in," he wrote in "Kern River," one of the finest of his semi-autobiographical songs.

The oil town was Bakersfield, and Haggard's part of it was Oildale, a shabby neighborhood north of the Kern River. He lived in an abandoned railroad boxcar that his father converted into a small house. (It is still standing on Yosemite Drive.) The house was half a block from the railroad tracks, and in the kitchen you could feel the freights as they rumbled by. When you stepped outside and looked straight down the tracks, beyond the horizon of spindly oil derricks you could see the snowcapped Tehachapi Mountains.

When he was fourteen, Haggard began to wish to shake loose from his life in Bakersfield and see where the freight trains went. "My problem was that I grew up too fast," he said. "I didn't want to go to school. I wanted to go to work. They wouldn't let me." And so he left town. Haggard and his good friend, Bob Teague, bought themselves a large supply of bologna and rode in boxcars and also hitchhiked their way from Bakersfield to Big Spring, Texas. Lefty Frizzell lived in Big Spring, and even at that time in his life, along with Jimmie Rodgers and Bob Wills—who Haggard once said "was more important to some of us than the President, and you know how everybody liked Harry"—there was nobody in the world he admired more than Lefty Frizzell.

As it turned out, they didn't see Lefty; he had moved on from Big Spring a year before they got there. "We just heard him all the way on jukeboxes," Haggard told me. Even so, it was quite a trip. Teague and Haggard visited San Antonio and El Paso, turned a car over in Arizona, and spent several days in the Los Angeles County Jail for somebody else's robbery. "I went to a whorehouse and got my first piece of ass and I bought my first pair of cowboy boots," Haggard said. "I was out on my own. For the first time there wasn't somebody hollering at me, telling me what to do. I enjoyed it. I had some certain things in my life I wanted to do. I wanted to hop a freight. I wanted to work in the oil fields. I wanted to play the guitar. There's a great choice of what to do in America. When I was growing up in America there was more choice than there is now. The parameters of excitement mean that for some people there's less choices now."

Sometime afterward, Haggard decided that instead of thumbing rides and jumping freights he would prefer to do his roaming in his own automobile. He and another lifelong friend, Dean Holloway—known to Haggard as Dean Row—acquired a jalopy. This was fine, except that they often had no money to pay for gas. One day, out on the road in Farmington, New Mexico, looking for work, they pulled in to a Shell service station and helped themselves to all the money in the safe. From then on, whenever the car's tank ran low, they always filled it up at Shell stations.

Because his methods of courtship bore similarities to his approaches to transportation, Haggard has been involved in not a few differences of opinion with indignant boyfriends and husbands over the years, and he is currently embroiled—and that is usually the right word for Haggard's romances—in his fifth marriage. A serious gambler, such as Haggard once was, would eagerly back a wager proposing that Haggard's appetite for comely women will never diminish. "He gets bored easily," Haggard's second wife, Bonnie Owens, told me. "He gets enough of something and he gets tired of it. The impression he gave me was, if I ever satisfy him, I'll be gone." Soon enough, of course, she did and she was.

"I was born the running kind, with leaving always on my mind," Haggard wrote in 1975, and the fact of his life has been that no matter what he is doing, after a time a feeling comes over him that he needs to be somewhere else, and he vanishes. Haggard is the child of refugees from the Dust Bowl, and so perhaps his restlessness was born into him. After James Haggard's barn burned down in 1934, he left Checotah, Oklahoma, and moved out to "Californy," as the Okies called it. He worked on a dairy farm for a while and then caught on as a carpenter with the Santa Fe Railroad. Merle Haggard came along just over two years later.

The Okies like James and Flossie Haggard who had migrated west across Route 66 found that the hot, cheerless workingman's town of Bakersfield, surrounded as it was by sprawling cotton and oil fields, reminded them a lot of Oklahoma. That so much of its population came from somewhere else gave Bakersfield the just-passing-through feel of a crossroads community. Although he was born in California, Merle Haggard has always regarded himself as a transplanted Oklahoman and, after his father died, he allowed his outlook to be formed by Depression experiences that he had, in fact, only heard about. Probably Haggard would have wandered from wherever he lived, but as someone who grew up with his feet in one place and his roots in another, the attraction to elsewhere was strong in him.

As a young man, Haggard accomplished another of those "certain things" he wanted to do by working for a while as a roughneck in the oil fields outside Bakersfield. He also harvested hay around Modesto, picked oranges and gathered up potatoes with the migrant workers in the San Joaquin Valley towns of Edison and Earlimart, worked as a short-order cook, dug ditches, and drove a truck. Mostly, though, he raised Cain, and such a lush crop of it that he completed his teens with the initials of a re-form school branded on his wrist and a protracted record of offenses that had progressed from truancy to check-forging to burglary. When people ask him why he got into so much trouble, he usually says he wanted to experience the rounder's life he heard about in Jimmie Rodgers's songs. "Wild hair's all it was," he explained to Paul Hemphill.

When he was twenty, Haggard and some friends got themselves very drunk on cheap red wine and tried to crowbar their way in through the back door of a restaurant that, unfortunately for them, was still open for business. (That's Haggard's version, anyway. Tommy Gallon, the Kern County sheriff who arrested Haggard, says he caught him climbing out of a building with a stolen check-cashing machine under his arm.) The ensu-ing two years and nine months' sentence to San Quentin Prison forever di-verted him from the criminal life, but prison did nothing to erode the edgy impulsiveness that is such a strong feature in Haggard's personality that it appears to run in dark tremors behind his eyes. More than ever, he had a strong dose of what he calls in one of his more famous songs "rambling fever in my soul," and it was the guitar that turned him loose at an honest wage.

With some help from Bob Teague, Haggard had taught himself to play the instrument as a kid. He gave his first concert at an Oildale landmark known as Beer Can Hill, where he played all night for a crowd of four. Bakersfield was dense with honky-tonks, and with country musicians. When Haggard was sixteen, Lefty Frizzell came through town and, after Haggard played for him backstage, Lefty invited him up onstage at the Rainbow Gardens. By then, Haggard was a familiar figure out on the Weedpatch Highway, begging rides to local towns where people might pay a little to hear him sing. Later, after he got out of prison, he became a regular performer in hardbitten little honky-tonks that were in every town up and down the San Joaquin Valley.

For a time, he kept this routine. On Sunday and Monday he sang at The Blackboard in Bakersfield. For Tuesday, Wednesday, and Thursday he moved over to The Lucky Spot. Then on Friday and Saturday nights, Haggard got into the car and headed a hundred miles south to The Porthole, a Navy bar in Ridgecrest, California. After he'd finished singing, he always went to Cy's Coffee Shop, a truck stop on the Edison Highway in Bakersfield, where he drank coffee until dawn. Then he drove over to the Kern River and fished for a few hours. Ten in the morning was bedtime. By late afternoon he was eating supper and getting ready to work. Years after he'd moved out of Bakersfield, he passed through town and stopped in at Cy's Coffee Shop, where the song "Kern River" came to him.

After signing on with Lewis Talley and his cousin Fuzzy Owen at Tally Records, Haggard played his first long-distance gig. It was at a strip bar in Kansas City and took place during the same week in March 1963 that Patsy Cline died. Since then, Haggard has been forever on the move. For a while, he kept the fact that he'd been in San Quentin a secret, but a conversation with Johnny Cash convinced him he should be forthcoming about it. "He said, admit it and there's nothing they can write in the tabloids," Haggard told me. "I think he was right." The

Haggard in the studio. "Merle doesn't realize that to young performers, he is what Lefty Frizzell and Bob Wills were to him."

years in prison, like so many of his other experiences, turned out to be so much research.

Haggard never forgot the faces on death row, the dusty men he mixed with in hobo jungles, or the canvas-covered labor-camp cabin where his Great-Aunt Willie Harp and his Great-Uncle Esker Harp lived. They were seasonal farm workers in Hughson, California, and had taken Haggard in for a while after his father died. Whatever had especially engaged him across the years turned up in his music, and the way he expressed it tended to be sifted through the abiding sympathy he felt for people who had been pushed around by life. He watched his mother's face beginning to show her age, and he noticed the grooves that unhappy love stories made under the eyes he met in roadhouses. As he traveled along the white-lined highways he thought about what they looked like to a truck driver; and because he'd been a truck driver he had a pretty good idea. "The songs," he told me, "are written from the back of your mind and the cushion of your experience." Forty-one of them became number-one country hits. Only Conway Twitty has ever had more.

Haggard's method of composing songs has included jotting words down on brown paper bags and, more often, dictating lines to someone else who writes them out for him. (Haggard has penmanship that even he finds inscrutable.) A frequent amanuensis is Bonnie Owens, whom Haggard married in 1965, twelve years after she'd been divorced from Buck Owens. Her marriage with Haggard eventually ended as well, but Owens remains a member of The Strangers and perhaps Haggard's closest friend. Her portrait of Haggard the songwriter sounds a lot like Hank Williams's description of his own writing method: "I pick up the pen and God moves it," Williams said. "It's amazing to me the things that come out of Merle's mouth when he's writing," Owens told me. "I never heard him *talk* like that. He'd say later, 'Bonnie, I don't ever remember saying those words. It's like God put 'em through me.' I knew he said them. I was there. I'd write them down. 'Today, I Started Loving You Again' was one of them. 'If We Make It Through December' was another. I'd say, 'Are you sure that's what you want?' and he'd say, 'Yeah, read it to me.' I would. Then he'd say, 'I do not remember saying that line.' He was just amazed." At 2:00 A.M. one night in Dallas in 1967, Haggard asked Bonnie to go down the street and get him a hamburger. This took her a few minutes. When she got back to their motel room, he'd written "Today, I Started Loving You Again" on a brown paper bag. He sang it to her and she burst into tears.

These days, Haggard remains more or less the same man he has always been, one who manages to couple abiding skittishness with vigorous loyalty to the things he loves. When he is away, which is mostly, Haggard prefers to take his meals at the Cracker Barrel, a chain of restaurants specializing in Southern cuisine that Haggard likes so well he bought stock in the company. Between Cracker Barrels, he and The Strangers ride the bus an average of 600 miles a day. While he rides, Haggard often listens to Lefty Frizzell, Bob Wills, and Jimmie Rodgers tapes. He will occasionally take a shift as bus driver. (According to some of The Strangers, Haggard and a gas pedal can be a moderately terrifying combination.) Haggard's band was named in 1964, after his first top-ten hit, "(My Friends Are Gonna Be) Strangers." Norm Hamlet has been a Stranger for twenty-nine years and Haggard's drummer, Biff Adam, has been with him for twenty-eight. There is still a lot about their boss that they find difficult to grasp.

Toward the end of that day when he'd left us for a sandwich, Haggard sent word up to the studio inviting me to meet him for breakfast at eight o'clock at his local morning haunt, the Night 'n' Day truck stop. When Abe Manuel heard about this date, he laughed. "You're having breakfast with Merle?" he said. "Well, soon as Merle says he's having breakfast with you, there'll be no breakfast. Or he'll decide to have breakfast at seven. If Nostradamus met Merle he'd have committed suicide." Abe Manuel has a nickname for Haggard. He calls him Merlin. This does not seem to displease Haggard.

I got to the truck stop a few minutes before eight, and there was Haggard with a John Deere cap on his head, leaning back from an empty plate. Breakfast had indeed been switched to seven. Haggard told me briefly why he'd left Bakersfield—where he lived for thirty-five years—and resettled in Northern California. "Doesn't rain enough for me in Bakersfield," he said. Then his chair scraped back and, with a friendly wave to a couple of veteran waitresses and an inquiry about the "Boss Lady's" health, he was gone.

As I ate my eggs I thought about the stories I'd heard of Haggard walking out on Ed Sullivan and abandoning his role in a production of *Oklahoma!* I'd driven down to the truck stop with Scott Moore, a rancher who, at the time, was both Haggard's manager and his bus driver. "Merle needs some action," he said. "Something going on around him." We drove back to the studio, walked inside, and there was Haggard standing by the door. "Anything you want to ask me," he said, "you go ahead."

In 1951, Lefty Frizzell recorded an album of Jimmie Rodgers's songs, which is how Haggard first heard of The Singing Brakeman. In 1968, Haggard decided to make his own Rodgers record, *Same Train, Different Time.* Two years later he did a Bob Wills album—*A Tribute to the Best Damn Fiddle Player in the World.* Wills combined frontier fiddle music with Dixieland to create an uninhibited, swinging form of orchestral music that owed a lot as well to Wills's love of blues singers like Bessie Smith. Haggard, who likes to refer to his own music as "country jazz," revered Wills as a musician and as a leader of men, but he particularly admired him for the freedom of feeling he brought to ensemble country music. The Wills tribute record is among Haggard's best, and it pleased Wills so much that before he died in 1975, he deeded his Stradivarius violin to Haggard. Over three months in 1968, Haggard had walked up and down the aisles in his bus teaching himself enough about the instrument to handle all of Wills's breakdowns on the album. "It was miserable," Biff Adam says. "We'd cover our heads with a pillow." But Haggard made himself into a fine fiddler. "The power of a fiddle is astronomical," he told me now. "You can make an audience hysterical. I saw what Bob Wills could do with it, and I wanted it in my bag of tricks, too. It goes through modes of importance to me. At the moment I'm trying to maintain enough top-drawer aptitude." He began cutting his fingernails. Somebody walked by and Haggard took the opportunity to solicit advice on how to treat a finger he'd burned on a cooking pot. A homemade salve that featured Preparation H was recommended. Suddenly, Haggard headed for the recording chamber.

All the musicians were waiting for him. Iris DeMent had came upon Haggard's credit-card receipt for his purchase of one of her records. She asked him if she could have it. "Sure," he said, sounding surprised. Scott Moore looked at me. "Merle doesn't realize that to young performers he is what Frizzell and Wills were to him," he said. Haggard announced that overnight he had done some thinking and had decided that the right way to record "No Time to Cry" was to add some "Mother Maybelle guitar." He was referring to the clean, limpid way Maybelle Carter simultaneously played the rhythm and the melody of a song. DeMent picked up the guitar on which Haggard recorded his tribute to his mother, "Mama Tried," to see if she could do a Maybelle. "I got to go see if I've still got a family," Haggard said. The door banged behind him.

◆ ◆ ◆

Haggard first took a liking to Northern California because of the fishing on Lake Shasta. He once lived in a houseboat, but has since relocated to the countryside outside Redding, a tidy town about twenty minutes south of the lake. Redding has the look of a place a man who wrote lines like "If you're runnin' down this country, man, you're walkin' on the fightin' side of me" would like. Plenty of American flags are in evidence, and driveways filled with Chevrolets and Buicks. Along the streets that head out of town, fresh-picked oranges and almonds are for sale at roadside stands and signs are posted declaring "Farmers Feed America" and "No Farms, No Food, No Future."

Shade Tree Manor is a spectacular place. It's built on the heights of a rolling hillside that looks out toward the snow-capped Lassen Peak and Mount Shasta to the north, with the long plain of the Sacramento Valley sprawling down in the other direction. On Haggard's property are lichen-crusted oak trees, sagging grape arbors, wild turkeys, and jackrabbits everywhere you look. A small creek runs nearby. One of the only things the place doesn't have is a beach, or it didn't, anyway, until Haggard decided he needed one. For an entire day dump trucks rattled over his cattle guards and deposited sand around a small pond. Then two palm trees were added.

When it didn't seem likely that Haggard would be back anytime soon, I decided to go for a walk out past the grape vines. But as I cut through the parking lot outside the studio, there he was. As ever, he was affable. Although I was beginning to get some idea, I asked how he'd managed to escape from prisons and reform schools so many times. "Seems almost like it was someone else," he said. "I guess I did do that. I was an amateur gymnast. I was very agile. I could dive right through that window"—he pointed at one—"hit the ground running. I've always been quick on my feet and able to disappear." I smiled. Haggard did not. "I'm actually very well calculated as a human being," he said. "How many people in the U.S.A. can tell you where they'll be 200 days from now? That's what I have to do. That's what Willie Nelson has to do." I said that all the bus travel must be hard on someone like him. "There's a kind of hatred you build up for the road," he said. "You feel confined amidst it all. Songs will not occur unless you do things somewhat spontaneously. One of the few things a guy has to defend himself against destiny is spontaneity. That way the devils don't know which way you're driving or which route you're taking." Then he nodded in a friendly way and left.

Throughout the rest of my stay, I had only brief glimpses of Haggard. Once he passed through the studio and told Abe Manuel, "You got to make it sound like you sat down on the floor and you're playing it for the first time and you happened to lay it down perfect." One of the reasons Haggard dislikes Nashville is his belief that the session players there are so practiced that they tend to bleed all the freshness from the music. A little while later, I saw him in another room, speaking on the telephone. He had put some autographed objects, including a baseball cap, up for auction to help sick local children and was now following up to see how they'd sold. "They knew the cap was real, didn't they?" he said. He listened and then shook his head. "No thanks necessary," he said. "Just glad to be involved." The telephone was on the desk of the Hag, Inc., office secretary. Her name is Debbie Parret, and she was Haggard's fourth wife. Haggard is friendly with all his former wives, except his third, Leona Williams. After he and Bonnie Owens divorced, Haggard asked her to be a bridesmaid in his next wedding, a role Owens performed graciously. "I gave up my slot," Debbie Parret told me. "We're still good friends most of the time."

The last time I saw Haggard, we talked about Lefty Frizzell, Jimmie Rodgers, and Bob Wills. "It's more than one thing with them," he said. "They each have a combination of ingredients that are encumbered in one personality. Iris DeMent has some of those elements too. Their intentions are so well executed without any pretense. They glide in and out of notes—they all have that in common. When they sing to you it's like someone delivering a great dramatic performance. And the melodic ability! To hear that, well . . ." He paused. Then he smiled and said, "Well, he that hath an ear, let him hear."

Iris DeMent is Haggard's most recent enthusiasm. He first heard her sing on his bus. A group of young singers and songwriters produced *Tulare Dust,* an album of their versions of their favorite Haggard songs. When Haggard heard DeMent's "Big City," his song about a young working stiff desperate for fun and freedom, "He thought it was the greatest thing ever," according to Biff Adam. "*That's* the way *I* wanted 'Big City' to sound," Adam remembers Haggard saying at the time. At the next opportunity during the trip, Haggard and Abe Manuel slipped off the bus and walked into a record store, where they bought *Infamous Angel* and

My Life, DeMent's first two albums. Haggard returned to the bus, slipped them into the tape machine, and found himself even more delighted with her writing than her voice. Besides her own songs, on each album DeMent included two compositions by other writers. After hearing her version of Lefty Frizzell's paean to his parents, "Mom and Dad's Waltz," Haggard decided that he had found a kindred spirit. He got on the telephone and invited DeMent out to Shade Tree Manor. He wanted to record two of her songs, he said, and he wondered if she would like to help him learn them. DeMent required very little persuasion.

As Scott Moore suspected, DeMent, thirty-three, had grown up listening to Haggard's records with the same kind of fervor the young Haggard had felt for Lefty Frizzell. Outside of visits to see relatives, during Iris DeMent's childhood her father, Patric Shaw DeMent, a man with a big family and a small paycheck, could afford to take his children on vacation only once. They happened to go to Northern California, where DeMent spent the week searching for Haggard, without success. "Iris would rather visit Merle than sell a million records," her husband Elmer says. "She's never sold a million records," he added. "But I feel sure of it." What DeMent liked so much about Haggard's music was that the people in his stories felt like her people. Although she grew up in California, she feels she comes from somewhere else, just the way Haggard does.

The DeMents' family story follows the classic rural Southern pattern of westward migration. DeMent's grandfather, William Tell DeMent, came to the Mississippi Delta from the Appalachians to farm the sandy loam. Pat DeMent grew up on a small island in the St. Francis River just outside the town of Paragould, along the Missouri border in northeast Arkansas. The whole area was thick with cypress trees that logging companies who supplied furniture builders in Chicago would soon begin to clear. Pat DeMent spent his childhood filling twelve-foot sacks full of cotton out in the fields with his brothers, sisters, and cousins, ferrying it all across the river on a small handmade barge, and taking it on to the gin by wagon.

"It was a hard way to make a living," said Clovis DeMent. Clovis is Iris DeMent's older cousin, and he was showing me around DeMent Island. Clovis grew up there with Pat DeMent and now owns a machine company outside Paragould. "We didn't have much, but we had everything we needed," he said. "We didn't know we were poor. We thought we were pretty well off, but I guess we were poor."

In those days there were only four houses on DeMent Island, and no shops of any kind. Despite its 150 cultivated acres, it was a truly wild place.

The shore was lined with black locust, swellbudded cypress, tupelo, and flowering willow trees that insulated the island from wind and sound. The trees could also be menacing. Sometimes snakes as thick as your wrist dropped out of them. The Cherokee Trail of Tears had passed nearby and the dirt was full of arrowheads and old bones. On some summer days, so many ducks filled up the sky that noon seemed like twilight. William Tell DeMent set up a grape arbor and made his own wine. He also had an apple and peach orchard. In winter, the DeMent kids walked across the frozen river and hiked along the levee three and a half miles to get to school. Otherwise, they rarely left the island, so that when, as an adult, Clovis gave up on farming and went north to St. Louis, the experience jarred him. "We didn't know anything about the city," he says. "If I could have, I would have come back. At first I was lonely there. But I had to work."

Pat DeMent stuck it out on the island a while longer. He farmed soybeans and corn in addition to the cotton, and he began his family. By the time his wife, Lola Rhee, was thirty-three, she had given birth to eight children. Six of them survived, but Lola Rhee didn't. "I think it was excessive childbirth," says Clovis. The dead infants were buried, without funerals, in unfinished pine boxes at the edge of a bean field in the rushes beside the river. Their mother was placed beside them. Several other DeMents were already there, including William Tell's wife, Eula DeMent, and Pat's brother, Joseph, who was thirteen in 1918, when he was fatally infected with influenza. Today, all the stones are hidden beneath a thicket of leaves and thorny brush. When you pull the brambles aside, you can see them—small, plainly worded markers, set close to one another. A family secret.

The DeMents like to think of themselves as stubborn, hardheaded people, but labor-intensive farming was giving way to machines, and eventually Pat DeMent decided he couldn't compete with tractors and combines. "One person could farm what forty did," says Clovis. "The other thirty-nine had to go and get a job. Pat had to leave the island and get a job or he'd have starved to death." Pat and his new wife, Flora Mae, tried farming on the mainland. When that went poorly, he found a house in Paragould and took a job at the Emerson Electric plant. After William Tell DeMent died, the family sold the island. There are no houses on it anymore.

Pat DeMent was fifty-one in 1961, when Iris, his fourteenth and last child, was born. In that same year, he was one of the leaders in a wildcat strike at the Emerson plant. The strikers hoped to form a union, but the company held firm and Pat DeMent walked a picket line for a year with eight little kids at home. When the strikers finally gave up, Pat knew he wasn't going back to work at the factory. There was no future for him in farming, either, and so, like James Haggard thirty years before him, he felt he had no choice but to pack up his house and move his family on out to California. He found a job as a janitor at the Movieland Wax Museum in Buena Park and kept it until he retired.

There were things to recommend the work. Pat met people like Mae West and Marilyn Monroe when they came in to have their figures made, and he thrilled his children when he brought the museum's Rolls-Royce home over the weekend so that they could wash and shine it. Still, life in California didn't make him happy. "The job wasn't satisfying to him," says Iris DeMent. "My whole family talked about Arkansas. My mom hadn't wanted to leave, but once she got out to California, she liked it and wanted to stay. My dad, he was always homesick. I know that my dad was very tied to his family and where he came from. I always had a sense of my dad as a person who was lonely for something, yearning for a past, the land he grew up on, his family. My dad grew up on this island, where he mostly saw nobody but his family. That went on into his forties, when he was torn away. It was an adventure to go to California, but it created a sadness in him, too. I always had a sense of that, so even though I didn't grow up on the island, I feel very much a part of it."

During her childhood, there was always music in Iris DeMent's house. Back in Arkansas, Iris's maternal grandfather, C.J. Cupp, had done a lot of the calling at local square dances, some of which were held in his living room. He'd invite twenty or thirty neighbors over, and clear the furniture off to the side, and either someone would turn out reels and hoedowns on a fiddle, or Grandpa Cupp would play records on his phonograph. He was partial to Jimmie Rodgers and The Carter Family, and soon enough, so too was his daughter, Flora Mae. Like every other family they knew, the Cupps listened to the *Grand Ole Opry* radio broadcasts from Nashville on Saturday nights and then sang around the house all week the new songs they'd heard. Flora Mae loved to sing. As an adult she would sometimes do so for hours as she washed and hung out the laundry, cleaned her house, and cooked dinner. She had a clear, resonant voice—you could hear it above everyone else's in church—and it gave her a lot of pleasure. She told Iris that if she'd known how to make herself a chance, she could have been an *Opry* star.

When he got to California, Pat DeMent, who had been saved in the later stages of his days in Arkansas, became a fervent member of a local Pentecostal church. Iris DeMent grew up in a house scattered with gospel hymnbooks. On Sundays, the family went to services in the morning, came home, and ate a huge fried-chicken dinner. Then they sat in a circle and sang songs like "Higher Ground" and "Heaven's Jubilee" before going back to church for another service. Three of her older sisters had a gospel group they called The DeMent Sisters and, says Iris DeMent, "We had a big old piano, and somebody was always playing it. Every now and then my mother would sit down and play it. She played it so loud."

DeMent liked some of the same music many American kids listened to in the 1970s—Bob Dylan, Joni Mitchell, James Taylor, as well as her favorites, Johnny Cash and Merle Haggard—but what she heard her mother sing moved her in ways she wasn't prepared to explain. Evangelical Christianity troubled DeMent because it seemed rigid and unsympathetic. The old-time country and gospel songs, however, felt just the opposite. "I'm so wrapped up in those sounds," she says. "It's more than music to me. It's kind of a place. I know this about those songs. It's music where people are sitting and writing about life, the things they're struggling with and the hard times. They're about trying to get through life and hope for the future. Whether you believe in heaven or not, heaven is an idea of hope, and hope can get you through life. For me, I'm drawn to that music because it's honest. It's written to help people, to give them a little courage to get through. For a lot of people, and for my family, that's all they were trying to do was get through life, and those songs helped a lot."

It wasn't until she was twenty-five and living in Topeka, Kansas, that DeMent began to write her own songs. The first time she'd driven through the Midwest, the little towns with their neat squares and crisp white picket fences pulled at her. "Something about those old brick buildings," she says. "You have a sense of the past in the Midwest. I like the people there. They're not so interested in what they look like and what they're driving. They seem more ordinary, and I like ordinary people. Plus it's more stable. They've been there for years. People from California all come from somewhere else."

That's largely what DeMent wrote about: the sense of time unfolding across ordinary lives. By the time she settled in Kansas City a couple of years later, she'd taught herself some guitar chords and had begun singing after work at local coffee houses. She was working as a waitress at a pizza parlor when a burly fireman stopped in for a beer. Elmer McCall had

Iris DeMent. "I'm so wrapped up in these sounds.
It's more than music to me."

fought in Vietnam and now took acting courses, but Iris DeMent loved him for the patient, forgiving sort he was. She had a temper. DeMent moved to Nashville for two years to establish herself in country music. When she returned to Missouri—she missed Elmer—she'd polished nearly enough songs to make a record. *Infamous Angel* was released in 1992. Two years later came *My Life*. When I met her, she was preparing a third collection, which is called *The Way I Should*.

DeMent uses simple language when she writes, and her songs tend to explore common experiences: the way timing and passion figure into love affairs; how it feels to spend a life in the same drab small town; the complicated ways people respond to death. Although the songs have the sound and feel of traditional country music, there isn't the vestigial longing for the retreating rural paradise that was such a common theme among the generation of country songwriters who were active in the middle decades of the century. It's probably more accurate to say that, like Merle Haggard, Iris DeMent writes regular people's songs rather than hillbilly or country music. Occasionally, one of them features sun-dappled portraits of children holding mason jars full of fireflies, but usually they are a little less sentimental than that. Her inclination is to think about people who have it rough, and she is also not, at times, immune to a strain of skepticism. In "Let the Mystery Be," a song that reveals her misgivings about religious and New Age dogma, she writes: "Some say once gone you're gone forever/And some say you're gonna come back/Some say you rest in the arms of the Savior/If in sinful ways you lack/Some say they're comin' back in a garden/Bunch of carrots and little sweet peas/I think I'll just let the mystery be."

DeMent tells stories in many of her songs, but they don't take the form of ballads so much as what, in the tradition of Loretta Lynn's "One's on the Way" ("Here in Topeka"), might be called life fragments. In the crushing "Easy's Gettin' Harder Every Day," she writes about a middle-aged working mother from small-town Idaho who leads a life of quiet desperation. The woman drops her child off at school and then "busts the lights" to get to work by nine so that she can spend the day counting the minutes until she punches out. At home, she watches "a bunch of folks who never heard of Idaho" on television. Then she and her husband "make love and then we kiss good night/He rolls over and he's out like a light/But I ain't mad about it, we got nothing to talk about anyway." By writing unsparing songs about people who don't have much, DeMent taps into both their sadness and their forbearance. In this way, her woman up in Idaho is really the female foil to Merle Haggard's workingman with the blues, or to his father, who, as Haggard describes him in "Mama's Hungry Eyes," prays "for a better way of life" and feels so acutely "that another class of people put us somewhere just below."

Like Haggard, DeMent first came to appreciate the frustrations of working-class Americans by growing up as the child of two of them. Sometimes her parents' lives serve as a prism for her imagination. Other songs are simply reproductions of their experiences. "Mama's Opry," for example, is a literal account of her mother's love for music, her unrealized dreams of singing on *The Grand Old Opry,* and the way her own private Opry gave her joy as she sang away days spent hanging clothes on the line and changing the latest baby's diapers.

Which gave DeMent an idea. When it came time to record *Infamous Angel,* she decided that the last song on the album would be her favorite old gospel number, "Higher Ground." She asked her mother to sing the lead vocal, and so at age seventy-four, Flora Mae DeMent had her Nashville debut. Pat DeMent died as DeMent was writing the songs for *My Life,* and her father's life more than her own became the album's true subject. Writing about him was a means of mourning, of thinking over how he'd lived. Music had meant as much to him as it had to her mother, something DeMent had only gradually come to understand.

So far as DeMent knew when she was a child, the only music that interested her father was religious music. Then, one day when she was seven or eight, DeMent was prowling inside her parents' closet, where she came upon a battered box next to a stack of quilts. She opened it and found a fiddle. For some reason, she felt frightened. She closed the box and hurried away. A few days later she was back for another peek at the fiddle, and then another. She kept this up until one day she brought the instrument out to the living room, handed it to her father, who was reading the paper, and asked him to play it. Her father opened the case and stared at the fiddle for a while. Finally, he took it out and played a few bars. Then he stopped. "I'm sorry, honey," he said. "I can't do it." He looked at the fiddle a little longer and then put it back in the case, snapped it shut, and handed it back to her.

There is a belief among some Southern fundamentalist Christians that stringed dance instruments are the tools of the devil. Bob Carter, the father of The Carter Family's A.P. Carter, had been a fine local musician who played at dances and didn't object to a little whiskey during breaks. After he became engaged to a young woman named Mollie from a strict

Methodist family, however, he quit playing the banjo and also stopped drinking. When A.P.'s younger brother E.J. was discovered with a banjo, Mollie threw it down a hill. A.P. himself gave up the fiddle in deference to his mother's religion.

At a family reunion many years after she first discovered the fiddle, DeMent finally heard her father tell the story of how he'd come to own it. He'd had a stroke by this time, and was confined to a wheelchair. One of her brothers pushed him out onto the lawn where everyone was sitting. He had his fiddle in his lap and he clenched it as he talked. "My dad said that one day when he was about five, my grandpa was out on the river and he saw this guy who was a fiddler-fisherman—a traveling fiddler who fed himself by fishing," she says. "It turned out he was pretty much in trouble. He needed money, and he offered to sell his fiddle to my grandpa. My dad was the youngest boy, and when my grandpa got home with the fiddle, he hung it on the wall and told my dad he couldn't touch it. He was too little and the fiddle was for older boys. Consequently, my dad really wanted to play it. He wanted to so badly that he watched my uncles playing songs on it, studying their fingers so attentively that he was learning to play in his mind. One evening he got his courage up and said to my grandpa, 'I believe if you'd let me try, I could play a tune.' He did, and when he finished, Grandpa said, 'Looks like that's your fiddle, Pat.'"

That was the end of the story. Pat DeMent put the fiddle he hadn't played in forty years in its case, gave it a gentle parting slap, and passed it on to his oldest son. In photographs, Pat DeMent looks like a patient, slightly forlorn man, inevitably surrounded by his throng of children. DeMent says that when he was near death with sickness, he would sit in his wheelchair and scold his pain by waving his arm and blurting "Goin' to Glory." The fiddle had been his best guess at the price of admission.

On a summer morning, Iris DeMent and I sat across a table in a West Tennessee Cracker Barrel restaurant. She is a plainspoken woman, as frank and emotional in conversation as she is in song. She began talking about what it must have been like for a five-year-old boy to receive the present of a fiddle from his father. "If you put this in the context that they were pretty poor people and there weren't a lot of luxuries, it was a pretty big event in my dad's life," she said. "I heard from my dad that my grandpa was a difficult person to gain respect from. A lot of people have told me that my dad played pretty well. My older brother Fred says Dad would come in from the fields and play for hours. I think my dad kept the fiddle in the closet all those years because it was something he loved very much. It meant a lot to him. A gift from his dad that came at a time and in a place when you didn't get a lot of gifts from your parents."

So far as DeMent knows, it wasn't for precisely the same reasons as Bob Carter that her father ceased doing something which brought him so much pleasure that a family friend told her, "When Pat played the fiddle, he was in another world." It was more that the fiddle represented his life before he was saved, and once he went right with the Lord, the church expected him to let the old things recede. Pat DeMent was a man who liked to test himself, even in mildly ascetic ways, and he saw putting away his fiddle as proof of his devotion to his newfound faith. "The music didn't stop," DeMent told me. "The fiddle stopped. It was his past life and something better left behind."

It so happens that the year DeMent discovered her father's fiddle was the same one that she first saw his island. That took place during a family reunion. "There were two carloads of us," she said. "We drove out and stopped at the cemetery. My dad and brothers got out and cleared some of the weeds. We all stood around and Dad talked about the dead relatives and I listened. We walked away from the graves, went over to the river, and got into a rowboat. My dad took each of us across. We'd walk on that land where my dad was from. They'd say, 'This was where the houses were.'" She stopped and began to cry. After a while she pulled herself together and continued speaking. "I remember," she said. "It was really neat. My dad said, 'That's where you kids are from.' They didn't have doctors. I think they'd just have the baby. There was a cluster of trees and Dad would say to my brother Fred, 'Fred, that's where you were born.' It's . . ." and she began to cry again. "I can't explain it," she said, finally. "This doesn't make me upset in a bad way. It's my dad talking about his life, which is my life. I can remember the feeling so vividly of being there and feeling so much a part of him even though he's gone now. I don't feel emotionally bound to California, where I grew up. I feel emotionally bound to DeMent Island. That's where I'm from, and I feel that I wouldn't be doing music if it weren't for my strong sense of connection to my ancestors I never met."

Merle Haggard's sister Lillian and his brother Lowell were teenagers when Haggard was born and both soon departed the household. Lillian told *The New Yorker:* "Merle hated being an only child. He hated it then, and he hates to be alone now. He used to give toys away to get neighbor kids to come play with him. Sometimes I think he's still doing that."

When Lillian's observation came up in one of my talks with Haggard, he said promptly, "Whatever she says probably fits the condition."

I was thinking about this during my last afternoon at Shade Tree Manor. It is really a playhouse. The huge game room is replete with a bar, a pool table, a jukebox, a tank full of tropical fish, and, this being Merle Haggard's playhouse, an electric train set. Off the kitchen is a den with a large-screen television. Guests have phone privileges and they are also free to open up the refrigerator, where they are likely to find something tasty like a freshly made jalapeño chicken salad. Haggard treats his friends generously, and it is important to him to remain close to them. Dean Row Holloway lived in a house on Haggard's property until recently, when he got married and moved to Sacramento. Haggard's manager, Fuzzy Owen, goes back more than thirty years with him.

It's the same way with The Strangers. They revere Haggard and know also that he genuinely cares about them. One of Haggard's best songs came as a result of watching his longtime guitar player, Roy Nichols, go through a period of personal turmoil. "Roy had been unable to make his marriages make it through December," Haggard told me. "It was something like five consecutive years that something unhappy had happened to him in December. I said, 'Roy, if you can make it through December you'll be all right.' He said, 'You ought to write that down.' I said, 'I will,' and I did." Haggard became a bandleader, with an eye toward Bob Wills. Like Wills, Haggard has excellent instincts for assembling ensemble talent, knows the strengths of his musicians, exacts a high level of performance, and rewards it by distributing solos. When, on the other hand, someone is not meeting his standards, his admonitions can be brutal. For all his skill at presiding over a band, however, Bonnie Owens believes Haggard is "a frustrated sideman" who "doesn't enjoy all the responsibility." The fact is that he can't, as his song confesses, hold himself in line.

Which is why all his guests were alone in the playhouse. After excusing himself to go get another sandwich, Haggard hadn't been around now for many hours. This practice had been going on for several days now, and accustomed to Haggard as they were—"That's Merle," they all kept saying—everyone seemed a little glum. Joe Manuel talked for hours on the telephone with his wife back in Tennessee. Lou Bradley listened to Haggard's old records. Iris and Elmer worked on their travel itinerary. Other people who drifted through shot pool or smoked languidly in front of the television set.

Abe Manuel seemed restless. Both Abe and Joe are fine musicians, but Abe is truly something special. At seventeen, he quit his job in a Louisiana oil field and taught himself the fiddle. Since then he has mastered just about every instrument you are likely to encounter in country music, including the accordion, the guitar, the harmonica, and even a pot full of grease (he can really bang it). Haggard has confided in friends that Abe is possibly the most talented musician he has ever met. Abe doesn't treat himself like anything special. He is a sardonic, profane, hard-drinking, chainsmoking man who, like Haggard, is always at the center of activity, although he is at heart a loner. Haggard seems drawn to him, and has come to regard Abe as a kind of Huck to his Tom. Abe is a trove of off-color stories and is a fearless practical joker who likes to walk up to well-dressed women he has spotted holding cellular telephones and inform them that he is expecting a call. Haggard gets a kick out of such antics. Mostly, however, he respects Abe's musical acumen. For a young man in his thirties, Manuel knows an amazing amount about country music, including all of Haggard's songs and enough of his stories to make you think he has been a Stranger all his life. The truth is that he has wanted to be a Stranger only as long as he can remember.

One thing that immediately endeared both Manuels to Haggard is their pedigree. Their father, Abe Manuel, Sr., was a Cajun musician who worked for Lefty Frizzell and was also, for a time, one of Bob Wills's Texas Playboys. He is now retired and owns Manuel's Country Store, a Cajun-style restaurant in the tiny town of Milton, Tennessee, an hour's drive outside Nashville. On summertime Friday nights at dusk, most of the town brings a lawn chair over to the restaurant, sets it down in the road—there isn't any traffic in Milton—and eats fried alligator and craw-fish étouffé while watching the Manuels and their friends play Cajun country music on the porch.

Everybody gets discovered somewhere, and for Abe and Joe Manuel it was the Pickin' Parlor in Nashville's Opryland Hotel, where they and Joe's first wife, Joanie, were playing Cajun country and western swing music. One day Merle Haggard walked in and sat down. The Manuels were, at the moment, well on their way to losing the job because of their refusal to play Garth Brooks and Tracy Lawrence songs. "We was the only group in Nashville that didn't play top forty," Abe told me. "We played what we wanted to. Somebody from the audience gave Joanie $20 to play Garth Brooks's 'Friends in Low Places.' I took it out of her hand and gave it back with $5 extra of my own money. I said, 'We'll play some songs you'll probably like just as much.' " Then they served up some Hank Williams and Bob Wills.

That trait is what Haggard admires most in Abe Manuel: his devotion to high musical standards. Everybody who lasts with Haggard has them. Though Haggard may exasperate them with his unpredictable ways, they know also that his quicksilver qualities feed the creative impulses that produce songs like his portrait of a man unable to make lasting connections with people or places, "I Take a Lot of Pride in What I Am." ("I guess I grew up a loner/I don't remember ever having any folks around/ But I keep thumbing through the phonebooks/And looking for my daddy's name in every town.") If you ask Haggard how he thinks up his best songs, he'll tell you they are likely to come to him just about anywhere so long as he remains fluid. "Mama Tried" was written "somewhere in Texas," and it was too many hours of "settin' in a bus pissed off at Los Angeles" that inspired "Big City." Haggard sometimes talks about the tension he feels between living as the man he is and the one he would like to be. He can't help himself, is the point, and somehow he must realize that if he could, something essential to him would be lost.

Farm on U.S. Highway 84, a few miles from Lubbock, Texas. "It's so stark,"
says Joe Ely. "When you're in a place that's really beautiful and gorgeous,
you kind of get insensitive to it. In Lubbock, you're more aware
of beauty. You have to train your eye."

PART SEVEN

TAKING IT FORWARD

*Emmylou Harris on stage. "You aren't conscious, you aren't really thinking,
you're just moving with a certain amount of abandon."*

EMMYLOU HARRIS

CONVERT

If there is a true diva in country music, it is Emmylou Harris. She has made close to twenty records of her own, many of them hugely successful, but by predilection she is that most deferential of performers, a harmony singer. "I love harmony singing," she was saying. "My real musical contribution is harmony singing and duet singing. It's always intriguing, the infinite combinations human voices can make together. There's a wonderful feeling singing with somebody else. I suppose it is like what Fred Astaire and Ginger Rogers felt. You aren't conscious, you aren't really thinking, you're just moving with a certain amount of abandon."

Harris's tremolo-infused soprano is agile enough for her to make subtle adjustments that enhance gifted singing partners and yet so attractive that she can function like a seasoned dollar-a-song taxi dancer stepping forward to make any slouch in a sportcoat look light and smart. Among the variety of men who have benefited from her vocal company are Roy Orbison ("That Lovin' You Feelin' Again"), Don Williams ("If I Needed You"), Rick Danko ("Evangeline"), Neil Young ("Star of Bethlehem"), Steve Earle ("Rivers of Babylon"), Ralph Stanley ("I Never Will Marry"), and Buck Owens ("Play 'Together Again' Again"). When I asked Owens what it was like to sing a duet with Harris, he shut his eyes and said, "It was just *mmm*." Then he said, "You know that whatever you do or however you sing, her part will complement it— always, always, always."

From Lulu Belle and Scotty Wiseman to Wilma Lee and Stoney Cooper, Loretta Lynn and Conway Twitty, June Carter and Johnny Cash, Buck Owens and Rose Maddox, George Jones and Tammy Wynette, to Porter Wagoner and Dolly Parton, the usual practice with country music duets has been to pair a man with a woman, singing either love or cheating songs. Yet since the first days of country recording, when Maybelle Carter performed with Sara, women have also sung with other women. Both Wilma Lee Cooper's and Kitty Wells's first singing partners were their sisters. The Coon Creek Girls were as popular late in the 1930s as another rural Kentucky-based all-female combo, The Judds, have been recently. For her part, Harris has sung with numerous women, including Nanci Griffith ("Are You Tired of Me Darling?"), Iris DeMent ("Mama's Opry"), and Dolly Parton and Linda Ronstadt, with whom she made the *Trio* recordings.

The point is, she can dance with anybody. It seemed to me that it must be a different experience waltzing with an old, lonesome tenor like Ralph Stanley than doing the frug with Steve Earle. Harris says not. "I'm an unschooled singer and it really is an unconscious process," she says. "If I thought about it, I would just mess it up."

"She's a great harmony singer because of the amount of heart she puts into it," Griffith says. "She has a great capacity to listen. That's such an important thing in singing harmony. I know a lot of really great singers who can't sing a lick of harmony because they don't listen in some way. They listen only to the melody line. My father taught me how to do it. Emmy, she's just a natural harmony singer."

It makes intuitive sense that a harmony singer gets along well with other people, and Harris is notoriously collegial. Bill Monroe's usual conversational policy is to offer up reluctant drops of vinegar. Every time he sees "Miss Immy," however, the Father of Bluegrass Music doles out eager spoonfuls of white sugar. "Mr. Monroe has always been nice to me," Harris said when I mentioned this to her. We were standing in her kitchen and Harris's teenage daughter, Meghann, ambled by just then. "Oh, Mom!" she groaned. "*Everyone* loves you."

At forty-nine, Harris is an elegant, well-spoken and poised woman who is often found in the company of people who lack her soigné. In particular, Nashville's best progressive songwriters treat the large white house she shares in the city with her mother, two daughters, and six dogs as New York fighters do Gleason's Gym; they are always coming by to try out their new combinations. On any night when Harris is in town, Jamie O'Hara, Kieran Kane, Rodney Crowell, Nanci Griffith, Steve Earle, or

Lucinda Williams may stop in to talk about music over lemon icebox pie. Earle is a talented performer who does not appear to get along easily with barbers or constables—he has kept both his hair and his rap sheet scruffy. Yet on the subject of Harris, he is a Father Steven, describing her as "a connoisseur of songs." Earle once punched a policeman in Dallas, and he spent years menacing himself by smoking crack and shooting heroin. Although Harris is the sort of conspicuously well-mannered woman who says "Well, bless your heart" at the slightest provocation, she has long gravitated toward such reckless characters—the torn-up people who tend to write the torn-up songs she likes best. It was one of country music's most renowned barroom hurricanes, Gram Parsons, who introduced Harris to country music and taught her to sing country harmony.

Harris was a young single mother working small clubs in Washington in 1971 when Parsons, the founding lead vocalist of the country-rock band The Flying Burrito Brothers, heard her sing a set in a room called Clyde's. He got up on stage and sang three songs with her, including Hank Williams's "I Saw the Light." Eventually, they made two albums together, *GP* and *Grievous Angel*. Harris refers to them as "regressive country," by which she says she means, "You have to draw on the past and you have to come up with something new. Gram's music was very contemporary and modern, but it was music that tipped its hat to the heart and soul of traditional country."

Harris has recently begun smoking cigarettes, which, given the pristine clarity of her legato and her generous nature, could well be a concession to the competition. She took a short drag now and said, "I came to country music late in life, through Gram. It was like I discovered this treasure that was right under everybody's noses, and it overwhelmed me. I'd listened to a little bit of country music as a teenager in Woodbridge, Virginia, but I'd never *heard* it until I started working with Gram. It was listening to the simplicity and restraint that gave me the vocal style that I have. It was an emotional thing. I don't remember telling myself that I shouldn't sing this or that way. It was just from singing all the time, following Gram's phrasing, and from singing along with countless George Jones and Tammy Wynette records. If you do more to it, then you're somehow negating the whole thing. I just called myself a country singer, but I never wanted to restrict myself to what people called country."

Harris's upbringing did not closely resemble that of any great country singer who came before her. Her mother, Genie Murchison, was a pretty girl from Birmingham, Alabama, who eloped with a decorated Marine jet pilot named Walter Harris while he was stationed in town during World War II. "He was a Yankee from New Jersey," says Harris. "It was a mixed marriage." The family settled in the Washington, D.C., suburbs when Harris was ten. Walter Harris flew air-sea rescue helicopters out of the base at Quantico, and his daughter took piano lessons and sang with her father in church. In high school she was the best student in a class of 400 and played in the marching band until she put aside her alto saxophone to become a cheerleader. Harris was already the great beauty she remains, with long, slender limbs, big brown eyes, and sunlit hair that fell past her shoulders, but she says that nobody invited her to the homecoming dance or much of anywhere else. "I was kind of isolated in high school," she says. "I might have been valedictorian, but there was nothing else to do. I sang all the time to myself. We lived in a tiny subdivision—off-base housing. This was a subdivision before malls. It was nowhere. If you didn't have a date you couldn't go into D.C., and nobody wanted to go hear Mississippi John Hurt with me anyway. So I stayed home and listened to folk music on the radio by myself." She wrote a worried letter to the folksinger Pete Seeger, telling him that she feared she hadn't suffered enough. "I felt, how could I be singing this music when I've lived such a sheltered life," she says. "He wrote me back and said, 'Don't worry. Life'll catch up with you. You'll suffer. Don't go hop a freight.'" She frowns in a cheerful way and says, "Oh, yes. Freight train found me. Almost ran me down."

She graduated from high school, left Virginia to study drama on a scholarship to the University of North Carolina at Greensboro, and then attended summer drama workshops at Tanglewood, in Lenox, Massachusetts. After a year and a half of college, she dropped out and went to New York to become a folksinger.

Harris spent two years in Greenwich Village, married, and mothered her first daughter. When the radical terrorists the Weathermen blew up a building in her neighborhood, Harris decided she wasn't raising a child in New York and removed to Nashville, where she was soon divorced. After that she bartended, waitressed, and, for a short time, collected food stamps. Then she went home to Washington, moved in with her parents, and found work handing out model-home brochures for a building company in Columbia, Maryland. This turned out to be a good way to practice her guitar. "I might see six people in a week," she says. "It was pretty nice. Shortly after that I began to get jobs in D.C. clubs." She was living with her boyfriend and performing six nights a week when she met her freight train—Gram Parsons.

Born Ingram Cecil Connor III, Parsons was bright, talented, and the sort of handsome hippie prince who wore fur collars, striped bell-bottoms, boots, and lots of crushed velour. Parsons's mother came from a family that made a fortune in the Winter Haven, Florida, citrus groves and then spent too much of it on liquor. His father, a Waycross, Georgia, business-man known as "Coon Dog" Connor, was from a prominent Tennessee family. He too struggled with alcoholism and shot himself to death when Parsons was twelve. Over the next few years, Parsons attended a private boys' school in Florida, spent some time singing at the folk clubs in Green-wich Village, and saw his mother drink herself to death. After briefly en-rolling at Harvard, he dropped out and became a full-time musician.

Country music at the time was associated with hardbitten working-class values and a strain of hawkish conservative politics that the New Left found so intolerable that in sections of Los Angeles and New York City, "Merle" and "Haggard" were fighting words. But Parsons was a young man filled with sorrows, and what he heard in the voices of people like Haggard, Hank Williams, and George Jones was their sympathy with suffering. He became the odd Southern aristocrat—and the rare hippie—who went around proclaiming how much he loved hard country. He idolized Williams, Elvis Presley, and Haggard, and it was his belief that if you paired traditional country vocals and instrumentation with up-tempo rock 'n' roll percussion, it would mean something to the college kids who were listening to his friends The Rolling Stones. By the time Harris met him, Parsons had made a record of just this stripe, *Sweetheart of the Rodeo,* with the folk-rock band The Byrds; left them to found The Flying Burrito Brothers; kept company in England, California, and on the French Riviera with The Rolling Stones—"I think I probably learned more from Gram than anybody else," Keith Richards said; become a heavy drug user—"He could get better coke than the Mafia," said Richards; married a teenaged blond Hollywood model; and outfitted himself in a custom-made jacket embroidered with naked women, pills, and marijuana leaves.

In 1972, Parsons was in Los Angeles, preparing to make his first solo record. He had lined up some of Elvis Presley's touring-band members to play the sessions and now, his biographer, Ben Fong-Torres, recounts, Parsons told a friend he needed a duet partner: "If you get a really good chick, it works better than anything, because you can look at each other with love in your eyes, right?" When he heard Harris sing that night in Washington, he was thoroughly smitten. "Oh, I've met this wonderful girl," he exulted to his sister. "This is the one. We just sound so good together."

Almost a year after meeting Parsons, Harris received an airline ticket to Los Angeles from him in the mail. "I decided I'd go," she says. "I'm surprised I didn't cash it in, but of course I wouldn't have. I'm too honest." Harris says that during her first few days in Los Angeles, she "couldn't figure out" what Parsons was after. One day he stopped by her hotel room at the Château Marmont and said, "Here's something I want you to listen to." It was a Louvin Brothers record, and when Harris heard the intricate harmonies the two brothers had worked out together in the northern Alabama cotton fields, she says "It really turned my head around. I love The Everly Brothers, but there's something purer and more raw about Charlie and Ira Louvin. It makes your hair stand up. I thought it was a girl singing. I went to Gram and said, 'Who's that girl?' He smiled and he said, 'That's Ira Louvin.' I thought it was so beautiful. It got me into duets. It really was like Fred Astaire dancing with Ginger Rogers. But in music it's even better because there are three combinations; you can hear those two voices separately, and you can hear them together."

After that, she found herself so taken with country music that she was like Chester Himes's people who are so poor they dream hungry; she just couldn't think much about anything else. "Once my ears turned that corner," says Harris, "I could hear what he was doing and what he was drawing from. I really heard George Jones for the first time. I just became obsessed with hearing this music. It was so straightforward and pure. I loved singing it and I loved singing harmony with Gram."

A sensitive harmony singer can work with a number of partners, and Harris certainly adjusts as well as anyone, but there are some pairs that truly flourish, and she and Parsons turned out to be one. In some ways they couldn't have been more different. When the band traveled on bus trips, sometimes Harris would sit down near the front and take out her knitting, while Parsons was in the rear using pint bottles to fight off his sad memories. Yet musically they understood each other. Parsons didn't always carry a tune perfectly, but his lightly twanging tenor had a triste, malty quality that seemed increasingly appealing the more you heard it. He thrived with Harris's pristine soprano floating just above him. In duets like "Hearts on Fire," "Song for You," and particularly "We'll Sweep Out the Ashes in the Morning," as the voices work their way through the song, each singer taking a phrase and then blending together toward the end of a line, there is something pretty and frayed about how they sound. "We'll Sweep Out the Ashes" is a song about a passion, and Parsons and Harris lend it a wistful flavor, so that besides the fire you also anticipate the embers.

Parsons died following a morphine-and-whiskey-fueled spree with a girlfriend at the Joshua Tree Inn in the California desert, east of Los Angeles. "He thought he had Keith Richards's metabolism," explains Parsons's friend and road manager, Phil Kaufman. "Gram was mistaken." His casket was to be sent to his stepfather, but Kaufman, acting, he says, according to a cremation pact he had made with Parsons, drove up to the airport in a Cadillac hearse and talked the mortuary air-service staff into turning the body over to him. He sped off for the Joshua Tree National Monument, where, at Cap Rock, he doused Parsons with five gallons of high-test gasoline and drank beer as he watched his friend sizzle.

Such macabre scenes, coupled with the surreal imagery coursing through some of his songs, helped Parsons in death to become a cult icon. Whereas some people once regarded him as another rich boy who couldn't hold his liquor, over time his music has eclipsed his excesses and he is now revered as the heavy-hearted honky-tonk hipster who melded two apparently discrete forms of music to winning effect. "Gram probably did more than anybody to sort of put a new face on country music," said Keith Richards. "He brought it into the mainstream." Over the years it has been Harris who has been his foremost champion. Because of her, Parsons is now widely acknowledged as "The Father of Progressive Country."

"When Gram died, I felt like I'd been amputated, like my life had just been whacked off," Harris told *Country Music* magazine in 1980. "I'd only been with Gram a short time, but it was like everything had become clear to me in that short period." If that sounded somewhat suggestive, so too did her elegy to him, "Boulder to Birmingham," in which she laments, "You really got me this time/And the hardest part is knowing I'll survive." To this day, when she talks publicly about her own music, Harris rarely hesitates to bring up Parsons, with the result that, says Nanci Griffith, "more people know Gram Parsons through Emmy than did during his lifetime." There is, however, something coy about the way she does it. Harris likes to mention Parsons, but she doesn't especially like to be asked about him in conversation. The effect is that you have been led into sensitive terrain by the same person who then wheels and warns you away. When I wondered why she had declined to talk to Parsons's biographer,

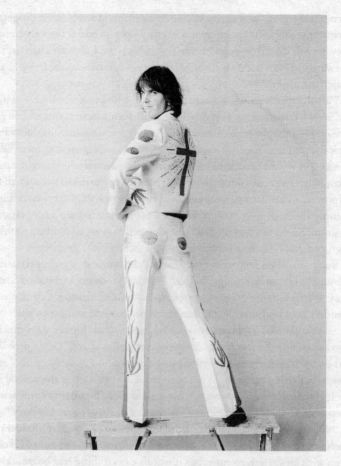

*Gram Parsons. "I'd never heard country music until I started
working with Gram," says Emmylou Harris. "I loved singing it
and I loved singing harmony with Gram."*

Fong-Torres, she said, somewhat sharply, "I have my own biography of
Gram. I don't want to be part of somebody else's."

And, in fact, she and her third husband, Paul Kennerly—Harris has
been three times divorced—did write a beautifully realized concept
album together, *The Ballad of Sally Rose.* It is the story of a woman who
apprentices herself to The Singer, a man with, according to the liner notes,
a "unique style" and "wild ways." Soon enough, The Singer is dead. In the

song "White Line," Sally says, "Seems like I was there from the start/A witness to your wild and reckless heart/You showed me the way but now you're gone . . . From night to night at every place I play in/The sweetness of your song remains/I'll be the keeper of the flame/Till every soul hears what your heart was saying." Speaking of the record, she said, "Obviously, it's inspired very much by Gram."

If you know what happened to Parsons and have some idea of how Harris felt about him, it's difficult to listen to their recordings now without hearing the personal experiences into the songs. The lines from "We'll Sweep Out the Ashes" that proclaim "We're two people caught up in a flame that has to die down soon/I didn't mean to start this fire and neither did you" seem even more romantic in retrospect than they did to begin with. Which, as Parsons had anticipated, was pretty sexy.

"They were both young and the harmonies were incredible," says Phil Kaufman. "They sang on the bus together, in hotel rooms, backstage before shows, backstage after shows. It was magical. They just complemented each other. It was a relationship that was consummated by music. It wasn't a physical consummation. If he hadn't been married, then definitely something would have happened between the two of them. If Gram had Emmylou it would have saved his life. Emmylou didn't have any of those habits. She might have leveled him off. They might be married today and have lived happily ever after."

Nashville resembles Tin Pan Alley in that most singers record songs written by other people. The singers are the celebrities, and the writers tend to seek out one another, worrying about the practical—where the next hit is coming from—and the profound—where country music is going. Like Patsy Cline, Emmylou Harris is a great singer who admires songwriters and counts many of them as close friends. Among the reasons that Harris likes to spend time with songwriters, and they with her, is that she shares their intense curiosity about music. "Emmy's always searched out different kinds of writers," says one of Harris's favorite writers, Lucinda Williams. "She likes people on the edge. Steve Earle and I, we write with a contemporary point of view but with reference to traditional music forms."

Country music has experienced many changes during Harris's twenty years in the singing business, and she has been at the hinges of those which have broadened public conceptions of the music. Her repertoire includes material by traditional country writers like The Louvin Brothers, Merle

Haggard, and Bill Monroe, and by writers whose work is associated with other musical genres—Jimi Hendrix, Neil Young, Paul Simon, and Kate and Anna McGarrigle. Throughout her career she has also sought out writers who elude easy classification. Earle is, of course, one. Another is that black-leather square peg in country's ten-gallon round hole—Lucinda Williams.

The granddaughter of two Methodist preachers, Williams grew up in little towns all over the South and most certainly would have been a traditional country singer and writer had she been of Kitty Wells's or Cindy Walker's generation. Instead, her father, the poet Miller Williams, had a shelf full of Bob Dylan and Robert Johnson records to go along with his Hank Williams collection. You can hear traces of all three in his daughter's music. Williams writes songs that are mostly about, she says in "Happy Woman Blues," "Trying hard to be a happy woman/But sometimes life just overcomes me." Filled as they are with small-town boys who "don't move fast enough," hard drinkers, loners, depressives, and relationships where people say "We can't seem to get along/The way we did before," Williams's are the songs that Patsy Cline might have written, had she been a writer. Williams wouldn't claim she writes country music. "To me, country is Loretta Lynn—American rural music," she says. "Emmy and I were both influenced by lots of different stuff. It's American roots music. That's the closest I can come to defining it. It's coming from different sounds, including country, but also blues and traditional folk. I think Gram Parsons and I are coming from a lot of the same places. He was somewhat of a maverick, blending lots of styles easily, and I've been told a few times that people connect me with him."

Williams has a voice that sounds thick and ripe the way pressed Delta sorghum tastes—she mostly grew up in Arkansas and Louisiana—and Harris contends that it's one of the flaws in current country radio that her music is never aired. She has a point. Williams's approach is, more or less, Jimmie Rodgers's; that is, she integrates elements of the many forms of popular music she grew up with into songs about the lives of average people. It's just that today, a Lucinda Williams can hear a surfeit of new sounds every time she walks into Tower Records. Naturally, her version of country is even more broadly informed than Rodgers's was.

Harris says she records blues, rock, and folk writers partly because she believes their songs contain the same elements she relishes in country songs: strong emotional content couched in readily accessible phrases set to deeply melodic music. Often her projects are regarded somewhat dubiously by the marketing departments at record companies, but she is known to be stubborn about what she likes.

"I've always felt that country music is a pure musical form and I believe that what is possible within its range is intensely varied," Harris was saying one night when I was visiting. We were sitting out on the back porch eating peach cobbler made, she pointed out, with Alabama peaches. "I never had a traditional country singing voice," she went on. "I choose to sing traditional material, but when I sing 'Making Believe,' it's a lot different than Kitty Wells singing 'Making Believe.' I make different interpretations of country material. I sing country songs with a noncountry voice but in the style of country singers, which is very restrained, very simple. Style is a product of your limitations. If everybody could do everything we wouldn't have anything distinctive. I adore Kitty and Loretta Lynn, but I can't do what they can do. In trying to do what they do, I came up with myself. I stepped on their stones to get there."

There is a guarded reserve to Harris. She keeps herself on some level opaque—a somewhat surprising quality in someone who has so much to say. Harris tends to speak in extended riffs in which one thought scampers quickly on to the next. Sometimes she builds up such momentum that an observation may dash across an intersection or pivot around a tall hedge at the corner, but she always ends up where she first implied she was heading. That is to say, Harris is full of vivid good sense and can occasionally be a bit of a trick to follow. Which makes her having such a pleasing voice something of a problem. Not every plangent singer also has a plangent speaking voice, but Harris does. There is a soft and gentle Alabama lilt to it, and it's so nice to listen to her say *anything,* that you can briefly sun yourself in the sound of her conversation, only to realize that you are now two thoughts behind her.

"Country music could only have happened in America," she was saying now. "Country music is the product of so many separate cultures of people coming together that the separate disappears and we're creating something else. It used to be that everybody wanted to get out of the country. Everybody wanted to get off the farm and get to the big city. In music you make it because you're a country boy or a country girl. Then you go get sophisticated pretty fast. Nowadays, everybody has cable television. A friend of mine worries that country as a genre is going to disappear the way the blues disappeared because it's getting so incorporated into the mainstream. But I wouldn't want to see country music now echoing the music of Hank Williams. Since country has always been rooted in the past, some people were against it because it represented that old hillbilly stuff. You have to begin with the past and move it forward. The Rolling Stones were so influenced by Muddy Waters, but then look what they did. They took it somewhere else."

One of her dogs came sidling onto the porch and she gave it a rub behind the ears and sent it on its way. "I don't know what it would be like to grow up surrounded by country music," she said. "I became fanatical about it— you know how converts are. And there was the added feeling after Gram died that I wanted to carry on his music in some small way. I also felt I could speak to some people like me who'd sort of looked down on country music. If I could be converted, so could they. I was kind of an ex-hippie—I was one of them. I also brought to it more than a love for traditional country. I could get really excited by a Louvin Brothers song, and I'd also cut a Beatles song. I was genuinely affected by both of these things. Country talks about emotional human issues: broken hearts, unrequited love, death, loneliness, fear, joy, losing your job, worry, God. In an everyday way it deals with issues that everyone from a blue-collar worker to a Yale literature professor experiences. Country music takes an enormous chance. Its aim is to go straight to the heart and when it makes it, it's a thing of beauty.

"But what is country, anyway?" Harris has thick, long hair that has prematurely gone whitish silver. It looks like a long diadem and when she shakes it, as she did now, it shivers into her eyes, a sight that many people find transfixing. (Among them are the editors of Nashville's alternative newspaper, *Nashville Scene,* which placed Harris on their list of the city's top five "babes" when she was just a couple of years shy of fifty. At her concerts, she sings above the din of besotted young men shouting out marriage proposals.) She moved her hair out of the way with her hand and went on talking. "I don't know. I know Buck Owens is country. George Jones is country. Merle Haggard and Loretta Lynn are country. But then there's this new generation who brought in new things. We're bringing a different experience to it and that's right. Mimicking the past because the past is a safe bet is the worst thing to do. With the old country music, the experiences were rural and that defined the sound and lyric content. Now we've got this enormous stage we live our lives on. Country music has to embrace that. The potential is limitless. We hear so little of it on the radio. Why shouldn't you hear Nanci Griffith and The O'Kanes and Trisha Yearwood and Lyle Lovett and Garth Brooks, Steve Earle, and Lucinda Williams. Lucinda!" She shook her head. "If I could write just one song like that I'd wave my hand and say, 'That's it—I'm really a babe!' "

Then she said, "We have so many colors, but on the radio it's like we have a painter who uses only charcoal. Wonderful things can be done with charcoal, but that's not the whole of it. I don't hear anything mysterious or creative in contemporary country music. To me Bruce Springsteen is more of a country poet because of the way he phrases, the simplicity and the passion of what he does—it's country even if it doesn't have a pedal steel guitar. Merle Haggard doesn't always have pedal steel, you know." Suddenly she brought herself up short, like someone who doesn't want it to be in their nature to grouse. "Look," she said. "Ultimately, complaining doesn't do any good. You have to do the music you love. I believe good music rises to the top and will always win out. I will record any song that intrigues me."

*The Flatlanders (Tony Pearson, Steve Wesson, Jimmie Dale Gilmore,
Joe Ely, and Butch Hancock). "We were all such vagabonds."*

JIMMIE DALE GILMORE *and* THE FLATLANDERS

LUBBOCK OR LEAVE IT

> *I thought happiness was Lubbock, Texas*
> *in my rear view mirror.*
>
> —MAC DAVIS

The reverence that the men and women of Massachusetts reserve for their meeting houses, Texans reserve for their dance halls. Halfway through the 1960s, James White opened a honky-tonk in his hometown, Austin. White called it The Broken Spoke, and over the years the Spoke established such a reputation for itself as a model gin mill that the State Historical Commission recently designated it a Texas landmark. It's a dimly lit, low-ceilinged place with space for more than 500 dancers, a handful of diners, a bar-length of whiskey drinkers, and a few pool hustlers besides. Out in front is a dirt parking lot, where White leaves the white Cadillac Coupé De Ville he bought because it's the same car Hank Williams was riding in when he died in the backseat on his way to a one-night show in West Virginia. Along the walls, photographs of many of the country musicians who have played The Spoke—Bob Wills, Ernest Tubb, and Willie Nelson are three—share space with neon and hand-lettered signs encouraging customers to eat chicken-fried steak, to drink, to dance, to buy "scientifically designed" condoms that will "totally stimulate her," and, should you happen to be a "misplaced husband," to park your car in the rear lot. Another one, which roils people down in the village of

Gruene—Gruene Hall is Texas's oldest operating dance hall—boasts that the Spoke is "The Last of the True Texas Dance Halls."

"This is the way a place like this looked in the 1940s and 1950s," James White was saying. "My parents would take me. In Texas you can take your kid. You can even give 'em beer if you want to as long as you're the parents. The good news," said White, who sometimes speaks in neon sign language, "is we ain't changin' nothin'." In his lifetime Austin has gone from a major stop on the Texas dance-hall circuit to the locus of progressive country music. There was a time when "longhairs" weren't welcome at the Spoke, but in recent years that has changed as people who value traditional country music like James White have observed that the liberal Austin musicians tend to bring more of the old feeling to their music than the hat acts in Nashville do.

"I'm definitely a country traditionalist," White said. "I'm hard-core country. I like Jimmie Rodgers, Roy Acuff, and Ernest Tubb. But I get along with the progressive country real fine. Jimmie Dale Gilmore probably falls more into the progressive country, but I like the way he sings. And Joe Ely. I like the way he phrases. Once he and Jerry Jeff Walker were here and Ernest Tubb was on stage, singing 'Walking the Floor over You.' They leaped up on stage and started singing with Ernest. Ernest went along with it. Ernest said, 'I think one of these boys wrote "Mr. Bojangles." ' Jerry Jeff got a kick out of that. I used to book Ernest here about three times a year until he died. He'd do all the beer-drinking, cigarette-smoking numbers." White pointed to a photograph of the Texas Troubadour wearing his trademark white cowboy hat and a vivid chartreuse checked sportscoat below it. "He liked green," White said.

We walked out onto the dance floor, which is out back, beyond the bar, and more than well scuffed. "People want me to change the floor, but it's sacred to me," White said. "Bob Wills stood here. Willie Nelson stood here. I never want to change it. I've got the roof fixed good now, but it used to have holes in it and I'd say, 'Bob Wills fiddled through there.' He did," White said. "He did."

The cigar-chomping Wills was a commanding bandleader who assembled a gifted group of musicians to produce dance music with brio. He mixed cow-in-Texas-country fiddle music and strains of big-band brass, back-room blues, and swinging Dixieland-style reed-inflected jazz. (Wills loved the blues so much he once rode fifty miles on a horse to hear "The Empress of the Blues," Bessie Smith, sing.) Hearing Wills's band for the first time was like encountering something pleasantly unexpected in familiar surroundings—a frisson of chicory in your coffee. Wills liked to overlay the music with improvised scatty riffs and wisecracking commentary, constant reminders that no matter how urbane some of their chords might sound, Son, Smokey, Eldon, Leon, and the rest were really just country boys having a good time. The gesture was appreciated by the dry-land farmers scattered across the plains of Oklahoma and Texas, who were also savvy enough about what came through their radios to recognize that Wills was making the most sophisticated ensemble country music anyone had ever heard. Wills became immensely popular all over the country. To prairie people he was legendary. Wills's music was so esteemed across West Texas that when he gave radio performances, entire towns tuned in. The singer Don Walser says that as a schoolboy on his way home from school in La Mesa, he heard Wills's music pouring out of every house he passed.

They still can't get enough of him. Wills died more than twenty years ago, but every year, during the last weekend in April, the living members of The Playboys reunite in his hometown, Turkey, Texas, and 15,000 people—many of them retired cotton choppers—show up to listen to them play "Cotton Patch Blues" one more time. That leaves the rest of the year for oldtimers like James White to tell anyone who will listen that not only was Wills so much musician that he could fiddle through the roof, he could also bake your bread without turning on the oven.

"Wills was the first legitimate star I ever had," White said. He was speaking quickly. "He walked in and everybody turned around, punched each other, and said, 'There he is!' He had on a big old cowboy hat, a cigar, a fiddle, and boots." White shook his head and a strain of incredulity came into his voice as he said, "They talk about him bein' gruff! He was real nice. He'd say to me, 'Tell me when to start and just let me take a little break in your office.' He'd set there and smoke. After he died his daughter came out here and she said, 'I'm gonna give you something.' So I think I'm the only man in the world with an over-fifty-year-old, half-smoked Bob Wills cigar." The stogie is a little larger than medium-sized and is resting daintily on an old-fashioned lady's lace hankie that once belonged to Wills's mother-in-law. "I visited his headstone," White went on. "It says 'Deep Within My Heart Lies a Melody.' That's a phrase from 'San Antonio Rose.' They'd always play 'San Antonio Rose' at least once a night in all the old dance halls. At the end they'd sing 'Good Night Irene.' Jimmie Dale Gilmore sang it here. Jimmie Dale knows all those old songs."

White was wearing a large cowboy hat himself, white sideburns, and a yellow leather vest that was as smooth as the skin on his face. The vest once belonged to his great-uncle, who was a Texas Ranger. White is descended from a long line of Texas Rangers and Indian fighters. "Dolly was in here just recently," he said. "She just got up here and sang. It was while she was making *Wild Texas Wind*. They wanted to call it it *Big T,* but NBC said, 'We're not puttin' out no movie called *Big T* with Dolly Parton.' " When he'd stopped chortling, White said, "Roy Acuff's been here. Tex Ritter, Hank Thompson, Floyd Tillman. Roy Acuff's daddy was a hard-shell Baptist preacher. All the drunks around the bar were saying, 'His daddy's a preacher. He don't play honky-tonks.' And then there he was. He said, 'What time does the other band start?' I said, 'You're the only band.' He said, 'Well, we're not much of a dance band.' I said, 'Whatever you play they'll love it.' They kept requesting 'Great Speckled Bird,' until he said, 'That's a sacred song and I don't usually play it in a dance hall, but I'll play it for y'all, but please don't applaud.' They did just what he asked and he went into the next song."

White pointed out a photograph of a well-barbered Willie Nelson taken in 1969, not long before the singer, despondent about his musical prospects, lay down in the middle of a Nashville boulevard and failed to get himself run over. When an attempt at a new career—pig farming in the Tennessee hills—also went awry, Nelson moved back home to Texas, bought a spread outside Austin, and turned the beautiful city beside the Colorado River into a refuge for renegade country musicians. He was a pigtailed free spirit by 1990, when the Internal Revenue Service disallowed several of his real-estate deductions and told him that he was $17 million in arrears on his taxes. "I used to book Willie's dad, Pop Nelson, and Willie'd come out for nothing and sing all night with him," White said. "When Willie had his problem we put a gallon pickle jar on the bar and people started giving donations. Before I knew it, the Associated Press put it out on the wire and people were sending in money from all over the country. I told him, 'Hell, I feel like your mailman.' Everyone's offering him the clothes off their back, a place to stay. I even got money from a guy in the Birmingham jail. You don't get more country than that. I sent Willie $10,000 in all. We had to do something to help Willie. He's helped everybody."

Willie Nelson still lives outside Austin, and when I talked with him about the city, it was the time of year when Austin's redbud trees and desert roses were blooming. Nelson said, "Austin to me represents freedom. Not only Austin, but Texas is still to me the wide-open space. There's room to think in Texas. Fortunately no one is in control." More than any other feature, it is Nelson's radiant, childlike smile that makes him look the way everyone hopes they feel when they're sixty-three years old. He flashed it now. Then he said, "*Lot* of music there."

Much of that is Nelson's doing. Nashville remains the undisputed center of the commercial country music recording industry, but it's to Austin that people head if they want to hear—or sign up—musicians with fresh approaches. The town is always swarming with A&R men because on any given night in Austin—a city approaching a million people—a hundred venues are offering live music.

Jimmie Dale Gilmore has played a lot of them. Even more than Nelson, who first was a successful Nashville songwriter before he remade himself into a friendly Texas outlaw icon who happened to sell millions of records, Gilmore is the classic Austin country singer: a man with a remarkable voice who arrives in town from somewhere else—in Gilmore's case that is the West Texas city of Lubbock—and spends his career in the musical penumbra because he hasn't enough of the good fortune, the ambition, the sense of timing, or the obvious mainstream appeal that thrusts a man up the country charts. Gilmore grew up on the music of Bob Wills, Hank Williams, and Johnny Cash, was leader of The Flatlanders, the best unsuccessful band ever to come out of Texas, and lately writes songs about crystal visions. Nobody is ever sure whether he is ahead of his time or behind it.

James White was standing in front of a photograph of Gilmore now. "He's a real Texan," White said. "Just like what I am. You know, they named him after Jimmie Rodgers. In Jimmie Dale you can hear that Jimmie Rodgers and that Hank Williams. He's got a special voice. A lot of people on the radio and so many of them are imitating George Strait. They're kind of getting away from the real country. Too smooth. But when Jimmie Dale sings it, you know it was him singing the song. I call it that high lonesome plains voice. When he sings 'I'm So Lonesome I Could Cry,' I can hear the whippoorwills and the robins and the leaves falling. I grew up in the country and I can see it all in my mind."

Gilmore was born on a dairy farm in Tulia, Texas, midway between Lubbock and Amarillo. His father, Brian Gilmore, played electric guitar in a small weekend dance combo and liked to watch Bob Wills on television. Some men play catch with their little boys. Brian Gilmore scooped his up and took him to see Webb Pierce. "Remember in the movie *The Commitments* how the father had a picture of Elvis above the Pope?" Gilmore said. "In my family, country music was more important than religion. I'm certain that my father would rather meet Ernest Tubb or George Jones than any of the Presidents. There may be a lot of families like that in West Texas."

The day I met him in Lubbock, Brian Gilmore led me to a seat in his living room and handed me a four-page elegy to his guitar that began "I saw her first in a music store." Then, speaking of his son, he said, "When Jimmie Dale was four, he could sing Hank Williams songs all the way through. He'd go out on the haystack with his aunt Janie. Jimmie would sing and Janie would cry."

The family left Tulia for Lubbock in 1951, when Gilmore was six. Brian Gilmore had served in the Army Air Corps in India and had decided to study bacteriology at Texas Tech on the G.I. Bill. "He was the first person in either my mom's or his family to get a degree," says Gilmore. "I'm at that convergence of where the rural met the urban. I was the last generation off the farm." After he graduated, Brian Gilmore took a job supervising the Texas Tech creamery and bought a house in the city.

Lubbock is a cotton marketplace of 190,000 people 340 miles from Austin, in the midst of a prairie that stretches hundreds of miles beyond the limestone cliffs west of the Colorado River. The land is dun-colored, flat as a tile, and seeded with tornadoes, sandstorms, and drought. Because there are no hills and very few trees to slow the wind, the gusts blow hard enough that "galloping" traffic lights are a local hazard. Anybody in town can tell you where they were when the great tornado of 1970 twisted the Great Plains Life Insurance building to licorice. The land is so level that when you are driving in the Texas Panhandle on U.S. 87, you can see whatever's coming up on the horizon—a thunderstorm, a farmhouse, a pump jack, a windmill—half an hour before it gets to you. Lubbock itself rises like a sand castle at the intersection of four highways, which is why it is known as "The Hub City of the Plains." Living in terrain like this makes people with imagination wonder what is past the horizon. Others tend to fix their sights a bit shorter. There can be friction between the two.

"Don't wear no Stetson, but I'm willing to bet, son, that I'm big Texan, as you are," wrote Terry Allen, one of a conspicuously large number of popular musicians—Buddy Holly, Roy Orbison, Waylon Jennings, Mac Davis, Jimmie Dale Gilmore, Joe Ely, Butch Hancock—who grew up in and around Lubbock. Their recurrent description is of feeling alienated from a desolate place where the cultural landscape was as bleak as the Amarillo Highway. Lubbock was a churchly city with a citizenry whose staunch Christian rectitude acted as a kind of moral windbreak fending off any but the most familiar breezes. Though Lubbock is livelier than it used to be, there is still no alcohol for sale in stores within the city limits, and the town also imposes evening curfews on children. I heard stories from musicians about restrictions placed upon Halloween and of school-district decisions to ban T-shirts decorated with a list of supposedly "satanic" symbols that included the Star of David. Local toughs roughed up Elvis Presley outside the Cotton Club when he came to town in 1956, and for many years after Buddy Holly died, the city fathers would not allow any kind of public memorial. After a concert honoring Holly drew many thousands of people in 1979, the city council refused permission for another one in the following year, explaining that the crowds might trample the buffalo grass. Buffalo grass draws its name from its ability to withstand the hooves of stampeding buffalo. "The most interesting thing to see in Lubbock is the lightning," Gilmore told me. Growing up there, he says, "was a lot like *The Last Picture Show,* without the sordid parts."

What got him through the 1950s and 1960s in Lubbock was the radio. Lubbock's KDAV was one of the first two all-country stations in the United States. "I think I'm a true folk musician in an older sense," Gilmore told me. "But I didn't just hear the fiddle player down the road or the local banjo man. My matrix was the radio. So I have a true love for the traditional as well as an openness to strange innovation. That's exactly the recipe." Most boys he knew could name any starting Southwest Conference backfield. Gilmore remembered the names of sidemen and the words to Blind Lemon Jefferson and Bill Monroe songs. "I know thousands of songs," he told me. "My wife Janet thinks that's why I'm incompetent at everything else. My mind is filled up with songs."

Gilmore, and the Austin musicians in general, represent a broadening of country music. (Their influences are a lot like Lucinda Williams's.) Part of the impetus for this change was that they grew up in a time when new and cheaper machinery fundamentally changed what backroads America listened to. The radio, the record shop, and the tour bus meant that a kid like Gilmore would hear a much richer variety of popular music than the young Kitty Wells or George Jones had. Not only was Gilmore the first generation off the farm, he was also the first who could sidle into a cinema, settle into a seat, and discover rock 'n' roll.

"I went to the old Midway Theater in Lubbock," he said, and then his voice grew excited. Gilmore speaks a kind of bop—there is no equivalent term for it in country music—stating a theme, bounding away to a succession of ancillary ideas, before returning, usually, to the initial subject. "I went to see *The Blackboard Jungle,*" he said. "The opening of that movie, "Rock Around the Clock," it hit me with such an impact. Probably changed my life. The movie really disturbed me, but the music, I absolutely loved it forever. I remember certain musical things more vividly than anything else from my childhood. I remember one day in the backseat of the car hearing this guy on the radio begin singing 'Good Golly Miss Molly.' Little Richard. I loved it." Soon he was explaining that it was modern society's familiarity with loud industrial noises that makes people mistake heavy metal for music.

When his father took him to see Elvis Presley open for Johnny Cash, Gilmore understood these two men to be saying that country music gave a man a lot more latitude than people had supposed. "I more than liked it," Gilmore said. "It set the course of my life. It was such a joyous sound. This was before the term 'rock 'n' roll' was getting around. Johnny Cash was bigger at the time than Elvis was. It was country music but it was so rhythmic and loud. The crowd was full of country music fans and they just loved it. After every song they were screaming. They knew 'Folsom Prison Blues,' and 'Hey Porter.' They didn't know Elvis's songs yet, but by the end of each show they sure did. Somebody pointed out that I sing like Johnny Cash. I'd never thought of that, but then I started listening to the Sun Records Johnny Cash and Elvis compendiums—everybody should have those albums—and I found out I knew every word on them. I hadn't heard those records in thirty years or something, but it was imprinted on me. And it's true my phrasing is very much like Johnny Cash's."

In 1995, a year after he released the record that included his stunning version of Hank Williams's "I'm So Lonesome I Could Cry," I had dinner with Gilmore at a Mexican restaurant in East Austin. He is a slim, gangly man with a loose-limbed, cheerfully indecisive way about him. All four of his grandparents gave him Cherokee blood, which accounts for the steep pitch of his cheekbones. His hair is long and dark, and now that he is past fifty and a grandfather, it is streaked with silver. He was saying that he believed he had spent his life in a kind of musical flux, caught somewhere between country and rock 'n' roll, between Lubbock and Tulia. "I can't find a slot that I am in," he said. "Well, I love Hank Williams and everything he represents. And I love Eddy Arnold and Bill Monroe. But the music that is my deepest love, Roy Orbison, The Everly Brothers, Buddy Holly, is what was eventually called rockabilly—country guys doing blues and pop music. The sense that I am a country singer is in the same sense that Roy Orbison is a country singer. The thing those guys all had in common, except maybe Johnny Cash, is that they were rejected by the country music establishment. They were country singers to begin with, but they were not marketed as country people."

Bruce Springsteen's longtime guitar player, Steve Van Zandt, says that when he and Springsteen were growing up in central New Jersey in the late 1960s, anyone who had long hair was bound to be your friend, and anybody who played in a band was tantamount to your brother. Things were the same in West Texas. Jimmie Dale Gilmore says that "the kind of people who were different in any way in Lubbock tended to find each other." It was Gilmore's good fortune to meet up with Butch Hancock, whose red hair covered a head filled with songs. Hancock was born on a cotton farm in New Home, Texas, grew up in Lubbock, and studied architecture at Texas Tech in Lubbock. Very few architects prefer to make their homes in house trailers, but Hancock does.

"In Lubbock we grew up with two main things," he was saying. "God loves you and he's gonna send you to hell, and that sex is bad and dirty and nasty and awful and you should save it for the one you love. You wonder why we're all crazy. I really felt as though I had landed on the wrong planet." One night as a boy, Hancock became convinced he was seeing a UFO descend from the sky. A game popular in his neighborhood may explain this impression. "After it rained, three days later there was a big crop of mosquitoes," he said. "Two days later they sprayed DDT through all the alleys where there were stagnant puddles of water for mosquitoes to breed in. Most all us kids jumped on our bikes and followed the trucks to see who could stay in the DDT fog the longest."

Like Gilmore, Butch Hancock can talk at some length about how eager he was to get out of Lubbock. Yet the city's very strictness seems to have been a tinder to their imaginations in a way that might not have happened in a more permissive setting. Lubbock stirred them when they were young and maintains an enduring, ambivalent appeal for both of them. The very place Hancock and I were talking in was a former Austin Studebaker showroom that Hancock has converted into an art gallery he calls

Lubbock or Leave It. On the walls are his photographs of the scenery in and around Lubbock and for sale is a collection of his songs he's titled *West Texas Waltzes and Dust Blown Tractor Tunes*. Hancock is a prolific songwriter whose lyrics ripple with bittersweet impressions of women and with clever turns of phrase—"She said babe, you're just a wave, you're not the water," is typical—but what gives songs like "When the Nights Are Cold" and "You've Never Seen Me Cry" their signature sad, stoic flavor is that they are set on the vast plains of West Texas:

> *The windmills and the watertanks all stand on solid ground*
> *The country mailman mutters as he motors into town*
> *The sunlight came, the sunlight went, the stars came out to see*
> *The way I laughed and the way I cried at the way you treated me*
> *The ocean, babe, is watered down but these plains are high and dry*
> *And though you've seen your share of dreams you've never seen me cry.*

Many of these songs were written in the cotton and wheat fields. "Second gear at two-thirds throttle on a John Deere tractor," Hancock said promptly. He is a vaguely stocky man with a rascal's light blue eyes, a wardrobe full of denim, and a reputation for squiring around attractive women whom he doesn't allow to get too attached to him. Hancock is fifty, and has never been married. "I was driving a terracing machine, working for my dad," he went on. "Soil conservation work. So on that old tractor I found out that that speed and gear was the key of G and you could play any song you wanted to in it. I got to carrying a notebook and jotting down songs out there. I'd go home at night and try them out on a guitar and they'd be done. In Lubbock, there's nothing between you and the clouds or you and the earth. It's kind of fascinating in a weird sort of way. Everything you see out there, every home, every grain elevator, seems out of place. You're standing on a floor, basically, and you wonder 'What's that tree *doing* there?' "

That night we were meeting up with Gilmore and another of their close friends from Lubbock who has since moved to Austin, the singer and guitar player Joe Ely. Both Ely and Gilmore have recorded Hancock's songs, so many, in fact, that they are often thought of as a kind of triumvirate. "We're like the expatriate Lubbock people living in Austin," Gilmore had said to me earlier in the day. "There was something about that place that drove us away. I regard myself as a professional. I'm ambitious. Probably even greedy. But because of them it concerns me more to produce something that is acceptable among my circle of friends than if it sells millions."

It was just by chance that Joe Ely, Butch Hancock, and Gilmore were all in Lubbock at the same time in 1971. Gilmore and Ely had known each other for years, but Hancock and Ely had never met. Hancock had gone off to California after leaving Texas Tech, and Ely was rarely in town. He was born in Amarillo and lived there ten years before his father took a job at a consignment store in Lubbock. Ely learned some guitar chords from Buddy Holly's teacher as a teenager and after that he dropped out of high school and began a footloose period of living in a state of what he calls "colorful misery." By the time he was thirty, Ely had hoboed on freights, worked in a traveling circus, taken a job driving concrete trucks down a mountain in Colorado, had a gun pulled on him in a Houston bar, played his guitar for change in the New York subways, been jailed repeatedly for vagrancy in Lubbock, and played billiards for high stakes with no money in his pockets at pool halls with names like The Golden Cue. "Out on the wire," he calls the last. Among the places he slept were beside Buddy Holly's grave, in a garbage can, on a beach, in a Greenwich Village attic, and on the Staten Island Ferry.

Gilmore had also been scuffling. He worked for a group of friends who were professional gamblers, singing their requests while they cleaned out college kids in poker games. Then he began playing some of the same Lubbock area "brown-bag" honky-tonks—the city was dry until a few years ago—where Bob Wills had once worked. In 1964, Gilmore married his high-school friend, the songwriter Jo Carol Pierce. Pierce had been raised by a mother who told her, "Marriage is no way for a woman to live." They were divorced in 1967. After that, Gilmore left for Austin, where he lived for a while before wandering on to Phoenix and Berkeley. Encountering Ely again back in Lubbock was as much of an accident as the record they soon made together.

"I'd been telling Joe, 'There's this old friend of mine who writes these unbelievable songs,' " says Gilmore. "I took Joe over to Butch's house and Butch played some of his songs. Joe was properly amazed. I might have written two good songs by that period. Butch already had pockets full of them. We sat down and we all had acoustic guitars. Here I was with the really country slant. Butch was the folk. Joe had more of a rock sensibility. But it was made somewhat evident that we all had something. This evening somehow cemented this bond between us. The whole thing about

The Flatlanders, its charm, was that we did not come together as a commercial enterprise. The connection was friendship."

They moved into a house together on Fourteenth Street in Lubbock and began playing weddings, funerals, gas stations, and goat roasts. A freelance producer auditioned them in his living room, and by March 1972, Gilmore, Ely, and Hancock were in a car headed for Nashville along with the bass player Syl Rice, the mandolin player Tony Pearson, the musical-saw player Steve Wesson, and the fiddler Tommy Hancock (no relation to Butch), who, Gilmore says, "was the only man in Lubbock with a beard." With Gilmore handling the lead vocals, among the songs they recorded were four by Butch Hancock, three of Gilmore's, Willie Nelson's "One Day at a Time," and "Jole Blon," the Cajun classic made famous by Harry Choates, an alcoholic fiddler who died in an Austin jailhouse at twenty-eight. As they played, someone on hand in the studio exclaimed, "It's funny that a bunch of flatlanders has to come to the hills of Tennessee to show us how to play country music."

And so they called themselves Jimmie Dale and The Flatlanders. At a time when many Nashville singers could easily be mistaken for lounge lizards, here were a shaggy bunch of guys from the countryside playing something that sounded like old-time music, but with an eerie, psychedelic tang to it. Several of the song lyrics featured vaguely surreal ideas ("She could never see/That this world's just not real to me," wrote Gilmore in "Tonight I'm Gonna Go Downtown"). Other numbers mention tripping, getting stoned, suicide, and "a new world where everyone is free"—not exactly what Bill Monroe was setting to mandolin breaks. The structure of the music owes more to Gilmore's interest in Jimmie Rodgers, Lester Flatt, and Hank Williams than it does to Bob Wills. Yet they had all listened to Wills with their fathers and in the part of the world where he was considered, says Gilmore, "the epitome of music." More to the point, they would share some of his miseries. Early in his career Wills was snubbed by a country music establishment offended that someone would so extravagantly stretch the limits of country instrumentation. The Tulsa, Oklahoma, musician's union wouldn't permit Wills and The Playboys to join for several months, explaining that because they didn't play music, they lacked the qualifications for membership. Gilmore and his friends were similarly ostracized.

The Flatlanders were a Southern string band determined to prove that straight country had wonderful places to go beyond where Roy Acuff and Bill Monroe had taken it. But nobody was quite ready for them. For reasons that remain murky, their watershed record wasn't released, except very briefly as an 8-track tape. (Something else that is still unclear is why the musical saw wasn't tempered a little.) This disheartened them, and gradually the band dissolved. After a while, Gilmore and the rest would brush off any talk about it by saying that The Flatlanders were "more a legend than a band." That's what Rounder titled the record when the company bought the rights and finally brought it out in 1990.

"**A**ll of us are glad the record was made," Joe Ely was saying. "It's a relic from the time. We were all such vagabonds that we left different things behind. That's the only thing that survived." Ely, Hancock, and Gilmore were having dinner at a café in Austin, where they have all lived for the past fifteen years. This is the sort of thing that happens more in Austin these days than anywhere else: three first-rate country musicians getting together to spend an evening talking about music. It was a cool evening, but not uncomfortably so. One of Austin's many virtues is a dry, gentle climate.

"For a month after we made the Flatlanders record, I thought it was real important and that something would come of it," said Gilmore.

Then they were all agreeing that the promise of success is not at all the reason to make music. "I'm always seeing guys who come to Austin from some far-off place and put a band together with the express purpose of making a record," said Ely. "It's like the music doesn't matter. We played music for years and we never thought of making records."

They did, of course, come from a far-off place themselves, and soon they were reminiscing about Lubbock. "Weird things would always happen there," said Ely. "A guy selling steel-guitar lessons door to door came by and my mother invited him in for a sandwich. He played his guitar and I was kind of fascinated. I was in fourth grade. Buddy Holly had made a musical awareness for young kids. I was always running into guys who Buddy Holly played with. In Amarillo, I saw Jerry Lee Lewis playing on a flatbed trailer at a Pontiac dealership in a windstorm. The wind was blowing forty miles an hour and you couldn't see across the street, the dust was so bad. I was up to my daddy's waist and here was this guy singing like crazy in a dust storm." He smiled and looked over at Gilmore.

"There was always this drive to play music and this drive to resist music," said Gilmore.

After The Flatlanders broke up, Ely assembled his own band and slung his guitar at the Lubbock honky-tonks with such bravura flair that late in the 1970s he received a record contract. He toured with The Clash, re-leased a spirited live album, *Live Shots,* and nearly made it big as a country star. But though the black-haired Ely is a dynamic live performer, nobody could ever quite manage to capture the full joyful vigor of his chops on vinyl, and he ended up back in Texas with a nickname—"The Godfather of Cowpunk"—which reflected his dilemma: he could sing like a roper but in his heart he wanted to rock.

"I saw Bob Wills at the Nat Ballroom in Amarillo," Ely was saying. "The dance floor there was built over the swimming pool. Lubbock and Amarillo are only 120 miles apart. And seventeen feet uphill. Lubbock had the university. Amarillo had the railroads and the hobos. My grand-dad worked on the Rock Island line for fifty years. Leadbelly must have wandered up that way, or else he just liked the name of it. He was from down South." He looked over at Hancock, who'd been listening quietly. "Y'all had this folk and bluegrass stuff I'd never heard of. Then once I heard Doc Watson through you two, I immediately learned his songs."

"It was the purity of his good taste," said Hancock. "He was a virtuoso picker and all, but it was also that it was the highest standard of good taste."

Earlier, Gilmore had told me, "Part of the magic of music for me is that music can evoke emotions that you can't even have otherwise, emotion there isn't even a word for. I remember when I was a little bitty kid hear-ing The Platters singing 'Harbor Lights.' I was from Lubbock; I didn't know what a harbor was. But the melody, the sound of the voices, gave me a feeling of pleasant longing that had nothing to do with anything that had yet happened to me. I wasn't old enough to have had sad love affairs." Now he said, "I've got this theory that music can evoke emotions you don't have at any other time."

They immediately knew what he meant. This subject was kicked around for a while, and then they began talking some more about Buddy Holly. After playing school dances and car-dealership openings in Lub-bock as a teenager, Holly had forged his enthusiasms for Hank Williams, Elvis Presley, and The Louvin Brothers into a string of seminal country-pop hits. His career was foundering a bit when, at age twenty-two, in 1959, he died in an airplane accident, a tragedy that made him into a rock 'n' roll martyr everywhere but in Lubbock.

"When I first moved to Lubbock I didn't associate Buddy Holly with Lubbock because the city completely did away with him," said Ely. He sounded angry. "Not a trace of him. It was only when a movie came out that they put up a statue. Now they're beginning to realize that people come there to see it because of the music. I moved to Austin because I realized that no matter what you tried to do there, you'd be pushed back."

"We didn't feel like we fit in any place in that town, so we ended up on each other's back porches," said Hancock. "Austin's the same way. It became the Texas magnet for artists and writers and all kinds of other crazy creative people."

Among them were musicians like Willie Nelson, Lucinda Williams, Lyle Lovett, Nanci Griffith, Jimmie and Stevie Ray Vaughan, and Jerry Jeff Walker, who liked to say, "I don't live in Texas. I live in Austin." The hellbent songwriter Townes Van Zandt was also an occasional resident until, as he explained to me, the nightlife wore him out. "I moved back down there ten years ago from Nashville, and decided I'm just gonna go hear all the live music, check out the scene," he said. "God, I was in jail four times for nothing serious. Got to where the police called me by my first name. They'd say, 'Townes, do you need the cuffs tonight?' and I'd say, 'I guess so.' So they'd put 'em on real loose. It's really too much fun for me."

Gilmore experienced some of that, too. Like all The Flatlanders, he had been coming to Austin for years—sometimes leaving Lubbock at midnight with ten other people crammed into one Volkswagen Beetle. He got there permanently in 1980, at the same time Ely did. (Hancock had been living in Austin since the mid-1970s.) Gilmore hadn't made any music since The Flatlanders. Well into middle age, he was still a gangly kid who had trouble growing up, a quality that helped furnish his life with more turmoil than recordings. Instead of writing, he'd been drifting, eventually taking cover for six years in a Denver mission run by a teenage Himalayan mystic called the Guru Maharaj Ji. (He remains fascinated by Beat mysticism, maintains a correspondence with the poet Allen Ginsberg, and practices Zen Buddhism.)

In Austin, he picked up his guitar and also far too much whiskey, women, and cocaine. Echoing what so many country musicians have told me when talking over the tension between singing sad and feeling sad, Gilmore said, "I felt like I identified with Hank Williams from the first time I heard his voice." But by 1987, Gilmore was playing Austin clubs like James White's Broken Spoke and the radical hippie–biker joint Emma-Joe's, named for Emma Goldman and Joe Hill. For a while he held the coveted job as the Wednesday-night regular at Threadgill's, a former Gulf station where Janis Joplin got her start early in the 1960s. All of this made him want to make records again. "Austin is extremely hospitable," he told me. He said he was thinking both of the city's physical beauty—the skies are usually sapphire blue, and when the sun sets, it does so in a blaze of ochre and pink—and of a population that is very receptive to musicians. "The music can thrive there because there is a great audience that is extremely supportive—that encourages innovation and appreciates both things that are old-fashioned and experimental."

Ely produced Gilmore's first record, in 1988, and since then Gilmore has made five more. The best of these records, *After Awhile* and *Spinning Around the Sun,* owe a lot to The Flatlanders. Gilmore's own writing leans toward the existential country love song, but whether he's singing about finding "my sweet El Dorado," or Hank Williams or Butch Hancock songs, the records reflect increasing confidence in the reedy, nasal tenor tremolo that James White had thought to call Gilmore's "high lonesome plains" voice. He is the most gifted singer of The Flatlanders, but his is the kind of voice that requires a little getting used to.

Back in 1978, Ely had also produced Hancock's first solo effort. They made the record for $7,000, and Hancock took it upon himself to sell all the copies himself, a practice he maintained with subsequent recordings until recently. "I remember Butch showing up with a vanload of records and saying, 'Now what do I do?' " said Gilmore.

"It was like a cousin I had who lived on a cotton farm," Ely said. "He noticed in a grocery store that garlic had a good price on it. So he grew a whole field of it and he went around to grocery stores and they'd say, 'Yeah, I'll take a pound of that.' Then a hailstorm came and pounded all that garlic into the ground." They were all laughing hard now. "Neighbors called from ten miles away," Ely went on. "The smell was *so* bad." He fixed Hancock a look. "Butch, you sell all of them records?" Butch had.

It seemed only fair now for Gilmore to tell an Ely circus story, and so he did. "We were out at Mom and Dad's house one night and we were watching the news and all of a sudden here came Joe leading a llama," Gilmore said. Ely was nodding ruefully. "My mama said, 'That's Joey!' " Ely, it turned out, soon left the circus when an ill-tempered horse mangled several of his ribs. After that he kept company with more predictable sorts, including a Lubbock man named Shallowwater Slim, who, said Ely, "could throw a die across a room and keep the five on the bottom every time."

They were hooting and giggling. "We can never write songs together because we end up laughing so much," Ely said.

"The lack of humor was what we hated about Lubbock," Gilmore said, a bit vehemently.

"A sense of humor was necessary to survive out there in the middle of the desert," Ely agreed. "It's so stark. When you're in a place that's really beautiful and gorgeous, you kind of get insensitive to it. There you're more aware of beauty. You have to train your eye to see it."

Street guitar pickers, Maynardsville, Tennessee, 1935.
"I grew up in Depression days with nothing much for enjoyment
and that helped me enjoy music more," says Earl Scruggs.

EPILOGUE

To CALL TODAY'S MAINSTREAM country music country at all is a misnomer. Hot Country is really pop rock music for a prospering, mostly conservative white middle class. It's kempt, comfortable music—hypersincere, settled, and careful neither to offend nor surprise. A lot like Disneyland, in some ways its model, contemporary country thrives because it is sleek and predictable, a safe adventure in a smoke-free environment.

Hot Country appears to be something of a passing fancy—already its sales figures are beginning to decline—but the suburban cowboy craze has been a painful one for the veteran practitioners of country music. The best country was always proudly devoid of affect, music that reassured its audience by going its own hillbilly way. Some popular music was designed to help you escape from the world. Country forced you to wake up on Sunday morning and confront your life. To see the music now so homogenized still has Johnny Cash a little shaken. "I think a lot of it's sex," he says. "These guys wear these tight jeans. They work out with a trainer three times a week. I can't see a lot of good country songs coming out of it. Individuality's missing. But it's working for them. It's like rivers and politics, you know. Bad stuff sometimes floats to the top. But I don't care. I'm still doing it my way. I just don't spend any time on Music Row, Nashville."

He doesn't have to. Cash, in fact, recorded his two most recent records with a California rap producer, something that emphasizes the notion that country music isn't limited to a particular style, people, or region anymore. It's versatile American music and full of possibilities, as musical innovators from Jimmie Rodgers to Cash to Iris DeMent have been making clear throughout this century. The Flatlanders probably made the point as well as anyone. They were a group of odd characters who didn't look like earlier country musicians, and whose music didn't quite sound like anyone else's either. They examined the country music that their parents grew up with, nodded at it respectfully, and then went their own way. That a Nashville record company essentially failed to release their one record for twenty years only made them like most distinctive artists across time: it took a while for people to get used to them. Now that recording is around for good.

Whether the singer is Rodgers, Bill Monroe, Hank Williams, or Emmylou Harris, what has bound traditional country together over this century is that it is simply worded, string-driven, melodic music concerned with subjects that are both quotidian and universal: faith, love, family, work, heartbreak, pleasure, sin, joy, and suffering. A lot of the best country is giddy, good-time music, but it is also more than that. The country that will last uses deceptively simple details to say profound things about the American experience. Because it rang so true to *their* experiences, good and bad, traditional country music braced the people who listened to it even as it entertained them—and it continues to. When the *New York Times* reporter Sara Rimer visited North Carolina farm country in the wake of Hurricane Bertha during July 1996, she met Julian Williford, a seventy-seven-year-old Beulaville tobacco farmer whose crop was wiped out by the storm. "We got to do like Hank Snow—keep moving on," he told her, citing "The Singing Ranger's" biggest hit.

The American singer whose music most obviously has this kind of social influence these days is the son of a Freehold, New Jersey, factory worker. Bruce Springsteen isn't usually associated with Hank Snow and Johnny Cash, but Emmylou Harris, who deplores Hot Country as "bloodless, cookie-cutter music," says, "I really think of him as a country singer." So does Don Everly of The Everly Brothers. "He's brilliant," he says. "He's wonderful. I'm a little disappointed in country music right now. Country music is supposed to be for working people. Ain't no working class in country anymore. But Bruce Springsteen, I can relate to that real well."

When Springsteen sings about migrant farm workers, Vietnam veterans, smalltime hoods, and mill workers out on the street celebrating the end of the week, he covers the sort of terrain that has appealed to the best country writers. Like Harlan Howard, Merle Haggard, or Hank Williams, Springsteen requires only three or four minutes to tell stories that pack the emotional force of great short fiction. One of them is his song about a dying factory city, "Youngstown." Nominally the story of the bitterness a family of iron scarfers feels after the big blast furnace they call "Jenny" closes, the song also expresses Springsteen's most familiar theme, the juxtaposition of a mythical American promised land where anything is possible with the crushing reality of a country that keeps letting hard-working people down.

> *From the Monongahela Valley*
> *To the Mesabi Iron Range*
> *To the coal mines of Appalachia*
> *The story's always the same*
> *Seven hundred tons of metal a day*
> *Now sir you tell me the world's changed*
> *Once I made you rich enough*
> *Rich enough to forget my name.*

Springsteen has, in fact, recently written a batch of what he offhandedly refers to as "South Jersey cowboy songs." He grew up on rock 'n' roll, but in his mid-twenties, after completing his record *Born to Run,* he became a great admirer of country singers like Hank Williams, George Jones, Charlie Rich, The Louvin Brothers, and of country music in general because it grappled with the grownup issues rock generally avoided. "Country asked all the right questions," he says. "It was concerned with how you go on living after you reach adulthood. I was asking those questions myself. Everything after *Born to Run* was shot full with a lot of country music—those questions."

Springsteen says, "I aspired to do work that meant something. I wanted to write about the way people lived and the possibilities of life"—and that's what all the best country writers have always done. If our America differs from Jimmie Rodgers's Depression-era America, or the postwar America Hank Snow saw in 1949 when he wrote "I'm Movin' On," it's still an America that inspires great country songs—songs that are among us. The Real Country boom has recently tended to obscure the most arresting country music, but Johnny Cash, Merle Haggard, Ralph Stanley, and George Jones are still making it, and so too are gifted younger singers like Jimmie Dale Gilmore, Junior Brown, Alison Krauss, Suzanne Cox, Dwight Yoakam, and Lucinda Williams. Because they have fresh things to say about life, and because their melodies sound clean, clear, and like nobody else's, young midwestern bands like Son Volt and Golden Smog, who play the alternative-rock-informed progressive country referred to as No Depression—after the Carter Family song and the Seattle-based magazine that covers this music—are more obvious heirs to Hank Williams and Gram Parsons than the bathetic head-twangers lately in favor along Music Row. Country music can come from anywhere, and it does.

The musicians I've met, and others like them, make me feel certain that there will always be men and women who seek to make compelling country music that has the spirit of the old songs in it. As Joe Ely said at the end of the evening I spent with him and the other Flatlanders, "You know, good stuff, eventually people'll want to hear it."

A woman says goodbye to her farm. "They offered the music of home for people who no longer had a home."

A Note on the Sources

With the exception of Jimmie Rodgers, Sara Carter, and Patsy Cline, who all died years before I began listening to country music, I spent time with each of the principal characters in this book. In the old days, if you wanted to meet up with a prominent country music singer, on Saturday night you went over to the Ryman Auditorium in Nashville where a kind sort like the *Grand Ole Opry* manager, Ott Devine, would take you backstage and introduce you around. The once glorious *Opry* is now a somewhat shopworn production and no longer a priority for many performers. Country music, meanwhile, has become so popular that even many older singers—who I mostly wanted to talk to—have become national celebrities with all the attendant difficulties in access that implies. I was fortunate to come into contact with a great number of helpful people—managers, publicists, record executives—who made the conversations I was seeking possible. The artists themselves sometimes assisted me in this respect. After I spoke with Chet Atkins, he put me in touch with Kitty Wells and Johnny Wright. Kitty and Johnny, in turn, told me how to reach Earl Scruggs and called ahead to provide an introduction. Harlan Howard was nice enough to telephone Buck Owens for me. I met Emmylou Harris at Harlan's birthday party. Emmylou then took me along to Bill Monroe's birthday party. And so it went.

Those interviews were supplemented by discussions with hundreds of other people, musical and not, who had something to tell me about the subject of each chapter. Many of the country singers and musicians I have written about no longer live in the place where they grew up. In most cases that place had a lot to do with their music, so I have gone to Dyess, Flint Hill,

Rosine, and the rest on my own, looked around, and talked with people who live there. (Quite a number of the people I met in those places were happy to talk about their hometown, but didn't want to be quoted or identified lest they say something that might make life in a small community difficult. Those interviews were used for background.)

Beyond this, I tried to read everything I could find about each of my subjects and, of course, to listen carefully to their music. I spent many months reading books and magazine and journal articles, looking through the extensive clip files, and listening to the massive record collection in the Country Music Foundation Library in Nashville, where Stephen Betts, Dan Cooper, Kent Henderson, Paul Kingsbury, Chris Skinker, Alan Stoker, and especially Ronnie "The Deacon" Pugh, my idea of a national treasure, were generous and patient with me. Closer to home, the New York City Public Library's Music and Recording Arts division at Lincoln Center was a valuable resource, as was the Bobst Memorial New York University Library. I was treated with exceptional kindness at the Southern Folklife Collection at the University of North Carolina, Chapel Hill, where I thank John Miller; at the North Carolina Collection at the University of North Carolina, Chapel Hill, where I thank Jerry W. Cotten; and at the Kern County Museum in Bakersfield, California, where I thank Carola Enriquez and Jeff Nickell.

I discuss particular sources in the notes to each chapter that follow, but here I need to express a series of more general debts. A book of this sort requires the cooperation of a vast number of people. Some of those who helped me along the way are: Sharon Allen; Christopher Brewer; John R. Burr; Julie Cahill; Keith Case; Roy Clark; Connie Conkwright; Willard, Marie, Evelyn, Sidney, and Suzanne Cox; Lane Cross; Mike Curb; Jason DeParle; Glen Dicker; Stuart Duncan; Minnesota Fats; Holly George-Warren; Don Gibson; Peter Guralnick; Kate Haggerty; Kelly Hancock; Monty Hitchcock; Ken Irwin; Dana Andrew Jennings; Danny Kahn; Rob Koss; Marilyn Laverty; Stephanie Ledgin; Kyle Lehning; Bill Malone; Robert Mann; Betty McInturff; Joan Myers; John Pennell; Alan Pepper, who kindly allowed me free run of his club, The Bottom Line; Ellen Jones Pryor; Lou Robin; Heidi Ellen Robinson; Jim Rooney; Barbara Roseman; William Sackus; Mark Satlof; Vin Scelsa; Michelle Schweitzer; Jim Shaw; Evelyn Shriver; Jerry Strobel, who on two occasions let me roam around backstage at *The Grand Ole Opry;* Elizabeth Thiels; Bob and India Waterson; Charles K. Wolfe.

The filmmaker Rachel (*High Lonesome*) Liebling was an enormous help to me at start and finish. Among other things, she helped me find many of the photographs.

◆ ◆ ◆

Several magazine editors took an interest in this project and commissioned articles which later, in different form, became book chapters. At *The New Yorker,* I thank Charles McGrath and Hal Espen. At the *New York Times Magazine,* I thank Alan Burdick, Gerry Marzoratti, Adam Moss, and Jack Rosenthal. At the *New York Times,* I thank Barbara Graustark. At the *New Republic,* I thank Andrew Sullivan. At the *Oxford American,* I thank Marc Smirnoff.

I am very grateful to The Corporation at Yaddo.

I owe particular thanks to several friends scattered around the country who shared my enthusiasm for this book and either put me up in their homes during my travels, read portions of the manuscript, accompanied me on research trips, or were particularly helpful in other ways they will recognize: Donald Antrim; Rebecca Brian; Alison Brown; Ted Conover; Dub Cornett; Rachel Dretzin; Donna Ferrato; Darcy Frey; Annette Hamburger; Larry Harris; Richard and Lisa Howorth; Peter Keane; Merrell Noden; Ann Patchett; Tom Powers; Tom Rush; Charles Siebert; Ilena Silverman; Jean Strouse; George Trow; Karl VanDevender; Garry West; Jonathan Wiener; Nicky Weinstock; Lucinda Williams; Jamie Wright; and Ginger Young. Melanie Thernstrom has, as Chet Atkins would say, been bein' nice to me the whole way through.

Kathy Robbins is to agents what Hank Williams is to sad songs—the best. I am also indebted to Bill Clegg and Tifanny Richards at the Robbins office. At Sterling Lord Literistic, I thank Jody Hotchkiss and Peter Matson. Many thanks as well to Stuart Krichevsky.

Dan Frank wouldn't like it if I went on about how special it is to work with him, but it is. At Pantheon I also thank Kristen Bearse, Marian Brown, Carol Devine Carson, Fearn Cutler, Altie Karper, Jeanne Morton, and Claudine O'Hearn, who devoted much energy toward making this a better book. At Vintage, Marty Asher, Katy Barrett, and Susie Leness are a great pleasure to work with.

This book is dedicated with much affection to my musical sister Sal and to my uncle Robert, who taught me so much of what I know about country music and other things too.

NOTES

PROLOGUE: THE SPIRIT OF JIMMIE RODGERS

♦ INTERVIEWS

Marty Brown; Corbert Byrd; Jimmie Dale Court; Holly Dunn; Larry Finch; Earlean Garry; Alison Krauss; Chris Lowe; Juanita M. Lynch; Florence Mars; Sam Marshall; Tim McGraw; Richard McWilliams; Shine Pogue; Mildred Pollard; Charley Pride; Conrad "Sonny" Rodgers; Tami Rose; Fonda Rush; Carolyn and Johnnie Shurley; Mayor John Robert Smith; Marty Stuart; Dorothy Thompson; Pam Tillis; Travis Tritt; Tanya Tucker; Lamarr Whitenton.

♦ BOOKS

Atkins, Chet, with Bill Neely. *Country Gentlemen.* Chicago: Henry Regnery Co., 1974.

Bishop, Edward Allen. *Elsie McWilliams (I Remember Jimmie).* Published by the author, 1985.

Caldwell, Erskine. *Tobacco Road.* Athens: University of Georgia Press, 1995.

The City of Meridian Annual Report, 1993.

Cobbett, William. *Rural Rides.* New York: Penguin Books, 1983.

Comber, Chris, and Mike Paris. "Jimmie Rodgers." In *Stars of Country Music,* edited by Bill C. Malone and Judith McCulloh. Urbana: University of Illinois Press, 1975.

Country Music Foundation. *Country: The Music and the Musicians.* New York: Abbeville Press, 1988.

Fairley, Laura Nay, and James T. Dawson. *Paths to the Past: An Overview History of Lauderdale County, Mississippi.* Meridian, Miss.: Lauderdale County Department of Archives, 1988.

Foote, Shelby. *The Civil War: A Narrative.* New York: Random House, 1963. This book contains General Sherman's wire.

Holtzberg-Call, Maggie. "The Gandy Dancer Speaks: Voices from Southern Black Railroad Gangs." In *Alabama Folklife,* edited by Stephen Maan. Birmingham, Ala.: Folklife Association, 1989.

Musical Roots of the South. A pamphlet published by the Southern Arts Federation, Atlanta, Georgia, 1992. Articles by Charles Wolfe and W. K. McNeil were very helpful.

Paris, Mike, and Chris Comber. *Jimmie the Kid: The Life of Jimmie Rodgers.* London: Eddison Press Ltd., 1977.

Percy, Walker. *Signposts in a Strange Land.* New York: Farrar, Straus & Giroux, 1991.

Porterfield, Nolan. *Jimmie Rodgers: The Life and Times of America's Blue Yodeler.* Urbana: University of Illinois Press, 1979.

Rodgers, Carrie. *My Husband Jimmie Rodgers.* San Antonio: Southern Library Institute, 1935.

Shank, Jack. *Meridian: The Queen with a Past.* 3 vols. Meridian, Miss.: Southeastern Printing Co., 1985–7.

Stearns, Marshall W. *The Story of Jazz.* New York: Oxford University Press, 1956. This book contains the Fats Waller anecdote.

Williams, Roger M. *Sing a Sad Song: The Life of Hank Williams.* Garden City, N.Y.: Doubleday & Co., 1970. This book contains Williams's comments to *Nation's Business* magazine.

◆ ARTICLES

Applebome, Peter. "Country Graybeards Get the Boot." *New York Times,* August 21, 1994.

Applebome, Peter. "Hank Williams, Garth Brooks, BR5-49?: As the Explosive Growth of the 90s Cools, Record Executives Are Looking for the Next Big Thing to Restore Nashville Momentum." *New York Times Magazine,* October 27, 1996.

At Home with Country Music's Hottest Stars. People, special issue, Fall 1994.

Brown, Patricia Leigh. "Reaching for the Stars: Nashville Fair Celebrates the Fans of Country Music." *New York Times,* June 14, 1992.

Cocks, Jay. "Friends in Low Places: Garth Brooks, Average Guy, Pleasant Singer and Hokey Holy Terror as a Performer, Is the Surprising New Face of Pop." *Time,* March 30, 1992.

"Country's Money Spinners." *Economist,* May 8, 1993.

Feiler, Bruce. "Gone Country: The Voice of Suburban America." *New Republic,* February 5, 1996.

Feiler, Bruce. "Has Country Music Become a Soundtrack for White Flight?" *New York Times,* October 20, 1996.

Jones, Malcolm Jr. "The Melody Lingers On: Before Great Singers, There Were Great Songwriters." *Newsweek,* November 20, 1995.

Meridian Star. Jimmie Rodgers Memorial Festival supplement, May 20, 1994.

Navarro, Mireya. "Florida Farm a Labor Battleground." *New York Times,* April 11, 1996.

Oermann, Robert K. "How Garth Conquered America." *Journal of Country Music,* Vol. 14, No. 3.

Painton, Priscilla. "Country Rocks the Boomers." *Time,* March 30, 1992.

Pareles, John. "Dolly Parton Heads from the Mountains Up to Carnegie Hall." *New York Times,* May 17, 1993.

"Rebirth of the Blues." *Economist,* May 4, 1996.

Revkin, Andrew C. "Harmony Rules a Country Music Fair." *New York Times,* June 15, 1996.

Rose, Tami. *The Believer Magazine,* February–April 1992 and February–April 1994.

Scherman, Tony. "Country Music: Its Rise and Fall." *American Heritage,* November 1994.

Schoemer, Karen. "Turning Pickup Trucks and Broken Hearts into Pure Platinum." *New York Times,* January 5, 1992.

"A Song for the City." *Economist,* April 23, 1994.

Williams, Lena. "A Black Fan of Country Music Finally Tells All." *New York Times,* June 19, 1994.

Nolan Porterfield's notes accompanying the complete Jimmie Rodgers recordings by Rounder Records were very helpful. Country record sales and radio statistics were supplied by the Country Music Association. The Merle Haggard letters were published in *Newsweek,* May 6, 1996. Official programs for every Fan Fair celebration are in the Country Music Foundation Library. I attended the Jimmie Rodgers Memorial Festival, May 1994, in Meridian, Mississippi, and Fan Fair, June 1994, in Nashville. I appreciate the help of the Jimmie Rodgers Museum, Meridian, Mississippi, and of Charles E. Riley at the Lauderdale County Archives, Meridian, Mississippi.

NOTES ON PAPER NAPKINS: HARLAN HOWARD

♦ INTERVIEWS

Pat Alger; Harlan Howard; Jan Howard; Melanie Smith Howard; Ralph Murphy; Buck Owens.

◆ BOOKS

Boswell, James. *Life of Johnson*. New York: Oxford University Press, 1953.

Horstman, Dorothy. *Sing Your Heart Out, Country Boy*. Nashville: Country Music Foundation Press, 1986.

Nelson, Willie, and Bud Shrake. *Willie: An Autobiography*. New York: Simon & Schuster, 1988.

Reid, Jan. *The Improbable Rise of Redneck Rock*. Austin: Heidelberg Publishers, 1974.

◆ ARTICLES

"Close-up on Harlan Howard, Nashville, April 1994." *Country Music Association Journal*, vol. 29, no. 4.

"Harlan Howard in His Own Words." *Country Song Roundup*, May 1970.

King, Larry L. "The Grand Ole Opry." *Harper's*, July 1968.

TAKING OUT THE TWANG: CHET ATKINS

◆ INTERVIEWS

Chet Atkins; Owen Bradley; Buster Devault; Garrison Keillor.

◆ BOOKS

Atkins, Chet, with Bill Neely. *Country Gentleman*. Chicago: Henry Regnery Co., 1974.

Flippo, Chet. "An Interview with Chet Atkins." In *Everybody Was Kung Fu Dancing*. New York: St. Martin's Press, 1991.

Ivey, William. "Chet Atkins." In *Stars of Country Music*, edited By Bill C. Malone and Judith McCulloh. Urbana: University of Illinois Press, 1975.

◆ ARTICLES

Hurst, Jack. "The Accent's on Atkins." *Chicago Tribune*, July 8, 1990.

Hurst, Jack. "From the Old School: Guitarist Chet Atkins Recalls a Less Businesslike Nashville." *Chicago Tribune*, September 4, 1994.

King, Larry L. "The Grand Ole Opry." *Harper's*, July 1968.

Millard, Bob. "Charley Pride: Alone in the Spotlight." *Journal of Country Music*, vol. 14, no. 2.

Siminoff, Roger H. "Chet Atkins." *Frets*, October 1979.

THREE WOMEN

Sara Carter

◆ INTERVIEWS

Janette Carter; Joe Carter; Johnny Cash; June Carter Cash; Bill Clifton; Rita Forrester; Edward A. Kahn; Mike Seeger; Jack Tottle; Charles K. Wolfe; Flo Wolfe.

♦ BOOKS

Atkins, John A., ed. *The Carter Family.* London: Old Time Music, 1970.

Atkins, John A. "The Carter Family." In *Stars of Country Music,* edited by Bill C. Malone and Judith McCulloh. Urbana: University of Illinois Press, 1975.

Bufwack, Mary A., and Robert K. Oermann. *Finding Her Voice: The Saga of Women in Country Music.* New York: Crown Publishers, 1993.

Carter, Janette. *Living with Memories.* Hiltons, Va.: Carter Family Memorial Music Center, 1983.

Cash, June Carter. *Among My Klediments.* Grand Rapids, Mich.: Zondervan Publishing House, 1979.

Cash, June Carter. *From the Heart.* New York: Prentice-Hall Press, 1987.

Kahn, Edward A. "The Carter Family: A Reflection of Changes in Society." Ph.D. thesis, University of California at Los Angeles, 1970.

Orgill, Michael. *Anchored in Love: The Carter Family Story.* Old Tappan, N.J.: Fleming H. Revell Co., 1975.

♦ ARTICLES

"The Carters in Virginia." *Journal of the American Academy for the Preservation of Old-Time Country Music,* no. 20, April 1994.

Also helpful were the TBS television special *America's Music: The Roots of Country* (Turner original production), which aired in the spring of 1996, and Tony Russell's liner notes to *The Carter Family* (Time-Life Records—Country & Western Classics). I visited The Carter Fold, Maces Springs, Virginia, in May 1996.

Kitty Wells

♦ INTERVIEWS

Chet Atkins; Owen Bradley; Martha Carson; Emmylou Harris; Loretta Lynn; Kitty Wells; Johnny Wright.

♦ BOOKS

Bufwack, Mary A., and Robert K. Oermann. *Finding Her Voice: The Saga of Women in Country Music.* New York: Crown Publishers, 1993.

Dunkleberger, A. C. *Queen of Country Music: The Life Story of Kitty Wells.* Nashville: Ambrose Printing Co., 1977.

Trott, Walt. *The Honky Tonk Angels: The Life and Legend of Kitty Wells, Johnny Wright—and Chronicling the Career of Johnny & Jack.* Nashville: Nova Books, 1993.

◆ ARTICLES

Creed, Dick. "Kitty Wells: Nothing Phony When She Belts One Out." *Winston-Salem Journal,* November 1, 1985.

Heironymous, Clara. "Kitty Wells' Secret—Personality Projection." *Nashville Tennessean,* November 15, 1959.

"J. D. Miller, Music Producer, 73; Wrote 'Honky-Tonk Angels.' " *New York Times,* March 25, 1996.

Oermann, Robert K. "Golden Memories Day for Kitty, Johnny." *Tennessean,* October 30, 1987.

The notes that accompany the Bear Family recording *The Golden Years—Kitty Wells,* by Bob Pinson, Richard Weize, and Charles Wolfe, are an excellent resource.

Patsy Cline

◆ INTERVIEWS

Bud Armel; Owen Bradley; June Carter Cash; Charlie Dick; Jack Fretwell; Harlan Howard; Judy Sue Huyett-Kempf; James S. Kniceley; Harold Madagan; Mel Tillis.

◆ BOOKS

Bego, Mark. *I Fall to Pieces: The Music and the Life of Patsy Cline.* Holbrook, Mass.: Adams Publishing, 1995.

Bufwack, Mary A., and Robert K. Oermann. *Finding Her Voice: The Saga of Women in Country Music.* New York: Crown Publishers, 1993.

Jones, Margaret. *Patsy: The Life and Times of Patsy Cline.* New York: HarperCollins, 1994.

Lynn, Loretta, and George Vecsey. *Coal Miner's Daughter.* New York: Warner Books, 1976.

Nassour, Ellis. *Honky Tonk Angel: The Intimate Story of Patsy Cline.* New York: St. Martin's Press, 1993.

◆ ARTICLES

Franklin, Ron. "It's Not the Same Town That Patsy Cline Knew." *USA Today,* October 10, 1985.

The *Winchester Star* clip file I reviewed often did not include publication dates of articles. I made use of pieces about Patsy Cline by *Star* staff writers Paul Blythe, Bill Hanlon, and Terri Higgins. The *Richmond Times-Dispatch* article that Harold Madagan has on the wall of his drugstore is dated September 3, 1995. Paul Kingsbury's notes that accompany MCA Records' complete Patsy Cline collection are an excellent resource.

The Winchester–Frederick County Chamber of Commerce has a small collection of Patsy Cline memorabilia. I saw the musical *Always Patsy Cline* performed at the Ryman Auditorium, Nashville, in the summer of 1994. *Sweet Dreams,* a movie about Patsy Cline's life, appeared in theaters in 1985.

FULL OF BEANS:
BILL MONROE AND RALPH STANLEY

♦ INTERVIEWS
Wendell Allen; Hoyt Bratcher; Alison Brown; Don Everly; Emmylou Harris; Frances Johnson Harvey; Alison Krauss; Rachel Liebling; Del McCoury; Jesse McReynolds; Fran Meade; Bill Monroe; Bill Porter; Hubert Powers; Bernard Rakes; Gary Reid; Jean Ritchie; Jim Rooney; Neil Rosenberg; Tom Rush; Earl Scruggs; Ricky Skaggs; Chris Skinker; Ralph Stanley; Tom Stanley; Marty Stuart.

♦ BOOKS
Rinzler, Ralph. "Bill Monroe." In *Stars of Country Music,* edited by Bill C. Malone and Judith McCulloh. Urbana: University of Illinois Press, 1975.

Rooney, James. *Bossmen: Bill Monroe and Muddy Waters.* New York: Dial Press, 1974.

Rosenberg, Neil, *Bluegrass: A History.* Urbana: University of Illinois Press, 1985.

Wright, John. *Traveling the High Way Home: Ralph Stanley and the World of Traditional Bluegrass Music.* Urbana: University of Illinois Press, 1993.

♦ ARTICLES
Altman, Billy. "Timeless Purity from the Soul of Bluegrass." *New York Times,* May 2, 1993.

Bliss, Gil. "Voices: Bill Monroe, Bluegrass Musician." *New Bedford* (Mass.) *Standard-Times,* October 16, 1988.

"Charges Against Monroe Dismissed." *Cleveland* (Tenn.) *Banner,* May 11, 1989.

Cole, William. "Side Glances at the Conference on Tomorrow's Children." *Mountain Life and Work,* Winter 1940. Note that I reviewed a great many issues of *Mountain Life and Work.*

Davis, Donna. "Monroe Glad Assault Charge Behind Him." *Nashville Banner,* May 11, 1989.

DeParle, Jason. "At Home with Bill Monroe: Lots to Sing, Little to Say." *New York Times,* June 9, 1994.

Gates, David. "Mountain-Music Summit Meeting." *Newsweek,* March 8, 1993.

Gordon, Douglas. "Ralph Stanley—Traditional Banjo Stylist." *Frets,* October 1979.

Henderson, Tom. Interview with Ralph Stanley. *Muleskinner News,* vol. 7, no. 1 (1976).

Hentoff, Nat. "Grass-Roots Bluegrass." *Wall Street Journal,* September 22, 1993.

Hornaday, Ann. "A Bluegrass Documentary with a Brooklyn Accent." *New York Times,* April 24, 1994.

Jennings, Dana Andrew. "Bluegrass, Straight and Pure, Even If the Money's No Good." *New York Times,* April 23, 1995.

King, Larry. "The Father of Bluegrass." *Pulse!* June 1988.

Kuykendall, Pete. "The Stanley Brothers." *Disc Collector,* no. 16, 1961.

Lawrence, Keith. "Battle for Uncle Pen's Cabin." *Owensboro* (Ky.) *Messenger-Inquirer,* October 13, 1991.

Lundy, Ronni. "Bill Monroe." *Louisville Times,* September 10, 1983.

Martin, Frank W. "The Hills—and Everywhere Else—Are Alive with the Sound of Bill Monroe's Unique Bluegrass." *People,* September 1, 1975.

Maslin, Janet. "A History of Bluegrass and Its Courtly Father." *New York Times,* April 29, 1994.

Mitchell, Larry. " 'Dr.' Ralph Stanley." *Pickin',* August 1977.

"A Music Legend Dies." *Tennessean,* September 11, 1996.

Oermann, Robert K. "High Lonesome Voice Stilled." *Tennessean,* September 10, 1996.

Oermann, Robert K. "Ricky Skaggs Remembers the Stanley Brothers." *Bluegrass Unlimited,* May 1981.

Orr, Jan. "The Power and Glory of Monroe's Music Will Echo into the Future." *Nashville Banner,* September 12, 1996.

Pareles, Jon. "Bill Monroe Dies at 84; Fused Musical Roots into Bluegrass." *New York Times,* September 10, 1996.

Ringle, Ken. "The Natural King of Bluegrass: Virginia's Ralph Stanley, the Old-Timey Singer Whose Time Has Come." *Washington Post,* March 20, 1993.

Rinzler, Ralph, "Ralph Stanley: Tradition from the Mountains." *Bluegrass Unlimited,* March 1974.

Rosenberg, Neil. "A Front Porch Visit with Birch Monroe." *Bluegrass Unlimited,* September 1982.

Scherman, Tony. "How a Child's Toy Begat Bluegrass." *New York Times,* September 18, 1994.

Thompson, Catherine. "Charges Against Monroe Dropped." *Tennessean,* May 11, 1989.

Tottle, Jack. "Ralph Stanley: The Stanley Sound." *Bluegrass Unlimited,* May 1981.

Wolmuth, Roger. "Bill Monroe: The Father of Bluegrass Music Still Calls His Own Tune." *People,* September 1, 1986.

Zimmerman, David. "Bill Monroe: Father of Bluegrass Influenced Generations of Music." *USA Today,* September 10, 1996.

Rachel Liebling's documentary film *High Lonesome* is an excellent introduction to bluegrass. John Rumble's liner notes to the MCA recording *The Music of Bill Monroe* are also a fine resource.

THREE FAST FINGERS: EARL SCRUGGS

♦ INTERVIEWS

Gretel Anthony; Bill Bolick; Alison Brown; Johnny Cash; Tywaina Kennedy; Del McCoury; Bill Monroe; Neil Rosenberg; Earl Scruggs; Louise Scruggs; Doc Watson.

♦ BOOKS

Bassham, Olan. *Lester Flatt: Baron of Bluegrass.* Manchester, Tenn.: Browning Printing Service, 1980.

Lambert, Jake, and Curly Sechler. *Lester Flatt: The Good Things Out Weigh the Bad.* Hendersonville, Tenn.: Jay-Lyn Publication, 1982.

Linn, Karen. *That Half-Barbaric Twang: The Banjo in American Popular Culture.* Urbana: University of Illinois Press, 1991.

Rooney, James. *Bossmen: Bill Monroe and Muddy Waters.* New York: Dial Press, 1971.

Rosenberg, Neil. *Bluegrass: A History.* Urbana: University of Illinois Press, 1985.

Rosenberg, Neil. "Lester Flatt and Earl Scruggs." In *Stars of Country Music,* edited by Bill C. Malone and Judith McCulloh. Urbana: University of Illinois Press, 1975.

♦ ARTICLES

"Paganini Ravioli." *The New Yorker,* August 26, 1996. This article contains the Franz Liszt quotation about Paganini.

Siminoff, Roger H. "Earl Scruggs." *Frets,* July 1981.

Neil Rosenberg's liner notes to the Flatt and Scruggs *Mercury Sessions* were a particularly good resource. I also found Mike Seeger's and Ralph Rinzler's notes for *American Banjo Three-Finger and Scruggs Style* (Smithsonian Folkways) very helpful.

The epigraph is taken from the chapter entitled "Panassié, Delaunay et Cie" in Whitney Balliett's *American Musicians* (New York: Oxford University Press, 1986).

HELL'S HALF ACRE: THE LOUVIN BROTHERS

◆ INTERVIEWS

Chet Atkins; Bill Bolick; Lorene Crye; Emmylou Harris; Gregory Heinicke; Charlie Louvin; Buford Trotman; Robert Trotman.

◆ BOOKS

Covington, Dennis. *Salvation on Sand Mountain: Snake Handling and Redemption in Southern Appalachia*. Reading, Mass.: Addison-Wesley Publishing Co., 1995.

Miller, Howard. *The Louvin Brothers from Beginning to End*. Published by the author, 1986.

Wolfe, Charles K. *In Close Harmony: The Story of the Louvin Brothers*. Jackson: University Press of Mississippi, 1996.

ARTICLES

Wolfe, Charles K. "The Louvin Brothers." *Journal of the American Academy for the Preservation of Old-Time Country Music,* February 1995.

I found Charles Wolfe's liner notes to the Bear Family collection *Louvin Brothers—Close Family* very helpful. Thanks also to the DeKalb County Chamber of Commerce, Fort Payne, Alabama.

JUST ONE OF THE PEOPLE: DOC WATSON

◆ INTERVIEWS

Chet Atkins; Clint Howard; Jimmie Dale Gilmore; Mitch Greenhill; Butch Hancock; Paul Kingsbury; Ruby Lanier; Jack Lawrence; Mark O'Connor; Penny Parsons; Jean Ritchie; Earl Scruggs; Ralph Stanley; B. Townes; Doc Watson; Nancy Watson; John Alexander Williams.

◆ BOOKS

Burton, Thomas G., ed. *Tom Ashley, Sam McGee, Bukka White: Tennessee Traditional Singers*. Knoxville: University of Tennessee Press, 1981.

Rinzler, Ralph, ed. *The Songs of Doc Watson*. New York: Oak Publications, 1971.

Ritchie, Jean. *Singing Family of the Cumberlands*. New York: Oxford University Press, 1955.

♦ ARTICLES

Bane, Michael. "A Chat with Doc Watson." *Country Music*, August 1976.

Flippo, Chet. "Doc Watson and His Tall Drink o' Water Merle." *Rolling Stone*, June 21, 1973.

Govert, Gary. "The Circle Is Unbroken: When Doc Watson Picks and Sings, the Music Bridges Generations." *Carolina Lifestyle*, August 1983.

Ide, Stephen. "Doc Watson: Nostalgia and Pleasure." *Dirty Linen*, June–July 1995.

Kingsbury, Paul. "A Visit with Acoustic Wizard Doc Watson: Fingerstylist, Flatpicker, Extraordinaire, and American Institution." *Country Guitar*, June 1994.

Ledgin, Stephanie P. "Father and Son: The Rich Musical Legacy of Doc and Merle Watson." *Acoustic Guitar*, March–April 1993.

Rhodes, Don. "Doc Watson." *Bluegrass Unlimited*, January 1978.

Sievert, Jon. "Doc Watson—Like Some Kind of Fine." *Frets*, March 1979.

Whittaker, H. Lloyd. "Doc Watson." *Bluegrass Unlimited*, November 1970.

Wolmuth, Roger. "After Years of Hard Traveling Mountain Maestro Doc Watson Looks to Find Some Easy Pickin' at Last." *People*, August 10, 1987.

Ralph Rinzler's notes to the Smithsonian Folkways recording *Doc Watson and Clarence Ashley* and Jeff Place's notes to the Smithsonian Folkways recording *The Doc Watson Family* were extremely helpful.

FADE TO BLACK: JOHNNY CASH

♦ INTERVIEWS

Charles Austan; Marilyn Bergman; Dr. Philip J. Boyne; Dr. Jeffrey B. Carter; Johnny Cash; June Carter Cash; Rosanne Cash; Jack Clement; Cheryl Crow; Bob Dylan; Mikal Gilmore; Marshall Grant; Merle Haggard; L. J. Hall; Reba Hancock; Emmylou Harris; Waylon Jennings; George Jones; Kris Kristofferson; Charlie Louvin; Willie Nelson; Tom Petty; Sam Phillips; Karen Robin; Lou Robin; Evelyn Shriver; Paul Simon; John L. Smith; Bruce Springsteen; Willie Stegall; Marty Stuart; Dr. Nat Winston.

♦ BOOKS

Carpozi, George Jr. *The Johnny Cash Story*. New York: Pyramid Books, 1970.

Cash, Johnny. *Man in Black.* Grand Rapids, Mich.: Zondervan Publishing House, 1975.

Cash, Johnny. *Man in White.* San Francisco: Harper & Row, 1986.

Danker, Frederick E. "Johnny Cash." In *Stars of Country Music,* edited by Bill C. Malone and Judith McCulloh. Urbana: University of Illinois Press, 1975.

Dolan, Sean. *Johnny Cash.* New York: Chelsea House Publishers, 1995.

Escott, Colin. *Sun Records: The Brief History of the Legendary Record Label.* New York: Quick Fox, 1975.

Escott, Colin, and Martin Hawkins. *Good Rockin' Tonight: Sun Records and the Birth of Rock & Roll.* New York: St. Martin's Press, 1991.

Govoni, Albert. *A Boy Named Cash.* New York: Lancer Books, 1970.

Guralnick, Peter. *Last Train to Memphis: The Rise of Elvis Presley.* Boston: Little, Brown & Co., 1994. This book contains the *Billboard* reference to Elvis's rendition of "Good Rockin' Tonight."

Guralnick, Peter. *Lost Highway: Journeys and Arrivals of American Musicians.* New York: Harper & Row, 1989. Waylon Jennings's disdainful comments about Johnny Cash and religion are quoted in this book.

Norman, Philip. *The Road Goes On Forever.* New York: Simon & Schuster, 1982.

Smith, John. L.. *The Johnny Cash Discography.* Westport, Conn.: Greenwood Press, 1985.

Wren, Christopher S. *Winners Got Scars Too: The Life and Legends of Johnny Cash.* New York: Ballantine Books, 1971.

◆ ARTICLES

Bowden, Bill. "Cash Ties Drug Bout to Ostrich." *Little Rock Democrat,* June 23, 1989.

Carr, Patrick. "Drug-free, Cash Finds Inner Peace." *Minneapolis Star,* March 20, 1989. Reprinted from *Country Music Magazine.*

DeCurtis, Anthony. "Recordings Their Way." *Rolling Stone,* May 19, 1994.

Dunn, Jancee. "Johnny Cash." *Rolling Stone,* June 30, 1994.

Farley, Christopher John. "Dream Album." *Time,* May 9, 1994.

Fricke, David. "American Stars n' Bars: Living History Steals the Show at SXSW." *Rolling Stone,* May 5, 1994.

Frook, John. "Johnny Cash: The Rough-Cut King of Country Music." *Life,* November 21, 1969.

Goldfarb, Susan. "Shocking Truth About Johnny Cash's Mystery Illness." *National Examiner,* May 30, 1995.

Hannah, Barry. "Big Country." *Spin,* July 1994.

Hilburn, Robert. "Q & A with Johnny Cash." *Los Angeles Times Calendar,* April 25, 1994.

Hoffman, Jan. "Some Girls Do: Rosanne Cash Walks Her Own Line." *Village Voice,* July 5, 1988.

"The House That Cash Built." *TV Guide,* March 27, 1971.

"Johnny Cash Checks Back into Alcohol, Drug Treatment Center." *Lakeland* (Fla.) *Ledger,* November 26, 1989.

"Johnny Cash on Life, Music and His Devotion to Family." *Cash Box,* June 14, 1980.

"Johnny Cash to Speak at National Conference on Drug, Alcohol Abuse." *Little Rock Gazette,* June 13, 1989.

La Farge, Peter. "Johnny Cash." *Sing Out,* May 1965.

McCall, Michael, and Rex Graham. "Johnny Cash to Have Heart Surgery." *Nashville Banner,* December 15, 1988.

Oermann, Robert K. "The Remarkable Journey of Johnny Cash." *Billboard,* 35th anniversary special issue, 1990. The issue also contains articles by Clive Davis, John Lomax III, Louis B. Robin, John L. Smith, and Gerry Wood.

Pond, Neil. "Johnny Cash: His Music, His Faith, His Demons." *Music City News,* May 1987.

Rader, Dotson. "I Can Sing of Death but I'm Obsessed with Life." *Washington Post Parade,* June 11, 1995.

Schoemer, Karen. "Johnny Cash, an Enduring American Icon." *New York Times,* May 3, 1992.

Shaw, Bill. "Easing Back with Johnny Cash." *People,* July 11, 1994.

Sutton, Terri. "This Godfather of Gloom Finds Light in the Darkness." *New York Times,* May 22, 1994.

Tosches, Nick. "The Second Coming of Johnny Cash." *Journal of Country Music,* vol. 17, no. 3.

Trakin, Roy. "An Exclusive *Hits* Dialogue with Johnny Cash." *Hits,* May 2, 1994.

Von Sternberg, Bob. "Tiny Town Hits Jackpot as Cash Draws a Crowd." *Minneapolis Star-Tribune,* August 19, 1989.

Wood, Tom. "Cash, Fans Mark 40 Years." *Tennessean,* April 23, 1995.

I made use of several clippings in the Cash file at the Country Music Foundation library that contain no bibliographical information. I looked over some old issues of the *Colony Herald* in Dyess, Arkansas, that people there had in their homes. One *Herald* article, undated, that was given to me is headlined "Dyess Was Home to J.R. Cash." Any information I found in this way I confirmed with Johnny Cash. Corey Johnson shared with me his clip file on Cash's most recent producer, Rick Rubin.

Gordon Jenkins's 1953 album *Seven Dreams* (Decca) contains lyrics and libretto.

Arthur Levy and Bill Flanagan's liner notes to the Columbia Country Classics' *The Essential Johnny Cash;* Frederick E. Danker's liner notes to the Time-Life Records—Country & Western Classics Johnny Cash collection; Colin Escott, Martin Hawkins, and Hank Davis's liner notes to the Bear Family's *The Sun Country Years: Country Music in Memphis 1950–1959;* Colin Escott's liner notes to the Bear Family's *The Man in Black: Johnny Cash 1959–1962;* and Cash's own "Album Thoughts" included with American's *American Recordings* and *Unchained* were all very helpful.

See also references listed under Sara Carter for background on June Carter Cash.

In the video library at the Country Music Foundation I saw Cash's 1959 appearance on *The Ed Sullivan Show;* his 1961 and 1963 appearances on *The Tonight Show;* several samples of *The Johnny Cash Show;* his Manhattan Center concert; and *The Pride of Jessie Hallam,* a film in which Cash plays an illiterate father.

JUST PUT THAT SAD BACK IN THE BOTTLE: GEORGE JONES

◆ INTERVIEWS

David Baker; Johnny Cash; Waylon Jennings; George Jones; Nancy Jones; Evelyn Shriver; Jimmy Velvet. Questions I had for Tammy Wynette were answered through Evelyn Shriver.

◆ BOOKS

Allen, Bob. *George Jones: The Saga of an American Singer.* Garden City, N.Y.: Doubleday & Co., 1984. This book contains the "It makes you sad . . ." and the "All my life it seems I've been running . . ." Jones quotations.

Carlisle, Dolly. *Ragged but Right: The Life and Times of George Jones.* Chicago: Contemporary Books, 1984.

Jones, George, and Tom Carter. *I Lived to Tell It All.* New York: Villard Books, 1996.

◆ ARTICLES

Allen, Bob. "George Jones." *Journal of the American Academy for the Preservation of Old-Time Country Music,* February 1994.

Costello, Elvis. "No-Show George Jones Shows Up." Andy Warhol's *Interview,* November 1992.

Gates, David. "George Is on Our Mind." *Newsweek,* March 14, 1994.

Hunter, James. "The Ballad of No-Show Jones." *New York Times Magazine,* March 15, 1992.

Hunter, James. "Honky-Tonk Men: George Jones and Keith Richards Pair Up for Jones' Upcoming Album." *Rolling Stone,* May 5, 1994.

Pareles, John. "Getting Just the Essence from a Country Singer." *New York Times,* November 14, 1992.

Tosches, Nick. "The Devil in George Jones." *Texas Monthly,* July 1994.

Zimmerman, David. "First Couple Rehash Their 'Golden' Era." *USA Today,* March 15, 1994.

STILL KICKING: SISTER ROSE MADDOX

♦ **INTERVIEWS**

Merle Haggard; Emmylou Harris; Rose Maddox; Buck Owens; Chris Strachwitz; Jonny Whiteside.

♦ **BOOKS**

Bufwack, Mary A., and Robert K. Oermann. *Finding Her Voice: The Saga of Women in Country Music.* New York: Crown Publishers, 1993.

Steinbeck, John. *The Harvest Gypsies.* Berkeley, Calif.: Heyday Books, 1988.

♦ **ARTICLES**

Kienzle, Rich. "Maddox Brothers and Rose in 'Buried Treasures.'" *Country Music,* September 1993.

Lee, Craig. "Maddox: The Rock of Rockability." *Los Angeles Times Calendar,* October 23, 1983.

"Rose Maddox: Greatest Woman Country Singer of All Time." *Unicorn Times,* July 1977.

Seeman, Charlie. "Maddox Brothers and Rose." *Journal of the American Academy for the Preservation of Old-Time Country Music,* August 1993.

"Three Paths Lead to the Country." *Oakland Tribune,* November 20, 1983.

Whiteside, Jonny. "Cowgirl in a Cadillac." *LA Weekly,* April 27–May 3, 1990.

There were several clips in the Rose Maddox file at the Country Music Foundation that contained no bibliographical information. I confirmed with Rose Maddox any information in them that I wanted to use. A good deal of information about Ashland, Oregon, was supplied to me by Susan Yates at the City of Ashland Department of Community Development. I looked at old photographs of Rose Maddox and The Maddox Family in back issues of the

Phoenix Gazette and the *Gridley* (Calif.) *Herald*. I found Chris Strachwitz's, Keith Olesen's, and especially Jonny Whiteside's liner notes accompanying the Arhoolie Records issues of Maddox Brothers and Rose material very useful. It is Whiteside who tells the story of Hank Williams asking about Sister Rose. His biography of Rose Maddox was in preparation when I was at work on this book. He was kind enough to send me a draft of *Ramblin' Rose: The Life and Career of Rose Maddox,* since published in 1996 by Country Music Foundation/Vanderbilt University Press. It's there I found the motel-checkout joke and the Woody Guthrie quotation.

HONKY-TONK MAN: BUCK OWENS

◆ **INTERVIEWS**
Tommy Collins; Merle Haggard; Harlan Howard; Loretta Lynn; Rose Maddox; Bonnie Owens; Buck Owens; Jim Shaw.

◆ **BOOKS**
Steinbeck, John. *The Harvest Gypsies*. Berkeley, Calif.: Heyday Books, 1988.

◆ **ARTICLES**
Milligan, Patrick. "The Buck Owens Discography." *Journal of Country Music,* vol. 16, no. 1.

Rich Kienzle wrote the excellent liner notes that accompany Rhino Records' *Buck Owens Collection*. Julio Martinez sent me a copy of *Bakersfield Country,* a documentary produced by Paula Mazur for KCET public television in Los Angeles, which contains interviews with Buck Owens.

GOING TO GET A SANDWICH: MERLE HAGGARD AND IRIS DeMENT

◆ **INTERVIEWS**
Lou Bradley; Clovis DeMent; Iris DeMent; Merle Haggard; Norman Hamlet; Emmylou Harris; Rose Maddox; Abe Manuel; Joe Manuel; Elmer McCall; Scott Moore; Biff Owen; Bonnie Owens; Debbie Parrett; Jim Rooney; Cindy Walker.

◆ **BOOKS**
Guralnick, Peter. *Lost Highway: Journeys and Arrivals of American Musicians*. New York: Harper & Row, 1989. The Merle Haggard chapter is called "In the Good Old Days (When Times Were Bad)."

Haggard, Merle, and Peggy Russell. *Sing Me Back Home.* New York: Times Books, 1981.

Hemphill, Paul. "Merle Haggard." In *Stars of Country Music,* edited by Bill C. Malone and Judith McCulloh. Urbana: University of Illinois Press, 1975.

♦ ARTICLES

Betts, Stephen L. "Regardless of the Tide: Iris DeMent Sails Outside the Mainstream." *Journal of Country Music,* vol. 17, no. 1.

Bowman, David. "The Life and Times of Merle Haggard, American Songwriter and Champion of the Working Stiff." *Pulse!* August 1996.

DeParle, Jason. "On the Bus with Merle Haggard." *New York Times,* July 29, 1993.

Di Salvatore, Bryan. "Ornery." *The New Yorker,* February 20, 1990.

Gates, David. "The Lion in Winter." *Newsweek,* April 15, 1996.

Giles, Jeff. "Songs in the Key of Life: Newcomer Iris DeMent Keeps the Faith." *Newsweek,* April 18, 1994.

Marks, Craig. "Home Is Where Her Heart Is: Iris DeMent Puts the Folk Back in Country." *Spin,* June 1994.

Ridley, Jim. "Straight from the Heart." *New Country,* July 1994.

Katy Reckdahl arranged for me to see Iris DeMent appear on *A Prairie Home Companion* at Town Hall in New York. Julio Martinez sent me a copy of *Bakersfield Country,* a documentary produced by Paula Mazur for KCET public television in Los Angeles, which includes interviews with Merle Haggard.

I found Daniel Cooper's liner notes to Capitol's Merle Haggard collection *Down Every Road* very helpful, as I did Iris DeMent's own notes to her record *My Life.*

CONVERT: EMMYLOU HARRIS

♦ INTERVIEWS

Nanci Griffith; Emmylou Harris; Phil Kaufman; Eugenia Murchison; Buck Owens; Eddie Tickner; Lucinda Williams.

♦ BOOKS

Bockris, Victor. *Keith Richards.* New York: Poseidon Books, 1992.

Bufwack, Mary A., and Robert K. Oermann. *Finding Her Voice: The Saga of Women in Country Music.* New York: Crown Publishers, 1993.

Country Music Foundation. *Country: The Music and the Musicians.* New York: Abbeville Press, 1988.

Fong-Torres, Ben. *Hickory Wind: The Life and Times of Gram Parsons.* New York: Pocket Books, 1991.

Griffin, Sid. *Gram Parsons: A Music Biography.* Pasadena, Calif.: Sierra Books, 1985.

Kaufman, Phil, and Colin White. *Road Mangler Deluxe.* Glendale, Calif.: White Bouke Publishing, 1993.

Southern, Terry, Michael Cooper, and Keith Richards. *The Early Stones.* New York: Hyperion Press, 1973.

Williams, Lucinda. *Sweet Old World.* Port Chester, N.Y.: Cherry Lane Music Co., 1992.

◆ ARTICLES

Arrington, Carl. "Singer Emmylou Harris and Producer Brian Ahern Make (and Record) Beautiful Music Together." *People,* November 15, 1982.

Bowman, David. "Young Enough to Start Over: Emmylou Harris Emerges from Daniel Lanois' Candle-lit Studio with Her Most 'Country' Album to Date." *Pulse!* October 1995.

Bradley, Bob. "Lucinda Williams: Passionate Wishes." *Journal of Country Music,* vol. 18, no. 2.

Cooper, Daniel. "Out of the Past." *Journal of Country Music,* vol. 18, no. 2.

DeParle, Jason. "On the Road with Lucinda Williams." *New York Times,* March 25, 1993.

Forte, Dan. "Emmylou Harris: The Alabama Angel." *Musician,* February 1983.

Gardella, Kay. "Emmy Winner: A Grand Ole Harris Takes Her Music Home to Original Opry Site for TNN." *Daily News* (N.Y.), January 12, 1992.

Gordinier, Jeff. "Leaving Normal: Emmylou Harris Goes Eccentric." *Entertainment Weekly,* September 29, 1995.

Hilburn, Robert. "How This Cowgirl Beat the Blues." *Los Angeles Times Calendar,* October 17, 1993.

Jarnigan, Bill. "Emmylou Harris: A Country Queen on the Move." *Truckers/USA,* vol. 5, no. 35.

Jerome, Jim. "Emmylou Harris." *People,* January 14, 1991.

Kirby, Kip. "Roses for You from Emmylou." *Country Music,* September 1980.

McCall, Michael. "For Harris, the Song Is All." *Nashville Banner,* May 11, 1989.

Mitz, Roman. "Emmylou Harris: A Dancer, Not a Yodeler." *Music Express,* February 1992.

Holly George-Warren's notes to Rhino Records' *A Tribute to Gram Parsons* were also helpful.

LUBBOCK OR LEAVE IT:
JIMMIE DALE GILMORE AND THE FLATLANDERS

♦ INTERVIEWS

Terry and Jo Harvey Allen; Mike Crowley; Mary Cutrafello; Joe Ely; Sharon Ely; Lanny Fiel; Brian Gilmore; Janet Gilmore; Jimmie Dale Gilmore; Nanci Griffith; Butch Hancock; Louise Hancock; Bob Horton; William Kerns; Shelby Meade; Natalie Merchant; Bobby J. Nelson; Willie Nelson; Rob Patterson; Alan Pepper; Barbara Roseman; Mark Rothbaum; Vin Scelsa; James M. White; Steve Van Zandt; Townes Van Zandt; Lucinda Williams; Eddie Wilson.

♦ BOOKS

Gleason, Ron, Mikal Gilmore, and Russ Parsons. *Honky Tonk Visions: On West Texas Music: 1936–1986.* Lubbock: Texas Tech University Museum, exhibition catalogue, 1986.

Nelson, Willie, and Bud Shrake. *Willie: An Autobiography.* New York: Simon & Schuster, 1988.

Reid, Jan. *The Improbable Rise of Redneck Rock.* Austin: Heidelberg Publishers, 1974.

Townsend, Charles. *San Antonio Rose: The Life and Music of Bob Wills.* Urbana: University of Illinois Press, 1976.

♦ ARTICLES

"Broken Spoke: A Country Music Landmark." *Austin American-Statesman,* December 17, 1988.

"Broken Spoke Keeps Smokin' Thanks to Bob Wills' Cigar." *Austin American-Statesman,* December 30, 1989.

Bruce, Bob. "Honky-Tonk Heavens." *Texas Highways,* February 1990.

Buchholz, Brad. "The Country Mystic: Tinting His Western Lyrics with Eastern Spirituality, Jimmie Dale Gilmore Sings a Whole 'Nother Twang." *Dallas Life Magazine, Dallas Morning News,* December 5, 1993.

Cocks, Jay. "Riding High with the Hard-Luck Guys: Joe Ely Keeps the Faith with the Past and Makes Good Music." *Time,* May 11, 1981.

Country Music: The Texas Connection. Houston Chronicle Magazine, special issue, September 30, 1979.

Cullum, Paul. "Joe Ely: The New Pride of Lubbock." *Ampersand,* May 1982.

Dougherty, Steve, and Anne Maier. "After Hard Times and a Decade in Eclipse, Willie Nelson Is Back in the Groove Again." *People,* June 21, 1993.

Fricke, David. "American Stars n' Bars: Living History Steals the Show at SXSW." *Rolling Stone,* May 5, 1994.

Fricke, David. "Home on the Strange. SXSW: A Texas Weekend of the Weird, the Wild and the Rockin'." *Rolling Stone,* May 13, 1993.

Fricke, David. "The Lone Star State of Mind: An Annual Texas Conference Showcases the Best of American Music." *Rolling Stone,* May 16, 1991.

Fricke, David. "Rockin' in the Heart of Texas: Unsigned Bands Reign Supreme at Austin's Annual Music Blowout." *Rolling Stone,* April 30, 1992.

Fricke, David. "Vision Thing: Singer/Songwriter Jimmie Dale Gilmore Takes Country Music Out of the Mainstream and into the Mystic." *Rolling Stone,* March 10, 1994.

Fruin, Deborah. "After Bitter Losses and Tragic Heartbreak, Willie Nelson Places His Hope in the Healing Hands of Time." *Country Fever,* August 1992.

George-Warren, Holly. "The Legend of Jimmie Dale Gilmore." *Men's Journal,* October 1993.

Gilmore, Jimmie Dale. "Family Reunion: Journey Through the Past and Elsewhere." *Austin Chronicle,* December 4, 1992.

"In Austin, an Appetite for Music as Big as Texas." *USA Today,* April 19, 1993.

Kalbacher, Gene. "Joe Ely: Livin' What He's Singin'." *Aquarian National,* June 10–17, 1981.

Kelp, Larry. "West Texas 'Flatlanders' Back Together Again." *Oakland Tribune,* July 18, 1989.

Kemp, Mark. "Searchin' for a Rainbow: A Country Without Borders." *Option,* November–December 1993.

Kennedy, Randy. "A Country Music Mecca in the Texas Outback." *New York Times,* May 4, 1994.

King, Larry. "An Eight-Track Tape as Holy Grail." *Pulse!* July 1990.

Kreilkamp, Ivan. "Rising Star: Jimmie Dale Gilmore Leads Country Toward El Dorado." *Boston Phoenix,* August 20, 1993.

McLeese, Don. "Butch Hancock Takes His Folk to Roadhouses." *Chicago Sun-Times,* February 19, 1989.

Morthland, John. "Jimmie Dale Gilmore: And the Beat Goes On." *Country Music,* November–December 1992.

Nash, Alanna. "Joe Ely." *Stereo Review,* October 1991.

Nichols, Lee. "Texas Songwriters Ain't Just in It for the Money." *Pulse!* May 1992.

Nichols, Lee. "Broken Spoke a Time Traveler with Trinkets from Past." *Austin American-Statesman,* February 27, 1990.

Pareles, John. "A Texas Conference with an Agenda You Can Dance To." *New York Times,* March 21, 1994.

Patoski, Joe Nick. "The Natural: In His New Release, Jimmie Dale Gilmore Sings Country the Way It's Supposed to Be Sung—Pure and Easy." *Texas Monthly,* September 1993.

Patterson, Rob. "Faces Behind the Doors: From Antone's to Zona Rosa: A Look at Who Runs Austin's Clubs." *Austin Chronicle,* May 20, 1994.

Patterson, Rob. "For the Sake of the Song: The Texas Musical Legacy of Townes Van Zandt and Guy Clark." *Austin Chronicle,* December 13, 1991.

Patterson, Rob. "The Hills Are Alive with the Sound of Music." *Austin Chronicle,* May 14, 1993.

Patterson, Rob. "Joe Ely's Highways and Heartaches." *Austin Chronicle,* October 19, 1990.

Patterson, Rob. "Keeping the Wills Tradition Alive: Ray Benson and Asleep at the Wheel." *Austin Chronicle,* May 13, 1994.

Patterson, Rob. "Lubbock and Leave It . . . for Austin." *Austin Chronicle,* December 4, 1992.

Perry, Claudia. "Joe Ely's Got Lubbock in His Rearview Mirror." *Houston Post,* July 15, 1990.

Rosenbaum, Ron. "The Ballad of Willie Nelson." *Vanity Fair,* November 1991.

Sandison, David. "Ely's Coming." *Melody Maker,* December 3, 1977.

Schoemer, Karen. "Deep in the Soul of Texas: In Austin the Fringe Is the Mainstream, Artists Are Heroes, and Even Bad Girls Can Feel Normal." *New York Times,* April 4, 1993.

Schoemer, Karen. "The Laid-Back No-Frills Road to a Music Conference in Texas." *New York Times,* March 18, 1992.

Schoemer, Karen. "The New Texas Troubadours: Jimmie Dale Gilmore and Friends Prove Lubbock Isn't a One-Icon Town." *Mirabella,* August 1993.

Spitzer, Nicholas R. "Bob Wills Is Still the King: Romantic Regionalism and Convergent Culture in Central Texas." *JEMF Quarterly,* Winter 1975.

Stout, Robert Joe. "Two-steppin' in Texas." *Texas Highways,* February 1990.

Tosches, Nick, and Joe Nick Patoski. "Texas Saves Country Music." Series of articles in *Texas Monthly,* October 1988.

Wald, Elijah. "Celebrating American Originals." *Boston Globe,* July 25, 1991.

Wilonsky, Robert. "Yin and Yang: Jimmie Dale Gilmore Is Texas' Last, Best Country-Music Philosopher." *Dallas Observer,* September 2, 1993.

Jo Rae DiMenno helped me to attend the 1995 South by Southwest Music Conference; I'm also grateful to Casey Monahan at the Texas Music Office, Office of the Governor. Terry Allen invited me to an Austin rehearsal of Jo Harvey Allen's musical *Chippy,* featuring Joe Ely and Butch Hancock. The show was later part of the "Serious Fun" festival at New York's Lincoln Center, Summer 1995. Don Walser's comments are taken from the notes to his record *Texas Top Hand* (Watermelon).

EPILOGUE: NO DEPRESSION

♦ **INTERVIEWS**

Peter Blackstock; Johnny Cash; Joe Ely; Don Everly; Emmylou Harris; Bruce Springsteen.

♦ **ARTICLES**

Applebome, Peter. "Hank Williams, Garth Brooks, BR5-49?: As the Explosive Growth of the 90s Cools, Record Executives Are Looking for the Next Big Thing to Restore Nashville Momentum." *New York Times Magazine,* October 27, 1996.

Feiler, Bruce. "Gone Country: The Voice of Suburban America." *New Republic,* February 5, 1996.

Rimer, Sara. "Storm Leaves North Carolina Farms in Ruins." *New York Times,* July 15, 1996.

SELECTED GENERAL BIBLIOGRAPHY

Note that I have repeated entries already listed under chapter headings only when that book in some way influenced my broader thinking about country music.

Balliett, Whitney. *American Musicians*. New York: Oxford University Press, 1986.

Balliett, Whitney. *American Singers*. New York: Oxford University Press, 1988.

Bane, Michael. *White Boy Singin' the Blues: The Black Roots of White Rock*. New York: Da Capo Press, 1992.

Barker, Garry. *Notes from a Native Son: Essays on the Appalachian Experience*. Knoxville: University of Tennessee Press, 1995.

Bayles, Martha. *Hole in Our Soul: The Loss of Beauty and Meaning in American Popular Music*. New York: Free Press, 1994.

Bufwack, Mary A., and Robert K. Oermann. *Finding Her Voice: The Saga of Women in Country Music*. New York: Crown Publishing, 1993.

Burt, Olive Woolley. *American Murder Ballads and Their Stories*. New York: Oxford University Press, 1958.

Cackett, Alan. *The Harmony Illustrated Encyclopedia of Country Music*. New York: Crown Publishers, 1994.

Caldwell, Erskine. *Deep South*. Athens: University of Georgia Press, 1995.

Cantwell, Robert. *Bluegrass Breakdown: The Making of the Old Southern Sound*. Urbana: University of Illinois Press, 1984.

Caro, Robert A. *The Years of Lyndon Johnson: The Path to Power.* New York: Alfred A. Knopf, 1981.

Carr, Patrick, ed. *The Illustrated History of Country Music.* Garden City, N.Y.: Doubleday & Co., 1979.

Carr, Patrick, ed. *The Illustrated History of Country Music.* New York: Times Books, 1995. (Updated and revised version of the Doubleday book.)

Cash, W. J. *The Mind of the South.* New York: Alfred A. Knopf, 1941.

Charles, Ray, and David Ritz. *Brother Ray: Ray Charles' Own Story.* New York: Da Capo Press, 1992.

Cooper, Daniel. *Lefty Frizzell: The Honky Tonk Life of Country Music's Greatest Singer.* Boston: Little, Brown & Co., 1995.

Corbin, Everett J. *Storm over Nashville: A Case Against "Modern" Country Music.* Nashville: Ashlar Press, 1980.

Country Music Foundation. *Country: The Music and the Musicians.* New York: Abbeville Press, 1988.

Davis, Francis. *The History of the Blues: The Roots, the Music, the People, from Charley Patton to Robert Cray.* New York: Hyperion, 1995.

Delmore, Alton. *Truth Is Stranger Than Publicity: The Delmore Brothers.* Edited by Charles K. Wolfe. Nashville: Country Music Foundation Press, 1995.

Escott, Colin. *Hank Williams: The Biography.* Boston: Little, Brown & Co., 1994.

Ferris, William. *Blues from the Delta.* London: Studio Vista, 1970.

Ferris, William, and Mary C. Hart, eds. *Folk Music and Modern Sound.* Jackson: University Press of Mississippi, 1982.

Fischer, David Hackett. *Albion's Seed: Four British Folkways in America.* New York: Oxford University Press, 1989.

Flippo, Chet. *Your Cheatin' Heart: A Biography of Hank Williams.* New York: Simon & Schuster, 1981.

Foote, Shelby. *The Civil War: A Narrative.* New York: Random House, 1963.

Goodman, James. *Stories of Scottsboro.* New York: Pantheon Books, 1994.

Grantham, Dewey W. *The South in Modern America.* New York: Harper-Collins, 1994.

Green, Douglas B. *Country Roots.* New York: Hawthorn Books, 1976.

Guralnick, Peter. *Feel Like Going Home: Portraits in Blues and Rock 'n' Roll.* New York: HarperCollins, 1989.

Guralnick, Peter. *Lost Highway: Journeys and Arrivals of American Musicians.* New York: Harper & Row, 1989.

Guralnick, Peter. *Sweet Soul Music: Rhythm and Blues and the Southern Dream of Freedom.* New York: Harper & Row, 1986.

Hemphill, Paul. *The Nashville Sound: Bright Lights and Country Music.* New York: Simon & Schuster, 1970.

Hentoff, Nat. *Listen to the Stories: Nat Hentoff on Jazz and Country Music.* New York: HarperCollins, 1995.

Heyman, Therese Thau, et al. *Dorothea Lange: American Photographs.* San Francisco: Museum of Modern Art, 1994.

Hilliard, Sam B. *The South Revisited: Forty Years of Change.* New Brunswick, N.J.: Rutgers University Press, 1992.

Horstman, Dorothy. *Sing Your Heart Out Country Boy.* Nashville: Country Music Foundation Press, 1986.

Howard, Jan. *Sunshine and Shadow.* New York: Richardson & Steinman, 1987.

Howard, John. *Stephen Foster: America's Troubadour.* New York: Tudor Publishing Co., 1934.

Hume, Martha. *You're So Cold I'm Turning Blue: Guide to the Greatest in Country Music.* New York: Penguin Books, 1982.

Judd, Naomi, and Bud Schaetzle. *Love Can Build a Bridge.* New York: Villard Books, 1993.

Karr, Mary. *The Liars' Club: A Memoir.* New York: Viking Penguin, 1995.

Kingsbury, Paul. *The Grand Ole Opry History of Country Music.* New York: Villard Books, 1995.

Klein, Joe. *Woody Guthrie: A Life.* New York: Ballantine Books, 1982.

Lees, Gene. *Meet Me at Jim & Andy's: Jazz Musicians and Their World.* New York: Oxford University Press, 1988.

Lingeman, Richard. *Small Town America: A Narrative History, 1620 to the Present.* Boston: Houghton Mifflin, 1980.

Lomax, Alan. *The Land Where the Blues Began.* New York: Pantheon Books, 1993.

Lynn, Loretta, and George Vecsey. *Coal Miner's Daughter.* New York: Warner Books, 1976.

McCloud, Barry. *Definitive Country: The Ultimate Encyclopedia of Country Music and Its Performers.* New York: Berkley Publishing Group, 1995.

Malone, Bill C. *Country Music U.S.A.* Austin: University of Texas Press, 1985.

Malone, Bill C. *Singing Cowboys and Musical Mountaineers: Southern Culture and the Roots of Country Music.* Athens: University of Georgia Press, 1993.

Malone, Bill C. *Southern Music, American Music.* Lexington: University Press of Kentucky, 1979.

Malone, Bill C., and Judith McCulloh, eds. *Stars of Country Music.* Urbana: University of Illinois Press, 1975.

Marcus, Greil. *Mystery Train: Images of America in Rock 'n' Roll Music.* New York: E. P. Dutton, 1975.

Morgan, Dan. *Rising in the West: The True Story of an "Okie" Family in Search of the American Dream.* New York: Alfred A. Knopf, 1992.

Naipaul, V. S. *A Turn in the South.* New York: Alfred A. Knopf, 1989.

Oliver, Paul. *The Meaning of the Blues.* New York: Collier Books, 1960.

Ondaatje, Michael. *Coming Through Slaughter.* New York: W. W. Norton & Co, 1976.

Oster, Harry. *Living Country Blues.* Detroit: Folklore Associates, 1969.

Palmer, Robert. *Deep Blues: A Musical and Cultural History of the Mississippi Delta.* New York: Viking Press, 1981.

Percy, William Alexander. *Lanterns on the Levee: Recollections of a Planter's Son.* New York: Alfred A Knopf, 1941.

Ritter, Lawrence. *The Glory of Their Times: The Story of the Early Days of Baseball Told by the Men Who Played It.* New York: Macmillan Co., 1966. This book is interesting given the similar backgrounds many old-time ballplayers shared with early country singers. Roy Acuff and Bill Monroe, among others, turned to music when poor health thwarted their promising baseball careers.

Rogers, Jimmie. *The Country Music Message: Revisited.* Fayetteville: University of Arkansas Press, 1989.

Rosenberg, Neil. *Bluegrass: A History.* Urbana: University of Illinois Press, 1985.

Schulman, Bruce J. *From Cotton Belt to Sunbelt: Federal Policy, Economic Development, and the Transformation of the South, 1938–1980.* Durham, N.C.: Duke University Press, 1994.

Steinbeck, John. *The Grapes of Wrath.* New York: Penguin Books, 1992.

Steinbeck, John. *The Harvest Gypsies.* Berkeley, Calif.: Heyday Books, 1988.

Terrell, Bob. *The Chuck Wagon Gang: A Legend Lives On.* Asheville, N.C.: Bob Terrell Pub., 1990.

Tichi, Cecelia. *High Lonesome: The American Culture of Country Music.* Chapel Hill: University of North Carolina Press, 1994.

Tillis, Mel, and Walter Wager. *Stutterin' Boy: The Autobiography of Mel Tillis.* New York: Rawson Associates, 1984.

Titon, Jeff Todd. *Early Downhome Blues: A Musical and Cultural Analysis.* Chapel Hill: University of North Carolina Press, 1994.

Tosches, Nick. *Country: The Biggest Music in America.* New York: Stein & Day, 1977.

Vaughan, Andrew. *The World of Country Music.* London: Studio Editions Ltd., 1992.

Williams, Roger M. *Sing a Sad Song: The Life of Hank Williams.* Garden City, N.Y.: Doubleday & Co., 1970.

Woodward, C. Vann. *The Origins of the New South, 1877–1913*. Baton Rouge: Louisiana State University Press, 1951.

Periodical publications I found especially helpful were:

Acoustic Guitar
Bluegrass Unlimited
Cash Box
Country Guitar
Country Music
The Devil's Box
The Journal of the American Academy for the Preservation of Old-Time Country Music
The Journal of Country Music
Nashville Scene
New Country
No Depression
Old-Time Country
The Old-Time Herald
Pickin'
Pulse!
Rolling Stone
Sing Out!
Spin

DISCOGRAPHY

(SUGGESTED LISTENING)

A complete discography for many of the musicians I've written about can fill and has filled an entire book by itself. And while the German Bear Family label has released the complete recordings of many country artists, most listeners will not require something that comprehensive. So instead of listing every last recording made by each performer, I want to suggest what I think are the best introductions to each artist. The advent of the compact disc has meant that many LPs have been re-released. In country that isn't quite as important as in jazz or rock, since older country albums were usually just the singles with some indifferent material tossed in to fill out the record. Still, if you are, say, a Merle Haggard or Gram Parsons aficionado, this is good news, because they did make full and excellent records and you can now find their best. Compact discs also mean that impressive compilations are available, because a little plastic can hold a great many cuts.

JIMMIE RODGERS

Rounder Records has released all of Rodgers's recordings. You can't really go wrong, but I'd begin with *America's Blue Yodeler,* the classic 1930–1931 recordings, which include "TB Blues," "In the Jailhouse Now," and "Blue Yodel 8," (which is "Muleskinner Blues.") The *First Sessions,* with the first "Blue Yodel" ("T for Texas"), "Sleep Baby Sleep," and an earlier rendition of "In the Jailhouse Now," are another obvious place to begin. Something else to try is Merle Haggard's excellent tribute album, *Same Train, Different Time* (Koch).

HARLAN HOWARD

While Harlan's own recordings of his songs are just back in print (Koch), his own rumpled singing voice doesn't do his great songs justice. Until someone has the good sense to put out a compilation of first-rate singers singing Howard's songs, they'll be searched out one by one. To get a sense of how much interpretative range his songs allow singers, listen to how different Johnny Cash's, Burl Ives's, and Ray Charles's fine versions of "Busted" are.

CHET ATKINS

The RCA two-disc box set *The RCA Years* includes a good introduction to Atkins's playing from the 1950s through the 1970s. Since then, I'm most partial to a Columbia recording he made with Mark Knopfler, *Neck & Neck*.

SARA CARTER

Rounder Records is in the process of releasing the complete Carter Family recordings. I'm partial to the 1927–1928 cuts, *Anchored in Love,* which include "Keep on the Sunny Side," "Wildwood Flower," "The Wandering Boy," "Little Darling Pal of Mine," and "The Poor Orphan Child." *When the Roses Bloom in Dixieland,* the 1929–1930 recordings, features "Motherless Child," "No Telephone in Heaven," "Wabash Cannonball," and "Jimmy Brown the Newsboy."

You can hear the famous first recordings of both Jimmie Rodgers and The Carter Family, as well as the Stonemans and everyone else of note whom Ralph Peer recorded in Bristol, Tennessee, in 1927, on the Country Music Foundation's two-disc compilation *The Bristol Sessions*. Rounder's *Lesley Riddle Step by Step* gives a feeling for this man who taught A.P. and Maybelle so much music.

KITTY WELLS

MCA Records' Country Music Hall of Fame Series has sixteen of Kitty's biggest hits on one disc. Besides "It Wasn't God Who Made Honky-Tonk Angels," you can hear her sing Harlan Howard's "Mommy for a Day."

PATSY CLINE

MCA's four-disc box *The Patsy Cline Collection* has it all. MCA also produces smaller "greatest" compilations, but Patsy, like Merle Haggard and Bill Monroe, is notably much more than her hits.

BILL MONROE

The MCA four-CD box set *The Music of Bill Monroe* is as good an introduction to his music as there is. For a less extensive taste of The Father of Bluegrass, the MCA Country Music Hall of Fame Series is a decent choice.

RALPH STANLEY

The Bear Family has released the classic 1949–1959 Stanley Brothers recordings on three compact discs. In 1992, Stanley assembled many of his favorite singers, including Emmylou Harris, Bill Monroe, Ricky Skaggs, George Jones, and Alison Krauss, to record some of the best Stanley material for an album he called *Saturday Night and Sunday Morning* (Freeland Recording Company). To my mind, this is one of the classic country-music recordings of all time.

EARL SCRUGGS

The Bill Monroe MCA box set contains a few of the recordings Earl Scruggs and Lester Flatt made with Monroe between 1945 and 1948. For more from this period, Rounder has released *Bill Monroe with Flatt & Scruggs: The Original Bluegrass Band*. Many classic Flatt & Scruggs recordings can be found on Rounder's *The Golden Era*. Smithsonian Folkways' *American Banjo Three-Finger and Scruggs Style* is a fine sampler that contains tunes played by several banjo pickers of note, including Snuffy Jenkins and Junie Scruggs. As for Uncle Dave Macon, The Smithsonian Institution's Folkways series offers a good selection of "The Dixie Dewdrop."

Note that an accessible modern introduction to bluegrass is *Old and in the Way* (United Artists), featuring David Grisman, Peter Rowan, Vassar Clements, and Jerry Garcia. A more traditional collection is the CMH soundtrack to the wonderful bluegrass documentary *High Lonesome*.

THE LOUVIN BROTHERS

I like Capitol's *Louvin Brothers,* a one-disc compilation, although you can't really go wrong with Razor & Tie's *When I Stop Dreaming—The Best of the Louvin Brothers* either. The Louvins' extraordinary *Tribute to the Delmore Brothers* is a Capitol recording. Various Blue Sky Boys and Delmore Brothers records are in and out of print. A nice place to start is RCA's *Various—Are You From Dixie?—Great Country Brother Teams of the 1930s,* which gives you a little Blue Sky Boys, a bit of the Delmores, as well as a general sense of some of the other things the Louvins were listening to as they grew up.

DOC WATSON

Smithsonian Folkways' *The Doc Watson Family* is a delightful compilation of songs Ralph Rinzler recorded not long after he "discovered" Watson. The best place to begin with Watson is *The Essential Doc Watson* (Vanguard). To hear Watson performing live with Clint Howard, try Vanguard's *Old Timey Concert.* As for Doc and Merle Watson, I like *Ballads from Deep Gap* (Vanguard) and *Down South* (Rykodisc) best, although you really can't go wrong with any record those two made. Two other Smithsonian Folkways collections worth considering are *Bill Monroe and Doc Watson Live Duet Recordings* and *Jean Ritchie and Doc Watson at Folk City.*

JOHNNY CASH

There are three places to visit with Cash. Rhino has released *The Sun Years.* Columbia's three-disc box set *The Essential Johnny Cash* is surely that. American's *American Recordings* is the recent masterpiece.

GEORGE JONES

The Legacy/Epic two-disc box set *The Spirit of Country—The Essential George Jones* has just about all the great ones. A good supplement is *Cup of Loneliness—The Classic Mercury Years.* Jones's Hank Williams covers are available on various Liberty and Mercury reissues. More recently, *And Along Came Jones* (MCA) was a fine, largely overlooked record.

ROSE MADDOX

Arhoolie Records' *The Maddox Brothers and Rose,* volumes 1 and 2, offers an excellent sense of "The World's Greatest Hillbilly Band."

BUCK OWENS

Owens and Rhino Records put a lot of effort into the three-disc set *The Buck Owens Collection,* and it shows. All the hits are here and even some of the misses.

MERLE HAGGARD AND IRIS DEMENT

Down Every Road, Capitol's four-CD box set, goes well beyond the hits and belongs in any country collection. Haggard's most recent disc, *1996* (Curb Records), with the wonderful "Truck Driver's Blues," is proof that the Hag still has it. As a rule, Haggard's LPs run deeper than anybody else's. Try *Big City* (Epic/CBS) for another typically fine one. *Tulare Dust—A Songwriter's Tribute to Merle Haggard* (Hightone) contains Iris DeMent's version of "Big City," as well as Haggard covers by Joe Ely, Lucinda Williams, Rosie Flores, and other talented younger Haggard acolytes. You can't miss with any of Iris DeMent's three records, although *My Life* (Warner) is probably the strongest.

EMMYLOU HARRIS

Harris has made many wonderful records, but *Pieces of the Sky* (Reprise), *Roses in the Snow* (Warner Brothers), and *Wrecking Ball* (Elektra) are as supremely accomplished as they are different. *Duets* (Reprise) is a decent compilation of her harmony recordings. Reprise has released Gram Parsons's albums *GP* and *Grievous Angel* on a single disc. There you can hear Harris's wonderful duets with Parsons. The place to begin with Lucinda Williams is *Lucinda Williams* (Chameleon). Steve Earle's MCA debut, *Guitar Town,* is a fine, fine record, but I'm partial to *Train a-Comin',* the stunning acoustic record he made for Winter-Harvest.

JIMMIE DALE GILMORE AND THE FLATLANDERS

The Flatlanders' classic *More a Legend Than a Band* is a Rounder recording. Jimmie Dale Gilmore's best recordings are *After Awhile* (Elektra-Nonesuch) and *Spinning Around the Sun* (Elektra). For years Butch Hancock put out his own records, and it's difficult to find anything better than the spare *West Texas Waltzes and Dust Blown Tractor Ballads,* which is available through Hancock directly at Lubbock or Leave It, in Austin, Texas. Sugar Hill Records has since released two Hancock collections, *Own & Own* and *Eats Away the Night.* I'd start with the first. Joe Ely's strongest LP is the dynamic concert recording *Live Shots* (MCA). Rhino has released a fine Bob Wills collection, *Bob*

Wills and the Texas Playboys Anthology. For a little Terry Allen, try *Lubbock on Everything* (Special Delivery), which includes his wonderful song "Amarillo Highway."

A record that brought a generation of people to traditional country music is the original 1972 *Will the Circle Be Unbroken* (United Artists) recording, a classic group of Nashville sessions hosted by the Nitty Gritty Dirt Band featuring Mother Maybelle Carter, Roy Acuff, Doc Watson, Earl Scruggs, Merle Travis, and Vassar Clements. If I were to suggest one record with which to begin a country collection, this would be it. Another way to go is Time-Life Music's massive *Country U.S.A.,* all twenty-three discs of it. This is available only through the mail or 800 telephone orders.

Other records that ought to be in every country music collection include Ray Charles's *Modern Sounds in Country and Western Music* (Rhino); Hank Williams's *40 Greatest Hits* (Polydor), and also his *Low Down Blues* (Mercury), a compilation in which Williams proves that a white boy certainly can sing the blues.

Simultaneously with the publication of this book, Compass Records in Nashville is releasing a sampler that includes at least one cut from every subject in the text. That record, *In the Country of Country,* is available at record and book stores or by telephone orders (1-800-757-2277).

INDEX

Italicized page numbers indicate photographs and their captions.

CREDITS

PERMISSIONS ACKNOWLEDGMENTS

Grateful acknowledgment is made to the following for permission to reprint previously published material:

Alpha Music, Inc.: Excerpt from "Happy Woman Blues" by Lucinda Williams. Copyright © 1980 by Alpha Music, Inc. All rights reserved. Reprinted by permission of Alpha Music, Inc.

Bug Music, Inc.: Excerpt from "Big River" by Johnny Cash. Copyright © 1986 by House of Cash, Inc. (BMI). Excerpt from "Delia's Gone" by Johnny Cash. Copyright © 1994 by Song of Cash, Inc. (ASCAP). Excerpt from "Man in Black" by Johnny Cash. Copyright © 1971 by Song of Cash, Inc. (ASCAP). Excerpt from "San Quentin" by Johnny Cash. Copyright © 1969 by Song of Cash, Inc. (ASCAP). Excerpt from "You've Never Seen Me Cry" by Butch Hancock. Copyright © 1990 by Rainlight Music (BMI). Administered by Bug Music, Inc. All rights reserved. Reprinted by permission of Bug Music, Inc.

Careers-BMG Music Publishing, Inc., Chancey Tunes, and Music Ridge Music: Excerpt from "Friends in Low Places" by Dewayne Blackwell and Earl Bud Lee. Copyright © 1990 by Careers-BMG Music Publishing, Inc. (BMI), Chancey Tunes, Music Ridge Music and Juan Ton Music. All rights reserved. Reprinted by permission of Careers-BMG Music Publishing, Inc., Chancey Tunes, and Music Ridge Music.

Copyright Management, Inc.: Excerpt from "White Line" by Emmylou Harris and Paul Kennerly. Copyright © 1984 by Franklin and Berks Music,

Merle Haggard. Copyright © 1968 by Sony/ATV Songs LLC (Renewed). Excerpt from "Sunday Morning Christian" by Harlan Howard and Lawrence Reynolds. Copyright © 1970 by Sony/ATV Songs LLC. All rights administered by Sony/ATV Music Publishing, 8 Music Square West, Nashville, TN 37203. All rights reserved. Reprinted by permission of Sony/ATV Music Publishing.

Wait & See Music: Excerpt from "Boulder to Birmingham" by Emmylou Harris and Bill Danoff. Copyright © 1979 by Wait & See Music and Cherry Lane Music Publishing Company, Inc. All rights reserved. Reprinted by permission of Wait & See Music.

PHOTOGRAPH CREDITS

Page vi   Fruit packers and guitar player. Courtesy Eudora Welty Collection, Mississippi Department of Archives and History.

Page 2   Signpost, Crossville, Tennessee. Photo by Ben Shahn. Courtesy Rachel Liebling.

Page 5   Jimmie Rodgers. Courtesy Country Music Foundation.

Page 9   Railroad crew laying track. Courtesy Rachel Liebling.

Page 11   Arnold Schultz and Clarence Wilson. Courtesy Rachel Liebling.

Page 17   Hank Williams. Courtesy Country Music Foundation.

Page 20   Crowds outside the Ryman Auditorium, 1940s. Courtesy Rachel Liebling.

Page 22   Harlan Howard and Waylon Jennings. Courtesy Harlan Howard.

Page 27   Auto workers outside Ford plant. Detroit. Courtesy Library of Congress.

Page 34   Kris Kristofferson, Harlan Howard, and Willie Nelson at Tootsie's. Bill Rouda, Nashville, Tennessee.

Page 38   Chet Atkins playing guitar. Courtesy Country Music Foundation.

Page 44   The Atkins family homestead in the 1930s. Courtesy Buster Devault.

Page 52   Girls in front of post office, Nethers, Virginia. Photo by Arthur Rothstein. Courtesy Rachel Liebling.

Page 57   The Carter Family. From the Gid Tanner Artist File #NF1996, The Southern Folklife Collection, Wilson Library, The University of North Carolina at Chapel Hill.

Page 62   A.P., Sara, and Janette Carter in front of store. Courtesy Country Music Foundation.

Page 64   Kitty Wells with husband, Johnny Wright, and his brother-in-law Jack Anglin. Courtesy Country Music Foundation.

Page 71   Patsy Cline and the boys. Courtesy Country Music Foundation.

Page 74   Patsy Cline. Courtesy Country Music Foundation.

Page 77   Apple stand outside Winchester, Virginia. Photo by Arthur Roth-stein. Courtesy Library of Congress LC-USF33-2196-M3.

Page 80   Bill Monroe at the old home. Photo by Charles Meyer. Courtesy Rachel Liebling.

Page 82   Bill Monroe and The Bluegrass Boys in the 1940s. Courtesy Rachel Liebling.

Page 91   Carter and Ralph Stanley. Courtesy Rachel Liebling.

Page 106   Bill Monroe and The Bluegrass Boys in the Blue Grass Special. Courtesy Rachel Liebling.

Page 107   Bill Monroe and baseball team. Courtesy Bluegrass Unlimited, Inc.

Page 112   Carolina banjo picker. Courtesy Library of Congress.

Page 123   Lester Flatt, Earl Scruggs, and The Foggy Mountain Boys. From the Gid Tanner Artist File #NF1996. The Southern Folklife Collection, Wilson Library, The University of North Carolina at Chapel Hill.

Page 127   Georgia textile factory. Photo by Jack Delano. Courtesy Library of Congress LC-USF34-46284-D.

Page 132   Baptism in the river. Courtesy Rachel Liebling.

Page 142   The Louvin Brothers on stage. Courtesy Country Music Foundation.

Page 148   Doc Watson and son Merle on porch. From the Gid Tanner Artist File #NF1996, The Southern Folklife Collection, Wilson Library, The University of North Carolina at Chapel Hill.

Page 163   Doc and Merle Watson. Courtesy Jim McGuire, Nashville.

Page 166   Boy with the family guitar. Courtesy Rachel Liebling.

Page 168   Johnny Cash and the people. Private Collection.

Page 179   Family picking cotton. Courtesy Rachel Liebling.

Page 191   Johnny Cash and June Carter. Source unknown.

Page 200   George Jones. From the Gid Tanner Artist File #NF1996, The Southern Folklife Collection, Wilson Library, The University of North Carolina at Chapel Hill.

Page 208   George Jones and Tammy Wynette. Courtesy Country Music Foundation.

Page 214   Oklahomans in the San Joaquin Valley, 1938. Photo by Dorothea Lange. Courtesy Romana Javitz Collection, Miriam and Ira D. Wallach Division of Art, Prints and Photographs, The New York Public Library, Astor, Lenox and Tilden Foundations.

Page 216 The Maddox Brothers and Rose. From the Gid Tanner Artist File #NF1996, The Southern Folklife Collection, Wilson Library, The University of North Carolina at Chapel Hill.

Page 223 The Maddox family in the *Oakland Tribune,* 1933. Courtesy Arhoolie Records.

Page 228 Downtown Bakersfield in the 1930s. The Collection of Christopher D. Brewer, Exeter, California.

Page 231 Young Buck Owens with guitar. Courtesy Country Music Foundation.

Page 239 The Blackboard Club, exterior and interior. Courtesy of Kern County Museum. Used by permission.

Page 245 Buck Owens and The Buckaroos. From the Gid Tanner Artist File #NF1996, The Southern Folklife Collection, Wilson Library, The University of North Carolina at Chapel Hill.

Page 248 Merle Haggard with Bonnie Owens. Courtesy Michael Ochs Archives/Venice, California.

Page 256 Merle Haggard in the studio. Courtesy Country Music Foundation.

Page 266 Iris DeMent. Courtesy Iris DeMent.

Page 274 Texas landscape near Lubbock. Photo by Butch Hancock.

Page 276 Emmylou Harris. Courtesy Country Music Foundation.

Page 284 Gram Parsons. Courtesy Sierra.

Page 290 Jimmie Dale Gilmore and The Flatlanders. Photo by Butch Hancock.

Page 308 Street guitar pickers, Maynardsville, Tennessee, 1935. Photo by Ben Shahn. Courtesy Rachel Liebling.

Page 313 A woman says goodbye to her farm. Courtesy Rachel Liebling.